Crabgrass Catholicism

HISTORICAL STUDIES OF URBAN AMERICA

Edited by Lilia Fernández, Timothy J. Gilfoyle, and Amanda I. Seligman
James R. Grossman, Editor Emeritus

Recent titles in the series

THE MENACE OF PROSPERITY: NEW YORK CITY AND THE STRUGGLE FOR ECONOMIC DEVELOPMENT, 1865–1981
by Daniel Wortel-London

METROPOLITAN LATINIDAD: TRANSFORMING AMERICAN URBAN HISTORY *by A. K. Sandoval-Strausz, ed.*

BUILDING THE METROPOLIS: ARCHITECTURE, CONSTRUCTION, AND LABOR IN NEW YORK CITY, 1880–1935 *by Alexander Wood*

IN THE SHADOW OF SLAVERY: AFRICAN AMERICANS IN NEW YORK CITY, 1626–1863, WITH A NEW AFTERWORD BY THE AUTHOR *by Leslie M. Harris*

IN LEVITTOWN'S SHADOW: POVERTY IN AMERICA'S WEALTHIEST POSTWAR SUBURB *by Tim Keogh*

THE GREAT AMERICAN TRANSIT DISASTER: A CENTURY OF AUSTERITY, AUTO-CENTRIC PLANNING, AND WHITE FLIGHT *by Nicholas Dagen Bloom*

CITY OF DIGNITY: CHRISTIANITY, LIBERALISM, AND THE MAKING OF GLOBAL LOS ANGELES *by Sean T. Dempsey*

NONPROFIT NEIGHBORHOODS: AN URBAN HISTORY OF INEQUALITY AND THE AMERICAN STATE *by Claire Dunning*

TO LIVE PEACEABLY TOGETHER: THE AMERICAN FRIENDS SERVICE COMMITTEE'S CAMPAIGN FOR OPEN HOUSING *by Tracy E. K'Meyer*

MAKING MEXICAN CHICAGO: FROM POSTWAR SETTLEMENT TO THE AGE OF GENTRIFICATION
by Mike Amezcua

MAKING THE SECOND GHETTO: RACE AND HOUSING IN CHICAGO, 1940–1960, WITH A NEW AFTERWORD BY N. D. B. CONNOLLY
by Arnold R. Hirsch

SUN RA'S CHICAGO: AFROFUTURISM AND THE CITY *by William Sites*

STEAM CITY: RAILROADS, URBAN SPACE, AND CORPORATE CAPITALISM IN NINETEENTH-CENTURY BALTIMORE
by David Schley

AFTER REDLINING: THE URBAN REINVESTMENT MOVEMENT IN THE ERA OF FINANCIAL DEREGULATION *by Rebecca K. Marchiel*

URBAN LOWLANDS: A HISTORY OF NEIGHBORHOODS, POVERTY, AND PLANNING *by Steven T. Moga*

BEYOND THE USUAL BEATING: THE JON BURGE POLICE TORTURE SCANDAL AND SOCIAL MOVEMENTS FOR POLICE ACCOUNTABILITY IN CHICAGO *by Andrew S. Baer*

RUNNING THE NUMBERS: RACE, POLICE, AND THE HISTORY OF URBAN GAMBLING *by Matthew Vaz*

THE WORLD OF JULIETTE KINZIE: CHICAGO BEFORE THE FIRE *by Ann Durkin Keating*

MURDER IN NEW ORLEANS: THE CREATION OF JIM CROW POLICING *by Jeffrey S. Adler*

THE IMPORTANCE OF BEING URBAN: DESIGNING THE PROGRESSIVE SCHOOL DISTRICT, 1890–1940 *by David A. Gamson*

NEW YORK RECENTERED: BUILDING THE METROPOLIS FROM THE SHORE
by Kara Murphy Schlichting

RENEWAL: LIBERAL PROTESTANTS AND THE AMERICAN CITY AFTER WORLD WAR II
by Mark Wild

THE GATEWAY TO THE PACIFIC: JAPANESE AMERICANS AND THE REMAKING OF SAN FRANCISCO
by Meredith Oda

A complete list of series titles is available on the University of Chicago Press website.

Crabgrass Catholicism

How Suburbanization Transformed Faith and Politics in Postwar America

STEPHEN M. KOETH

The University of Chicago Press
Chicago and London

The University of Chicago Press, Chicago 60637
The University of Chicago Press, Ltd., London
© 2025 by The University of Chicago
All rights reserved. No part of this book may be used or reproduced in any manner whatsoever without written permission, except in the case of brief quotations in critical articles and reviews. For more information, contact the University of Chicago Press, 1427 E. 60th St., Chicago, IL 60637.
Published 2025

34 33 32 31 30 29 28 27 26 25   1 2 3 4 5

ISBN-13: 978-0-226-82996-8 (cloth)
ISBN-13: 978-0-226-84220-2 (paper)
ISBN-13: 978-0-226-84219-6 (e-book)
DOI: https://doi.org/10.7208/chicago/9780226842196.001.0001

Library of Congress Cataloging-in-Publication Data

Names: Koeth, Stephen M., author.
Title: Crabgrass Catholicism : how suburbanization transformed faith and politics in postwar America / Stephen M. Koeth.
Other titles: Historical studies of urban America.
Description: Chicago : The University of Chicago Press, 2025. | Series: Historical studies of urban America | Includes bibliographical references and index.
Identifiers: LCCN 2024056917 | ISBN 9780226829968 (cloth) | ISBN 9780226842202 (paperback) | ISBN 9780226842196 (ebook)
Subjects: LCSH: Catholic Church—New York (State)—Long Island—History—20th century. | Catholic Church. Diocese of Rockville Centre (Long Island, N.Y.)—History. | Catholic Church—United States—History—20th century. | Suburban churches—New York (State)—Long Island—History—20th century. | Social change—United States. | United States—History—1945-
Classification: LCC BX1407.S8 K64 2025 | DDC 282/.7472109045—dc23/eng/20250110
LC record available at https://lccn.loc.gov/2024056917

For my parents . . .
. . . with unspeakable love and gratitude for, literally, everything

CONTENTS

List of Abbreviations / ix   List of Figures and Tables / xi

Introduction / 1

ONE / An Urban Catholic World: Agrarianism,
Urbanism, and the Ethnic Parish / 13

TWO / The Suburban Church: Postwar Suburbanization
and Catholic Institutional Expansion / 37

THREE / From Church to Home: Spaces for Prayer, Education,
and Charity in the Suburban Parish / 67

FOUR / Priests and Parishioners: Lay Associations, Parish Councils,
and Church Leadership / 101

FIVE / Suburban Parish Boundaries: Race, Ethnicity,
and Mixed Parishes in Suburbia / 131

SIX / Suburban Catholic Education: Parochial Schools, CCD,
and Ecclesiastical Polarization / 155

SEVEN / Politics in Catholic Suburbia: State Funding, School Prayer,
and Political Realignment / 187

Epilogue: The Suburban Church and Religious Disaffiliation / 219

Acknowledgments / 225   Appendix / 229
Notes / 235   Index / 301

ABBREVIATIONS

AANY	Archives of the Archdiocese of New York
ACUA	Archives of the Catholic University of America
ADB	Archives of the Diocese of Brooklyn
ADRVC	Archives of the Diocese of Rockville Centre
UNDA	Archives of the University of Notre Dame
CARA	Center for Applied Research in the Apostolate
CCD	Confraternity of Christian Doctrine
CEF	Citizens for Educational Freedom
CFM	Christian Family Movement
CPPS	Missionaries of the Precious Blood
CSC	Congregation of Holy Cross
CSJ	Congregation of St. Joseph (Josephites)
CSP	Missionary Society of St. Paul the Apostle (Paulists)
CSSR	Congregation of the Most Holy Redeemer (Redemptorists)
CWV	Catholic War Veterans of America
CYO	Catholic Youth Organization
FHA	Federal Housing Administration
HLIS	Housing Legislation Information Services
HOLC	Homeowners Loan Corporation
HUD	US Department of Housing and Urban Development
ICRC	The Intra-Church Relations Committee
LIAL	The Long Island Association of Laymen

NCCM	National Council of Catholic Men
NCEA	National Catholic Educational Association
NCRLC	National Catholic Rural Life Conference
NCWC	National Catholic Welfare Conference
NORC	National Opinion Research Center
NUE	National Center for Urban and Ethnic Affairs
NYCLU	New York Civil Liberties Union
NYSCC	New York State Catholic Conference
OFM	Order of Friars Minor (Franciscans)
OP	Order of Preachers (Dominicans)
POAU	Protestants and Other Americans United for Separation of Church and State
RLB	Rural Life Bureau of the National Catholic Welfare Conference
SAD	Social Action Department of the National Catholic Welfare Conference
SJ	Society of Jesus (Jesuits)
USCCB	United States Conference of Catholic Bishops
VA	Veterans Administration
YCS	Young Christian Students
YCW	Young Christian Workers

FIGURES AND TABLES

FIGURES

I.1. Ss. Cyril and Methodius Church (1963)
1.1. NCRLC: "Standing on Two Feet" pamphlet cover (1947)
2.1. Norwich-Green Homes advertisement (1952)
2.2. Morewood Oaks Homes advertisement (1959)
2.3. Parishes of Nassau and Suffolk Counties over time
2.4. Parishes of Nassau County by year
2.5. Parishes of Suffolk County by year
2.6. Dioceses of Metro New York
2.7. St. Agnes Church, Rockville Centre (1935)
3.1. Aerial photograph of St. James Parish (undated)
3.2. Fundraising drive at St. Frances de Chantal Parish (undated)
3.3. St. Gerard Parish, Mass in rectory kitchen (1969)
3.4. Brochure for St. Anne Drive-In Church (undated)
3.5. St. Elizabeth Parish Home CCD class (1969)
4.1. Marriage Encounter meeting (1971)
4.2. Pro-life marchers from St. Frances de Chantal Parish (1970)
6.1. Our Lady of Grace School Building, West Babylon (undated)
6.2. Opening day of St. Frances de Chantal School, Wantagh (1956)
6.3. Diocese of Rockville Centre High School campaign brochure (1963)

6.4. St. Anne School classroom (1946)

6.5. St. Bernard Parish home visitation program (1974)

6.6. Protesters at Nassau Coliseum rally to save high schools (1984)

TABLES

6.1. Nassau and Suffolk County parishes founded, 1945–1957

6.2. Nassau and Suffolk County parishes founded after 1957

Introduction

On July 6, 1963, Bishop Walter P. Kellenberg of the Diocese of Rockville Centre dedicated the new church, school, rectory, and convent of Ss. Cyril and Methodius Parish in Deer Park, New York. The day's festivities—including Kellenberg's blessing of the buildings and a solemn pontifical Mass—marked the parish's seventh anniversary and the first time in the history of the suburban Long Island diocese that an entire parish plant was dedicated at once.[1]

The hamlet of Deer Park, halfway along Long Island on the western edge of Suffolk County, was first settled in the 1600s but it was not until 1930 that a group of twenty-five Catholic families purchased an unused schoolhouse, converted it into a chapel, and petitioned Bishop Thomas E. Molloy of Brooklyn for a priest.[2] They had to borrow one at first, and then could only share one. In 1934 Molloy established Our Lady of the Miraculous Medal Parish in neighboring Wyandanch and its pastor also served the mission chapel in Deer Park, which was named in honor of Saints Cyril and Methodius.

After World War II, as housing developments sprung up in Deer Park to accommodate veterans and their families, Ss. Cyril and Methodius outgrew its schoolhouse chapel. In June 1949 Bishop Molloy consecrated a new, 340-seat, colonial-style church for the mission. But the pace of Deer Park's expansion only quickened. By the time Molloy raised Ss. Cyril and Methodius to parish status in July 1956, 10,000 people were attending its Sunday Masses and the newly appointed pastor, Fr. James J. Behan, was celebrating additional Masses in the local movie theater and the VFW hall. So, Behan obtained seven acres of land and began fundraising for a new parish plant. The parish's mostly young and middle-income families contributed their dimes and quarters, as one associate pastor put it, raising nearly $30,000 at a single parish dance, all in hope of having a church and school of their own.[3] The parish plant they built cost $2.25 million.

The parish's facilities were extensive but they were barely enough. The rectory contained the parish offices and living quarters for the parish's priests, while the convent—with its own chapel—provided room for ten nuns, with the possibility of adding lodging for ten more. The two-story school, which was opened in September 1962 and staffed by the Sisters of Saint Joseph from Brentwood, contained twenty-four classrooms for more than 1,000 students, as well as a library, offices, nurse's room, teachers' lounge, supply room, and cafeteria.[4] But with nearly 800 parish baptisms a year and a waiting list just as long, the building was still too small. Over 6,200 children who attended public schools received religious instruction in the parish's Confraternity of Christian Doctrine (CCD) program, one of the largest in the diocese. Because the parish's territory covered thirty-five square miles, transporting those public school students to the parish plant for religious education was exceedingly difficult, so classes were held in 180 parishioners' homes and conducted by 230 lay volunteer teachers.

It was the church, however, that was the crown jewel of Ss. Cyril and Methodius's new plant. The cruciform nave held 1,200 congregants and allowed for unobstructed sightlines to the altar. The basement contained a parish library, a soundproofed mothers' room, and a 1,000-seat auditorium where parishioners attended overflow Masses on Sunday mornings. While these features made the structure "unusually functional," one observer remarked it was also "striking in its beauty" thanks to "historical refinements," including "Byzantine touches, mosaic-tiled columns, and terrazzo floors." The emphasis, nonetheless, was clearly on the modernity of the design. A parish journal exuded that the church's "clean architectural details, its bright and luminous atmosphere, depart from the traditional to exemplify the spirit of the young progressive parish whose prayers and devotion" had made it possible.[5] According to *The Long Island Catholic* diocesan newspaper, it quickly gained a reputation as "a shrine to see."[6]

The story of Ss. Cyril and Methodius's explosive development, and the scene of bishop, priests, sisters, and laity proudly dedicating their new, modern facilities, are emblematic of American Catholicism in the years after World War II. Those postwar years were halcyon days for the Church marked by population growth, large numbers of priestly and religious vocations, institutional expansion, and a steady, if uneasy cultural acceptance of Catholicism that had no more powerful a symbol than the election of an Irish

Figure I.1. The sanctuary, nave, and transept of Ss. Cyril and Methodius Church (1963). *Source*: Ss. Cyril and Saint Methodius Church, Deer Park, Long Island, New York (Assorted Parish Journals file, ADRVC).

Catholic president, John F. Kennedy. The immigrant church of the previous generation gave way. In its place rose the suburban church.

Over the course of the nineteenth century, successive waves of immigrants from Europe had landed on America's shores, massively expanding the Catholic Church in the United States and shifting its centers of power from the countryside to the cities of the Northeast and Midwest. Historian Jay Dolan labeled the urban, ethnic, insular, and working-class Catholicism that emerged from this sea change the "Immigrant Church," and many of its features endured through World War II.[7] But between 1945 and 1965, American Catholicism experienced unprecedented growth. The Catholic population almost doubled from 23.9 million to 45.6 million members and the numbers of priests, religious sisters, and Catholic institutions expanded accordingly. Crucially, the number of students in Catholic colleges and universities tripled in large part due to the tuition assistance offered by the GI Bill.[8] These gains in educational attainment, combined with the nation's postwar economic boom and the increase of employment opportunities in management positions, meant that by the mid-1960s American Catholics had achieved or exceeded the national averages for education and income.[9]

As Catholics moved up into the ranks of the college-educated middle class, they also moved out into the nation's rapidly expanding suburbs, collapsing the walls of the urban Catholic ghetto. Thanks to the aging of the prewar housing stock, federal mortgage assistance for veterans, the construction of the interstate highway system, and the normalization of car ownership, the suburban housing market boomed. As the Catholic population in suburbia grew, so too did the ecclesial infrastructure of parishes and schools that was necessary to serve it. In 1945 there were only 295 parishes on Long Island and 214 of those were in the New York City boroughs of Brooklyn and Queens. By 1960 the number of parishes in the two boroughs remained unchanged, but in Nassau and Suffolk Counties the number had jumped from 81 to 114. The Catholic presence on Long Island had grown so much that the Holy See established a separate diocese, the Diocese of Rockville Centre, to administer the Church in the two suburban counties. It was the first entirely suburban diocese in the United States. As similar demographic patterns developed outside cities across the country, it would not be the last.[10]

The millions of Catholics who moved to the suburbs in the postwar period changed American Catholicism, American religion, American society, and American politics. As historian Thomas Sugrue has pointed out, however, this dramatic shift has largely gone unstudied by urban, political, and religious historians, including scholars of American Catholicism.[11] *Crabgrass Catholicism* argues that understanding the United States in the twentieth century requires a firm understanding of the suburban Church. Employing Dolan's *The Immigrant Church* as a model, it explores the effects of postwar suburbanization on American Catholicism by examining the formation and transformation of dioceses and parishes on Long Island over a forty-year period between 1945 and 1985. For Dolan, nineteenth-century New York was the "capital of American Catholicism," and "the most conspicuous example of what was taking place in many cities across the country."[12] The same is true of postwar New York, as its suburbs became iconic examples of the era's demographic change. Throughout the 1950s and 1960s the newspapers of New York's dioceses had national circulations and Francis Cardinal Spellman, the archbishop of New York, became one of America's most influential churchmen.

This study is especially focused on the Diocese of Rockville Centre, which throughout the 1960s was one of the fastest-growing Catholic communities in the nation.[13] "A diocese is Catholicism in miniature" as Kathleen Cummings, Timothy Matovina, and Robert Orsi have written; the "major nexus of contact between church and world," and therefore the "most relevant unit of historical study" for understanding how suburbanization reshaped American Catholicism.[14] When the Diocese of Rockville Centre was founded in 1957—the year before Pope John XXIII began his transformative reign as pope—commentators nationwide saw its creation as a sign of the Vatican's interest in addressing the unique challenges of suburban life. They urged the faithful to see Rockville Centre not only as a prototype for the suburban church, but as a model for the future of the Church as a whole..

Crabgrass Catholicism begins by describing the urban ethnic communities that generations of Catholic immigrants built and sustained, and the symbiotic relationship that existed between parish and neighborhood. At the same time, chapter 1 details Catholic leaders' historic ambivalence toward urban life and their advocacy of a return to the land. Exploring the reasons for the laity's exodus from the city—including the postwar housing crisis and theological rhetoric framing homeownership as the foundation of healthy family life—the chapter concludes by narrating the irony of Catholic intellectuals' newfound appreciation for the city amid the urban crisis of the 1960s and 1970s.

Chapter 2 surveys the demographic and institutional expansion of Catholicism into the suburbs of metropolitan New York. Arguing for Catholicism's importance in the processes of suburban development, it details how pastoral leaders and the faithful made decisions about establishing and funding new dioceses, parishes, and schools in the suburbs, and how developers and lay fraternal associations encouraged Catholics to purchase suburban homes based on their proximity to parish complexes. The chapter shows how power struggles within the hierarchy were an important element in decisions about diocesan restructuring. It briefly summarizes the largely negative reaction of Catholic public intellectuals, including priest-sociologist Andrew Greeley, to the rise of suburbia and argues that, in many ways, Church leaders attempted to simply transplant an urban model of the parish into the new suburban context. This failure to adapt models of ministry to the new suburban reality and their focus on the needs of city dwellers and urban parishes, led some commentators to suggest that by the 1970s the Church had "lost the suburbs."

Chapter 3 explores how space shapes religious practice. It begins by investigating how suburban parishes were established and financed by dioceses and parishioners. It then describes the variety of spaces in which suburban Catholics prayed, instructed their children in the faith, and performed acts of charity. Practical considerations regarding suburbia's spatial arrangement helped shift the center of Catholic practice from the parish plant to the family home and from public and communal expressions of piety to domestic and private forms of prayer. Because new parishes often lacked sufficient buildings and suburban transportation options were limited, gatherings that normally occurred in parish buildings—including Mass and religious education classes—had to be held in private homes. Suburbia also stripped the parish and the home of their deep association with ethnic identity and placed tremendous emphasis on domesticity and the nuclear family. As a result, more generically American forms of devotion and domestic rituals—such as home Masses, block rosaries, and self-guided retreats—rose in popularity, replacing communal devotions rooted in immigrant traditions. So, too, did Catholic charity and activism—including ecumenical outreach and efforts to improve race relations and civil rights—become centered in the home. Such changes undermined the traditional sense of the parish as a permanent, sacred space, at the same time that overcrowding in suburban parishes further diminished a sense of true community. These changes signaled the rise of a less communal, more individual understanding of the faith. Religious practice increasingly became one more personal choice that American Catholics made amid a panoply of social possibilities. Suburbanization therefore led to the wholesale questioning of the parish as the dominant means of structuring Catholic life.

Suburbanization also shifted the balance of power between priest and people, from the leadership of clergy to greater involvement of the laity in the Church's organization and mission. The suburban Church thereby anticipated the reforms of the Second Vatican Council and paved the way for their acceptance by the laity. Chapter 4 details how an increasingly well-educated laity helped found new suburban parishes, spearheaded building drives, formed parish school boards, and led religious education classes in the absence of women religious.

Suburban laity were also the driving force behind the explosive growth of new family apostolates, including the Christian Family Movement, the Cana Conference, and Marriage Encounter. Such experiences of parish leadership, along with new roles in the liturgy and the spread of parish and diocesan councils in the wake of Vatican II, fueled the laity's expectation of greater influence in Church affairs. But parish councils did not live up to their promise. By the 1980s, the councils had been hobbled by class and ideological divisions within the laity, differing expectations regarding their role in the parish, and concerns from priests and laity alike that they might undermine the rightful leadership role of the clergy. While councils rarely became instruments through which the laity influenced the day-to-day management of parish affairs, the number of lay men and women in positions of diocesan and parish leadership nevertheless continued to expand and meet the approval of the faithful.[15]

Chapter 5 explores the roles that race and ethnicity played in the formation and life of suburban parishes. Catholic migration to the suburbs reduced the importance of ethnicity—understood as a form of group association based on a combination of region of origin, ancestry, language, cultural traditions, and religion—in parish life.[16] Whereas urban parishes were often defined by the ethnic heritage of their parishioners, in the suburbs laity who once had seen themselves as Irish, Polish, or Italian Catholics came increasingly to see themselves simply as Catholic, and the religious rituals and social gatherings of parishes ceased to be informed by the traditions of European homeplaces. Long Island's high rate of racial segregation also led suburbanites to identify themselves as white. Despite the efforts of Church leaders and some suburban Catholics to support civil rights and parish integration, others among the laity chose their parish based on its racial exclusivity. As Latin American immigration to Long Island increased in the 1970s and 1980s, the Diocese of Rockville Centre wrestled with how best to serve a new community whose practice of the faith was so closely linked to its language and ethnic culture. Some white Catholics, wishing to recover their lost ethnic identity, responded by trying to revive religious traditions associated with their European heritage and with the urban ethnic neighborhood. The Church was thus forced to grapple with how race and ethnicity should inform religious practice even as parishes attempted to unite and serve faithful from diverse backgrounds.

Chapter 6 examines how the financial and social pressures of the suburbs forced American Catholics to rethink how they educated young people in the faith. In suburbia, amid a postwar baby boom, the bishops' long-desired goal of educating every Catholic child in a parish school slipped further and further from reach. Contrary to legend, many of Long Island's earliest postwar parishes took nearly a decade before they opened a school. Even in the 1950s and early 1960s, as suburban dioceses rushed to build new parochial schools, there were never enough teaching sisters or classrooms to provide every Catholic child with a parochial education. This highlights the central role religious women played in the passing on of the faith and in the faithful's day-to-day experience of the Church, as well as the significant troubles caused by an insufficient number of religious sisters. Both a lack of open desks and the increased tuition costs needed to hire lay faculty drove more and more Catholic parents, who were already struggling under the weight of suburban mortgages and property taxes, to choose public schooling for their children.

Responding to such practical concerns and to Vatican II-era changes in catechetical theology, some educational theorists, parents, and pastoral leaders questioned the benefits of maintaining a parallel Catholic school system. Instead, they called for greater investment in afterschool programs of religious education. By the late 1960s and 1970s, even Long Island parishes that could afford to construct school buildings were operating "catechetical centers" instead of traditional parochial schools. Chapter 6 argues that debates over parochial schools and the religious education of children—like debates over civil rights, differing interpretations of the Second Vatican Council held in Rome between 1962 and 1964, and responses to Pope Paul VI's 1968 encyclical, *Humanae Vitae*, on the morality of artificial contraception—created left-right divisions within the Church. The chapter concludes with the rise of Catholic school closures in the early 1980s, the laity's reaction to those closures, and concerns about the success of afterschool catechetical programs in passing on the faith to the next generation.

Chapter 7 details how the demographic and economic pressures that suburbia exerted on Catholic education had profound effects on Catholics' participation in postwar politics. The fiscal crisis threatening Catholic schools in the 1950s and 1960s led America's Catholic bishops to redouble their efforts to obtain state aid for nonpublic schools. By narrating the 1967 defeat of a revised New York State constitution that would have allowed some state funding of nonpublic schools, chapter 7 shows that Catholic voters ultimately prioritized tax relief and local control over obtaining state aid for parochial schools. Suburban Catholics became increasingly dissatisfied with New Deal liberalism and increasingly open to conservative political positions. Catholic parents on Long Island who were attempting to secure religion's place in their children's public schools, drove some of the Supreme Court's most consequential postwar rulings on church and state. Such efforts foreshadowed the conservative coalition-building role that Catholics would play in the gathering culture wars. The chapter concludes with the 1980 presidential election, the US Senate election of Alfonse D'Amato, and the role that suburban Catholic voters on Long Island played in the so-called Reagan Revolution as they abandoned the New Deal coalition and became suburban swing voters.

Just as suburbanization drove profound political change, the epilogue suggests, it also ultimately contributed to a crisis of religious disaffiliation. In the era of the suburban church the faith became one more consumer choice, parishes struggled to pass the faith on to the next generation, and political polarization and the trauma of clergy sexual abuse drove more of the faithful from the Church. The emergence of crabgrass Catholicism in the postwar period thus continues to shape and reshape the US Church even today.

Crabgrass Catholicism places religion at the center of scholarship on the growth of suburbs and on suburban life and politics. It demonstrates that it is only through accounting for the religious lives of suburbanites that we can fully understand the processes of suburbanization and the experience of suburbia. Its title is a tribute to Kenneth T. Jackson's 1985 landmark text, *Crabgrass Frontier*, which signaled suburban history's emergence as a robust subfield.[17] But Jackson, like many of the earliest scholars of suburbanization, overlooked how religion organized suburban space and shaped suburban economics, politics, and family life. The so-called new suburban history, which emerged after 2000, countered claims that suburbs were "homogenous, conformist, and bourgeois," highlighting suburbia's racial and class diversity.[18] Other studies explored the consumer culture of postwar suburbs, the lives of suburban women, and even the suburban seeds of the environmental movement.[19] But the "new" suburban history was no more attentive to the importance of religion than the "old." Surveying several of the most important contributions to the new suburban history, Michelle Nickerson assesses that historians have ignored the religious lives of suburbanites, how religion helps organize suburban space, and how religion shapes suburban politics and economics.[20]

Even historians of American Catholicism have typically noted but glossed over the processes and effects of suburbanization.[21] A flurry of Catholic commentary on suburbia in the late 1950s and early 1960s—highlighted by the publication of Andrew Greeley's *The Church and the Suburbs* in 1959—receded quickly and, in the sixty-plus years since, Catholic suburbanization has been woefully understudied.[22] US Catholic historians have focused instead on those faithful who remained in the urban core, on the cultural upheavals of the 1960s, and on the religious reforms of the Second Vatican Council. Gerald Gamm's *Urban Exodus* and John McGreevy's *Parish Boundaries*, for example, both explore the cultural, theological, and organizational explanations behind Catholics' relative reluctance to leave their urban neighborhoods. They address the conflicts that erupted between these Catholics and newly arriving African American residents over racial integration and civil rights.[23] But the suburban experience is largely omitted from these stories, which hampers our understanding of how Catholicism evolved in postwar America. This is especially regrettable because Catholic historians have long lamented that mainstream histories of twentieth-century America rarely engage with Catholicism despite the fact that one in four Americans is Catholic, and they comprise the nation's largest denomination.[24]

Such engagement with American Catholics requires meeting them where they live. The history of suburbia is particularly useful in correcting this scholarly omission, because as Kevin Kruse and Thomas Sugrue have argued, the "transformation of the United States into a suburban nation" is central to the story of postwar America.[25] American Catholics were essential to the formation of postwar suburbs. *Crabgrass Catholicism*, indeed, shows how the study of US Catholicism, with its hierarchical leadership and its structure of archdioceses, dioceses, and parishes, allows for a truly metropolitan approach to urban, political, and religious history. It argues that the ecclesial institutions Catholics built, and the faith communities they formed, were crucial in creating suburban infrastructure and culture. It also shows, in turn, how suburban life intensified Catholics' assimilation, transformed their practice of the faith and their role in the Church's institutions, and reshaped their political priorities and allegiances.

More than that, *Crabgrass Catholicism* puts American Catholics at the center of the most significant political developments of the late twentieth century. Recent scholarship on the politics of the suburbs has focused almost exclusively on evangelical Protestants and the rise of the right in the Sunbelt South.[26] Meanwhile, recent scholarship on Catholics and postwar politics has stressed how racial backlash and opposition to abortion drove Catholic voters toward an alliance with conservatives.[27] But this study shows how, from at least the 1950s, the economic pressures of suburbanization led bishops to redouble their quest for state funds for parochial schools, and led lay Catholics to demand relief from skyrocketing suburban taxes.[28] This not only opened a fissure between the political concerns of the hierarchy and the laity, but also indicated the laity's growing disaffection with the state and New Deal liberalism.[29] The pressure of suburban mortgages and taxes also drove Catholic parents to place their children in public schools and, in turn, to exert influence on school boards to include prayer and moral formation in those schools. These local efforts by Long Island Catholics had national consequences in legal debates and Supreme Court cases about the presence of religion in public life. This book thus shows how postwar suburbanization, taxation, and education reshaped the issues that motivated Catholic voters, transformed them into swing voters, and prefigured the tax revolts, culture wars, and political polarization that would reorient American politics in the decades to come.[30]

Crabgrass Catholicism also offers a distinctive argument within the growing body of scholarship that explores the antecedents, implementation, and reception of the Second Vatican Council.[31] Rather than portraying the Council as a sudden and revolutionary event driven by theologians and conciliar documents, *Crabgrass Catholicism* stresses the grassroots origins of religious reform.[32] Crucially, the book argues that conciliar reforms amplified changes that were already occurring in Catholic conceptions of the parish, in the roles of priests and laity, in parish associations and devotional life, and in religious education, all because of the material conditions of postwar suburbanization.[33] The rise of suburbia, its structural organization, its familial ideal, and the "ethnic amalgamation" it helped accomplish undermined the devotional ethos that had defined urban and ethnic Catholicism. Catholic spiritual life and parish worship was thus transformed even before the liturgical changes mandated by the Second Vatican Council.[34] In suburbia the center of Catholic life shifted from the parish to the home. Traditional lay associations and forms of piety gave way to new family apostolates and domestic liturgies. The pioneering of new suburban parishes opened leadership opportunities for the laity who spearheaded funding drives and took up membership on parochial school boards. This led to greater expectations of shared responsibility even before parish councils were established in the wake of the Council.

Altogether, *Crabgrass Catholicism* is therefore a new history not merely of how religion shaped Long Island's postwar suburbs, nor even of how suburbanization altered American Catholicism, but of how suburban Catholics were at the center of some of the most significant social and political developments of the postwar era. Through a metropolitan approach to urban, religious, and political history, *Crabgrass Catholicism* tells a much broader and vitally important story of transformations in global faith and national politics.

ONE

An Urban Catholic World: Agrarianism, Urbanism, and the Ethnic Parish

Throughout the 1950s and 1960s, as America struggled to address an urban housing crisis and the suburbs boomed, a debate played out in the pages of American Catholic periodicals between those who preferred city life and those who longed for a home in the suburbs. In March 1950 Muriel Reno wrote in *America* about the urban housing project into which she, her husband, and son had moved in New York City. Projects like it had "mushroomed in large cities throughout the nation," she wrote, and in her estimation, they were "a practical, if not ideal, solution" to the nation's housing demands. Reno catalogued the advantages the project offered its youngest members, including playgrounds, organized recreation, and ample playmates. She also celebrated the expansion of nearby parishes and parochial schools to accommodate the new project's residents. A third neighborhood parish had just been founded, the two original churches had added extra priests and Masses, a $1-million Catholic school had been opened, and the parishes' social programs expanded to provide "card parties, dances, and discussions of family problems" for the project's residents.[1]

In July 1955 Harry Schlegel penned his own defense of city life in the pages of *The Sign*. Having lived in the suburbs, he knew the expense of patching the driveway and repairing the washing machine and he longed for the convenience of the city's subways and laundromats. In the same spread in *The Sign* Art Smith argued in favor of the suburbs. Despite there always being "something that needs fixing" in a suburban home, Smith couldn't keep from dreaming about owning one. "Did you ever try being *proud* of an apartment?," he asked readers. "It can't be done."[2] And in the very same volume in which Schlegel and Smith's debate between "Town and Country" appeared, an article about the Archbishop Walsh Homes in Newark,

New Jersey, touted the public housing complex's safety, amenities, and community. And yet Catholic resident Jeanne Daugherty said that she and her husband combed the real estate section of the newspaper every evening. "We don't plan on staying here forever," she laughed. "A home of our own—that's our aim; it always has been."³

This Catholic debate over the relative merits of city and suburb was played out against a long history of American Catholic thought about and creation of urban life. It was European immigration from the 1820s to the 1850s that first made the US Catholic Church a highly urban and ethnic institution. In an era of rapid urbanization Catholic immigrants built American city life by fusing the neighborhood with the ethnic parish which was dominated by its priests and religious sisters, centered on its church and school, and bound together by its communal worship and devotions. At the same time, these immigrants built an entire parallel Catholic world—what John McGreevy has labeled a Catholic "milieu"—of educational, social, and service institutions to rival Protestant and secular peers.⁴

Despite the fact that the Church in the United States had become an overwhelmingly urban institution, many Catholic leaders in the late nineteenth and early twentieth centuries denigrated the city and idealized rural communities as bulwarks of faith and family. As World War II was ending, and the nation was confronted by a massive housing shortage, Catholic advocates of rural life imagined a postwar world in which the faithful enjoyed the best of both worlds, working in industrial cities while remaining close to the land on suburban plots. Other Catholic leaders and organizations advocated for increased public housing and mortgage assistance to address the housing crisis. Whatever solution they proposed, these commentators argued for the necessity of quality housing in maintaining healthy family life. The rhetoric they employed only served to heighten the laity's desire for homeownership, which increasingly meant life in the suburbs.

The form of urban parish life built by European immigrants largely continued through World War II until Catholics began moving to the suburbs in the postwar period. Researchers and critics explored why people were embracing suburbia and highlighted its purported benefits for family life and leisure. Many of these Catholic elites celebrated the demise of the urban ethnic parish, which they saw as a stultifying ghetto. But even as the laity fled inner cities for the suburbs, Catholic intellectuals and pastoral leaders in the 1960s and 1970s turned to ridiculing suburbia and adopted a newfound appreciation for metropolitanism thanks to the civil rights movement and the urban crisis.

Catholic Urbanization and Agrarianism

Until the first two decades of the nineteenth century, the majority of American Catholics—like the vast majority of Americans in general—lived on small farms and in rural villages. The epicenter of Catholicism in the United States was Maryland where, in 1789, the Vatican had established the nation's first and only diocese in the once-Catholic colony. In April 1808 the Vatican elevated Baltimore to the status of archdiocese and established new dioceses in New York, Philadelphia, Boston, and Bardstown, Kentucky. While doing deference to the nation's original See city, the Vatican's restructuring presaged a sea change in American Catholic demographics. Between 1820 and 1920 a wave of European immigration flooded America's shores, expanding the Catholic population "by an overwhelming 1,300 percent, from about 318,000 in 1830—3 percent of the total American white population—to 4.5 million in 1870, representing about 13 percent of that population."[5] As the Church expanded, its center of power also shifted to the cities of the Northeast and Midwest where the majority of Irish and German immigrants settled, thus making "the American Church simultaneously urban and ethnic."[6]

However much they may have wanted to pursue farming in their new homeland, many Catholic immigrants found they lacked the financial wherewithal and knowledge of American farming conditions necessary to succeed. Meanwhile, the United States was rapidly urbanizing during the nineteenth century and cities' expanding economies offered immigrants numerous opportunities for employment. In cities Catholic immigrants also found support from a community of their compatriots and coreligionists. Catholic leaders were especially concerned about the possibility of losing immigrant faithful to Protestantism—a process that was referred to as "leakage." This threat was particularly acute in rural areas that lacked sufficient Catholic institutions and were marked by nativist politics or successful Protestant missionary activity.[7] Some bishops, most notably the formidable Archbishop John Hughes of New York, therefore supported the urban settlement of Catholic immigrants.[8]

But despite the threat of leakage, the majority of Catholic leaders remained convinced that rural life was morally superior to life in the city, which they saw as a breeding ground of individualism, vice, violence, and secularism. Catholics' experience in their European homelands and their adoption of a Jeffersonian "faith in the yeoman farmer" convinced them that rural living supported a life of family, virtue, and faith, as well as the local institutions that served as crucial intermediaries between the individual and the state.[9] The bishops therefore entertained various schemes for the establishment of financially self-sufficient Catholic farm colonies centered on a parish church and school.[10] Although these colonization efforts met with only marginal success, their greatest advocate, Bishop John Lancaster Spalding of Peoria, Illinois, helped popularize the theory that because urban birth rates were lower than those in the country, American Catholicism's future was inextricably linked with the health of rural communities.[11]

Concern for the health of the Church in rural areas led Edwin V. O'Hara, a priest of the Archdiocese of Oregon City and later bishop of Great Falls, Montana and Kansas City, Missouri, to found the most influential Catholic agrarian movement, the National Catholic Rural Life Conference (NCRLC). Born and raised in rural Minnesota and ordained in 1905, O'Hara earned a national reputation for his innovative approach to rural education and his interest in health care, farm management, and economic cooperation. In 1923, along with seventy other rural life leaders, O'Hara established the NCRLC to coordinate meetings, facilitate decisions, and serve as a clearinghouse for successful rural aid programs.[12] Parallel Protestant and Jewish organizations served as important models and early collaborators for the NCRLC, but even more important, the NCRLC operated alongside other Catholic organizations involved in agrarian concerns, including Francis C. Kelley's Catholic Extension Society, Frederick P. Kenkel's Central Verein, the Grail Movement, and the Catholic Worker Movement founded by Dorothy Day and Peter Maurin.[13]

In concert with these other groups, the NCRLC was highly successful at convincing even urban Catholic leaders of the importance of rural life for the continued health of the Church. David Bovée has summarized that "most of the nationally circulated Catholic periodicals of the day either editorialized or carried articles on the subject" and "in all cases they supported O'Hara's approach." Even the great social reformer, Msgr. John A. Ryan, who was overwhelmingly concerned with issues of the industrial economy, endorsed O'Hara's theories.[14] As the NCRLC's membership expanded from the late 1930s through the late 1950s, its annual conference and its numerous publications helped spread the conference's agrarian message.[15]

An Urban Catholic World

Even as American Catholic leaders voiced criticisms of urban conditions and support for rural life, nineteenth-century Catholic immigrants from Ireland and Germany settled in urban centers where they encountered a vital Church that was increasingly defined by parish life. Urban parishes flourished as a crucial means of serving immigrants' needs, defending against nativist hostility, and both preserving ethnic culture and assisting in assimilation. As urban neighborhoods grew into what Jay Dolan has called "ethnic villages," parishes were increasingly distinguished by the ethnicity and language of their immigrant residents and, in turn, the towers and steeples of parish churches marked "the boundaries of the city's neighborhoods."[16] The parish was often the first institution that immigrants encountered and it became "their principal means of identification with the city," regulating most of their activities outside of work.[17] Well into the twentieth century Catholics defined where they were from in their city by the name of their parish church, not by the name of their neighborhood or district.[18]

Although the mid-nineteenth century saw a proliferation of "manuals of prayer, catechisms, and devotional literature" intended to help the laity maintain and transmit the faith, it was mainly through the parish that immigrants preserved the beliefs and rituals of the old country. With little space and few valuables of their own, immigrants considered the architecture, art, liturgy, and music of the parish church and of Sunday Mass and public devotions a source of pride.[19] Parishes typically held three to five Masses as well as Vespers and Benediction on Sundays, and some form of instruction or devotions several evenings a week. Public forms of prayer such as novenas, Eucharistic processions, Marian feasts, and Forty Hours devotions marked the neighborhood's calendar. Most of all, the parish mission—a kind of communal retreat held in the church over the course of several nights—flourished as a means of revivifying personal faith and parish life.[20]

The number and size of Manhattan's parish churches, and their schedule of services, however, suggest that in the 1860s only about half of New York's Catholics were regularly attending Sunday Mass. As a result priests and laity alike dedicated themselves to expanding the number of the city's parishes in order to attract a greater number of faithful in an ever-growing population. Between 1840 and 1864 Archbishop John Hughes had founded 61 new parishes but his successor, John Cardinal McCloskey, established another 88 new parishes between 1864 and 1885. Thus the Church in New York went from having 70 parishes and 109 priests to serve 202,000 Catholics in 1850, to having 277 parishes and 534 priests to serve 800,000 faithful in 1880—even as the counties of northern New Jersey were detached to form a new diocese.[21]

Beyond their parish church, Catholic immigrants' desire to maintain the faith amid the shock of cultural change and in the face of anti-Catholic nativism, also led to the creation of a parallel world of schools, hospitals, orphanages, and other institutions. By the end of the nineteenth century they had built "a thriving subculture within the confines of most large American cities," which has been dubbed "the Catholic ghetto."[22] At the heart of this parallel institutional world was the American nun. Beginning around 1820 the number of women religious outstripped that of priests, but there were still fewer than 500 nuns in the United States in 1830.[23] Thanks to waves of antebellum immigration that number grew rapidly, however. By 1860 there were over 5,000 American nuns and by 1900 there were approximately 50,000 nuns who operated almost 4,000 parochial schools.[24]

More than any other element of this parallel world, it was the parish school that became the "hallmark of American Catholicism." Although some critics questioned the advisability of isolating from the broader culture by not using the public school system, the majority of lay faithful desired a Catholic education for their children. In 1850 New York had 17 Catholic schools educating 9,120 students, and by 1880 the system had grown to 209 schools with 76,392 pupils. And yet there were still insufficient facilities, funds, and personnel to provide a Catholic education for every student who desired one. In 1880 only 39 percent of Catholic children in Brooklyn and 20 percent of Catholic children in New York attended parochial schools.[25]

As immigration swelled the ranks of women religious, and made the urban parish the center of American Catholic life, the role and ministry of priests evolved. No longer an itinerant missionary responsible for vast rural territories, the American priest became an urban institution builder. "Brick-and-mortar" priests, as they have been called, were remembered most for having built or renovated parish buildings and established parish organizations.[26] The success of these builder priests was especially impressive in light of the constant financial problems that parishes faced as they tried to serve a rapidly growing number of members with limited financial resources. Although the laity continued to initiate the founding of new parishes and raised necessary funds "through fairs, parties, and other social functions," lay trustees no longer built and owned parish churches as they had in a previous era. Now the bishop's hand was strengthened as he came to hold all of the Church's property as *corporation sole*. This strengthening of the institutional structure of the Church and the centralization of authority with the bishop and his chancery were necessary, in part, to mitigate against the possibility that tensions between the immigrant ethnic groups of an increasingly diverse local church would lead to schism along national lines.[27]

Despite the rising authority of the clergy, more and more of the laity participated in associations of the faithful for devotional, social, cultural, and charitable purposes. Usually segregated by sex, these spiritual organizations based in the parish wed prayer to socialization and good works. While Catholics were suspicious of, and largely uninvolved in, major reform movements such as abolition, women's rights, prison reform, and public education, they did participate in and support charitable efforts to provide for the poor, homeless, and orphans of their own community.[28]

Between 1880 and 1930 the American Catholic Church absorbed an even greater wave of immigrants. These new immigrants hailed principally from Eastern and Southern Europe, especially from Italy, and so parishes evolved to serve the demands of "a bewildering array of unique immigrant groups." National parishes, formed to provide for the needs of an ethnic community rather than the residents of a particular geographical location, were founded in ever-greater numbers. In Manhattan, for example, half of the new parishes opened between 1902 and 1918 were national parishes and one-third of those served Italian immigrants.[29]

The devotional life of parishes also continued to evolve. The singing of Sunday Vespers virtually disappeared from parishes in this period, but Holy Hours of Adoration became popular, the number of Sunday Masses increased, and the practice of setting aside one of those Masses for the children of the parish school was developed.[30] Most importantly, within national parishes especially, feast days and festivals celebrating a regional saint or Marian devotion became a popular means of maintaining the traditions of the old country.[31] Although pastors often resented the laymen who organized such events, and lamented that the devotions "overemphasized local and village saints to the neglect of more central teachings of the Church," they were forced to tolerate the processions through the streets of a saint's statue because they proved to be lucrative fundraisers for parishes. Parishes also employed pew rents, special collections, and various benevolence societies, which raised funds by hosting social gatherings but also offered their members a spiritual benefit for their investment of time and money. Parish societies and sodalities of all kinds proliferated and included a higher percentage of parishioners than ever before. Between 1880 and 1900, for example, the number of parish conferences of the St. Vincent de Paul Society doubled.[32]

The number of parishes with a school also steadily increased between 1880 and 1930, so that by 1930 69 percent of Brooklyn parishes operated a school. The percentage of Catholic children attending parochial schools also jumped significantly, though still less than half of all Catholic children attended a parochial school. Still, the urban ethnic parish was highly successful in inculcating the faith in the younger generation of Catholics as is indicated by the era's low number of marriages outside the faith and its high number of vocations to the priesthood and religious life.[33]

Between 1930 and World War II, as federal legislation stemmed the tide of immigration, the Church turned its attention from the needs of newly arrived immigrants to "consolidating and stabilizing the parochial system." Increasingly removed from the experience of immigration, Catholics slowly began to define themselves less by ethnicity and more by religion. While some parishes continued to be associated with particular ethnic communities, and parishes remained insular, the parish's role as an "ethnic fortress diminished and it became a religious fortress." Accordingly, the number of new national parishes being founded dropped and many previously national parishes were converted into, or merged with, territorial parishes.[34] A nascent religious solidarity across ethnic lines provided the Church increased institutional and political power and offered individual Catholics a larger pool of coreligionists in which to seek potential marriage partners.[35]

The clergy continued to be concerned with the building and maintenance of the parish plant—the assemblage of church, school, rectory, convent, and gymnasium that often comprised an entire city block—and with the constant fundraising and debt reduction it required. Even newer parishes were forced to expand their facilities within just a few years in the face of increasing demands. Parishioners continued to provide remarkable financial support to their parishes and financing was increasingly available to parishes from the diocese. In the 1930s and 1940s bishops established Diocesan Loan Funds to provide parishes with low interest loans, and made every effort to ensure that newly established parishes were given land and start-up funds from the diocese.

The number of parish schools rose steadily but the Catholic school system continued to educate only a minority of all Catholic children. Fears that many youths went without any religious education led to the expansion of Confraternity of Christian Doctrine (CCD) programs, which provided Catholic children attending public schools afterschool religious instruction. Concerns over juvenile delinquency also led to an explosion of parish recreational activities and athletic clubs for youths under the direction of Catholic Youth Organizations (CYO).[36]

Although the folk religion of the immigrants lost much of its hold on their American-born descendants, subsequent generations of urban Catholics attended Mass in even higher numbers than their forebears and maintained a robust ritual and devotional life.[37] The 1920s through the 1950s represented the height of devotional Catholicism in which the rosary and novenas to the saints were highly popular, annual parish missions continued to flourish, and public devotions such as Miraculous Medal novenas drew thousands of worshippers weekly.[38]

Membership in lay associations also expanded significantly and new parish organizations were established. This was especially true for sodalities of women, but Catholic men also joined parish Holy Name Societies in record numbers. Indeed, the 1930s saw the adoption in the United States of the European concept of Catholic Action, which had developed after World War I in Italy and rapidly spread internationally. Conceived in part as an alternative to fascism, Catholic Action argued that modern social changes required an increase in the laity's participation in the apostolic ministries of the hierarchy. The concept was given papal approval in the writings of Pope Pius XI in the late 1920s and early 1930s, though a number of lay associations dedicated to its principles were already thriving, including the Young Christian Worker Movement in Belgium, and the New York Catholic Benevolent Society, which worked to care for orphaned children.[39] Programs of Catholic Action taught participants to "see, judge, and act" in response to the needs of society, and inculcated in the laity a sense that their apostolate, or activity as Christians in the world, was of vital importance.

The concept of Catholic Action was wed to and advanced by the liturgical movement, which aimed to improve the quality and beauty of the Church's sacramental worship, art, and music, to deepen the laity's involvement in communal worship, and to harness the power of the Mass to the advancement of social reform.[40] Like Catholic Action, the liturgical movement had its origins in Europe, but in the 1920s Fr. Virgil Michel of St. John's University in Minnesota spurred the movement's spread in the United States. Michel and his fellow liturgical reformers were convinced that the theological symbols of the liturgy and the cycles of the liturgical seasons would be better appreciated by those faithful who lived in close contact with the land. They therefore advocated the revival of traditional rural rituals such as rogation days, and cooperated with Catholic agrarians who advanced liturgical renewal by sponsoring retreats, devotions, and liturgy weeks.[41]

Altogether, the 1930s and 1940s were "a time of minimal internal change in the Catholic parish" as "the established patterns of parish life persisted and were elaborated."[42] The eve of the Second World War was a kind of golden age for the parish, in which the parallel Catholic world built by successive waves of European immigrants and their children was largely preserved within urban parish boundaries. The parish remained a fortress that delimited assimilation, perpetuated Catholic difference, defended against anti-Catholic bigotry, and successfully passed the faith to younger generations. It was still dominated by its pastor, its spiritual and associational life continued to center on its church, and its school was still the focus of formation in the faith.

Just beneath the surface, however, seeds of change were gestating. Within the Church, the small groups of reformers leading the liturgical renewal and Catholic Action would, over time, help transform understandings of lay involvement in the Church's ministry and prayer. Some thirty years later, in the 1960s, these theological and pastoral developments would help inspire and be fulfilled in the documents of the Second Vatican Council.[43] But changes in the laity's lived experience of the Church were also being driven by forces outside the Church. As suburbanization began to transform the metropolitan landscape, the urban Catholic world built by generations of Catholic immigrants would be transformed and the laity who abandoned the city for the crabgrass frontier would refashion the parish and their role in it.

Prewar Suburbanization and the Postwar Housing Crisis

Even as the immigrants of the 1830s through the 1890s established the urban parish as the most important institution in American Catholicism, cities were already beginning to be transformed by suburbanization. As historian Kenneth T. Jackson has shown, between 1815 and 1875 a pattern of demographic and spatial change took hold of American cities resulting in "suburban affluence and center despair."[44] In the New York metropolitan area Brooklyn was growing in population at a faster pace than Manhattan by 1830 and, according to one midcentury journalist, this was resulting in "the desertion of the city by men of wealth."[45] The same phenomenon began to affect New York's Catholic parishes as well. By the end of the nineteenth century, Monsignor James McGean, the pastor of the oldest Catholic parish in New York State, St. Peter's Church on Barclay Street in Manhattan, "was complaining of the exodus of his better-off parishioners to Brooklyn and New Jersey."[46]

The rapid expansion of the region's Catholic population due to immigration, and the changing distribution of that population across urban, suburban, and rural areas in the mid-nineteenth century resulted in a reorganization of metropolitan New York's Catholic dioceses. In 1847 the Vatican established new dioceses in Albany and Buffalo, removing those northern cities and their surrounding counties from the jurisdiction of the Diocese of New York. Three years later, in July 1850, New York was elevated to the status of metropolitan archdiocese. Another three years later, in July 1853, the counties of northeastern New Jersey were established as the Diocese of Newark, and all of Long Island—then comprising Kings, Queens, and Suffolk

Counties, and after 1899 adding the newly created Nassau County—was established as the Diocese of Brooklyn. This left the Archdiocese of New York with governance over Manhattan, the Bronx, Staten Island, and the northern counties of Dutchess, Orange, Putnam, Rockland, Sullivan, Ulster, and Westchester, which it maintains to this day.[47] The establishment of a separate diocese in Brooklyn made pastoral sense at the time as Brooklyn had achieved legal status as an independent city in 1834.

Nationwide, suburban migration skyrocketed after World War I, propelled by the normalization of the automobile, rising wages, falling housing prices, and the passage of real estate tax exemptions.[48] In the New York metropolitan region suburban development in Brooklyn and Nassau County "picked up steam between 1900 and 1929 resulting in the decline of the Catholic population of the Archdiocese from 1,350,000 in 1900 to about 1,000,000 in 1940."[49] Suburbanization also shifted the growth regions within the archdiocese to the outskirts of Staten Island and the Bronx, and especially from the boroughs of New York City to the cities and suburbs to the north. Yonkers, for example, had just two parishes in 1890, but nine by 1900, and twenty by 1931. And in 1929 alone, Westchester County saw the addition of five parishes.[50]

The burgeoning process of suburbanization slowed considerably, however, during the Depression and World War II. The deprivations of the Depression and war rationing limited the financing and the availability of materials needed to maintain existing homes and build new ones. The volume and quality of the nation's housing stock declined as existing housing went unmaintained and new housing starts slowed to a trickle. During the New Deal programs were put in place that transformed the government's role in homebuilding and set the stage for a postwar suburban building boom. The Home Owners Loan Corporation (HOLC), signed into law in 1933, proved revolutionary because it normalized home buying through a "self-amortizing mortgage with uniform payments spread over the whole life of the debt." It also instituted a system for appraising a neighborhood, its residents, and its housing stock to determine its suitability for home loans. This system formed the basis of redlining, in which loans were not granted in neighborhoods deemed to be "at risk" especially because they were inhabited by African Americans.[51]

By war's end the nation had endured sixteen years of minimal home construction. The need for new quality housing was especially pressing because veterans were returning stateside, marrying, and starting families. Wilson Wyatt, who served as President Harry S. Truman's housing czar through 1946, estimated that the nation required an additional 5 million houses or apartments by the end of that year to accommodate demobilizing veterans.[52] Over the summer of 1946, the Bureau of the Census found that in most cities between 25 and 40 percent of married veterans were without homes of their own, that "more than two million families doubled up in homes, and more than a quarter million families were living in hotels, rooming houses, tourist camps, and similar places."[53]

Catholic Responses to the Housing Crisis

Catholic leaders were vocal about the urgent need to address this housing crisis, which Boston's Richard Cardinal Cushing referred to as "the problem most vitally affecting the nation's wellbeing and the future of family morality."[54] In their 1949 letter on "Christian Family," the US bishops lamented that social legislation to provide suitable housing for families was "slow, fumbling, and inadequate" and failed to remove "the great difficulties that lie in the way of those who wish to marry and establish homes."[55] Earlier that same year Congress had finally passed the Taft-Ellender-Wagner Housing Act, which the bishops had supported over the course of several years through a series of legislative setbacks.

The bishops' point man on housing for the better part of a decade had been Msgr. John O'Grady, the founding dean of the Catholic University of America's School of Social Work, and later the secretary of the National Conference of Catholic Charities.[56] O'Grady became involved in the housing issue in the 1930s and was a founding member of the National Housing Conference. Although he was initially focused on providing public housing for poor families, by the mid-1940s O'Grady was backing efforts to provide housing for middle-income earners. He served as an advisor in the drafting of the Taft-Ellender-Wagner Bill and repeatedly testified before Congress in support of the bill's passage. He also served as chairman of Housing Legislation Information Services (HLIS), a pro-housing lobby with thirty-one member organizations including the American Federation of Labor (AFL), Congress of Industrial Organizations (CIO), and the National Association for the Advancement of Colored People (NAACP).[57] O'Grady wrote editorials in *Catholic Charities Review* explaining the legislation's benefits and spoke in favor of the bill to skeptical audiences, including a 1946 convention of the American Legion.[58] He also organized some fifty meetings of Catholics across the country, orchestrated a meeting of ecumenical religious leaders, and personally lobbied President Truman all in hopes of getting the bill passed.[59]

Catholic periodicals, too, shined light on the housing crisis, proposed solutions, and advocated the passage of housing legislation. Between 1945 and 1950 *America* magazine ran frequent articles and editorials on the housing sector and potential policy solutions. Its coverage of the housing crisis revealed a suspicion of "the excessive individualism of builders, their lack of planning and cooperation," and their "opposition to price controls." While stating a preference for employing "as little government intervention as possible," the journal backed industrial planning, price controls, rationing of construction materials, and the employment of mass-production techniques.[60] The editors gave strong support to the Taft-Ellender-Wagner housing bill and, over the course of several Congresses, closely followed the bill's progression through committees to its ultimate passage.

Lay organizations, especially veterans' groups, were also invested in the housing issue. The Catholic War Veterans of America (CWV) had been founded in 1935 by Rev. Edward J. Higgins at the Church of the Immaculate Conception in Long Island City, Queens. After World War II veterans swelled its ranks and the organization grew to more than 200,000 members nationwide.[61] Although the CWV had posts across the country, none were "as large, as effectively organized, and as politically active" as those in Brooklyn and Queens and these posts "dominated the national organization for decades."[62] At the height of the Cold War the CWV would become notorious for supporting Senator Joseph McCarthy's brand of anticommunism. But the CWV was founded "For God, For County, and For Home," and in the late 1940s it worked with Jewish War Veterans, the American Legion, and Veterans of Foreign Wars (VFW) on the national housing crisis.[63] Robert F. Wagner Jr., son of the US senator and later mayor of New York City, served as chairman of the CWV's Housing Committee. In the spring of 1948 Wagner and the association's newspaper, *The Catholic War Veteran*, gave their full support to the bill sponsored by his father, the Taft-Ellender-Wagner Bill, which became the Housing Act of 1949. He argued the bill would provide sufficient financing for private industry to build homes that middle-income families could afford and would provide low-rent public housing for low-income families.[64]

At the heart of Catholic concern over the housing crisis was the conviction that adequate housing was essential for the overall health of family life. Church leaders were especially concerned that the only housing available to many families—living with relatives, slum apartments, and public housing alike—"failed to provide sufficient living room and privacy for families" with two or more children and would therefore lead to familial strife, juvenile delinquency, and "the almost automatic limitation on family size."[65] Father Daniel U. Hanrahan, pastor of Sacred Heart Church in St. Alban's, Queens, told the St. Vincent de Paul Society of Brooklyn that "the lack of space in which children can entertain their friends at home" forced children to "seek companionship in the streets" and was thus the "cause of much juvenile delinquency."[66] Others worried that "compact modern apartments" made "parents dread the arrival of another child for which additional space is unavailable" and noted that the nation's large cities, many of which had high concentrations of Catholics, were no longer showing "significant population increases."[67]

"Standing on Two Feet"—a Postwar Agrarian Vision

If postwar public housing and city apartments were too small or too expensive, what housing options remained for Catholic families concerned about domestic conflict, delinquent children, and the limitation of family size? For decades Catholic agrarians had been warning about the ill effects of urban life on birth rates and family size, and advocated that Catholic families return to the land. Such concerns about declining birthrates thus preceded by decades the late 1960s debate about the morality of contraception and complicates the typical account of Catholics and birth control use prior to *Humanae Vitae*.[68] And yet, agrarian arguments were not limited to the NCRLC's own publications or to its mostly midwestern membership. Rather, throughout the 1940s and early 1950s even national Catholic periodicals and urban diocesan newspapers advanced the "agrarian myth" for their largely city-dwelling readers.[69]

In the August 2, 1940, edition of *Commonweal*, Msgr. Luigi Ligutti of NCRLC published an article provocatively entitled "Cities Kill." While calling for more serious study of Catholic demographics, Ligutti argued that urban Catholics had "stopped even reproducing themselves." Ligutti ruefully noted that states with the lowest birthrates—New Jersey, Connecticut, Massachusetts, and New York—were also the states with the largest Catholic populations. "I recently shocked a Communion breakfast audience in the East," Ligutti wrote, "when I asked them to pray for Long Island, calling it the concentrated graveyard of Catholicity."[70] Even New York's Catholic periodicals published articles and editorials backing the NCRLC's take on the ill effects of urban living and the need to strengthen rural communities. A November 17, 1945, editorial in the Archdiocese of New York's *Catholic News* argued that the urban character of the US Church "placed most Catholics in an environment where the rearing of a family is most difficult," and where the population dwindles in the absence of immigration. And a March 20, 1948, editorial in *The Catholic News* urged bishops to ensure that rural communities with the highest birth rates had sufficient parishes and schools to pass on the faith.[71]

Figure 1.1. The cover of a 1947 NCRLC pamphlet. *Credit*: Department of Special Collections and University Archives, Raynor Memorial Libraries, Marquette University Archives.

As World War II was nearing its completion, Catholic agrarians dreamed of a postwar economy based on a large class of family farmers and proposed that veterans use the GI Bill's home loans to purchase small farms.[72] But after the war technological advancements encouraged agriculturists to further pursue economies of scale, and income disparities between city and farm increased. Many NCRLC leaders began urging urban workers to at least take up part-time suburban agriculture as a means of insulating themselves from the city and reconnecting with the land.[73] This project became known as "standing on two feet." Having one foot in the industrial city and another on the soil of farming would allow families who owned "homes with small acreages" to keep standing during economic upheaval.[74] In 1947 Walter John Marx thus admonished readers of *The Sign* to save enough money to pay cash for a couple of rural acres and then live in a tent while they used "the money they would have spent for rent, telephone, gas and electric" to purchase the building supplies needed to build their own home.[75] In a letter to the editor of *America* in 1949 Morton A. Hill, SJ, similarly recommended that Catholics "work in the city, and live in the country" in homes they built themselves and recommended several books that could provide them with building plans.[76] Even the director of the Social Action Department for the Diocese of Brooklyn, Fr. William F. Kelly, wrote in support of the two-footed economy. In 1950, in the diocesan newspaper *The Tablet*, Kelly rehearsed the agrarians' contention that the modern city was "the greatest sterilizer of human beings the world has ever known" and lamented that it was likely "too much to hope" that a slowdown in urban expansion might eventually lead to a "'foot on the farm and a foot in industry' arrangement in American life."[77]

The Appeal of the Suburbs and Homeownership

In 1957, as American suburbs boomed, Monsignor Ligutti welcomed the unfolding suburban exodus as "an ideal opportunity to strike a blow for healthier family life." In the agrarian tradition, he celebrated the opportunity "to show the people the advantages of getting a few acres . . . when they move away from the city."[78] But this was wishful thinking at best. In the decade after the war, it had become abundantly clear that Catholic agrarians' dire predictions about the demographic collapse of American Catholicism had not come to pass.[79] The ethnic national parish successfully maintained the faith of urban dwellers, rural birthrates declined to be on par with urban birthrates, and the postwar baby boom—which boosted the American population despite declines in rural communities—proved to be neither rural nor urban, but substantially suburban.[80] The two-footed living that Ligutti proposed, and the expansion of the highway system he thought it required, ultimately spawned a "crabgrass frontier," not the return to the land for which he had hoped.[81] Membership in the NCRLC peaked in 1958 at over 10,000 members, but began declining in 1959 and only leveled off at about 3,000 members in the mid-1960s.[82]

Still, strands of agrarianism's influence endured in the Church's promotion of homeownership and especially in the laity whose embrace of the postwar suburbs echoed the agrarian critique of urban life and its fervent belief in the virtues of homeownership and decentralized government. Throughout the postwar housing crisis, Catholic rhetoric made clear that inadequate housing was a threat to family life and society and that homeownership made for "better living, better youth, better morals and a better nation."[83] In 1951 the editors of *America* therefore celebrated that for the first time in American history more families owned their own homes than rented them and expressed hope that 60 percent of American families might be homeowners by 1960, if not by 1955.[84] In that same spirit Boston's Cardinal Cushing instructed graduates in Stonehill College's class of 1953:

> Whatever you be, be a friend to the future of the family and the sanctity of the home. . . . Aspire to own your own home at the earliest possible date. Identify your career and your eventual home. Make the first a means to the attainment of the second as your home, in turn, should be a means to the perfection both of society and of yourself.[85]

Unfortunately, the first wave of houses then appearing in suburban developments, including the iconic Levittown on Long Island, were deemed by some Catholic critics to be no better than small city apartments. Writing in *America* in 1949, James Bernard Kelley lamented that the $10,000 homes being built outside of New York City had only five rooms. Although they were advertised as "capable of expansion," Kelley called the expansion attic "the greatest fraud ever perpetuated on the American public." Without a basement for storage, or a garage for a car, these "jerry-built affairs" were also so far from the city that homeowners had to spend fifteen to twenty dollars on commuting costs to only see their children on the weekends. "Instead of being the start of a home for a growing family," Kelley railed, such a basic house "forcibly restricted" family size and was a "millstone" around a homebuyer's neck. In 1952 the editors of *America* concurred, referring to the prevalence of suburban "birth-control housing" and suggesting that Planned Parenthood Association of America was "exerting pressure on room-space in proposed new housing units" in order to promote smaller family size.[86]

In 1959 Fr. Andrew M. Greeley—a priest of the Archdiocese of Chicago who would go on to become a prolific sociologist of American Catholicism—published *The Church and the Suburbs*, a survey of suburban Catholicism based on his experience as a newly ordained priest assigned to a suburban parish. Greeley interrogated the reasons why so many Catholics were flocking to the suburbs and acknowledged the role played by federal policies, developments in transportation, and the advent of mass-construction techniques in propelling suburbanization. But he prioritized the "social and psychological reasons" behind suburbanization. A suburban house, Greeley summarized, fulfilled homebuyers' instinctive desire to "have a place they can call a home of their own." Homeowners deemed the suburbs ideal for family life, precisely because they were "a happy compromise between the bliss of the countryside and the convenience of the city."[87] Suburbia's fresh air, open space, and backyard swimming pools were insurance against the youth delinquency that was bred in apartment houses and on crowded city streets.

Most other Catholic commentators agreed that Catholic suburbanites sought homes of their own in which to raise their children outside the overcrowded and polluted city. Jesuit Father Neil Hurley wrote that, "the desire to leave the soot, concrete, crowds and noise of the large cities was always strong among American families."[88] Dennis Clark concurred that, repelled by the "inhuman dimensions of city life," and longing for "home, land, and family," suburbanites were seeking "permanence, tradition, and communally held values." And Fr. Robert Howes agreed that suburbia's "schools, air, space, and light" for the raising of children were "the most powerful magnet" for new suburbanites. Almost alone among Catholic commentators, Howes added that "the pursuit of localism" also drove suburbanites to flee the "one party" city for the chance at "genuine civic action" in more personal, less bureaucratic suburbs.[89]

Despite framing suburbanization as a flight from the problems of the city, Greeley did not explicitly attribute the suburban exodus to racist white flight. Greeley was more than willing to challenge suburban racism and lamented that Catholic suburbanites had been "far more interested in escaping from the oncoming minority groups . . . than in saving the old neighborhood." But he recognized that many white Catholics had "always wanted to escape" urban neighborhoods in order to own their own homes and have a small plot of land.[90] Even Dennis Clark, who served as director of the Catholic Interracial Council of New York and as editor of the *Interracial Review*, decried opposition to the racial integration of neighborhoods, but suggested that white Catholics feared losing property value and social status in an integrated neighborhood more than they feared the proximity of Blacks.[91]

Because Greeley and other commentators emphasized that suburbs were a place to live the "good life," and that the "golf, gardening, bridge clubs, casual clothes, landscaped lawns," and innumerable time-saving gadgets of suburbia made life "like one long vacation," they largely ignored the economic incentives that drove suburbanization. As Eli Lederhendeler has argued, postwar suburbanization "was not necessarily causally related to racial issues" but rather, "economics and status considerations" explained much of the suburban exodus.[92] Joshua Zeitz notes that between 1940 and 1960 some 340,000 white residents fled Brooklyn for suburban sections of Queens, Staten Island, and Nassau County. But he argues this "had nothing to do with the expansion of New York's black population," and was rather indicative of the fact that "many returning GIs were simply eager to avail themselves of housing opportunities otherwise unavailable in Brooklyn."[93] Especially during the earliest wave of postwar suburbanization, federal subsidies of highways and mortgages made it such that purchasing a suburban home was more affordable for white veterans than renting. Employment considerations, too, drew city dwellers to the booming suburbs. Between 1954 and 1956 90 percent of the New York metropolitan region's new manufacturing plants were built in the suburbs outside of the city. On Long Island, the Cold War and, in turn, the space race drove the expansion of jobs in the area's longstanding aerospace industry. Whereas in the late 1940s three of four residents of Levittown commuted to work in New York City, by the early 1960s the proportion had nearly reversed with six out of ten residents employed in Nassau County.[94]

Postwar Catholic Urbanism

While elements of the agrarian myth persisted in those who flocked to suburbia, it became clear in the decade following World War II that the agrarian indictment of urban life and its effect on the faith had been far too sweeping. The urban neighborhood—which Andrew Greeley claimed Catholics invented via the "incredible mixture of the precinct and the parish"—had, in fact, been at the heart of a thriving Catholic subculture. As Benjamin Looker has written, the church, school, pious societies, and social clubs built by generations of Catholic immigrants were formative institutions "infusing religious sensibilities into the daily life of the urban village," and thereby successfully passing on the faith to subsequent generations.[95]

Despite these successes, in the heady days after World War II, many Catholic intellectuals began questioning the merits of this separatist subculture and critiqued the urban ethnic parish for ghettoizing Catholicism. In a widely debated 1955 article priest-historian John Tracy Ellis set the tenor of the coming era by arguing that a "self-imposed ghetto mentality" had stifled Catholic intellectual life and kept them from rising into the nation's elite.[96] Encouraged by the full participation of Catholics in World War II, and by the theological speculation that would fully flower during Vatican II, many Catholic liberals—especially a younger generation of clergy and laity—saw the urban ethnic parish as an obstacle to full engagement in American life and therefore celebrated that suburbanization was precipitating the collapse of the ghetto. The prominence in the early 1960s of "the two Johns"—Irish Catholic President John F. Kennedy, who was inaugurated in 1961, and Pope John XXIII, who opened the Second Vatican Council in 1962—seemed to confirm that American Catholicism was emerging from its urban ghetto to engage modernity and take an active role in American society.[97]

Nostalgia for rural life was thus replaced by futuristic hopes for the modern metropolis, and throughout the 1960s and 1970s the city came to occupy a privileged place in secular academic, Protestant, and Catholic thought.[98] In a 1961 jeremiad against suburbia, *The Suburban Captivity of the Church*, Episcopalian ethicist Gibson Winter also critiqued neighborhood-based churches claiming that they "become exclusive and antimetropolitan," contributing only to "a desperate clutching for some straw of similarity on which to build racial or religious community."[99] Then, in 1965, Harvard Divinity School theologian and Baptist minister Harvey Cox published his highly influential book, *The Secular City*.[100] Cox admitted that urbanization, with its characteristically "anti-traditional, innovative, mobile," and "complex" way of living and thinking, was a secularizing force. But Cox asserted that urban secularity allowed for greater human freedom, and argued that as a missionary community the church should learn from and be changed by the secular city so as to be at the forefront of societal change.[101]

Liberal Catholics found resonance between *The Secular City* and *Gaudium et Spes*, the Second Vatican Council's Pastoral Constitution on the Church in the Modern World, which was promulgated the same year and affirmed the Church's duty, even amid religious pluralism and secularization, to scrutinize "the signs of the times," learn from the world, and serve its needs.[102] Inspired by the civil rights movement, they rejected the segregated ethnic neighborhood and advanced a more metropolitan view of the city, which they saw as the all-important site of Christian action.[103] Thus, in the 1960s and 1970s local and national conferences and dozens of books and articles discussed the city and the burgeoning urban crisis at length, and young priests and women religious celebrated urban ministry, especially to poor minorities, as the cutting edge of ecclesial and social reform.[104] Women religious, in particular, took advantage of funding from President Lyndon Johnson's Office of Economic Opportunity, and other federal agencies associated with the War on Poverty, to develop urban ministries to African Americans.[105] Because their focus was on the inner city, on the old neighborhoods abandoned by suburbanites, on the racial minorities who now dominated those neighborhoods, and on those white ethnics who remained, if they discussed the suburbs at all it was to critique their racial exclusivity and consumerism and to explore the role suburbanites should play in solving urban problems.

Meanwhile, the white ethnic Catholics who remained in racially homogenous sections of the city defended their neighborhoods, from both Catholic critics and fiscal disinvestment.[106] Whereas the link between the health of ethnic neighborhoods and parishes and the health of the Church itself had long been self-evident to urban-dwelling Catholics, defenders of the ethnic neighborhood now had "to develop a self-conscious language of urban community, an explicit set of terms with which to defend localist values," without resorting to racism. Postwar debates over racial integration and competing visions of the city proved particularly divisive for American Catholics and heightened questions about how the Church could pass the faith on to future generations absent the institutions, traditions, and symbol system of the ethnic ghetto.[107]

In the 1970s select Catholic intellectuals and activists mounted a defense of ethnic neighborhoods and their embattled Catholic subculture as part of a white ethnic revival.[108] These defenders of the ethnic neighborhood were liberals inspired by the civil rights movement and Vatican II, and their localist strain of Catholic urbanism posited that healthy ethnic neighborhoods could still be a refuge from the upheavals plaguing the Church and nation, and a springboard for a multiracial, multiethnic, working-class coalition to combat urban disinvestment.[109] Michael Novak's *The Rise of the Unmeltable Ethnics* was the "chief programmatic statement of the white-ethnic revival," arguing that the Anglo-Protestant elite had destroyed the local experiences that white ethnics cherished through programs of Americanization, slum clearance, and urban renewal.[110] Monsignor Geno Baroni established the National Center for Urban Ethnic Affairs (NUE) to support community organizing and ameliorate the economic crisis that plagued white working-class neighborhoods, fueled political alienation, and undermined efforts at interracial coalition building. He was especially interested in reinvigorating the cultural and religious resources that he felt could have assisted white ethnics in better responding to job flight, declining public services, and rising property taxes. He accused Catholic leaders of making white ethnics the scapegoats for racial turmoil and of funneling financial and personnel resources toward the building of suburban parishes and schools.[111]

Andrew Greeley rejected Catholic progressives' dismissal of the ghetto, their thirst for cultural assimilation, and their argument that self-imposed isolation had left Catholics underrepresented in politics, academics, and business.[112] By the 1970s Greeley warned of a growing divide between the 'neighborhood' of grassroots Catholics and the 'downtown' of the bishops, clergy, and ideologues who were so focused on debates over women priests, birth control, and the Vietnam War but had forgotten how to address the spiritual needs of average Catholics.[113]

Conclusion

It is an irony of history that while the American Catholic community was overwhelmingly comprised of city dwellers, from the 1830s through the 1950s, a significant number of Catholic elites denigrated urban life and championed an agrarian myth that depicted the rural countryside as the soul of the nation and the spiritual and demographic salvation of the Church. Echoes of this agrarian myth were evident in urban laity who abandoned the city in the postwar period for a slice of the suburban dream.[114] Borrowing themes from agrarians' anti-urban rhetoric, these Catholics celebrated the virtues of homeownership and the fresh air and sunlight available outside the confines of the city. Equally ironic is the fact that, just as the epicenter of the US Catholic population was shifting away from the city to the suburbs, the Second Vatican Council, the civil rights movement, and the urban crisis of the 1960s and 1970s led Catholic intellectuals, activists, and pastoral leaders to celebrate the city as they never had before.

The average Catholic layperson could reasonably have been confused about precisely where the experts thought they should live. In August 1957, just months after the erection of the Diocese of Rockville Centre and as postwar suburbanization was radically altering the demographics of American Catholicism, an editorial in the Brooklyn diocesan newspaper, *The Tablet*, indicated just such confusion. The editorial lamented that, on one hand, Catholic intellectuals were "criticizing the state of Catholicity in the suburbs," worrying that an "inability to build churches and schools, and to staff the same, as well as increased taxation" posed a serious threat to the suburban Catholic family. On the other hand, critics warned that "family disintegration and lax community spirit" threatened parish life in the city. Catholics "contemplating marriage or purchasing a home may be confused by such reports," the editors wrote, entitling their piece, "Where Shall We Live?"[115] Large numbers of laity simply voted with their feet and the Catholic expansion into the suburbs marched on.

TWO

The Suburban Church: Postwar Suburbanization and Catholic Institutional Expansion

On May 26, 1957, Bishop Walter P. Kellenberg, the first bishop of the newly erected Diocese of Rockville Centre, took canonical possession of his See. Tracing a path traveled by many of the suburban families in his new Long Island flock, Kellenberg departed his mother's apartment on Mosholu Parkway in the Bronx at a quarter-to-two that afternoon. A ten-car motorcade led by New York City Police motorcycles conveyed Kellenberg, his eighty-four-year-old mother, and clergy from his former diocese of Ogdensburg, New York, across the Bronx, through Queens, and into Nassau County where the party was joined by civic officials. En route to the diocese's newly designated Cathedral of St. Agnes in Rockville Centre, Kellenberg stopped to be greeted by the pastors of Blessed Sacrament and Holy Name of Mary parishes in Valley Stream, Our Lady of Peace Parish in Lynbrook, and St. Raymond Parish in East Rockaway. Arriving in Rockville Centre, Kellenberg was cheered by 15,000 people, including Nassau County executive A. Holly Patterson, and escorted by a welcome parade to the cathedral. There Kellenberg paid his respects to St. Agnes's aged pastor Msgr. Peter Quealy and formally presented the papal decree naming him bishop to Msgr. Edward P. Hoar, the administrator of the Diocese of Brooklyn from which the new diocese was being carved.[1] The following morning, Kellenberg celebrated a Solemn Pontifical Mass of Installation in the presence of Francis Cardinal Spellman, three archbishops, twenty-six bishops, and over 400 priests.[2]

Few could be blamed for seeing Kellenberg's reception and installation as proof of Catholicism's power and prestige at the apex of the American century, and of the optimism and excitement that marked the Church's expansion into the rapidly developing suburbs. Indeed, Msgr. William J. McKenna, who spoke on behalf of the new diocese's clergy at Kellenberg's installation reception, said: "We justly rejoice, that a rural village has been raised to the exalted excellence of an Episcopal see and that a once obscure country church has assumed the dignity and majesty of a Gothic Cathedral."[3] For many new suburbanites, this optimism and excitement was the dominant feature of Catholic life on Long Island through the 1950s and early 1960s as new parishes, schools, and various other Catholic institutions were sprouting like weeds.

But McKenna went on to speak in decidedly darker terms of the challenges facing the Church on Long Island and its new bishop. In just ten years, the population of Long Island's two counties had grown from 650,000 to 1,400,000, almost a quarter of whom were Catholic. As McKenna summarized:

> That incomparable increase had begotten a multiplication of parishes and parishioners, perplexing pastors and people and begetting depressing if not discouraging problems, defying solution. Overflowing congregations, numerically inadequate sacerdotal aid, parochial schools filled to capacity, as many outside as in, the staggering figures of 400 and 500 Baptisms a year, the pleading of parents begging in tears for the benefit of a Catholic school education, and the inevitable negative answer, and varied other relevant circumstances challenge our zeal, our energy, our spirit of sacrifice unto the heroic.[4]

If the erection of a new diocese on Long Island was proof of Catholicism's ascendancy, it was also an indication of the challenges that postwar suburbanization would pose for the Church in the years to come.

The rapid expansion of postwar housing developments on Long Island, propelled by innovations in federal financing and construction techniques, resulted in the demographic and institutional expansion of Catholicism in the suburbs of metropolitan New York. Catholics played a crucial role in shaping this suburban landscape as developers and lay fraternal associations spurred suburbanization by encouraging Catholics to purchase homes near existing or planned parish complexes. In turn, the huge population of newly suburbanized Catholics funded an unprecedented number of religious building programs. This building boom not only created an entirely new Catholic infrastructure in the suburbs to rival and surpass what had existed in the urban core, but it also gave shape to new suburban communities, and shifted the epicenter of American Catholicism from city to suburb. So, too, power struggles over institutions and funds within metropolitan New York's episcopal leadership resulted in the establishment of a new diocese for suburban Long Island's Catholics. The erection of the Diocese of Rockville Centre was seen as a boon to Long Island's burgeoning civic life, but first and foremost as a sign of US Catholicism's suburban future and the challenges suburbia posed for the Church.

The birth of the Diocese of Rockville Centre coincided precisely with the height of commentary on suburbia from US Catholic intellectuals and pastoral leaders in the late 1950s and early 1960s. This commentary was overwhelmingly critical of suburbia and fearful of the way suburban living would change the practice of the faith. Catholic critiques of suburbia were, however, reflective of concerns over modernity, economic prosperity, consumerism, assimilation, and the decline of ethnic religiosity as much as they were a specific response to suburban living. While Catholic laity, especially laywomen, penned defenses of suburban living, Catholic leaders largely failed to head pundits' calls for a pastoral strategy capable of addressing the new realities of suburban living. They thereby contributed to what other commentators referred to as the Church's "loss of the suburbs."

The Suburban Boom

The national housing crisis caused by the Depression, wartime rationing, and postwar demobilization was ultimately solved through the mass production of affordable suburban homes. Although the Federal Housing Authority (FHA) and the mortgage benefits of the GI Bill helped create a massive new market of moderate-income homebuyers, other government policies continued to thwart efforts to provide veterans with sufficient new housing. Wartime price controls remained in effect until early 1947, keeping the price of a single-family home at $10,000, much more than most veterans could afford. When the Levitt and Sons development company announced, in 1947, their plan to build an affordable veterans' housing community on Long Island, they were "received as heroes." Founded in 1929 Levitt and Sons was already well known in New York for building upscale custom homes on Long Island's Gold Coast.[5] During the war the Levitts built wartime housing for shipyard workers in Virginia, practicing the methods of mass construction that would change American homebuilding forever, and preparing to build the development that would make them a household name. They began buying up potato fields on the eastern end of Long Island's Hempstead Plain and stockpiled building supplies. The Levitts envisioned building "stabilized communities" for returning war veterans "that would feature restrictive covenants, zoned shopping areas, and recreational facilities."[6]

Immediately after the war the Levitts experimented with different building materials, and different home sizes and layouts, in developments built in Westbury, Albertson, and Carle Place. In Carle Place houses were built without basements on a concrete slab, a design feature that required a change in building codes, which the Levitts achieved with the support of veterans' groups. In addition to a kitchen and living room, the homes had two bedrooms and a bath, and a stairway to an unfinished attic, and sold for $7,500. After trial and error, the Levitts had finally found the formula for the homes they would build in Levittown.[7]

On May 7, 1947, a *Newsday* headline announced that the Levitts would build 2,000 homes, to be rented to veterans for $60 a month, surrounding a central "village green" with commercial and recreational facilities. Long lines formed at the leasing office and by the end of the month over 6,500 applications had been filed for the initial offering of homes.[8] Overwhelmed by the response, the Levitts acquired adjoining parcels of land over the coming four years and increased the size of the development until it encompassed six square miles sprawling over Wantagh and Westbury in the Town of Hempstead and Hicksville in the Town of Oyster Bay. The firm perfected their mass-production techniques reducing the homebuilding process to twenty-six steps, employing subcontractors for every stage of construction, and keeping costs low by purchasing fixtures and appliances directly from manufacturers. At the height of production the Levitts were building more than thirty houses a day and, with the creation of federal loan guarantees, the Levitts were able to boast "the largest line of credit ever offered a private home builder."[9] They switched their development from rentals to sales, offering homeownership with a thirty-year mortgage, little to no down payment, and monthly costs on par with rentals. As the *New York Times* architectural critic Paul Goldberger has written, the Levitts "turned the detached, single-family house from a distant dream to a real possibility for thousands of middle class American families."[10]

When the building came to an end on November 21, 1951, the Levitts had built a total of 17,447 homes, "several village greens, ten swimming pools, numerous playgrounds, baseball fields, and a $250,000 community center."[11] Levittown became the largest-ever housing development built by a single builder, and both its size and its public reception were indications of the tremendous demand for suburban housing.[12] Indeed, the construction of Levittown was just the start of a tremendous expansion of housing and population across Long Island:

> To the west of Levittown, Uniondale and East Meadow spread across former farm fields. The older communities of Hicksville and Farmingdale expanded as their surrounding farm homesteads disappeared into housing developments and the open lands of Island Trees, Plainview and Bethpage

were rapidly subdivided. . . . Older villages such as Freeport, Rockville Centre, Hempstead, Valley Stream, Long Beach, and the Five Towns area were intensively developed. . . . The western unincorporated portion of the Town of Hempstead was also completely subdivided during this period, with New Hyde Park, Elmont, Franklin Square and West Hempstead growing out across empty farm fields.[13]

Thanks to natural population growth, the arrival of workers during World War II, and the first wave of suburban immigrants into developments like Levittown in the late 1940s, Nassau County's population had grown to 672,765 by 1950. But during the next decade, from 1950 to 1960, the county's population would nearly double to 1,300,171.[14] The Town of North Hempstead grew at a slower pace, from 142,613 residents to 219,088, because the North Shore's incorporated villages had larger building plot requirements, which limited housing development. But the Town of Hempstead "lived up to its boast of being the fastest-growing community in the United States," adding over 40,000 residents in 1950 and a record 55,000 residents in 1951. By 1960 Hempstead's population had almost doubled from 448,092 to 767,211 people." And by the end of the 1950s the Town of Oyster Bay had increased its population 282 percent from 82,060 to 313,872, adding over 30,000 new residents a year between 1953 and 1956.[15]

Nassau County's exponential growth came to an end around 1960. Whereas the county's population had grown by 93.3 percent between 1950 and 1960, the pace of growth was only 9.8 percent between 1960 and 1970, with the majority of this rise coming from the natural increase of an enormous population.[16] The suburban boom in Nassau was, however, an early and intense example of a demographic shift that was occurring throughout the New York metropolitan region and across the country. In the 1950s the US urban population grew by only 11 percent, and between 1950 and 1970 the population of American cities grew by just 10 million people. Meanwhile, suburbs in the 1950s grew by nearly 50 percent, from 41 million to 60 million residents, and between 1950 and 1970 American suburbs gained a total of 85 million residents.[17]

Between 1950 and 1970 New York City's population grew by only 2,905 residents. Even this relative stability masked the fact that the city's population was shifting within the five boroughs. Middle-class whites were moving out of Manhattan, Brooklyn, and the Bronx, to newly developed suburban sections of Staten Island and Queens. Staten Island's population skyrocketed from 174,441 to 295,443 between 1940 and 1970 and Queens's increased from 1,297,631 to 1,986,473.[18] The city's population stability also concealed the fact that a tremendous influx of immigrants from places like Puerto Rico was replacing the tens of thousands of New Yorkers who were leaving the city entirely for neighboring suburban counties.[19] Between 1950 and 1960 Suffolk County's population increased by 141.5 percent; Westchester County's by 29.3 percent; and Rockland County's by 53.2 percent. Then, over the ensuing decade, Suffolk County's population continued its increase by 68.7 percent; Westchester County by 10.6 percent; and Rockland County by 68.1 percent.[20]

Although statistical data on the religious makeup of this suburban exodus "is variable and inconclusive," it is abundantly clear that suburbanization had especially significant effects on Catholics in New York and across the nation.[21] Between the mid-1950s and the late 1960s, among white Catholics who lived in the nation's metropolitan regions, "the proportion who lived in suburbs rather than central city areas increased very dramatically from 42 percent to 68 percent."[22] The suburban trend only continued in the decades to come. Whereas in 1952 half of the nation's Catholics lived in central cities and only one-third in suburbs, by 1980 only a quarter of Catholics lived in cities and half resided in the suburbs and countryside.[23] Such changes were evident in Detroit, where the Catholic population declined from 1 million to 100,000; in Baltimore, where the Catholic population shrank from 150,000 just prior to World War II to 33,000 in the mid-1990s; and in San Francisco where Sunday Mass attendance fell from 120,000 in 1961 to 47,000 in 1994.[24]

In the Archdiocese of New York, parishes in New York City "lost 166,956 people between 1940 and 1970," but the archdiocese's seven suburban counties gained 774,669 people, almost half of whom—some 323,129 Catholics—lived in Westchester.[25] While some city parishes saw an influx of Puerto Rican arrivals, other parishes in neighborhoods that became heavily African American saw their parish rolls dramatically depleted. In the South Bronx's St. Jerome Parish, for example, the total attendance at Sunday Masses "dropped from 6,100 in 1950 to 795 in 1975."[26] Meanwhile, on Long Island, the suburban migration led to Catholics representing an increasingly large percent of Nassau County's population, "so that by the early 1960s between 42 and 46 percent of the county's population was Catholic."[27]

Catholic Institutional Expansion into the Suburbs

Many American bishops were concerned that this postwar migration to the suburbs would devastate the Church's ability to maintain its urban parishes and require tremendous expenses to replicate Church infrastructure in the suburbs. Some, including Bishop Joseph Burke of Buffalo, New York, therefore tried to convince their congregants to remain in the urban core.[28] However, many members of the hierarchy cooperated with urban planners and developers in order to maximize the Church's real estate holdings and to anticipate where the Church would need to expand in order to serve its suburbanizing flock. Lay organizations and the Catholic press promoted the suburban housing blitz by publishing articles and advertisements and by sponsoring model-home shows. And Catholic laity decided which suburban home to purchase, in part, based on its proximity to a parish church and school.

Between 1949 and 1960 CWV chapters in Brooklyn, Queens, the Bronx, and Westchester sponsored more than a dozen model-home shows with multiple homes on offer each year between 1951 and 1953. These shows were an opportunity to raise funds and to promote the organization's ideals of God, Country, and Home, which in the midst of the Cold War were seen as crucial antidotes to the spread of Communism. Since all of the model homes were located in expanding suburban neighborhoods within either the Archdiocese of New York or the Diocese of Brooklyn, the CWV could not be accused of promoting the depopulation of these dioceses. But the home shows certainly provided builders and home-furnishing retailers the opportunity to display their latest designs and to encourage the dream of suburban homeownership within their visitors. In some instances parishes in suburban areas of the city worked with developers to build dream homes that were toured by prospective homebuyers and raffled off as a means of fundraising. In 1958 Our Lady Star of the Sea Parish in the Huguenot section of Staten Island built and furnished a six-room, brick, ranch-style dream house and the women of the parish served as hostesses for those who toured the home. In turn, the funds raised were used to add a kindergarten classroom to the planned parish grade school, which opened the following year and expanded social services in the rapidly developing neighborhood.[29]

The pages of New York's three diocesan newspapers were also littered with advertisements for real estate and home sales, for department stores selling the latest furniture, appliances, and consumer goods, and for contractors prepared to modify and improve starter homes with attic expansions, replacement windows, and swimming pools.[30] Similarly, developers advertised their homes in the pages of the metropolitan area's three diocesan newspapers, attempting to reach the lucrative market of Catholic homebuyers and to assure prospective buyers of ready access to ecclesial services from their new suburban homes.[31]

Figure 2.1. Advertisement for Norwich-Green by Kern Realty Homes in East Norwich, near St. Dominic Parish. *Source*: *The Tablet* 45, no. 11 (May 3, 1952): 20.

Catholics were thus crucial players in giving America's postwar suburbs their shape and texture. This contribution was most obvious in the churches, schools, and other structures for charitable institutions which the Church designed, financed, and built in suburbia. The nationwide explosion in suburban house building and the postwar baby boom led to a

Figure 2.2. Advertisement for Morewood Oaks Homes in East Northport near St. Anthony of Padua Parish. *Source: The Tablet* 52, no. 24 (July 25, 1959): 7.

massive expansion of buildings for all religious denominations. Throughout the 1950s and 1960s the number of newly constructed churches, schools, rectories, convents, gymnasiums, and other religious facilities such as hospitals, charity centers, and youth camps resulted in a record amount of money being spent on religious building projects. The trend began in 1947, when $126 million was spent on church construction. By the 1950s Americans "were spending $2 million dollars a day on the construction of religious buildings, representing an estimated 70,000 'worship units' and 12,500 structures for education." The trend peaked in 1965 at some $1.2 billion spent that year.[32]

Population expansion, and the demands it placed on institutions and buildings were especially pronounced among American Catholics whose overall population numbers grew by 35.8 percent between 1950 and 1960, accounting for 41 percent of the nation's population increase.[33] In 1948 a nationwide survey estimated that Catholic institutions would spend $10 billion over the coming decade to build a projected 38 hospitals, 316 churches, 83 high schools, and 236 grade schools, among numerous other categories of buildings. The Archdiocese of New York was said to lead the way with $25,489,000 in construction already underway.[34] At the end of the decade, a forecast by the trade journal *Catholic Building and Maintenance* predicted that the pace of building would continue in 1959: $1.75 billion would be spent that year on the construction of churches, schools, and hospitals alone, with the building of rectories, convents, and other buildings raising that figure significantly. Notably, grammar and high schools represented the bulk of the predicted projects with churches representing only 10 to 15 percent of the expected projects for 1959.[35]

A significant portion of this building blitz was occurring in the suburbs. From 1940 to 1970 thirty-two of the forty-five new parishes established in the Archdiocese of New York were located in its suburban counties, and some eighty-four parochial schools were opened in Westchester and Rockland Counties alone.[36] In the Diocese of Brooklyn Archbishop Thomas E. Molloy established eighty-eight new parishes between 1922 and 1953. Only thirteen were in Brooklyn, but there were forty in Queens, twenty-five in Nassau, and ten in Suffolk. In the final six years of that timeframe, from 1948 to 1953, the last twenty-five of those eighty-eight new parishes were organized. Their distribution indicates an even greater shift toward Long Island's two suburban counties: eight new parishes were formed in Suffolk and twelve in Nassau, but only five were in Queens and there were no new parishes in Brooklyn.[37] This pattern was replicated across the country. Between 1940 and 1962 the Archdiocese of San Antonio established twenty-seven new

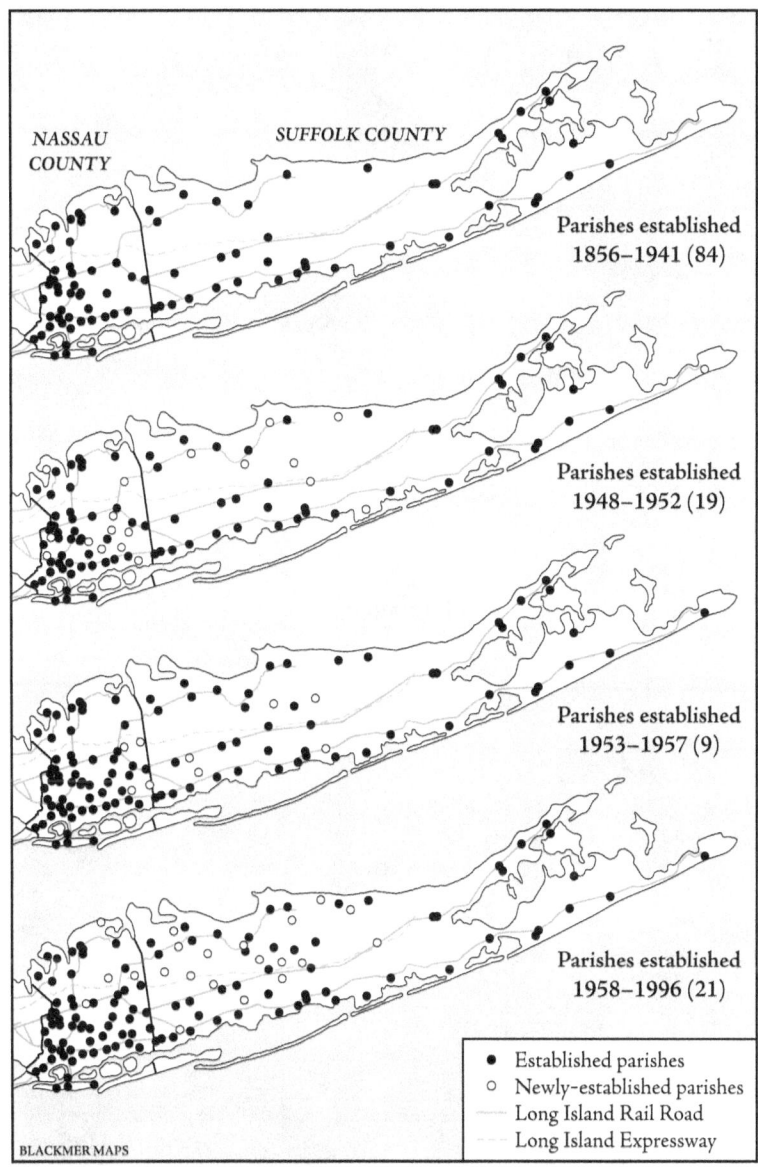

Figure 2.3. Catholic parishes of Nassau and Suffolk Counties over time.

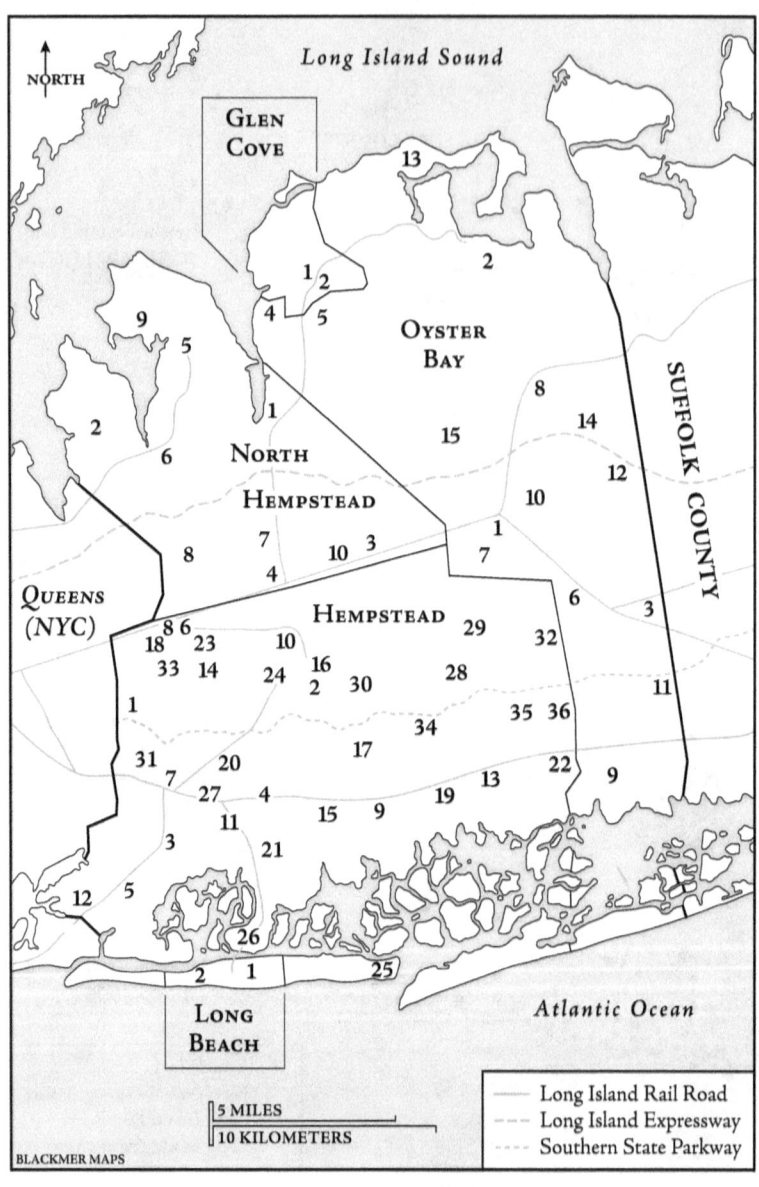

Figure 2.4. The Catholic parishes of Nassau County, Long Island, by year of establishment

Glen Cove
1. St. Patrick, Glen Cove (1856)
2. St. Rocco, Glen Cove (1937)

Hempstead
1. St. Boniface, Elmont (1858)
2. Our Lady of Loretto, Hempstead (1871)
3. St. Joseph, Hewlett (1872)
4. St. Agnes, Rockville Centre (1894)
5. St. Joachim, Cedarhurst (1894)
6. Holy Spirit, New Hyde Park (1897)
7. Holy Name of Mary, Valley Stream (1902)
8. St. Hedwig, Floral Park (1902)
9. Our Holy Redeemer, Freeport (1903)
10. St. Joseph, Garden City (1905)
11. St. Raymond, East Rockaway (1909)
12. Our Lady of Good Counsel, Inwood (1910)
13. St. Barnabas the Apostle, Bellmore (1912)
14. St. Catherine of Sienna, Franklin Square (1913)
15. St. Christopher, Baldwin (1915)
16. St. Ladislaus, Hempstead (1915)
17. Queen of the Most Holy Rosary, Roosevelt (1919)
18. Our Lady of Victory, Floral Park (1921)
19. Curé of Ars, Merrick (1926)
20. Our Lady of Lourdes, Malverne (1926)
21. St. Anthony, Oceanside (1927)
22. St. William the Abbot, Seaford (1928)
23. St. Anne, Garden City (1929)
24. St. Thomas the Apostle, West Hempstead (1931)
25. Our Lady of the Miraculous Medal, Point Lookout (1937)
26. Sacred Heart, Island Park (1938)
27. Our Lady of Peace, Lynbrook (1940)
28. St. Raphael, East Meadow (1941)
29. St. Bernard, Levittown (1948)
30. St. Martha, Uniondale (1949)
31. Blessed Sacrament, Valley Stream (1950)
32. St. James, Seaford (1951)
33. St. Vincent de Paul, Elmont (1951)
34. Sacred Heart, North Merrick (1952)
35. St. Frances de Chantal, Wantagh (1952)
36. Maria Regina, Seaford (1955)

Long Beach
1. St. Mary of the Isle, Long Beach (1918)
2. St. Ignatius Martyr, Long Beach (1926)

North Hempstead
1. St. Mary, Roslyn (1871)
2. St. Aloysius, Great Neck (1876)
3. St. Brigid, Westbury (1892)
4. Corpus Christi, Mineola (1901)
5. St. Peter of Alcantara, Port Washington (1901)
6. St. Mary, Manhasset (1912)
7. St. Aidan, Williston Park (1928)
8. Notre Dame, New Hyde Park (1941)
9. Our Lady of Fatima, Manorhaven (1948)
10. Our Lady of Hope, Carle Place (1987)

Oyster Bay
1. St. Ignatius Loyola, Hicksville (1872)
2. St. Dominic, Oyster Bay (1895)
3. St. Killian, Farmingdale (1896)
4. St. Boniface Martyr, Sea Cliff (1898)
5. St. Hyacinth, Glen Head (1909)
6. St. Martin of Tours, Bethpage (1923)
7. Holy Family, Hicksville (1951)
8. St. Edward the Confessor, Syosset (1952)
9. St. Rose of Lima, Massapequa (1952)
10. Our Lady of Mercy, Hicksville (1953)
11. Our Lady of Lourdes, Massapequa Park (1955)
12. St. Pius X, Plainview (1955)
13. St. Gertrude, Bayville (1959)
14. Holy Name of Jesus, Woodbury (1962)
15. St. Paul the Apostle, Brookville (1962)

Figure 2.4. (*continued*)

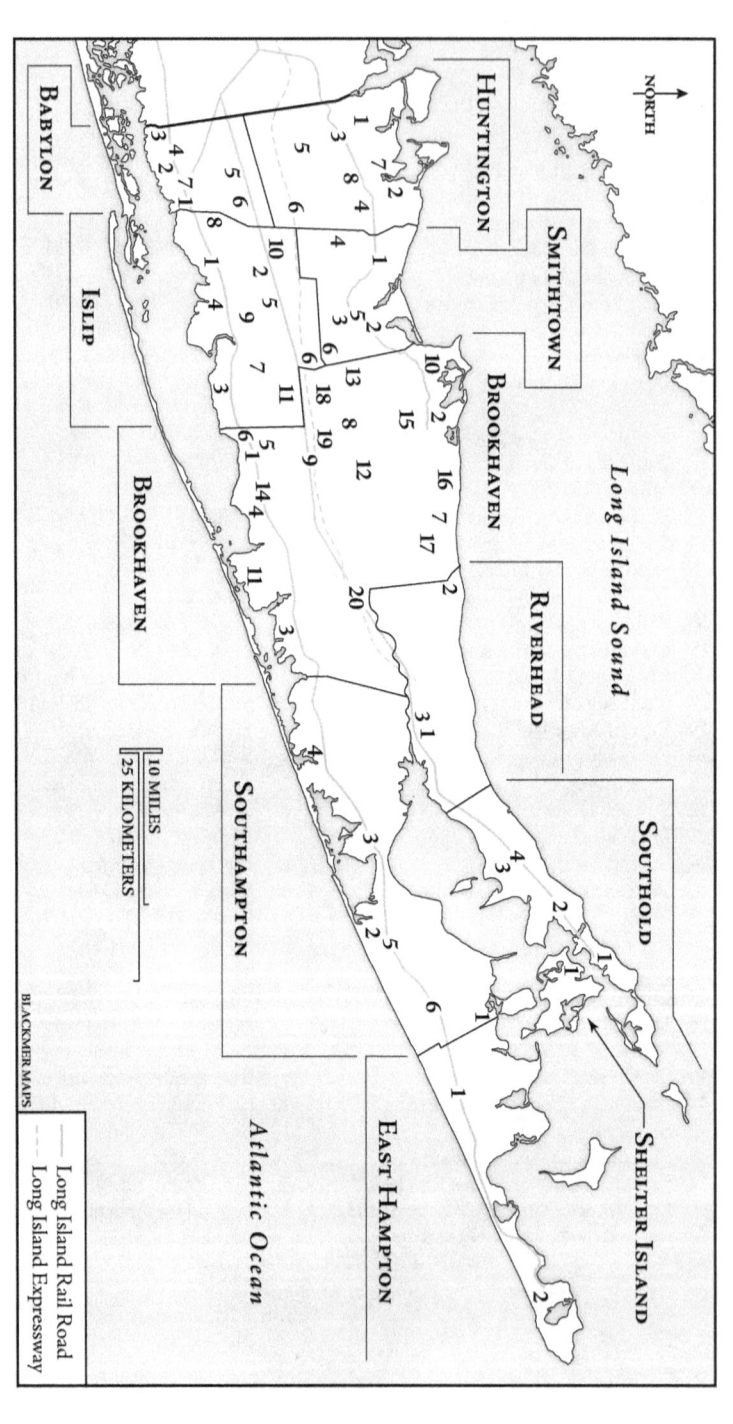

Figure 2.5. The Catholic parishes of Suffolk County, Long Island, by year of establishment

BABYLON
1. St. Joseph, Babylon (1877)
2. Our Lady of Perpetual Help, Lindenhurst (1894)
3. St. Martin of Tours, Amityville (1898)
4. Our Lady of the Assumption, Copiague (1929)
5. Our Lady of the Miraculous Medal, Wyandanch (1936)
6. Ss. Cyril and Methodius, Deer Park (1956)
7. Our Lady of Grace, West Babylon (1962)

BROOKHAVEN
1. St. Francis de Sales, Patchogue (1879)
2. Infant Jesus, Port Jefferson (1903)
3. St. John the Evangelist, Center Moriches (1903)
4. Mary Immaculate, Bellport (1907)
5. Our Lady of Mount Carmel, Patchogue (1918)
6. Our Lady of the Snow, Blue Point (1920)
7. St. Anthony of Padua, Rocky Point (1948)
8. St. Margaret of Scotland, Selden (1948)
9. St. Sylvester, Medford (1948)
10. St. James, Setauker (1949)
11. St. Jude, Mastic Beach (1949)
12. St. Francis Cabrini, Coram (1953)
13. Assumption of the Blessed Virgin Mary, Centereach (1955)
14. St. Joseph the Worker, East Patchogue (1955)
15. St. Gerard Majella, Port Jefferson Station (1968)
16. St. Louis de Montfort, Sound Beach (1971)
17. St. Mark, Shoreham (1973)
18. St. Elizabeth Ann Seton, Lake Ronkonkoma (1988)
19. Resurrection, Farmingville (1988)
20. Ss. Peter and Paul, Manorville (1996)

EAST HAMPTON
1. Most Holy Trinity, East Hampton (1907)
2. St. Therese of Lisieux, Montauk (1950)

HUNTINGTON
1. St. Patrick, Huntington (1860)
2. St. Philip Neri, Northport (1893)
3. St. Hugh of Lincoln, Huntington Station (1913)
4. St. Anthony of Padua, East Northport (1951)
5. St. Elizabeth of Hungary, Melville (1962)
6. St. Matthew, Dix Hills (1965)
7. Our Lady Queen of Martyrs, Centerport (1966)
8. St. Francis of Assisi, Greenlawn (1966)

ISLIP
1. St. Patrick, Bay Shore (1883)
2. St. Anne, Brentwood (1895)
3. St. Lawrence the Martyr, Sayville (1895)
4. St. Mary, East Islip (1898)
5. St. John of God, Central Islip (1904)
6. St. Joseph, Ronkonkoma (1910)
7. St. John Nepomucene, Bohemia (1919)
8. Our Lady of Lourdes, West Islip (1956)
9. St. Peter the Apostle, Islip Terrace (1962)
10. St. Luke, Brentwood (1965)
11. Good Shepherd, Holbrook (1970)

RIVERHEAD
1. St. John the Evangelist, Riverhead (1869)
2. St. John the Baptist, Wading River (1922)
3. St. Isidore, Riverhead (1903)

SHELTER ISLAND
1. Our Lady of the Isle, Shelter Island (1911)

SMITHTOWN
1. St. Joseph, Kings Park (1892)
2. Ss. Philip and James, Saint James (1907)
3. St. Patrick, Smithtown (1952)
4. Christ the King, Commack (1959)
5. St. Thomas More, Hauppauge (1967)
6. Holy Cross, Nesconset (1988)

SOUTHAMPTON
1. St. Andrew, Sag Harbor (1859)
2. Sacred Hearts of Jesus and Mary, Southampton (1896)
3. St. Rosalie, Hampton Bays (1904)
4. Immaculate Conception, Westhampton (1913)
5. Our Lady of Poland, Southampton (1918)
6. Queen of the Most Holy Rosary, Bridgehampton (1922)

SOUTHOLD
1. St. Agnes, Greenport (1886)
2. St. Patrick, Southold (1865)
3. Sacred Heart, Cutchogue (1901)
4. Our Lady of Ostrabrama, Cutchogue (1912)

Figure 2.5. (*continued*)

parishes, almost all of which were "in new outlying areas."[38] Of the seventy-two parishes founded in the Archdiocese of Philadelphia between 1945 and the mid-1970s, sixty-two were in the suburbs and just ten were in the city.[39]

This extended period of ecclesial construction spawned several publications dedicated to assisting religious institutions in planning, building, and financing churches, schools, and hospitals. These included *Catholic Building and Maintenance*, *Church Property Administration*, and *Catholic Market*.[40] Annual Catholic building conventions were also held to discuss new building technologies as well as problems such as material shortages and rising construction costs. The nationwide religious building boom also led to legal battles over zoning laws prohibiting the building of churches and private schools in residential zones, and to debates over the tax-exempt status of religious organizations.[41] Some municipalities attempted to use zoning restrictions as a means of excluding religious minorities. Advocates of restrictive zoning also argued that churches and schools created vehicular traffic that disturbed suburban quiet, safety, and health.[42] Most often, suburban municipalities desperate for tax dollars to fund schools, libraries, and emergency services tried to use zoning laws to keep tax-exempt churches and religious schools from developing land that might otherwise provide needed tax revenue. In 1956, however, justices of the New York State Court of Appeals ruled 5–1 in favor of the Diocese of Rochester's bid to build St. Thomas More Church and School in a suburban residential area, stating that "churches and schools are more important than local taxes."[43]

Establishing A New Suburban Diocese

The postwar expansion of suburban populations and ecclesial infrastructure led to a restructuring of New York's Catholic dioceses. When Pope Pius IX established the Diocese of Brooklyn in 1853 Brooklyn was still an independent city, and a large and rapidly growing one at that. Brooklyn was the nation's seventh-largest city in 1850 with a population of 96,838 and by the next census, in 1860, it had climbed to the third-largest city in the country with a population of 266,661. By 1890 Brooklyn's population had soared still further to 806,343 and showed few signs of slowing.[44] Pope Pius's decision to establish a Diocese of Brooklyn separate from the Archdiocese of New York across the East River thus seemed perfectly justified. But when, on January 1, 1898, Brooklyn and Queens joined Greater New York as two of the city's five boroughs, this meant that two different bishops and dioceses administered portions of New York City's Catholic population. This ecclesial organization complicated the Church's relationship with city administration and threatened to undermine the Church's influence on city affairs if it failed to speak with one unified voice. At numerous points since 1898—including Francis Spellman's ascension as archbishop of New York in 1939, the death of Brooklyn Bishop Joseph McEntegart in 1968, and the arrival of John O'Connor as archbishop of New York in 1984—New York churchmen have suggested an ecclesiastical restructuring that would return Brooklyn and Queens to the Archdiocese of New York so that the Church in New York City could more easily speak with one voice.[45]

At the same time, it had also long been rumored that because the archdiocese's territory was so vast, and because the interests of the city and the rural northern counties were so divergent, some portion of those counties north of New York City would be removed from the archdiocese's control to form a new diocese.[46] It was even said that a parish in Poughkeepsie, New York, had a cathedra, or bishop's chair, in its basement in anticipation of the church being named the cathedral of a new northern diocese. In February 1954 Msgr. Joseph P. Christopher, a professor at the Catholic University of America who had studied in Rome with Francis Spellman, wrote Msgr. Florence D. Cohalan, professor of history at Cathedral College in Manhattan, speculating that a new diocese would be established in Poughkeepsie and that Archbishop Thomas E. Molloy of Brooklyn had recently traveled to Rome to advocate such a division. Christopher also wondered "what recompense" Spellman would receive for the loss of territory from the archdiocese.[47]

Christopher's letter hints at a competition that existed between the Archdiocese of New York and the Diocese of Brooklyn, or more specifically between Spellman and Molloy.[48] Indeed Molloy is said to have pointedly commented: "there is more than water that separates Brooklyn from New York."[49] At various points Spellman is also reported to have suggested—jokingly or not—that because so many Manhattan residents had relocated to Queens that the borough should be returned to the control of the archdiocese and that the Diocese of Brooklyn could have Staten Island in a trade.[50] Bishop James J. Daly, an auxiliary bishop of the Diocese of Rockville Centre, speculated that Spellman's interest in Queens was ultimately financial. The Archdiocese was "having its own financial difficulties," Daly suggested, "and Queens was a gold mine."[51]

It was also widely rumored that the cardinal supported a plan to divide the Diocese of Brooklyn and create a new diocese for Nassau and Suffolk Counties. Conscious of power dynamics, Spellman was presumably concerned that his archdiocese was being outpaced in population growth by Brooklyn, already the nation's largest diocese and buoyed by the tremendous growth of Queens and Nassau County. During Molloy's thirty-five-year tenure in Brooklyn, from 1921 to 1956, he established 102 new parishes, 45 of which were in Queens, and by the early 1950s Nassau County was the fastest-growing county in the nation. As one priest from Brooklyn, put it: "we were so big and threatening next to New York . . . it had been rumored that the diocese would be split."[52]

It is unclear if, as Msgr. Christopher suggested, Molloy's visit to Rome in 1954 had anything to do with advocating a breakup of the Archdiocese of New York or if, as others have postulated, it had more to do with Molloy "quietly and effectively" opposing Spellman's proposed division of the Diocese of Brooklyn.[53] Bishop Daly even speculated that Molloy made use of his contacts in the Vatican and made strategic monetary contributions to Roman officials to forestall his diocese's division.[54] Whatever the precise nature of their conflicting proposals, it is eminently clear that Spellman was the most powerful member of the American hierarchy—the "American pope," as John Cooney has called him—and he won the day with Molloy's death in November 1956.[55] Within just five months—and only weeks before Walter O'Malley would announce that the Brooklyn Dodgers were leaving New York for Los Angeles—Spellman told priests gathered at St. Patrick's Cathedral for the annual Holy Thursday Chrism Mass that Pope Pius XII had established the Diocese of Rockville Centre to administer the church in Nassau and Suffolk Counties.[56] Protocol indicated that the announcement should have been made by the Vatican's Apostolic Delegate to the United States, Archbishop Amleto Cicognani; that it was not was widely considered to be an indication of Spellman's role in and satisfaction with the decision.[57]

The bishops appointed to shepherd Long Island's two dioceses were also an indication of Spellman's power. Bishop Bryan J. McEntegart, the former executive director of Catholic Relief Services then serving as rector of the Catholic University of America, was named the fourth bishop of Brooklyn, now consisting of just Kings and Queens Counties. Brooklyn became the nation's smallest diocese geographically at just 179 square miles, yet it remained the most populous diocese in the United States and held the distinction of being the first entirely urban diocese in the country. Bishop Walter P. Kellenberg, who had served as an auxiliary bishop to Spellman in New York and succeeded McEntegart as bishop of Ogdensburg in 1954, was named the first bishop of Rockville Centre, which covered the 1,222 square miles from the New York City line to the tip of Long Island 100 miles to the east.[58] Both McEntegart and Kellenberg had been ordained as priests of the Archdiocese of New York and owed their ascension into the ranks of the hierarchy to Spellman's powerful patronage.[59]

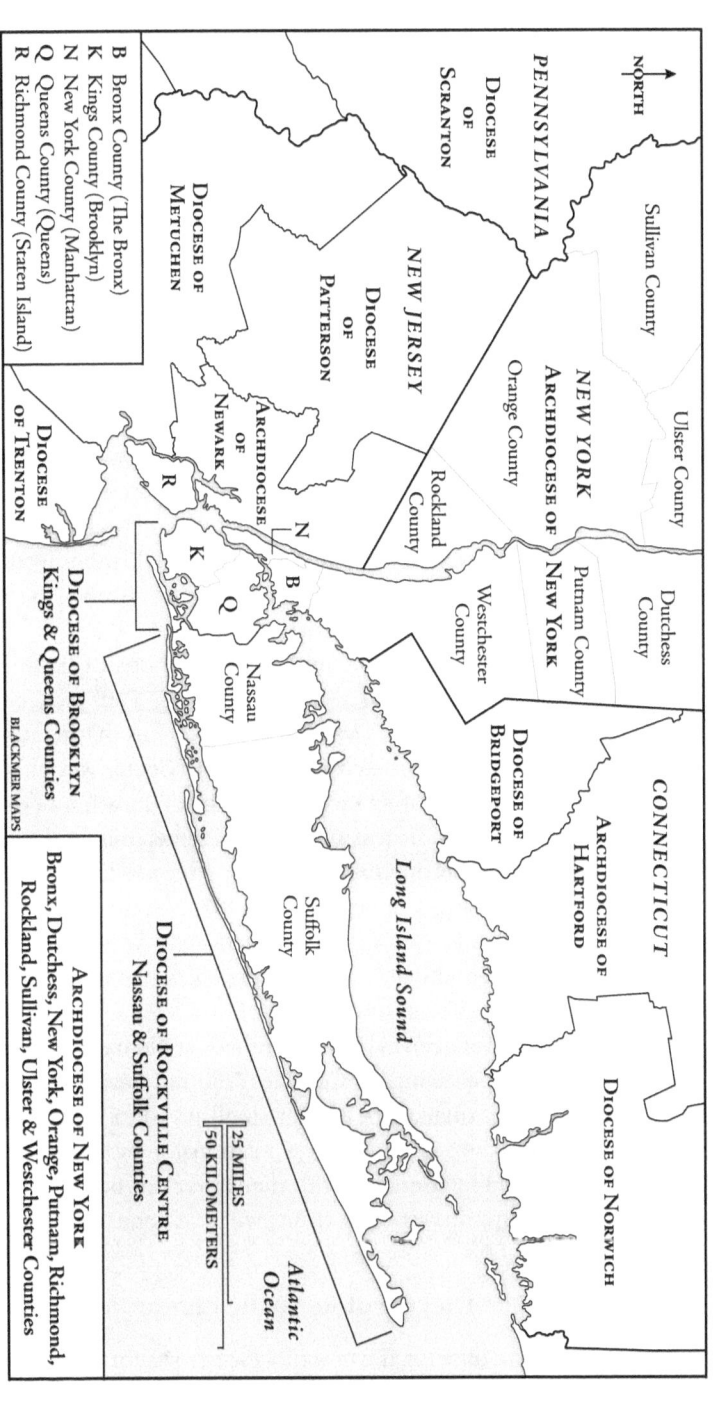

Figure 2.6. The dioceses of metropolitan New York and surrounding region

Speaking at Kellenberg's installation in Rockville Centre, Spellman recalled that New York's second archbishop and America's first cardinal, John McCloskey, had been born in Brooklyn. Spellman cast Kellenberg's installation as an instance of New York trying "to settle an ancient debt with the Diocese of Brooklyn" by offering its onetime chancellor to the new Diocese of Rockville Centre.[60] Most observers, however, saw the two appointments as clear proof of Spellman's tremendous influence in Rome and of his intention to have a hand in the administration of his two neighboring dioceses.[61] Writing to Monsignor Cohalan in February 1957, Monsignor Christopher reported that McEntegart and Kellenberg would be named as bishops of the two dioceses and predicted: "Spellie will run them, so indirectly N.Y. will be the great overlord."[62] Just how much influence Spellman tried to exert on his protégés is difficult to determine. It seems likely he simply trusted that their loyalty and expertise would benefit him and the Church, whatever their day-to-day decisions. However, the creation of the new Long Island diocese and the relationship between the metropolitan region's bishops would have a profound impact on the Church's political lobbying efforts, especially its attempt to secure state funding for parochial schools.

Despite the fact that the people, priests, and bishops of the Brooklyn and Rockville Centre dioceses had a shared history, Fr. Paul McKeever said that the splitting of the dioceses "was a bad chapter" in that relationship. "The antagonism between Brooklyn and Rockville Centre was enhanced" by debates over the division of financial assets, the delineation of diocesan borders, and the control of diocesan real estate, cemeteries, and especially the major seminary in Huntington.[63] However, after meeting with Kellenberg to discuss these matters in September 1957, McEntegart confidently reported to Spellman that "our mutual problems will be solved in a spirit of understanding and good will."[64] This ultimately seems to have been the case. In 1973 the chancellor of the Diocese of Brooklyn suggested that the division of assets had not been as contentious as it could have been because the parishes of Nassau and Suffolk Counties "did not have a great deal of assets because most of them were new or small parishes."[65] And in 1981 Bishop James J. Daly assessed the dioceses' relationship by saying: "we were blessed to have a good relationship with the Diocese of Brooklyn . . . and Brooklyn has been supportive of everything we have done."[66]

The Diocese of Rockville Centre

The Vatican decree establishing the new diocese gave its formal name as *Dioecesis Petropolitana in Insula Longa*: The Diocese of Rockville Centre in Long

Island.[67] Most dioceses derive their names from the city of the episcopal seat, but Rockville Centre was neither Long Island's center of population and industry nor its geographic center. Located twenty-five miles from Manhattan, ninety miles from the eastern end of Long Island at Montauk Point, and midway between Long Island's north and south shores, and only sixty-five years old at the time of the diocese's founding, Rockville Centre lacked heavy industry and high-rise apartments and had gained half its population of 25,000 residents since the end of World War II. Indeed, Rockville Centre was an incorporated village, not a city, making it the only such diocesan seat among the nation's then 122 dioceses and archdioceses.[68] The new diocese's name seemed to reflect the fact that Rockville Centre's salient characteristic was that it was largely indistinguishable from the dozens of other suburban towns the diocese was intended to serve. Rockville Centre is "representative of nearly every place on the Island and within the Diocese," one commenter noted, "and, indeed, of suburban villages everywhere."[69]

What Rockville Centre was able to boast was "a church imposing enough to serve as a cathedral," which, in the establishment of suburban dioceses, was a not-insignificant factor in the selection of a diocesan seat. It had long been said that Msgr. Peter Quealy built Rockville Centre's St. Agnes Church in 1935 with an eye to it one day serving as the cathedral for a second Long Island diocese. Monsignor Edmond Trench, who grew up in St. Agnes Parish, recalls his boyhood pastor proudly predicting: "Someday this is going to be a cathedral."[70] During his fifty years as pastor of St. Agnes, Quealy had also established a parish grade school and high school, and purchased land for what would become Holy Rood Cemetery, Mercy Hospital, and Malloy College.[71] Many of his parishioners even credited Quealy with having convinced the Vatican to establish a new Long Island diocese owing to his ecclesial connections. It was not at all surprising that when Bishop Kellenberg arrived in Rockville Centre his first visit was to the ailing but highly esteemed Quealy.[72]

In one sense, Walter Kellenberg's background made him an eminently wise choice for the first bishop of a new diocese. As *Newsday* commented upon his death in 1986, Kellenberg's appointment to Rockville Centre was "the ideal meeting between a diocese without a past and a man who knew how to build a future."[73] Kellenberg was born in Lower Manhattan, on June 3, 1901, and his family had moved to the Bronx by the time he was five. He graduated from Cathedral College, the archdiocese's high school seminary in 1922, and after theological studies at St. Joseph's Seminary in Dunwoodie, was ordained a priest on June 2, 1928. The young Father Kellenberg must have showed considerable promise because, just six years later, Cardinal

Figure 2.7. St. Agnes Church, later Cathedral, shortly after its erection in 1935. *Source: Building, Past, Present, Future Diocese of Brooklyn* (Brooklyn, NY: Diocesan Building Commission, 1936): 52. Used with permission of the Diocese of Brooklyn, All Rights Reserved.

Hayes brought him to work in the archdiocesan chancery while studying real estate, insurance, and business administration at Columbia University. In 1935 he was named assistant chancellor under then-Monsignor James Francis McIntyre, later Cardinal Archbishop of Los Angeles. Placed in charge of the Archdiocesan Building Office, Kellenberg was responsible for planning new parishes and diocesan buildings, hiring architects, negotiating contracts, and supervising building contractors. Kellenberg was named secretary to Cardinal Spellman in 1939 and served in that capacity until 1947 when he was named chancellor of the archdiocese. Ordained an auxiliary bishop on October 5, 1953, Kellenberg was appointed the sixth bishop of Ogdensburg, New York, five months later, but was only in the upstate diocese for three years before being named to Rockville Centre in 1957.[74]

Just fifty-six years old, tall and strapping, when Kellenberg arrived in Rockville Centre, his vast knowledge of the inner workings of a diocesan chancery, and his training in real estate and building, prepared him well for the task of creating an entirely new diocesan administration and for overseeing the massive building programs that the suburban expansion on Long Island demanded. But having spent the overwhelming majority of his twenty-nine years as a priest in administrative positions, Kellenberg had only minimal experience of parish ministry and had never been the pastor of a parish. The emergence of the suburban church undeniably called for "builder" bishops like Kellenberg to provide the necessary infrastructure for Catholic life in the suburbs. However, a focus on institutions and infrastructure may also have kept the Church from cultivating leaders capable of developing a novel pastoral program for the parishes' new suburban context.

At the time of its establishment, the Diocese of Rockville Centre was comprised of 112 parishes serving almost a half a million Catholics out of a total population of 1,778,000.[75] In the first five years of the diocese's existence, between 1957 and 1962, the number of Catholics grew by nearly 50 percent whereas the overall population of Nassau and Suffolk Counties increased by 29 percent.[76] Then, between 1962 and 1963, the diocese increased by 6 percent in a single year, an increase that was three times the national Catholic growth rate and made the Diocese of Rockville Centre the nation's fifth-largest diocese, behind Brooklyn, Hartford, Pittsburgh, and Cleveland, and topping Trenton and Providence.[77] At various points throughout the 1960s anywhere from 42 to 46 percent of Nassau County residents identified themselves as Catholic.[78] Even when the national Catholic population decreased for the first time in a century, in 1970, the Catholic population of Rockville Centre continued to grow.[79] In 1970 Catholics accounted for half of Long Island's total population growth and the Diocese of Rockville Centre rose to become the second most populous diocese in the nation behind its mother-See, the Diocese of Brooklyn.[80] By 1982, despite a decline in the rate of its growth, the diocese continued to add population, comprising 40 percent of Long Island's total population, twice the national average.[81]

Having been raised in the parishes and schools of Brooklyn and New York, the clergy and people of the new suburban diocese sought to build for themselves and their children the same network of institutions they had known in the city, attempting to replicate in the suburbs the community of the urban parish.[82] They joined together to form "the usual societies, confraternities, activities, and programs that characterized the typical parish of their experience," and despite struggling with the financial burdens of mortgages and taxes, they donated generously to parish and diocesan building campaigns. These contributions built out the institutional footprint of the new diocese, but in so doing they also assisted in providing infrastructure for suburban development on Long Island. Prior to the erection of the diocese in 1957 there were already 112 parishes, seventy parochial schools, three Catholic hospitals, two Catholic Charities offices, and a Catholic women's college on Long Island. In just the first four years of its existence, the Diocese of Rockville Centre and its parishes spent over $65 million to build twenty-eight new elementary schools; twenty-seven additions to existing parochial schools; three high schools; eleven churches and five church expansions; eighteen convents and eight convent expansions; seven rectories; twenty-two parish auditoriums; a CYO day camp; a preparatory seminary; and a building for the diocesan chancery. The diocese also opened a fourth hospital, two additional Catholic Charities offices, and two outpatient psychiatric clinics. In addition to the growing number of parish-based St. Vincent de Paul Societies, the diocese's Catholic Charities offices became the largest nongovernmental social service agency on Long Island, with up to half of its clients being non-Catholics.[83]

Catholic Responses to Suburbia

The creation of the Diocese of Rockville Centre was widely hailed as indicative of the American Church's suburban future. Writing in *Commonweal*, Dennis J. Geaney evaluated that in "establishing a suburban diocese on Long Island with the village of Rockville Centre as the see 'city,'" the Vatican had recognized that the dominant parish type in the United States was no longer the "rural, downtown, or national parish, but the parish on the edge of the city or just beyond it in the lands of suburbia." Jesuit Father Neil P. Hurley added in *America* that the division of Long Island's suburban counties from the urban Diocese of Brooklyn gave "evidence that eventually dioceses will be born which can focus on Suburbia's unique problems."[84]

The diocese was therefore said to be showing the way forward. James G. Murray wrote in *Catholic Market* that Rockville Centre was "a model, or pilot study, of future trends in American Catholicism" and might "also become a prototype." In *America* Robert A. Graham, SJ, labeled Bishop Kellenberg the "Bishop of Suburbia" and predicted: "the rest of the country will watch Rockville Centre closely" to see how it met the challenges posed by suburban life. Graham warned that the diocese's greatest challenge would be to provide "adequate religious and education facilities in fast-growing communities." Although the young couples who predominated in the diocese were "in the lower-middle-income brackets with their homes still to be paid for," Graham held out hope that their concern for "the spiritual welfare of their growing families" would help them solve "the problem of the Church in Suburbia."[85]

These responses to the establishment of the Diocese of Rockville Centre came as Catholic commentary on suburbia reached a fever pitch in the late 1950s and early 1960s, amid much broader secular, Jewish, and Protestant conversations about the effects of suburbanization and corporatization, the nature of the religious revival of the 1950s, and the so-called suburban captivity of the churches.[86] Catholic periodicals published a wave of reflections by Catholic pastoral leaders, social scientists, and lay commentators, assessing suburban life and its likely effects on the Church. As reactions to the new diocese's creation indicate, many of these reflections were critical of suburban life, fearful of the influence it would have on the life of faith, and anxious for the hierarchy, clergy, and laity to answer the challenge that suburban living posed for the Church.

Andrew Greeley's *The Church and the Suburbs*, published in 1959, was the single most important contribution to this dialogue. Although it was largely overlooked by the secular and Protestant press it was well received by its handful of mainly Catholic reviewers.[87] And Greeley's questions and insights reached an even broader audience through articles he published in popular Catholic periodicals.[88] Greeley was principally interested in how suburbanization was altering the contours of parish life, the ministry of priests and their relationship with the laity, and the Catholic formation of young people. In three chapters at the heart of his book Greeley outlined the principal social, psychological, and religious problems he saw arising from the Church's move to the suburbs and how the Church might evolve to meet suburbia's unique needs, just as national parishes had provided for the needs of immigrants.

Greeley and his contemporaries universally agreed that "the peculiar conditions" of suburbia posed "an apostolic gauntlet" for the Church, that the suburban parish was "quite different from its predecessors," and that to address suburbia's "distinct challenges" the parish would need to adapt itself to "an expression of Catholic life" that was based on socioeconomics rather than ethnicity.[89] They defined the suburbs as a "way of life" premised on an "unbelievable array of gadgets," including "television, air conditioners, 'hi-fi,' power lawn mowers, deepfreezers, electric dishwashers, automatic dryers, automobiles, back-yard swimming pools, and tranquilizing drugs." Knowing that the postwar consumer economy was geared toward "constantly expanding human needs," they worried about how the Church would reconcile its "traditional teachings of Christian frugality" with "the material prosperity of Suburbia." Such theological questions surrounding money had particular import because the first and most important characteristic of the suburban parish was that it faced the challenge of financing and building, within five to ten years, "a school with a hall which can be used for Mass, a convent, rectory, church, and perhaps a social center." As a result, the suburban parish was burdened almost immediately by a huge debt and by facilities that quickly become insufficient for its ever-expanding population, even as its parishioners were "mortgaged to the hilt" and struggled "paying high taxes for poor public service and an expensive public school system."[90]

Critics universally agreed that Catholic suburbanites were "successful, educated, and independent" and "the most intelligent group of listeners" the Church had ever known. But because they had "been taught to question things" they felt "free to disagree" with the clergy "and to do so forcefully and persistently." Greeley worried that priestly authority was almost certain to decline. With suburban parishes becoming vast social service organizations, a pastor was required to be "a good preacher, a skilled counselor, a lively socializer, a gifted organizer, an accomplished diplomat, a shrewd coach or athletic director, a wise planner and builder, and a genius with teenagers." Such vast demands on pastors, combined with the suburban parish's "never-ending financial crisis," and the laity's rising competence and expectation of leadership, was inspiring "radical innovations" in which the laity took on tasks formerly reserved to the clergy including administrative work such as "book-keeping, census work, planning, fund raising," and ministerial functions like teaching home religion classes.[91]

Greeley and his contemporaries also worried about the suburban parish's ability to maintain its central religious meaning and to inculcate the faith in families—especially in the next generation—absent the web of relationships, traditions, and institutions that had marked the ethnic urban experience. Suburbia was "the ultimate melting pot," they feared, and Catholic suburbanites might become "*too* American," surrendering Catholic positions on matters like "birth control, divorce, and premarital sex,' and ultimately sharing "the common American notion that one religion is practically as good as another."[92] On the other hand, they also worried that because the suburbs were excessively focused on children, and on the problems caused by rapid growth, that the suburban parish might be seen as "a glorified day-nursery" and become apathetic about "larger economic and social questions of the day."[93]

Such a development was especially concerning to Catholic commentators because, despite their critiques of suburbia, they recognized its importance in addressing pressing social concerns. Amid the civil rights movement and the burgeoning urban crisis, there was a tendency among Catholic critics to view the suburbs merely as a means of saving the inner city.[94] By the late 1960s Andrew Greeley lamented that *The Church and the Suburbs* had not defended suburbs strongly enough and he derided an "inner city mentality" in which young priests and nuns felt "that they will only be doing the work of the Church if they move into apartment buildings of the inner city." But while advocating for pastoral ministry aimed at the material and spiritual poverty of suburbia, even Greeley focused more on metropolitan organizations capable of marshalling the wealth and vitality of the suburban lay apostolate to solve urban problems.[95]

The Defense of Suburbia

Greeley's *The Church and the Suburbs* was broadly emblematic of Catholic commentary on the suburbs, dwelling as it did on suburbia's "darker aspects."[96] The exceptions include positive evaluations of suburban life by a handful of Catholic women who wrote in defense of suburbia, motherhood, and homemaking, among whom Phyllis McGinley stands out as the most important.[97] Born in Oregon and raised in Colorado and Utah, McGinley was a graduate of the University of Utah who moved to New York in 1929 and worked as a junior high school teacher in New Rochelle. In 1937 she married Bell Telephone Company employee Charles Hayden and they moved to Larchmont, New York, where they raised two daughters. McGinley proudly labeled herself a "housewife poet," and her light verse and essays were widely published in the 1950s and 1960s, including in *Ladies Home Journal, The Atlantic, Saturday Review,* and *The New Yorker.* She won the 1961 Pulitzer Prize and in June 1965 appeared on the cover of *Time* magazine, one of only nine poets to receive the honor in 100 years. Her 1951 collection, *A Short Walk from the Station*, with an introductory essay entitled "Suburbia, of Thee I Sing," defended suburbia from critiques that it was a conformist and materialist wasteland, arguing that "in a world of terrible extremes," future generations would look back on the postwar suburbs as "the safe, important medium." When Betty Friedan, in her landmark

Feminine Mystique, criticized McGinley for glorifying housework, McGinley responded with a collection of essays entitled *Sixpence in Her Shoe*. She celebrated the fact that whether a housewife liked or loathed her "daily round of chores," or worked outside the home or not, that it was into the hands of women that "life had dropped its most significant duties."[98] Her collection spent more than six months on *The New York Times* bestseller list and far outstripped Friedan's book sales.[99]

Letters to the editors of national Catholic publications, interviews in diocesan newspapers, and occasional op-eds indicate that the majority of Catholic suburbanites agreed with McGinley and defended suburbia from its frequent critics. When Catholic publications printed suburban jeremiads such as Paul Brindel's "A Pox on Suburbia," lay readers wrote to defend their new communities. Marjorie Sillers of Brooklyn wrote that she and her family had lived in city and suburb "and decidedly vote for the fields and fresh air." Adelaide D. Katz of Hicksville argued that suburbanites were quite happy with their way of life, and that although homeownership brought responsibilities, new suburban parishes were thriving precisely because parishioners had "grateful appreciation of their little piece of land, something of their very own to work for." Conversely, when *The Long Island Catholic* reprinted Joyce Sentner Daly's essay "I Like Suburbia," reporter Antoinette Bosco found that Long Island laywomen responded, "we like suburbia, too." Sentner Daly argued that suburbia was a new continent of spiritual growth and a "frontier of individualism" because suburbia offered women "the freedom, the impetus, to become whatever she will." Bosco's respondents emphasized that suburbia was friendlier, quieter, more relaxed, and more comfortable than the city, and Mrs. Al Schryver of Christ the King Parish in Commack dismissed the caricature of suburban conformity. Employing remarkably contemporary theological language, she insisted that how much one conformed in suburbia was "a matter of choice and a matter of conscience."[100]

Conclusion

The period of Catholic commentary on suburbia was short-lived. After *The Church and the Suburbs* there were no other book-length projects exploring Catholic suburbanization and the number of articles on Catholicism in suburbia fell off precipitously. The US Catholic bishops sponsored no conferences on the Church in the suburbs and organized no committees or research groups to explore the phenomenon or to advise church leaders about how to adapt their strategic planning to respond to the suburban boom. In fact, throughout the 1960s and 1970s, local and national conferences and dozens of books and articles discussed not the suburban church but the city and the urban parish, even as the majority of American Catholics came to reside in the suburbs. When commentators and theorists spoke of the metropolis or megalopolis, which encompassed both the urban core and the surrounding suburbs, their focus was not so much on the needs of suburbs but on the role suburbanites should play in solving urban problems.[101]

On the one hand, researchers and critics were turning their attention back to the inner city in the mid-1960s because of pressing urban concerns of poverty, crime, and racial riots.[102] At the same time, the lack of express focus on the suburbs is indicative of the fact that the Church in the United States had, to a significant extent, simply become suburban.[103] Whenever theologians, pastoral leaders, and sociologists talked about the Church in America after the 1960s they were talking about a largely suburbanized church whether they named it such or not. When Catholic activists of various stripes urged liturgical and spiritual renewal, increased lay involvement, or changes to catechetical theory and method, they were largely addressing suburban Catholics, in suburban parishes and schools, and grappling with social, cultural, and economic realities created by, or exacerbated by, suburbanization. This is also to say, that when Catholic critics spoke of suburbia they were not only thinking of the ways that space, geography, and location reshaped Catholicism. They were also speaking with concern about the ways that various elements of modern life—rising levels of educational attainment and income, materialism, ecumenism, secularization, and changes to family structure, to name but a few—were reshaping Catholicism. They recognized that suburbia represented an encapsulation and a heightening of all of these factors.

Andrew Greeley and other surveyors of the suburban landscape feared that if the Church did not "effectively adjust itself to the new suburban humanism" it would face ever-greater challenges in the years to come.[104] They called for the development of a suburban spirituality that channeled the advantages of suburban living in order to address the threats suburbia posed to authentic Christian living, including consumerism, isolation, and apathy. But there is very little indication that the bishops or individual dioceses succeeded at developing a pastoral approach that was unique to the suburbs. At best, Catholic suburbanites were recruited to the service of the city as a means of solving the urban crisis. By the early 1970s, as Mass attendance, participation in parish societies, religious and priestly vocations, and enrollments in parochial schools all declined precipitously, some experts warned that efforts to form the consciences of and to mobilize suburban Catholics "should be done as an end in itself, not as a means to solve the urban crisis." In a May 1970 speech to a "Symposium on Metropolis" held at the Catholic University of America, sociologist Dorothy Dohen warned that the Church in the United States had already "come dangerously close to losing the suburbs."[105]

THREE

From Church to Home: Spaces for Prayer, Education, and Charity in the Suburban Parish

On June 26, 1955, approximately 260 station wagons and sedans pulled into the Fifth Avenue Drive-In in Brentwood, New York. But the occupants of those family cars weren't there to see a double feature. They were there to attend Sunday Mass. St. Anne Parish in Brentwood was founded in 1895, but remained a small country parish until the suburban boom overwhelmed its shrine church in the 1950s. To relieve overcrowding at the church, which had just 276 seats to accommodate 2,200 worshippers at five Sunday Masses, the pastor, Fr. Thomas I. Conarty, planned for two, and eventually four, Masses to be said at the drive-in theater. Parish volunteers constructed a three-sided shed at the base of the movie screen in which the priest celebrated Mass. Ushers distributed bulletins, envelopes, and missalettes as the cars arrived, and collected parishioners' donations as they drove away. Microphones relayed the voice of the celebrant to speakers at each parking spot and priests would ask drivers to flash their headlights if they could hear him. Congregants stayed in their cars during Mass and when it was time to receive Holy Communion, they walked up to the covered altar rail in front of the presider's shed. After that first Sunday of drive-in Masses, Father Conarty declared the experiment a success that had garnered the enthusiastic support of even those parishioners who had initially objected to the outdoor liturgies. Still, he insisted that the drive-in Masses would only last through the summer. "That summer lasted until 1968 when the drive-in was sold," and St. Anne Parish held Masses indoors at the Brentwood Theatre until its new church was completed in 1969.[1]

Space shapes religious practice. In what Andrew Greeley has called the "sacramental imagination" of Catholicism, the physical—everything from water, bread, and wine to the light of a candle, the smell of incense, and the sound of music—is understood as capable of being imbued with spiritual meaning.² Within this worldview, the parish has traditionally represented the sanctification of space and territory. In the cities of the late nineteenth and early twentieth centuries, the Church built parish churches, spaces in which ritual objects and actions spiritually transformed the faithful who experienced them. But as the faithful spilled out of these churches in processions, festivals, and the rhythms of daily life, the parish lent sacred meaning to the entire ethnic neighborhood and the two became one and the same. Streets and sections of the city were known by the name of the parish church that stood at the center of, and gave an air of permanence to, the world that Catholic immigrants built. In turn, the contours of urban spaces and places shaped the faithful's experience of the Church.³ In the urban village, Catholics regularly encountered priests, nuns, and fellow parishioners not just at Mass, but at a vast array of social events, and on the streets of the neighborhood. This web of interactions reinforced a communal understanding of the faith and fostered high levels of participation in the life of faith.

But the suburban setting changed the Church's understanding of, and the laity's interaction with, the parish because, in the postwar suburbs, the concept of the neighborhood was radically altered and sometimes lost entirely. With it the Catholic conception of the parish was stretched to the breaking point and was increasingly rejected as a viable means of structuring Catholic life. The suburban parish was divorced from the ethnic neighborhood and Catholic religious practice became less the expression of an ethnic and religious community and more a familial and individual observance. The suburban housing development, which was spread over a much wider area than the urban neighborhood, was often unwalkable. The automobile, which helped give rise to the suburb, delimited the suburbanite's world, making the church inaccessible to nondrivers and lessening the frequency with which parishioners passed by or entered their parish church, or encountered their priests and fellow parishioners on the streets.⁴

The suburbs were also comprised of single-family houses in which, especially in the earliest days of suburban development, a single generation of young veterans lived with their wives and children cut off from the extended family networks that long held the ethnic parish together. Newly and rapidly expanding suburban parishes lacked sufficient facilities in which to host Sunday Mass, religious education classes, pious devotions, retreats, missions, and various forms of charitable activities and social interaction. All of this drove parish life from the public spaces of the parish plant to a variety of temporary spaces, and especially to the private space of the family home. These temporary and secular spaces not only diffused the parish community, but they undermined the sense of the parish as a permanent and sacred space. And even after a suburban parish built a church and school, it served such a huge number of families that the formation of true community was exceedingly difficult. In the suburbs, just as the church was no longer at the physical heart of a neighborhood, the parish was no longer the psychic center of American Catholicism. This development had profound effects on the levels of commitment to and practice of the faith.

Establishing Suburban Parishes

When Catholics moved out of the city in the early postwar period, they helped create a new kind of parish—the suburban parish—where before Catholic commentators, pastoral theologians, and sociologists had categorized parishes as either urban or rural. But because canon law defined parishes territorially, and because of the hierarchical nature of Catholicism, Catholic suburbanites formed communities in ways that were entirely consistent with how new parishes were always established. Most frequently, when a Catholic family moved to a new suburban community, they simply began attending Mass at a previously established parish that was suddenly transformed from a small rural parish into a massive suburban parish. In many instances, this resulted in parishioners and pastors petitioning the diocese to establish new parishes by breaking territory, and therefore parishioners, off of unmanageably large parishes. Less often, landowning Catholics donated property to the diocese in the hopes of providing space for the creation of a new church and school in their community. Finally, dioceses occasionally speculated in land in advance of suburban housing developments anticipating the need for new parishes and schools in a given area. In all of these instances, bishops relied on the advice of pastors, priest consultors, and building commissions to make recommendations about the establishment of new parishes based on the size of parish populations, the distances between parishes and the transportation options for parishioners, and the availability of land and of priests to staff new parishes.

The first St. Ignatius Loyola Church was built in Hicksville in 1859 when a local carpenter donated two lots of land and built a simple 100-seat church for his fellow German Catholics. St. Ignatius Loyola Parish steadily expanded, building a second, larger church in 1891, which was then doubled in size in 1926. The parish also built a grade school for 100 students in 1907 and then a replacement building for 350 students in 1923.[5] But the parish's population truly exploded after World War II, as suburban housing developments, including Levittown, sprouted up within its boundaries. In 1948 a survey of the area found that farmland that previously housed just

100 people now contained 63,000 people.[6] One parish could not possibly provide for the number of Catholics flooding the area. That same year, the Diocese of Brooklyn created St. Bernard Parish in Levittown, breaking territory off from St. Ignatius Loyola Parish. The diocese purchased the Centre Island Airport building and 1,200 parishioners attended the first Mass of St. Bernard Parish on November 7, 1948.[7] But as the area's population continued to boom, the territory once served by St. Ignatius Loyola Parish was further subdivided to establish Holy Family Parish in Hicksville in 1951, St. Edward Parish in Syosset in 1952, Our Lady of Mercy in Hicksville in 1953, St. Pius X Parish in Plainview in 1955, and finally, St. Paul the Apostle Parish in Jericho in 1962.[8]

In establishing new suburban parishes, dioceses considered specific requests from the lay faithful who felt ill served by their parish because it was either too far away or overcrowded.[9] Beginning in 1909 priests from Our Lady of Loretto and St. Ladislaus parishes in Hempstead ministered to the Catholics of Uniondale in an old two-room wooden schoolhouse that was purchased for $150. In 1914 this 175-seat mission chapel was rededicated to St. Martha. When the surrounding potato fields gave way to suburban homes, Lloyd Brown petitioned the Diocese of Brooklyn to send a resident pastor to Uniondale and establish its mission chapel as a parish. Brown's efforts were rewarded when, in 1949, Archbishop Molloy assigned Fr. John J. Byrne as first pastor of St. Martha Parish.[10]

Catholics in Wantagh similarly complained of having to travel to either St. Barnabas the Apostle Parish in Bellmore or St. William the Abbot Parish in Seaford for Sunday Mass. In January 1946 they enlisted George Caffrey to spearhead efforts to convince the Diocese of Brooklyn to establish a parish in Wantagh. Caffrey served as chairman of the Committee for the Erection of a Catholic Church in Wantagh and with his daughter Dorothy went door-to-door to collect signatures for a petition to the diocese. After a series of correspondences between the committee and the diocese, and consultation with the pastors of St. William and St. Barnabas parishes, Archbishop Thomas Molloy established a mission chapel in Wantagh and beginning in June 1948, Sunday Mass was celebrated in the Wantagh Fire Hall. Finally, in January 1952 a resident pastor was assigned to Wantagh and St. Frances de Chantal Parish was established.[11]

Occasionally, Catholic landowners donated property to the diocese so that much-needed suburban parishes could be established, or laity offered use of buildings they owned so that a fledgling parish had a place to gather for Sunday Mass. Even after St. Ignatius Loyola Parish in Hicksville began to have new parishes carved from its territory, far-flung parishioners still

Figure 3.1. Aerial photograph of St. James Parish plant under construction, undated. *Source*: Archives of St. James Parish, Seaford, NY.

clogged the roads on Sunday mornings making multiple trips to and from the parish ferrying family members and neighbors without cars to Mass.[12] In September 1953 the Diocese of Brooklyn therefore established a new parish in Hicksville, Our Lady of Mercy Parish, located on South Oyster Bay Road where John J. Froehlich had donated five acres of property for the establishment of a parish. Until a new church could be built, however, John and Helen Pelkowski lent a vacant barn to house Sunday Mass and Froehlich assisted in purchasing a model home as the parish's first rectory. Within the first six months, Our Lady of Mercy conducted six Sunday Masses in the barn-church and two Sunday Masses in the rectory basement and still many parishioners were left to hear Sunday Mass standing outside the buildings. So many families moved into the area that even the establishment of St. Pius X Parish in Plainview on October 13, 1955, which diminished Our Lady of Mercy's territory, did not ease the overcrowding.[13]

Anticipating the need for new parishes and schools in rapidly expanding suburban areas, dioceses also purchased undeveloped land in advance of housing developments. In December 1960 the Diocese of Rockville Centre purchased two parcels of land totaling thirty-eight acres in West Babylon from members of the Van Bourgondien family, which had operated a garden center in the area since 1919. Two years later, in June 1962, Bishop Walter P. Kellenberg announced the establishment of Our Lady of Grace Parish and named Fr. Thomas Bannon the first pastor. When Bannon died unexpectedly just a few months later, the new parish already had 6,000 families.[14]

Dioceses clearly worked in consultation with private developers and city planning commissions—including "master builder" Robert Moses—to determine where housing development would necessitate the establishment of new parishes.[15] In July 1959 the Diocese of Brooklyn worked with the pastor of St. Clare Parish and a real estate developer to determine the need for and boundaries of a new parish in Rosedale, Queens, near Idlewild (later John F. Kennedy) Airport on the borough's border with Nassau County. At the time, 2,364 homes existed in the area and about 1,276 of them were Catholic. Already some 500 new homes were planned and future development was speculated to bring another 2,250 families to the area. In 1960 the Diocese of Brooklyn established St. Pius X Parish in Rosedale from the southern section of St. Clare Parish.[16]

That same year the Diocese of Brooklyn prepared for a new parish in the area of Mill Basin and Bergen Beach in Brooklyn. The diocese purchased property on Island Avenue between 69th and 70th Streets for $120,137 and paid a builder $26,350 for a house at 2017 E. 68th Street to serve as a rectory. The builder assured the diocese that 300 homes would be built directly across the street from the diocese's property. In May of the following year, the New York City Planning Commission announced that some 3,500 additional housing units could be developed on 200 acres of land in neighboring Paerdegat Basin. The staff of the Diocesan Projects office reported that although the area had a high concentration of Jewish residents, Italian Catholic families were moving into the area and Bishop Bryan McEntegart wanted to "assure a continuation of this trend." On June 30, 1961, the Diocese established St. Bernard Parish and Fr. Patrick J. Kenny was named pastor. The parish's first Sunday Masses were celebrated on August 20 in a tent erected on the property purchased by the diocese. A total of 1,762 parishioners attended one of the six Masses held that Sunday and the parish's first census indicated that 700 Catholic families already lived within St. Bernard's boundaries.[17]

The lay faithful did not just write to the bishop to request that he establish a new parish. They also wrote to complain that, because of their address, they now belonged to a newly established parish despite having happily belonged to the mother parish from which it was created. John Verbeeck lived in Uniondale and he and three generations of his family had belonged to Our Lady of Loretto Parish in Hempstead and attended that parish's school. But when St. Martha Parish was established in Uniondale in 1949, that became his territorial parish and his children were no longer eligible to enroll at Our Lady of Loretto. St. Martha's, however, did not open a parish school until 1957 and Verbeeck complained that parents had to organize carpools to shuttle their children to Our Holy Redeemer School in Freeport.[18] When the Diocese of Rockville Centre instituted parish councils in the late 1960s, pastors and parishioners wrote to Bishop Kellenberg asking if faithful who resided outside a parish's boundaries were still eligible for election to the council of the parish where they were active. The diocese attempted to reinforce parish boundaries, universally answering that the faithful could only serve on the council of the parish within which they resided.[19] But the mobility of suburbanites and the constant shifting of parish boundaries as more and more new parishes were created eroded the territorial meaning of the parish and with it the sense of the parish as a sacred space.

Funding Suburban Parishes

Pastors and parishioners of new parishes were spared the expense of purchasing property when lay Catholics donated land for the establishment of a parish, or when dioceses speculated by purchasing property for a parish near future housing developments. But all new parishes required a significant amount of capital to renovate an existing space for Sunday worship or to purchase or erect basic facilities for Mass, for the religious education of youth, and for the housing of the parish's priests and religious sisters. In some instances, the bishop of Brooklyn directed that the pastors of well-established and financially secure parishes provide donations to the pastors of newly created parishes.

In June 1961, when Bishop Bryan McEntegart named Fr. Patrick J. Kenny pastor of the newly established St. Bernard Parish in Mill Basin, Brooklyn, the bishop also wrote to inform him that five parishes had, at his instruction, donated a combined $300,000 to the new parish. The bishop stated that such generosity was proof of "an admirable Priestly solidarity" and suggested that Father Kenny visit each of these pastors to personally thank them for their generosity.[20] In reality, of course, it was the parishioners of established parishes who were providing these funds through contributions they had expected would be used to support their own parish. Writing to Bishop McEntegart to provide the requested donation for St. Bernard Parish, Fr. Joseph J. Tschantz of St. Gerard Majella Parish in Hollis assured the bishop that "this transfer of funds will not hinder or inconvenience us in our plans for the future of this parish." Although Father Tschantz had not announced the transfer of parish funds to his parishioners, he assumed that they would "all be in full agreement with your Excellency's policy in these matters."[21]

Similarly, when St. Jude Parish was established in Canarsie, Brooklyn in 1961, a total of $320,000 was donated to the new parish by nine well-established parishes.[22] In 1964, when St. Laurence Parish in East New York, Brooklyn, was created, six established parishes and an anonymous donor gave a total of $200,000 to assist the new community.[23] And when St. Columba Parish in Marine Park, Brooklyn was formed in 1967, six established parishes each made $50,000 donations to the new parish.[24] Records of all these financial transactions indicate that donating pastors were to list the expenditure as a contribution to "Home Missions," that the diocese held donated funds in escrow until the new parishes needed them, and that the pastors receiving donations were to maintain confidentiality lest his parishioners "feel there is no reason to give their full measure of support" to the new parish.[25] Such secrecy also ensured that congregants from the parishes making these donations did not question why their contributions were being redirected to other parishes. Undoubtedly, in some cases the donation of funds from long-established parishes to newly created parishes meant that money was following the very parishioners who had financially sustained urban parishes as they moved to homes near newly erected suburban parishes. But this transfer of wealth from urban to suburban sections of the diocese undeniably paralleled federal and state legislation that subsidized the expansion of the postwar suburbs at the expense of funding for inner-city neighborhoods.

It is not clear if this policy of providing new parishes with seed money from established parishes was in effect when the Diocese of Brooklyn created new parishes in Nassau and Suffolk Counties between 1945 and 1957. Once the Diocese of Rockville Centre was established in 1957, its oldest parishes were, up until that time, small-town and rural parishes that were themselves expanding rapidly and were not capable of providing sizable donations to newly established parishes. Bishop Walter Kellenberg did, however, establish a diocesan loan account in which parishes with sufficient financing voluntarily deposited surplus monies in a diocesan fund that then lent to parishes needing financial assistance with their building projects. Monsignor Edmond Trench, a former chancellor and finance director for the Diocese of Rockville Centre, credited the diocesan loan account with building much of the diocese's infrastructure. But, as in the examples cited above, Trench

Figure 3.2. Tabulating pledges for St. Frances de Chantal Parish's fundraising drive, n.d. *Source*: Box 99, Item 3, Archives of St. Frances de Chantal Parish, Wantagh, NY.

clarified that the decision to participate in the diocesan loan account was made by the pastor. Only with the advent of parish councils in the late 1960s did pastors need to convince their parishioners to participate "for the good of the Church on Long Island." But Trench noted that priests then faced the problem that "when money gets tight everybody gets very provincial."[26]

Most new suburban parishes acquired their property and built their first buildings by borrowing and then, over time, fundraising to finance that debt. A history of Our Lady of Grace Parish in West Babylon summarizes that young suburban families "spent their time and energy raising money for the parish" through "card parties, cocktail parties, dances, bake sales, fashion shows, talent shows, hat sales," bazaars, and raffles—including raffles for brand-new cars.[27] Suburban Catholics were exceedingly generous in supporting the diocesan and parish building campaigns that created an entirely new suburban infrastructure of churches, schools, and hospitals, and many of them still fondly recall the pioneer days of their parish. Not only did these faithful build buildings, but their fundraising efforts also built strong community bonds and a sense among the laity that parishes belonged to them. Over time, however, there were also increasing complaints from the laity about pastors who seemed incapable of preaching about anything other than the parish's financial needs.

The Rapid Expansion of Suburban Parishes

Between World War II and the erection of the Diocese of Rockville Centre in 1957, the Diocese of Brooklyn established twenty-eight parishes on Long Island, fifteen in Nassau County and thirteen in Suffolk County. After the war new parishes were established in 1948 and added every year except 1954, with four parishes added in 1951 and five parishes established in 1952. The first area to develop was the broad plain of farmland at the center of Nassau County near Hicksville. Father Lawrence Ballweg's first assignment after his ordination in 1940 was to St. Ignatius Loyola Parish in Hicksville, where he remained for the next twenty-six years, eventually becoming monsignor. When he arrived, Hicksville was still "a small town" and St. Ignatius was "a real country parish" with about 400 families and a church that accommodated about 350 people. Only after World War II did Hicksville expand as potato farmers sold their land to developers building houses for veterans. "There were hundreds completed every week," Ballweg recalled, "and many of the people who moved here were Catholic and they came from Brooklyn and New York. . . . Suddenly this became one of the biggest parishes in the whole country." Before six parishes were created from its original territorial bounds, St. Ignatius had five Sunday Masses on the hour in its little country church, until it built a 1,000-seat auditorium, "the largest meeting room in all of Nassau County," where it still held six Sunday Masses to accommodate all its parishioners. So many young couples were starting families that Ballweg remembered baptizing twenty-eight newborns in just one hot summer afternoon.[28]

Uniondale's Catholic population surged in the late 1940s as returning veterans and widespread car ownership turned the area into a bedroom community for New York City. Elevated from mission church to parish in 1949, St. Martha Parish in Uniondale grew from less than 500 members to more than 4,500 parishioners in its first ten years. At first, Masses were held in the tiny mission church that was previously a two-room schoolhouse. Parishioner John Verbeeck recalled that the mission church was "dismal" and with room for fewer than 200 people "the overflow for the Masses extended into the street." Excavating the chapel's basement doubled the number of Masses and parishioners who could be accommodated, and Masses were said at the Labor Lyceum so that the total number of Sunday Masses climbed to eleven. It was still not enough.[29] In March 1952 150 volunteers began conducting a pledge drive to build a parish church. Within three months a 700-seat brick colonial church was under construction, and within ten years St. Martha's had built and paid for a rectory, the $350,000 church and a $950,000 school with twenty-two classrooms for 1,000 students, and was planning a $300,000 convent for twenty-five sisters.[30]

After the erection of the Diocese of Rockville Centre in 1957, as undeveloped land in Nassau County disappeared and development moved further out on Long Island, the pace of new parishes slowed and their location shifted into Suffolk County. At the fifth anniversary of the diocese in June 1962, Bishop Kellenberg established five new parishes: St. Elizabeth in South Huntington; Our Lady of Grace in West Babylon; St. Peter the Apostle in North Great River; St. Paul the Apostle in Jericho; and Holy Name of Jesus in Woodbury. The new diocesan newspaper, *The Long Island Catholic*, highlighted that, "almost all the parishes are located near the Nassau-Suffolk County line and are evidence of the growing population of Long Island. During the past ten years," the paper noted, "the population of Nassau County has almost doubled while the population of Suffolk County has nearly tripled."[31] Indeed, during the first fifteen years of the new Diocese, sixteen new parishes were established and thirteen of these were in Suffolk County.

Throughout the early 1950s, the minutes of the Diocese of Brooklyn's Building Commission are filled with references to Long Island parishes in desperate need of expanded facilities to accommodate their exploding populations. In 1951 St. James Parish in Wantagh planned for an auditorium to be added onto the existing chapel because in just the two months since the parish's first Mass over 1,000 congregants were attending Sunday Mass. The following year, Our Lady of the Snows Parish in Floral Park similarly planned an auditorium to accommodate its ballooning congregation. In 1955 the pastor of St. William the Abbot Parish in Seaford proposed building an auditorium and a school expansion "to keep abreast of the rapid growth in his community."[32]

As a newly ordained priest in 1956, Emil Wcela was assigned to Maria Regina Parish in Seaford just two years after the parish was founded. He recalled that, "there were still some potato farms" in the area but that "the population was exploding." All the parishes in the area "were new, just a year or two old," and with 2,000 families Maria Regina was "pretty typical."[33] Just a few years later, in 1961, Msgr. Anthony Savastano was assigned as associate pastor of Christ the King Parish in Commack, which had been established two years earlier. "Migration was coming out from Brooklyn and Queens and settling into the western part of Suffolk," Savastano recalled. "You would start off with 1,800 families and then the following year you'd have 2,500 and then the following year you'd have 3,500. It was just burgeoning."[34]

Temporary Spaces for Suburban Parishes

New suburban parishes were characterized by such rapid and overwhelming population growth that temporary and makeshift facilities were required for parish gatherings, most pressingly for Sunday Mass.[35] Perhaps the quickest and most temporary solution was for the parish to erect a tent on property the parish owned or rented. In 1960 the newly established Our Lady of Hope Parish in Middle Village purchased a house as a temporary rectory and erected a 600-seat tent on a vacant lot next-door. On July 3 3,000 people attended the parish's first Masses in the tent. That winter, when the tent collapsed under the weight of a major snowstorm, parishioners worked through the night to ensure the tent was restored for Masses the next morning.[36] The following summer, St. Bernard Parish was established to cover the Bergen Beach, Mill Basin, and Flatbush Garden neighborhoods of Brooklyn, and it too erected a tent as its first church. On August 20, 1961, a total of 1,762 parishioners attended the six Masses offered in the 300-seat tent and the pastor, Fr. Patrick J. Kenny, reported to Bishop McEntegart that "the tent has proven to be an attraction to the people here. We have more people looking it over than would come to see a cathedral being built."[37]

The luckiest of new parishes found old churches and chapels they could purchase from other congregations. In 1942 Fr. Charles L. Sullivan, the founding pastor of St. Raphael Parish in East Meadow purchased the former Williston Park Reformed Church for $1,500 and paid $395 to have the building moved to the new parish's property.[38] Other pastors arranged for Masses in public buildings such as firehouses and schools. In 1948 St. Frances de Chantal began as a mission which gathered for Sunday Masses in the Wantagh Fire Hall. By the time the mission was made a parish in January 1952, the community had outgrown the fire hall and it gathered for Mass in the Beech Street School until a church was completed in June of that year.[39] Holy Family Parish celebrated its first Mass on October 14, 1951, in the Northside School of Levittown, and when Our Lady of Lourdes Parish in Massapequa was established in 1952, it too held Sunday Mass in a public school.[40]

New parishes also used private clubs, restaurants, ballrooms, stores, and industrial buildings. When Our Lady of Grace Parish in West Babylon was founded in 1962, the Republican Club on Great East Neck Road lent its space for the 6,000 families of the parish to gather for Sunday Mass, and when that space proved too small Mass was held at the local Democratic Club as well. When the parish outgrew both halls, it rented a warehouse on Route 109 that parishioners affectionately referred to as "the Fort."[41] In 1962 the new St. Paul the Apostle Parish in Jericho was offered use of the Jericho Jewish Center, the Lions Club of Hicksville, and the Jericho Firehouse for its Sunday Mass sites. On Christmas Eve 1952 St. Rose of Lima Parish in Massapequa Park was only three months old and held its first Midnight Mass in a former saloon called the Wagon Wheel. St. Bernard Parish, founded in Levittown in 1948, held its first Masses in an airplane hangar purchased from the Centre Island Aircraft Company and St. Luke Parish in Brentwood, founded in 1965, conducted Masses in a former casket factory.[42]

Given that many of the postwar housing developments in Nassau County were built on former farmland, it is unsurprising that numerous new parishes converted barns into temporary churches. When Blessed Sacrament Parish was formed in Valley Stream in July 1950, the parish's "physical plant consisted of an old farmhouse and a barn on North Central Avenue," which parishioners worked to convert into a church by Christmas. On Christmas Eve the following year, St. James Parish in Seaford was only three months old and held its first Midnight Mass in a chicken coop that had been transformed into a chapel. And parishioners in St. Pius X Parish, founded in Plainview in 1955, spent two weeks "in painting, sewing, carpentry, wiring, and borrowing necessary furnishing for the sanctuary" of their first church, housed in Mr. and Mrs. John Hartman's empty barn on Old Bethpage Road.[43]

Since suburban parishes were formed to serve the many families moving into newly built developments of single-family homes, the first building many parishes purchased, not surprisingly, was a house that served as a residence for the parish's priests, and as a site for smaller parish gatherings like daily Masses and Confessions. When Holy Family Parish was formed in Hicksville in 1951, founding pastor Fr. Martin O'Dea bought a ranch-style house at 2 Crocus Lane in Levittown to serve as the rectory. Daily Masses, Confessions, and even Baptisms were held there. Christ the King Parish in Commack, founded in 1959, began in a split-level house with the garage turned into a chapel. In 1962 a private home was purchased as the priests' residence for St. Paul the Apostle Parish in Jericho and the den was converted into a chapel. That same year, Fr. Thomas Bannon founded Our Lady of Grace Parish in West Babylon from a house at 666 Albin Avenue and its two-car garage was converted into a daily Mass chapel. At St. Matthew Parish in Dix Hills, a family home was purchased as a rectory in 1965 and the

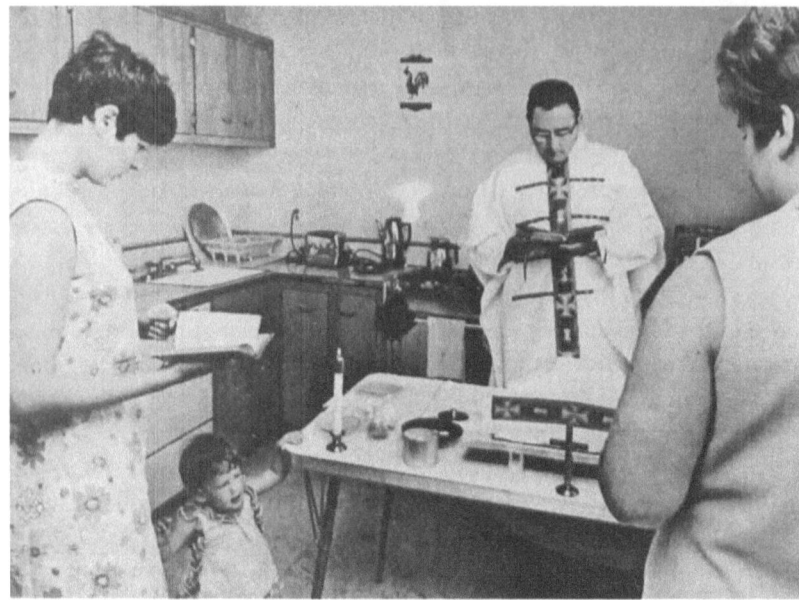

Figure 3.3. Fr. Theodore J. Howard of St. Gerard Parish in Terryville celebrates Mass in the kitchen of the temporary rectory. *Source*: "Priests Have Opinions, But It's People Who Make New St. Gerard's Parish 'Go,'" *Long Island Catholic* 8, no. 9 (June 26, 1969): 3.

living room became a daily Mass chapel. And in 1967, a year after founding St. Francis of Assisi Parish in Greenlawn, Fr. Joseph F. Keyes purchased a house on Northgate Drive to serve as a rectory. He "emphasized to his parish that they were to regard the new rectory as their own house" and "made it clear that the lovely house was a 'people's building' as he put it."[44]

Perhaps the most telling of the temporary settings in which parishes celebrated Sunday Mass was the drive-in movie theater that St. Anne Parish in Brentwood used between 1955 and 1968. Understandably, new parishes in both urban and suburban settings had frequently made use of theaters as temporary churches, given that these spaces were physically and acoustically designed for large gatherings of people to see and hear a performance. Holy Family Parish in Hicksville held Masses at the Meadowbrook Theatre in East Meadow when the parish was first established in 1951. So, too, did St. Jude Parish at the Canarsie Theater in Brooklyn in 1961, and St. James Parish at the Three Village Theatre in Setauket in 1965.[45] The associate pastor of Christ the King Parish in Commack joked that his young parishioners got so used to going to Mass in the Mayfair Theatre "that when they went to the movies they genuflected."[46]

But in the postwar suburbs, America's love affair with the automobile gave rise to the drive-in movie theater. "By 1958 more than four thousand outdoors screens dotted the American landscape," notes historian Kenneth T. Jackson, and pioneering ministers across the country were eager to attract worshippers to their Sunday services by holding them in drive-in theaters.[47] By far the most famous of the nation's drive-in churches was the Garden Grove Community Church in Garden Grove, California, founded by Rev. Robert Schuller in 1955. With a $500 grant from the Reformed Church in America, Schuller began his church in a drive-in theater before building, in 1958, a unique building to accommodate both walk-in and drive-in congregants. Schuller's motto for his church was "Come as you are in the family car."[48] In 1980 Schuller's ministry, which had expanded to include televangelism, would move into the iconic Crystal Cathedral designed by Philip Johnson.[49]

Schuller was not unique, however. The same year he opened his first drive-in church, St. Anne Parish on Long Island held Sunday Mass at the Fifth Avenue Drive-In in Brentwood. What was intended as a temporary measure to relieve overcrowding lasted for thirteen years. Over that period of time, "occasional problems" emerged with the venue. Cold and snow,

Figure 3.4. Brochure for St. Anne Drive-In Church, n.d.
Source: Archives of St. Anne Parish, Brentwood, NY.

rain and mud, made priests' hands turn blue, dirtied parishioners walking up for Communion, and trapped their cars. The shed housing the altar was once blown down in a storm, and if there was insufficient time between Masses, traffic for the next Mass "would back up on Fifth Avenue and the police would call the rectory."[50]

Even more importantly, the drive-in venue fundamentally altered the nature of participating in Mass. Worship became much more informal and isolating. Parishioners recall, as children, being piled in the back of the family's station wagon still in their pajamas or wearing their swimsuits for a day at the beach, a practice that in hindsight they deemed a "very informal, almost sacrilegious" way to attend Mass.[51] Worshippers sat not in pews, with other parishioners, but in the car with only other members of their family. Historian Maureen Fitzgerald, who grew up on Long Island in the 1960s, recalled her family's visits to St. Anne's Drive-in Church as "the most alienating of our suburban Catholic experiments." Writing in a 2007 essay, Fitzgerald narrates an experience from when she was about nine years old and "literally got lost coming back from Communion, which was given at a makeshift altar under the screen. It was easy to find the screen but hard to differentiate the sea of station wagons a quarter mile back," she writes. "When my father finally found me, we got into the car, drove off, and did not return. The absurdity and profound sense of loss in this experience was palpable."[52]

Fitzgerald's parents had grown up in the city and their urban parishes "were central to how they defined neighborhood and community." But the local drive-in, and suburban churches that were "architecturally indistinct from a gymnasium," hardly satisfied her mother's "search for peace in sacred space," and the priests' constant preaching about "the need to put more money in the collection plate," stymied her father's desire for "intellectual engagement" and a "more sophisticated Catholicism."[53] Even as suburban parishes replaced temporary spaces with new parish buildings, the shift toward the familial, individual, and private that the Drive-In Church signified continued. While pastors worked to recreate the urban parish plant, the expediencies of the suburban parish and the domestic focus of suburbia combined to shift the center of parish life from the parish plant to the private home.

The Suburban Home as a Place of Prayer and School of Religion

Once a parish had secured a location for its mushrooming population to attend Sunday Mass, the next most pressing need was to find space in which the hundreds of children in the parish could receive religious instruction.

In some instances, established but suburbanizing parishes had small parish school buildings that could also be used for the afterschool religious instruction of children who attended public schools. But the majority of parishes did not yet have any educational facilities of their own. As a 1963 article in *The Long Island Catholic* summarized: "In most cases public facilities are closed to religious instruction classes; often there are no centrally located private facilities available. The answer to this problem is the bringing of religion classes into private homes in the parish."[54]

Sacred Heart Parish in Island Park was founded in 1938 and ran Sunday School classes in its parish hall for the small number of youth in the parish. But in 1953, "due to the large number of children and the danger of the wooden frame building," Fr. Aloysius J. Palko established a Confraternity of Christian Doctrine (CCD) program in parishioners' homes to provide afterschool religious instruction for children who attended public schools.[55] That same year, Fr. Louis J. Schwebius, the founding pastor of Our Lady of Mercy Parish in Hicksville, "asked for female volunteers who were willing to conduct religious instruction classes in their homes for the children in their immediate neighborhood." Crucially, the new parish did not have any nuns to teach the parish's children and it was impossible to provide transportation to and from a single location for all the parish's children. Forty-five classes were held in homes throughout the parish and over the first three years of the program 1,100 children received instruction for their First Holy Communion.[56]

When Bishop Emil Wcela arrived at Maria Regina Parish in Seaford as a newly ordained priest in 1956, he recalled that the parish's religious education "was all in homes. It was in people's basements."[57] Wcela's fellow associate pastor, Msgr. Robert Emmet Fagan, added, "we had about 3,000 children and about 90 homes." It was his responsibility to assign children to classes based on the streets they lived on, and he recalled years later how the tedious process took days to complete.[58] In the early 1960s, at Christ the King Parish in Commack, Fr. William Koenig directed an "in-home catechetical program" with 400 parent volunteers teaching approximately 2,000 students in classes of five to ten students.[59] Similar programs were established at Our Lady of Grace Parish in West Babylon in 1962 and at St. Elizabeth Parish in South Huntington in 1963.[60] The in-home religious education program at St. Francis of Assisi Parish in Greenlawn was established in 1967 and had more than 100 houses in which religious instruction was held. The author of a parish journal stated, "The home classrooms have performed their role faithfully and well. . . . Home and church have thus knit together in the effort of raising the children in the faith of the Trinity"[61]

Figure 3.5. Mrs. Rose Cordes leads a fifth-grade in-home CCD class in St. Elizabeth Parish, South Huntington. *Source*: "The Parish Councils: Response Sought at St. Elizabeth's," *Long Island Catholic* 8, no. 34 (December 18, 1969): 9.

However, the qualitative change this brought about in the experience of religious formation cannot be underestimated. The longstanding expectation had been that Catholic children should receive instruction five days a week, for six hours a day, while wearing a uniform, at the hands of habited religious women in a Catholic school building. Ideals about Catholic education presumed that, in addition to classroom content and pedagogical method, everything from the school's schedule and decor to the attire of students and teachers created a Catholic environment in which children were not merely instructed in dogma but formed for religious practice.[62] But in the fast-growing suburbs, where the only option was that religious instruction be limited to an hour a week, in the kitchens and basements of family homes, and led by laywomen and -men, religious formation was domesticated, privatized, and isolated from other subjects.

It is no surprise, then, that the use of family homes for afterschool religious education was usually a temporary measure that parishes abandoned once they had the resources to build a parish school or at least a religious education center. By the late 1960s, however, many parishes once again began holding religious education classes for teenagers in private homes, and classes for engaged couples moved from rectories and parish centers to the private homes of host couples.[63] This is reflective of the fact that the move away from the public and communal space of the parish to the private and familial space of the home was rooted not merely in practicality, or in the domestic ideals of the 1950s, but also in a theological shift that emphasized the home as a place of prayer and as the essential setting for religious education, especially of children. Reflecting in 1988 on his childhood on Long Island in the late 1950s and 1960s, Msgr. Thomas Hartman boldly stated, "I see religion as something that you experience outside the Church. Your love for God is experienced most directly through your family; those with whom you are working in the market-place. You go to the church to celebrate that, to reinforce that," he argued, before adding "the substance of my own faith really came in the home."[64]

Amid the postwar housing crisis, Catholic authors worried that "the first principles of *home*-building" were "lost in the battle for *houses*."[65] The National Catholic Rural Life Conference (NCRLC) and the National Catholic Welfare Conference (NCWC) Family Life Bureau, along with proponents of the liturgical movement, published practical guides for families to turn their house into a home through what was called "the family liturgy." The laity were encouraged to build home altars or shrines and to employ ritual objects just as their Catholic ancestors had for generations. But as ethnic traditions were waning, the laity were now encouraged to root their family prayer squarely in the liturgical life of the Church through seasonal devotions such as Advent wreaths and Holy Thursday commemorations.

Catholic women played a particularly important role in proposing and enacting this vision of the domestic church. Lay Catholic writers like Mary Perkins Ryan encouraged Catholic wives and mothers to view their care for their husbands, children, and home as "a vital force in orienting families to Christ," thus showing that laywomen had "great potential to act as leaders and nurturers" of the Church.[66] In that very spirit, the women of St. Pius X Parish's Legion of Mary "arranged for a parish-wide blessing of 6,000 homes on Epiphany Sunday," 1957, to help families understand their home as sacred space.[67] And at Our Lady of Grace Parish in West Babylon the parish magazine encouraged parents to include religious articles such as crucifixes, statues, and religious paintings in their homes because such "sacramentals" preserved the "divine contact between altar and family and they help to turn pagan houses into Christian homes."[68]

Devotions such as novenas and the praying of the rosary also moved from citywide celebrations in the streets, and parish-wide celebrations in the church, to family celebrations in the cul-de-sac and private home. Suburbanization and the collapse of the urban and ethnic era of Catholicism brought an end to the large citywide Catholic rallies and Eucharistic congresses that had once been popular in cities across the urban north.[69] In the New York metropolitan area, the citywide rallies and processions sponsored by lay associations like the Legion of Mary and the Holy Name Society, which in the early 1950s still attracted tens of thousands of Catholics, diminished significantly over the rest of the decade and virtually disappeared by the 1960s.[70] Somewhat anomalously, the Legion of Mary in the Diocese of Rockville Centre began hosting a regional Rosary Rally at Roosevelt Raceway in Westbury in 1967. Although it continued into the 1980s, its steady decline in participants—from a height of 20,000 in 1969 to 5,000 in 1977—also indicates that mass devotional gatherings no longer held the same appeal.[71]

The overall decline in the popularity of the rosary and other pious devotions in the late 1960s and 1970s is often explained as an effect of the Second Vatican Council's privileging of the Mass and the reading of Scripture. But an equally important, and in many ways prior explanation for this decline is that suburbanization, and the breakup of the ethnic neighborhood, had inspired even in the late 1940s and '50s a shift from the public devotions of the parish to the private devotions of the home. While ethnic Catholicism had long encouraged various forms of domestic rituals, as such pious practices waned by the 1940s, in middle-class suburbs Catholics were encouraged to take up Americanized forms of devotion like the family and block rosary, both as a means of strengthening family life and recapturing some of the old spirit of the neighborhood parish.[72]

Father Patrick Peyton, CSC, whose motto was "the family that prays together, stays together," was the great apostle of the family rosary. In 1950 he produced an hour-long Easter Sunday television program, *The Triumphant Hour*, which promoted the family rosary and was viewed by a record audience of 42 million people.[73] The block rosary was a communal devotion that gathered neighborhood families once a week in one another's homes or yards to pray the rosary together. A movement to promote the block rosary began in the late 1940s and by the early 1950s there were "many units flourishing at Jamaica Estates" in Queens.[74] By 1958 there were approximately forty prayer groups a week in Orange County, New York; on Long

Island, St. Pius X Parish in Plainview had formed the area's first parish block rosary.[75] Parishioners of St. Martha Parish in Uniondale participated in a hybrid form of the block and family rosary. The parish's Rosary Crusade, begun in 1961, involved 150 families of the parish passing "a statue of Our Lady of Fatima and a large pair of rosary beads" from house to house. Each night, in the home hosting the statue, the father led "his family in the recitation of the rosary" and then took "the statue and beads to the next house" where the rosary was said the next night.[76]

Retreats for lay Catholics also shifted from communal spaces to the privacy of the home. During the 1930s and '40s, retreats for lay Catholics increased in popularity and religious communities of priests and sisters opened retreat houses to host single-sex, weekend-long retreats for the laity. While there is an essential aspect of all retreats that is personal and private, retreatants in this era were often at retreat houses with other members of their parish or the lay organization that was sponsoring the retreat. These gatherings were always more common among men, in part because women found it more difficult to break free from their domestic duties for a weekend.[77] In the 1950s enclosed retreats remained popular but increasingly attempts were made to provide the laity with opportunities to do a retreat in their own homes. In 1953, as television was rapidly expanding in popularity and Bishop Fulton Sheen was building the audience that would make his *Life Is Worth Living* the most watched religious series in television history, The National Council of Catholic Men produced "A Living Room Retreat," which was aired on NBC stations across the country as part of *The Catholic Hour* television program.[78] Over the course of four Sunday afternoons in March, Fr. Bertin Roll, OFM, who was "well-known for his work with mothers and children on home life," served as a "living room retreat master" leading his viewers in prayer and meditation. Roll also gave a brief sermon and suggested "certain practices which might be adopted in every home."[79] In 1962 *The Long Island Catholic* recommended that its readers make use of Jean Kelleher's new book, *Halo for a Housewife*, which provided spiritual readings and prayers for each morning, afternoon, and evening of a three-day, personal, at-home retreat for women. The review was quick to point out that this was "not intended to be a substitute for an enclosed retreat," but admitted that it could "well fill-in until a weekend retreat is possible."[80]

In 1974 Dorothy Horstmann, a housewife from St. Thomas More Parish in Hauppauge, and Sr. Mary Sullivan, a Sister of the Cenacle, launched what became an international program of At Home Retreats. The two women began offering thirteen-week retreats based on the Spiritual Exercises of St. Ignatius of Loyola to small groups of seven to twelve young housewives, usually between twenty-seven and forty years of age. There remained a communal component to the retreat, as participants gathered one evening a week in the home of the lay retreat leader or one of the retreatants to discuss the fruit of the week's prayer. But the retreatants' principal commitment was to remain "in the world, confronting day-to-day responsibilities," while performing fifteen minutes of personal prayer in their homes. The retreats proved so popular that Horstmann and Sullivan trained other teams to lead retreats, published a booklet about the retreats entitled *Come Follow Me*, and expanded to provide retreats for men and married couples.[81] By 1977 seventy-seven retreats had been held on Long Island and more than 900 people had participated. With diocesan approval, At Home Retreats incorporated as a not-for-profit and formalized the retreat's format and the training of retreat leaders. By 1979 the organization had spread to all fifty states and to Great Britain, Ireland, Holland, Belgium, Canada, and Bermuda.[82]

The founders of At Home Retreats insisted that they were "not a parish program," but always strived to be "in dialogue with the parish" and often found that retreatants became "more rather than less involved in parish activities."[83] As the organization's name indicated, however, the crucial aspect of the retreat was that it took place at home. "The retreat is always given in the home, never in a convent or parish center," Fr. Robert E. Lauder noted in a 1983 column in *The Long Island Catholic*. He felt that this home setting symbolized "that religion is not something confined to a specifically religious setting," but he also saw a practical benefit to this approach:

> I know many of my lay friends who at one time in their lives would not miss making an annual retreat. Now I know none. I can understand how difficult it is to get away to some retreat house. Family obligations make weekend retreats just about impossible for many. I think the At Home Retreat is the answer for my friends.[84]

Lay participants agreed. "I could not get away for a weekend retreat and a day of recollection was never long enough," one participant wrote. A "retreat in a home was exactly what the doctor ordered."[85]

For a brief period of time in the late 1960s the family home was considered to be a uniquely advantageous setting even for the Mass, the most important rite of the Church and the center of parish activity. Central though it was, prior to Vatican II the Mass was not an especially participatory gathering for the laity who prayed silently as the priest celebrated the sacred ritual quietly, in Latin, while facing away from the congregation and toward the altar. In the drive-in churches, and overcrowded, temporary worship spaces of suburbia, the liturgy seemed all the more individual in nature. With the reforms of Vatican II the faithful were given more vocal and active roles in the liturgy, heightening their sense that the Mass was a corporate action of the Body of Christ. While both the practicalities of suburban life and theological considerations were making the private space of the family home a place of parish prayer, the faithful were increasingly excited to experience the Mass as a communal activity.[86]

In the summer of 1967 Bishop Walter Kellenberg thus gave permission to the priests of St. Anne Parish in Brentwood to undertake an "experimental diocesan project in parish renewal," centered around celebrating Mass in parishioners' homes. Father Peter Chiara, who was assisting with the renewal program, felt that "in the intimate atmosphere of a home, fellow parishioners would be able to develop more personal—or community—relationships." By the end of the summer, Mass had been said in forty-five homes for 1,200 people, and Father Chiara found that people who had not been going to Mass regularly were attending the home Masses.[87] The experiment was apparently deemed such a success that by the end of the summer Kellenberg had extended his authorization of home Masses to all the parishes and priests of the diocese, making him one of only seven bishops in the entire country to grant such far-reaching approval of home Masses.[88] Parishes across the diocese enthusiastically embraced this movement of the Mass "from very public to intimate" spaces.[89] Monsignor John Alesandro was a newly ordained priest assigned to St. Thomas the Apostle Parish in West Hempstead where he recalls: "we had 100 home masses and study groups . . . and there were many parishioners involved in it." St. Mary Parish in East Islip observed a "Teen Week" in which 540 teenagers gathered around dining room tables for one of the five home Masses celebrated every night for a week.[90]

Adults of St. Mary's who participated in a similar program commented that "the home Mass experience helped to clarify and bring across the beauty of the new emphasis that 'salvation must be achieved as a family rather than as an individual.'"[91] Parishioners who attended home Masses in other parishes agreed. Dr. Joseph Serio of West Hempstead said that the home setting and the nearness of the priest made the homily "much more meaningful," and Mrs. Frederick Dri of Brentwood felt that Mass was "much better in a family group."

Priest celebrants, too, embraced home Masses. Father William R. Geary of St. Agnes Cathedral Parish in Rockville Centre enthused that "they are the greatest experience in my priesthood."[92] And Fr. James Richter wrote that the informality of the home Mass did not "lessen the reverence and respect for divine worship" but rather "deepened and enriched it," and helped "answer the universal complaint that our suburban parishes are too large and that most people feel like strangers at our overcrowded Sunday Masses."[93]

The popularity of the home Mass was, however, short-lived. In just a few years, what was briefly "a highly successful program," was deemed to be waning. As early as October 1968 the newsletter of the Christian Family Movement had soured on home Masses, commenting that they had "no lasting effect" and that "everyone returns to the little world of their own."[94] Father William R. Karvelis of St. Ignatius Loyola Parish in Hicksville commented in August 1970 that home Masses were "certainly not catching on like wildfire now." Explanations for the drop-off varied, but centered on the busyness of both parishioners and priests. Father Arthur J. Kane of St. Elizabeth in South Huntington said that his parishioners were commuters who could not host a home Mass "before 8 or 8:30 at night." Father Charles J. Murphy of Our Lady of the Snow in Blue Point said that parishioners weren't requesting home Masses because they recognized there were too few priests in their parishes and that it was difficult for them to "get away in the evenings" given their various responsibilities.[95] The rapid decline in the popularity of home Masses in the late 1960s may also indicate that they were unable to speak to the tumultuous events of the era. Within just months of home Masses being permitted, the year 1968 witnessed the assassinations of Martin Luther King Jr. and Robert F. Kennedy, the Soviet invasion of Prague, and the riots at the Democratic National Convention in Chicago. As the Christian Family Movement newsletter suggested, perhaps parishioners preferred to retreat to the domestic refuge rather than invite the world in.[96]

The noted exception was at Our Lady of Grace Parish in West Babylon, where home Masses were "celebrated at least twice a week," and the parish's Vestment Guild prepared kits to provide families with all that was needed, including "a cross, cruets, candles, wine, hosts (large and small), altar linens, alb, missal, Greek antemensium (needed in place of an altar stone), and a set of white vestments."[97] The parish even suggested that First Communions take place as part of a home Mass, announcing through the *Our Parish* magazine in April 1971 that, "as many families as possible are urged to let the child first receive Jesus at a Home Mass with his family, friends, and relatives in his own home."[98]

If the Mass was the single-most important event in a parish's communal life, the annual parish mission was among the next most important and best-attended parish celebrations from the 1930s into the 1950s. But in suburbia, parish missions, like retreats and the Mass itself, moved "out of the church pulpits and into the living rooms of parish homes." In 1967 St. Peter the Apostle Parish in Islip Terrace instituted the diocese's first-ever home mission, entitled "Christ Visits His People." Fathers Aloysius Dlag and Peter Ryan "wanted to create an atmosphere of Christian love" in their parish and "felt that the way to do this was to start with small groups within homes." Over the course of six nights, groups of parishioners gathered in four different family homes to share Bible readings, prayer intentions, and an open discussion. At the time, Bishop Walter Kellenberg had not yet approved home Masses in the diocese, but later that year when St. Mary Parish in East Islip held its first home mission, it was premised on home Masses. Father William J. Connors, CSSR, a Redemptorist priest who visited the parish to assist with the mission reflected that, "in the home setting, you really got to see the needs of the people."[99]

When the priests of Our Lady of Fatima Parish in Manorhaven wanted to give parishioners "a fuller understanding of the parish as a community," they recruited Jesuit priests from St. Ignatius Retreat House in Manhasset to lead a three-week renewal program in which six families met in parishioners' homes. The mission culminated "with the celebration of the Eucharist in homes of parishioners."[100] In 1971 St. Brigid Parish in Westbury was one of the largest parishes in the diocese. Covering territory nine miles long by six miles wide, the parish had 4,440 families, celebrated twenty-one Sunday Masses in four locations, and educated 1,400 children in the parish school and 2,000 children in the CCD program. Father Patrick Callan, the associate pastor, lamented, "We reach people only in a fleeting manner. People come to Mass, and it's all so impersonal—as if they were coming to their spiritual gas station. They drop in for a refill of grace once a week." In an "attempt to eliminate the impersonality" of such a huge parish, St. Brigid's undertook "a program of decentralization" that divided the parish into four quadrants, and then into sections, with an area leader for each. In each section parishioners would "gather in each other's homes for Masses, socials, discussion groups, adult education, and CCD" classes for Catholic students in public schools.[101] That same year, St. Gerard Parish in Terryville conducted a nine-week mission to provide parishioners with a "new vision of how to 'personalize' a parish." Because parishes were so big, "most people in the same parish remain strangers to each other." Father William Connors was therefore "convinced that a parish must be broken down into small, manageable neighborhood groups." Conducted by four Redemptorist priests, the mission featured home Masses and discussion groups aimed at forming a network of small communities.[102]

The Suburban Home as a Site of Charity and Activism

In suburbia even the forms of charity offered by the institutional Church and practiced by the average parishioner came to center on the family home. One of Andrew Greeley's greatest fears about suburbia's effects on the Church was that the suburban parish would be "so concerned with its own problems of growth" that, like the suburbs themselves, it would be isolated from the needs of the broader city and world, and thus fail to be a "platform for social action."[103] A 1969 article in *The Long Island Catholic* concurred, calling "the apathy of a care-less 'silent majority' who live apart from the inner cities nestled in their impenetrable suburbs" one of the most serious threats to American society.[104] Writing in 1989 Catholic historian Jay P. Dolan seemed to confirm that Greeley's worst fears had come to pass. Dolan assessed that suburban parishes were white and middle class, lacked "concern for issues of social justice," and failed to "bridge the chasm separating the urban church from the church in the suburbs."[105]

More recent scholarship on the postwar suburbs has complicated their image as universally white, middle-class, and politically apathetic by uncovering the racial and economic diversity in suburbia and detailing the political activism that originated in suburban homes.[106] A closer examination of Catholic suburbia reveals that charity and activism did not disappear, but that the forms and setting of that service evolved according to the changed circumstances of suburban Catholics. No longer immigrants themselves, and at a remove from their places of employment, suburban Catholics shifted their charitable efforts and activism from communal spaces like union halls and the parish to more private and personal spaces like the family home. So, too, their charity and activism shifted from supporting Catholic immigrants and blue-collar laborers to caring for nuclear families in crisis and reaching out beyond the Catholic community.

The first and simplest charitable concern of suburban Catholics was to care for their fellow parishioners, especially those who were new to suburbia, by forming welcoming communities in their parishes. In 1967 a group of women in St. Peter of Alcantara Parish in Port Washington recognized that in many suburbs "people tend to become very anonymous" and that increased mobility meant that one often did not see familiar faces at Sunday Mass. Convinced that "a parish should be a neighborhood," these women formed a committee to welcome the twenty-five new families their parish registered each month. But believing that a less formal "party atmosphere of coffee and dessert" would best make newcomers feel that they belonged, these welcome events were hosted in volunteers' homes, not at the parish itself.[107] Similarly, when St. Anne Parish in Brentwood wanted to "restore a sense of community" among its 6,000 families, teams of priests, seminarians, and sisters undertook a parish-wide project of home visitations. Not only did the parish see attendance at daily Mass skyrocket, at least one person was reported to have converted to Catholicism because of the home visit she received.[108]

Door-to-door surveys of all the homes within a parish's bounds were often undertaken as a means of inspiring conversions to Catholicism and of encouraging fallen-away Catholics to return to the faith. In 1962, for example, the 107 Legion of Mary chapters across the Diocese of Rockville Centre made a total of approximately 14,000 home visits, resulting in 603 people returning to weekly Mass, 159 Baptisms, 647 people joining religious instruction, 474 children receiving First Communion, 166 Confirmations, 55 marriages being validated, and 353 people joining a parish society.[109] But even as ecumenical dialogue suddenly replaced proselytism as a focus of Catholic action, the home remained the preferred venue of interfaith interaction. After the Second Vatican Council gave an imprimatur to interfaith dialogue in its 1965 Decree on Ecumenism, *Unitatis Redintegratio*, the National Council of Churches and the National Confraternity of Christian Doctrine published *Living Room Dialogues*, a workbook for groups of Protestants and Catholics meeting "in informal, local-level groups" to discuss "the worldwide movement toward Christian unity."[110] The following year, when Bishop Walter Kellenberg issued "Interim Directives for Ecumenical Activities in the Diocese of Rockville Centre," he recommended *Living Room Dialogues* and said that open houses were helpful in "getting local congregations to become better acquainted."[111] Considering the mutual suspicion and vitriol that marked Catholic–Protestant relations for over four centuries, such openness to interfaith dialogue was revolutionary.[112] And it is especially noteworthy that the suburban family home, not the parish, church, or some other public space, was envisioned as the ideal setting for such ecumenical exchanges.

Newcomers to suburbia often lacked relatives and friends in the area. When illness or maternity made household duties difficult for a housewife, she had few avenues of support. In 1949 Catholic Charities in Nassau County addressed this need by launching an emergency "homemaker service" in which an aid worker did shopping, cared for children, and did housekeeping for the family while the father of the house was at work. Between 1949 and 1950 Catholic Charities in Nassau County saw a 64 percent increase in its casework and emergency homemaking was the most requested service.[113] Recognizing that even middle-class families faced with a sudden crisis often needed immediate financial help, a group of women at St. Rose of Lima Parish worked with Diocesan Catholic Charities to established St. Rose of Lima Community Services in 1964. The charity helped Catholics and non-Catholics alike to "get jobs, pay bills, get help in their homes" and to "transport people to clinics" and "help put food on the table." That same year, the Family Services Division of Diocesan Catholic Charities reported that it provided 394 families with emergency homemaker services and approximately 1,300 couples with marriage counseling.[114]

Among the social justice issues that most concerned Catholic activists, and critics of suburbia, throughout the 1950s and '60s were race relations, open housing, and the urban crisis. Catholic commentators judged that suburbanites had fled cities and absolved themselves of their obligation to address the needs of urban minorities. Some suburban Catholics—especially members of the diocesan Interracial Council—were, however, active in antiracism, focusing their efforts on establishing open housing and on increasing interracial understanding and urban-suburban partnerships. Once again, the family home was seen as the ideal setting for forming such personal relationships.

In June 1964, just weeks before the Civil Rights Act of 1964 was passed in Congress, the Interracial Council sponsored a Home Get-Together program "to get whites and Negroes together on a social basis," and thus break down "the barriers of fear, prejudice and ignorance." In its first year, more than 900 people took part in these gatherings.[115] The following year the Council partnered with Protestant and Jewish groups in the Nassau Interfaith Committee for Interracial Visits to sponsor two Home Visit Days. On May 16, 1965, some 500 white families attended a "getting-to-know-you afternoon" in one of 130 African American homes to get "a glimpse of what the racial revolution means to them." The day was so successful a second was held on November 14. Ann Luna of Notre Dame Parish in New Hyde Park, the Catholic representative to the Nassau Interfaith Committee, commented, "the great value of Home Visit Day is that it provides a relaxed and friendly setting for personal contact." For many, "this was their first time in a Negro home and vice-versa," Luna said, and the gatherings were "successful in dispelling misunderstandings and ignorance."[116]

Suburban homes were also the site of attempts to form interracial bonds across the urban-suburban divide. In 1964 Edward T. Croll, a twenty-nine-year-old Irish Catholic from Hartford, Connecticut and a graduate of Fairfield University, founded the Revitalization Corps, which on Long Island was best known for running "Operation Suburbia" beginning in June 1969. This was a program in which white families invited Black youngsters from the inner city to spend a weekend or a summer vacation with them in the suburbs to "begin dialogue and personal relationships between people in the city and those in the suburbs." Curtis Jackson, a social worker at the Bed-Stuy Youth in Action Home Study Project, saw participation in "Operation Suburbia" as a way for "black youngsters to come in contact with whites" and come to "see white people as people, as individuals." In St. Francis of Assisi Parish in Greenlawn, white parishioners saw summer visitations as a way of expressing the "concern of the parish over the plight of black people in the city" and as a means of "establishing bonds that would transcend racial and economic differences." Over the summer of 1970 parishioner Leone Barrington recruited twenty-six families in the parish to host "twenty-seven Negro Children," ranging in age from seven to twelve, from St. Peter Claver Parish in Brooklyn. During their week on Long Island, the children were said to have "breathed clean air" and "enjoyed all the happy activities that middle-class suburban kids accept as a matter of course."[117]

A Loss of Confidence in the Parish

The emphasis that suburbia placed on the home, and the shift from public to private space that this brought about, contributed to fears over the health of the parish, and to attempts to redefine the parish. Concern about the health of parish life was a consistent theme in Catholic pastoral writing from at least the 1940s through today. Even in the 1940s Catholic leaders worried that parishes were mere sacramental "service stations" where the faithful came briefly, once a week, for a distribution of spiritual graces but did little real engagement with the Liturgy, their priests, or their fellow parishioners, and failed to build real Christian community.[118] The decline of the ethnic parish, suburbanization, the explosion of parish size in the suburbs, and, after the late 1960s, the decline in Sunday Mass attendance, all compounded this problem in the minds of critics.

Some Catholics became convinced that the territorial parish, and the conception of the parish as a physical space, should be abandoned entirely. A 1968 article in *The Long Island Catholic* argued that "on suburban Long Island, people become fellow parishioners on a strictly geographic basis, because they happened to buy a house in a certain area and not because of any interest, work, education, or philosophical relationship." But this did not lend itself to "the development of community" and without that a true parish could not be said to exist. "Perhaps there should be some redefining of exactly what a parish is," the article suggested, adding that "the tendency to identify the parish with structures and buildings" had to go.[119]

Throughout the 1970s and early 1980s Catholics experimented with methods of redefining the parish, of reaching the faithful where they were, and of organizing the faithful into communities of worship and service.

In 1969 Pat and Patty Crowley, the Chicago couple who founded the Christian Family Movement, warned that suburbanization had negatively affected the sense of community in Catholic parishes. The Crowleys lamented the depersonalization that plagued both society and the Church. Commuting in bumper-to-bumper expressway traffic, suburbanites were "very close to one another and yet so far," isolated in their own cars and "unable to communicate with each other. So too," the Crowleys said, "with our parishes." Suburban parishes were "large and getting larger," and so suburban Catholics stood "next to strangers at Mass, wondering who they might be." Dashing to clear the parking lot "for cars coming in for the next Mass," parishioners only had time to wave at their associate pastor, who was "rushing toward the basement church-hall to help in the distribution of Communion." During the week, the Crowleys feared, the automobile and the television were among the "too many things to do, too many voices, too many distracting influences" which kept parishioners "away from parish activities."[120]

Priests in the Diocese of Rockville Centre had similar concerns about the sense of community in suburbia and its effects on parish life. Reminiscing a half-century later, Fr. John Cervini contrasted the "neighborhoods of the City" he knew growing up in the 1940s in Our Lady of Sorrows Parish in Corona, Queens, with the suburban, "isolated neighborhoods" of Long Island. In the city, neighborhood and community "was very real," but on Long Island "people don't know . . . the name of the street two blocks away from their house. They just know how to get from the Southern State Parkway right to their home." He lamented that people had lost the sense of community that was necessary for parish life "because of the shift to individualism." Cervini's observation resonated with sociologist Robert Putnam's argument that after 1965 Americans' participation in traditional civic organizations declined significantly.[121] Drawing on his experience as a missionary in the Dominican Republic, and on the concept of "base communities" popularized in the late 1960s and 1970s by Latin American liberation theology, Cervini advocated the creation of pastoral teams, responsible for the development of small neighborhood communities that would gather for prayer, Bible study, and reflection. He hoped that when the members of these small communities came to the parish for Mass, they would not just be "plugging into the gas station," but would rather bring "their neighborhoods and their neighborhood's problems with them to the Mass."[122]

Parishioners and priests also critiqued the temporary, makeshift, or overly functional spaces in which suburban parishes gathered for Mass, and the overcrowding in suburban parishes that made the formation of community nearly impossible. In 1968 a *Long Island Catholic* survey found that "many lay people complain that in a Church-auditorium where you have upwards of 1,200 people, Mass is an impersonal experience." However, the article's author also contended that, "in all practicality, there is no solution to the numbers problem at Sunday Mass on Long Island."[123] At St. Bernard Parish in Levittown, Fr. Lawrence Ballweg said that "instead of being joyous and happy occasions" Masses in the parish auditorium were "generally lifeless." The parish's liturgy committee recommended that the altar in the auditorium be moved down from the platform, onto the floor, so that the congregation could at least sit around it in a circle.[124]

These critiques of parish worship spaces continued into the 1980s. Father William Donovan was born in Brooklyn in 1953 and, as a child, moved with his family to Copiague. He was ordained a priest of the Diocese of Rockville Centre in 1979, spent five years at Ss. Cyril and Methodius Parish in Deer Park, "one of the largest parishes in the Diocese," and in 1986 was named as head of the diocese's Office of Research and Planning. In an oral interview a few years after that appointment, Donovan lamented that whereas parishes in Brooklyn were within walking distance, and Catholics identified themselves by their neighborhoods and parish, this was "certainly not the case on Long Island." Long Island parishes were farther from where people live, and while "the average parish in the United States is about 500 families," Donovan argued "the average parish on Long Island is about 3,000 families," six times the national average. Because of the diocese's rapid growth, and its exceedingly large congregations, Donovan felt that parishes were "providing worship space in a large hall" but were not providing any real sense of community. "People have the feeling that they could be gone from the parish for ten to fifteen years," Donovan said, "and no one would ever know they were gone." He added that the functional auditoriums that parishes had built to accommodate their mushrooming congregations were "fine when the parishes were first expanding," but that they were "starting to wear on people now." Donovan was incredulous that many parishes still had Mass in an auditorium decades after their founding, and felt that it had "taken a toll on the Diocese as far as people's sense of what is reverent and sacred." Without a sense of the parish as a community that lives and worships together as a unit, Donovan warned, "we are losing people to born-again churches."[125]

The Diocese of Rockville Centre and its parishes attempted to build a greater sense of community, and to reach parishioners and fallen-away

Catholics in their homes, by employing various forms of media and communications, and by experimenting with different parish structures and ministries. Beginning in the 1960s many parishes organized a local newspaper or magazine as a means of reaching parishioners in their homes and communicating with them about the activities of the parish's organizations. This was in addition to the diocesan-wide newspaper, *The Long Island Catholic*, which was founded in 1963 and which Bishop Walter Kellenberg insisted every Catholic in the diocese receive a copy. Parishes and lay associations, like the Legion of Mary, also tried to reach suburbanites in the secular settings in which they gathered, most especially the shopping mall. In 1967 the Legion launched an "Apostolate to the Crowds," a program of proselytizing in shopping centers, and in 1970 the diocese founded an experimental and ecumenical ministry in the Smithhaven Mall, which developed a particular focus on ministering to teenagers.[126] Finally, in 1964, the Diocese of Rockville Centre became the first Catholic diocese in the country to receive a Federal Communications Commission (FCC) license to operate an instructional television station. By late 1968 a Diocesan television center had been built in Uniondale and by 1970 content was being produced and transmitted to parochial schools across the diocese on one of four channels. In 1976, with the advent of satellite and cable television, this educational television station was adapted to produce content to reach Catholic and non-Catholic families in their homes.[127] As with so many of the experiments aimed at developing the cohesive community once provided by the parish, these efforts met with mixed success at best.

Conclusion

From the mid-1960s through the 1970s, the Church in the United States witnessed a broad disengagement from parish life and the practice of the faith. Nationwide, the rate of Catholics leaving the Church doubled to 14 percent, and by the late 1970s 16 percent of those raised in the Church had left by adulthood.[128] Even for those who remained practicing Catholics, parishes no longer played the central role they had for previous generations in the ethnic neighborhood and at the dawning of the suburban church. The Notre Dame Study of Catholic Parish Life, a wide-ranging national study conducted in the early 1980s, found that fewer Catholics "than ever, especially in the suburbs," saw their parish as "the center of their social lives" or as capable of fulfilling their social or spiritual needs.[129] Parishes were therefore increasingly incapable of creating the kind of community that could insulate Catholics from assimilation or support families in passing the faith to the next generation.

In 1982, when the Diocese of Rockville Centre celebrated its twenty-fifth anniversary, Bishop John McGann optimistically reported to Vatican officials that while Mass attendance had declined nationwide, on Long Island it had been "consistently maintained."[130] And yet, Long Island's Catholic leaders recognized the desperate need to revitalize parish life and to stem the tide of Catholics who were abandoning the practice of the faith. To mark the diocesan anniversary, McGann launched a campaign to invite fallen-away Catholics back to church. A "Come Home for Christmas" program sent personalized greetings to 11,000 such people. "Re-membering" sessions, designed "to stir up memories of their Catholic heritage," were held across the diocese and attendees were encouraged to "renew their 'membership' in the Church."[131]

The urban ethnic parish had developed as a highly successful means of providing for immigrants, perpetuating ethnic culture, and passing the faith on to future generations. Whatever their faults, the parishes of the urban Catholic world wove geography, education, culture, family, and faith into a "resilient social fabric" that "sustained faith while structuring a genuine community life."[132] But transplanting this model of parish in suburbia proved problematic. Formed by rapid population expansion, the suburban parish faced the challenge of finding the space and the methods of bringing large numbers of the faithful together to form community, practice charity, and pass on the faith, absent the binding forces of ethnic religiosity. In the postwar suburbs the parish was no longer the lodestar of a Catholic's spiritual and social world. Private spaces, especially the family home, held more prominence in suburbanites' lives than the common space of the neighborhood, and Catholic leaders encouraged the faithful to see the home as the center of prayer and faith formation.

Priest and sociologist Andrew Greeley had feared that in the suburbs, absent the reinforcing communal context of the ethnic neighborhood and parish, adherence to the practices and values of the Church would simply become another life choice made amid a panoply of social possibilities, not unlike the consumer choices to which suburban Catholics were becoming accustomed. That the suburban context made the private home the principal site of religious activity and gave the laity greater authority in the Church's ministries certainly seems to have deepened the laity's conviction that they could make their own decisions about their practice of the faith. As Greeley had ruefully predicted, in the era of the suburban church American Catholics' rates of weekly church attendance, use of artificial contraception, and views on abortion increasingly aligned with those of the general population.[133]

FOUR

Priests and Parishioners: Lay Associations, Parish Councils, and Church Leadership

In 1968 the Diocese of Rockville Centre announced the erection of a new parish in the Terryville section of Suffolk County and purchased ten and half acres for a future parish center. St. Gerard Majella Parish was carved out of territories previously belonging to Infant Jesus Parish in Port Jefferson, St. Margaret Parish in Selden, and St. James Parish in Setauket, and had approximately 2,000 Catholic families within its boundaries. The temporary rectory was described as "symbolic of the new spirit in St. Gerard's" because it was a development house that had been modified by parishioners. The parish's first Sunday Masses were celebrated in East Setauket's Fox Theatre and, until a parish center could be constructed, Masses were said three days a week in the rectory. A number of parishioners also took teacher-training courses and launched the parish's religious education program in parishioners' homes.[1]

In all these details, St. Gerard Majella was like so many of the suburban parishes established in Nassau and Suffolk Counties in the two decades after World War II. However, St. Gerard Majella Parish was portrayed as something entirely new: a "layman's parish," which embodied the vision of Vatican II for lay leadership in the Church. Father Philip J. Reehill, the parish's founding pastor, spoke at length with *The Long Island Catholic* about how he and his parishioners would relate to one another. "Every priest likes to have the chance to build a new parish," Reehill confessed, but this new parish would be "lay run," he promised, "with members of the community becoming actively involved in all its phases of growth and development." Reehill claimed not to have "any guidelines or cut and dried blueprints for how things should proceed" and expressed the hope that he would "never have to say 'no' to the people." Nine months after the parish's founding, Reehill reported that he and his associate pastor had thrown "the parish at the people" and they had come "out strong in grabbing it. We express opinions, not answers," Reehill said.²

Suburban parishes dramatically altered the balance of power between clergy and laity by transforming priestly ministry, the religious associations the laity joined, and the role laymen and -women played in the leadership of the Church.³ Reehill's rhetoric about the founding and development of St Gerard's reflected the spirit of Vatican II, as Reehill himself stated. And yet, the new parish—or at least the pastor's description of it—represents not so much a break from the suburban parishes of the prior two decades as the fruition of the changes that suburbanization wrought on Catholic parishes, lay associations, priests, and laypeople. As discussed in chapter 1, calls for the faithful to take up the lay apostolate and Catholic Action dated back at least to the 1930s, but postwar suburbanization accelerated and diversified lay participation in the ministries and administration of the Church and led to a gradual transfer of authority from clergy to laity. In newly built suburbs, power structures were "often completely open and flexible," even in Catholic parishes.⁴ The laity who forged these communities felt a greater sense of ownership over their parishes, and the suburbs' insufficient number of clergy and religious drove the laity into previously unthinkable areas of ministry, most especially the religious instruction of youth.

Suburbia's emphasis on domesticity and family life also changed the types of lay associations that the faithful joined. Traditional parish societies like the Holy Name Society and the Rosary Society, which were single gender, met in parish facilities, and focused on bringing members together for ritual prayer and service to the parish community, gave way to family apostolates. These new associations welcomed couples, were based in family homes, and were aimed more at training members for family life, building small community, and providing avenues of service to the broader community than providing a communal spirituality. Unlike traditional parish societies, the family apostolates were also founded and led by laypeople, which furthered the expectation that a highly educated laity would now be able to provide leadership within the Church.

All of these changes preceded the Second Vatican Council. Although the Council is often perceived as opening the possibility of lay leadership in the Church, in actuality it validated and advanced a vision of lay responsibility that was already developing in apostolic associations and suburban parishes. In particular, the theology underpinning the lay apostolic associations helped shape the Council's proclamations on the laity's role in the Church.⁵ In the wake of the Council, the excitement around the establishment of school boards and parish councils represented hopes for the full flowering of the laity's involvement in the Church's decision-making. This hope was short-lived, however. Despite undeniable improvement in the leadership opportunities available to laypeople, class and ideological divisions within the laity, a lack of preparation for lay ecclesial leadership, and the traditional centrality of priesthood to authority in the Church all undermined attempts to form a unified lay voice in Church affairs.

A Shortage of Priests

The suburban church was formed amid a growing shortage of priests. Between 1942 and 1952 the number of priests in the United States increased by 21.5 percent, while the US Catholic population expanded by 30.4 percent, resulting in a decreasing priest-to-people ratio.[6] This growing shortage of priests was particularly acute in new suburban dioceses like the Diocese of Rockville Centre. The paucity of priests compared to the vast number of suburban faithful helped transform expectations of parish clergy and of lay involvement in the administration and ministries of the parish.

In 1945 there were approximately 175 diocesan priests assigned to work in the parishes of Nassau and Suffolk Counties. As suburbanization ballooned the Catholic population in those counties, the number of priests increased—to 371 by 1957—but never kept pace with the expansion of the populace.[7] In Brooklyn, as in most dioceses, the wealthiest, most vibrant, and therefore most desirable parishes to which a priest could be assigned were in the city and an assignment to a rural parish was seen as a kind of exile.[8] It was understood that the Diocese of Brooklyn assigned to the hinterland of Long Island priests who were inexperienced or had proven incapable of administering a large city parish, who had rabble-roused among the clergy, or who were known to struggle with alcoholism. As Monsignor Edmond Trench put it in a 1981 interview, "Long Island was the dumping ground for Archbishop Molloy. . . . It was the place where he put his problems, his alcoholic priests, his troublesome priests."[9]

This preexisting pattern of priestly assignment came to have greater import when the Vatican established the Diocese of Rockville Centre in 1957. Catholic institutions on Long Island were divided between the Brooklyn and Rockville Centre dioceses based on where they were located, but so, too, were the priests of the previously singular diocese. Priests became members of the diocese in whose territory they were working when the dioceses were split regardless of their preference, where they had been raised, or where their families lived—a process referred to as being "frozen in place." This division of priests meant that the Diocese of Rockville Centre began its existence with an insufficient number of priests for the number of faithful who had and would continue to pour into its suburban parishes. It also meant that Bishop Walter Kellenberg had very few priests with leadership experience to assign to diocesan administration, and that priests in Rockville Centre were made pastors at an earlier age than their peers in the Diocese of Brooklyn.[10]

Given this shortage of priests, the first major project that Kellenberg undertook—within his first year as bishop—was the establishment of a preparatory seminary for the recruitment and training of high school–aged aspirants to the priesthood. Kellenberg described the opening of a seminary "before all other schools" as a "logical necessity" because of the central importance of priests in the life of a parish. "What good would more parishes and churches be," he said, "if we did not have priests to staff them?"[11] The fundraising for, and dedication of, St. Pius X Preparatory Seminary was an important source of unity and pride in the young diocese.[12] On September 3, 1961, when a purpose-built seminary was dedicated, 20 bishops, 600 priests, 350 religious, and some 7,000 lay faithful attended the ceremonies, presided over by Cardinal Spellman. Nassau County Police chief inspector Francis J. Looney said that "the only time he could recall a larger crowd was for a visit of the country's president."[13]

In September 1958, a month before the election of Pope John XXIII, St. Pius X Seminary had opened in temporary facilities with 106 freshmen and, by 1962, had 415 high school seminarians and 52 seminarians in a new junior college department. Thanks to a program of vocations promotion, which *The Long Island Catholic* hailed as "one of the most extensive of its kind," the Diocese of Rockville Centre also saw a significant increase in the number of young men in the major seminary during the diocese's first five years. When the diocese was established in 1957 it had only 51 seminarians, but by 1962, in addition to the 415 high school seminarians at St. Pius X, there were 107 seminarians for the diocese, an increase of 110 percent. Still, because of a high rate of attrition, and the length of seminary formation, the number of priests in the diocese rose only 1.5 percent between 1957 and 1962, from 379 priests to 383. Meanwhile, the total population of Nassau and Suffolk Counties grew by 18.5 percent (from 1,706,689 to 2,021,167) and the Catholic population of Long Island increased by 39.5 percent (from 497,855 to 694,497). This resulted in a 13 percent decrease in the priest-to-people ratio in the diocese, from one priest for every 1,312 Catholics, to one priest for every 1,484 Catholics. Nationally, there was one priest for every 771 Catholics, meaning that a priest of the Diocese of Rockville Centre "had to care for almost twice as many Catholics as the national average."[14] By the diocese's tenth anniversary in 1967, the priest-to-people ratio had worsened. A study by the Center for Applied Research in the Apostolate (CARA) in Washington, DC, found that Rockville Centre had one priest for every 1,781 Catholics.[15] This was the second lowest priest-to-people ratio in the country, with only the Diocese of Brownsville, Texas, having more people per priest.[16]

Changing Expectations of the Clergy

Despite the diocese's dearth of priests, the size of its parishes, and its poor priest-to-person ratio, clergy and laity basically attempted to transpose the models of priestly ministry and parish life they had known in their urban parishes to their new suburban parishes. This meant that the clergy continued to play the dominant role in the organizational and ministerial life of the parish. Bishop Emil Wcela recalled that when he was a newly ordained priest assigned to Maria Regina Parish in Seaford, "the only parish staff was the three priests."[17] His fellow associate pastor, Msgr. Robert Emmet Fagan, agreed, recalling, "you had wonderful people who would do anything," but "the priest had to be always in the leadership position."[18]

At the same time, the staggering size of suburban congregations and the diversity of their needs required priests to involve the laity as much as possible in building up the parish. In 1955 the *Homiletic and Pastoral Review* invited Msgr. Josiah G. Chatham, the founding pastor of St. Richard Parish in Jackson, Mississippi, to offer advice to priests tasked with establishing a new suburban parish. "In two years," Chatham warned, "the parish will probably double in size. There is going to be more work, spiritual and temporal, than any one or two men can possibly do. You are going to need the wholehearted cooperation of the laity. . . . Make your parish a parish of the Lay Apostolate!"[19] Chatham captured the attitude evident in many of the founding pastors in the Diocese of Rockville Centre. John Verbeeck, a parishioner of St. Martha Parish in Uniondale, recalled the parish's founding pastor as being solicitous of lay input and involvement. Although parish councils didn't yet exist in 1949, Verbeeck remembered that "none of the planning was finalized before Father Byrne spoke to and consulted with all the societies and interested people of Uniondale."[20]

The need to bring the laity into greater involvement in parish life significantly altered expectations for a priest's ministry. On top of being a builder and maintainer of facilities, a prayerful liturgist, a compassionate confessor, and a wise counselor, he also needed to be an animator and overseer of the lay apostolate. Such expectations were only confirmed by the Second Vatican Council's call for greater participation of the laity in the ministry of the Church. As Fr. James B. Richter, pastor of St. Bernard Parish in Levittown, summarized, this made the priesthood "a harder job than ever before. . . . You have to be authoritative but not too authoritarian; you have to provide leadership, but you have to realize it's not a one-man show. You have to recognize the charisms you see in people, but be faithful to the deposit of faith."[21]

As early as 1959 Andrew Greeley had feared that the heightened expectations suburban laity placed on priests would inevitably lead to "savage criticism" of the clergy.[22] By 1970, in the wake of the Second Vatican Council, and the social and political tumult of the 1960s, the editors of *The Long Island Catholic* assessed that clergy increasingly "came in for a thorough lambasting" from conservative laity who thought priests were "involving themselves too much in outside-the-parish affairs," and from liberal laity who thought clergy were "suffocating the spirit of Vatican II."[23]

The rapidly evolving expectations of priestly ministry brought on by suburbanization and the reforms of Vatican II had tremendous effects on priestly identity and morale. In just six years between 1966 and 1972 one in ten American priests left the priesthood with some 600 priests leaving active ministry each year between 1969 and 1972 alone.[24] Even still, when the US bishops commissioned Andrew Greeley to conduct a study of American priests in 1971, he declared it surprising that even more priests had not left active ministry. "We've broken with patterns that have existed half a millennium," he said, "and we've done it in five years."[25] Father Andrew L. Millar of Our Lady of Grace Parish in West Babylon expanded on that theme in the parish's magazine. In the urban ethnic ghetto, Millar argued, the priest "was the father-figure par-excellence . . . it was his church, his school, his rectory, his convent." But "all of that has suddenly changed," Millar lamented, and "like every other father-figure" the priest "is in big trouble. He is under both the microscope and the lash."[26]

The shocking departure of so many men from the priesthood in the late 1960s and early 1970s only exacerbated the Diocese of Rockville Centre's shortage of clergy and its priest-to-people ratio. In eight years between 1969 and 1977 the number of active diocesan priests in Rockville Centre declined from 495 to 386, a loss of over 20 percent of the presbyterate from active ministry for reasons of departure, retirement, or ill health.[27] The diocese attempted to alleviate this shortage of priests by welcoming foreign-born priests to serve in its parishes. By 1977 there were at least thirty-five such priests in the Diocese of Rockville Centre. Whereas in previous generations, foreign-born priests serving in the United States were immigrants working among other immigrants from their native land, this newest wave of foreign-born clergy consisted of missionary priests from putatively priest-rich dioceses in Asia and Africa.[28] As Fr. John E. Murray, the director of Rockville Centre's priest personnel board admitted, this resulted in "criticism of the use of foreign-speaking priests because of the language barrier and cultural differences."[29] In August 1984 an anonymous letter to *The Long Island Catholic* questioned "whether the spiritual needs of God's people will be fulfilled when they cannot understand the readings and prayers of the Mass, when the homilies can be unrelated to American cultural life, when the celebrations of weddings and funerals leave the participants confused and, in some cases, angry."[30] This critique elicited both a pledge from the diocese to better assist missionary priests in adjusting to the United States and expressions of appreciation for foreign-born priests from other priests and laity.[31] Supporters were especially grateful that the presence of foreign-born priests highlighted the universal nature of the Church, and Fr. Francis X. McQuade of St. Hugh Parish in Huntington Station wondered how much "subtle racism or xenophobia" played a role in shaping the laity's criticisms."[32]

Parish Pioneering on the Crabgrass Frontier

The faithful who poured into Long Island's postwar suburban parishes were young and energetic married couples who enthusiastically participated in parish life by attending Sunday Mass and joining parish associations, like the Rosary Society and the Holy Name Society. These were the backbone of lay involvement in the urban parishes in which they grew up. Through these traditional parish societies, the laity volunteered their time and organized fundraising efforts to support the growth of their new parish. They also found opportunities to build friendships and community in suburbia, and were able to prove a commitment to their parish, thereby fulfilling a requirement frequently placed by pastors on the admission of children to the parish school. Although starting a new parish posed many challenges, priests and people alike reported a sense of excitement about being pioneers. The laity gained a strong sense of ownership over their parish.

Perhaps the most important aspect of parish life to which suburban laity contributed was the expansion of Confraternity of Christian Doctrine (CCD) programs for students attending public schools. With vast numbers of young people needing religious education, suburban parishes had to organize sufficient CCD classes without the benefit of classroom facilities or teaching sisters, who were in short supply for many parishes even when the number of religious vocations were at their peak. Lay people recruited to teach religion in their homes needed training in pedagogy and theology. The programs developed to provide it were the first wave of what would become a vast array of adult education programs and discussion groups attempting to answer an educated laity's growing demands for formation in the faith. Altogether, the challenges and opportunities posed by suburbanization and the baby boom transformed the laity's relationship with their parish and their priests, and spurred their expectation of greater involvement in the Church's mission.

Having been "raised in the traditional churches of Brooklyn and the Bronx," suburban Catholics "saw the parish as the social as well as the spiritual center of their community," and throughout the 1940s and 1950s they swelled the ranks of traditional parish associations.[33] In interviews nearly twenty-five and fifty years after Maria Regina Parish in Seaford was founded in 1955, Bishop Emil Wcela recalled that in the parish's early days almost all of the parishioners were "in their twenties and thirties" and "there was great interest in the Church. . . . You could get volunteers for lots of things," he recalled. When the parish held Rosary Society meetings, 400 women would attend and, when asked, "Why are you all here?" they would answer, "Because it's a way to get out of the house. . . . All the young mothers needed time away from their homes and families."[34] On top of socialization, involvement in parish societies helped secure Catholic schooling for one's children. "Everyone knew," Wcela recounted, that "if you wanted to get your children into the parish school . . . you had to get your name on the list and score points for parish participation."[35]

Parish societies were also crucial in organizing volunteer labor to repurpose temporary facilities into churches and to organize fundraising drives to finance the purchase of land and the construction of parish buildings.[36] Tales of fundraising efforts, via card parties, dances, bake sales, fashion shows, bazaars, and even automobile raffles are legion in parish histories of the era.[37] As Fr. Donald Campion, SJ, and Dennis Clark noted in *America* in 1956, these "increasingly popular, highly organized fundraising operations," which were necessary to "meet the overnight demands for church and school expansion," yielded not only financial profits, but "social and spiritual dividends" as well.[38] Shared sacrifice and recreation fostered a sense of community cohesion that helped convince parishioners that they had both the right and the competency to contribute to the leadership of their parish communities.[39]

Although founding parishioners recalled the early days of their parish as a "gypsy experience," and "the closest thing to pioneering this century," the successful completion of a parish church or school brought a "profound sense of accomplishment" and a sense of ownership over the parish.[40] As Ann Matuza Sessa of Our Lady of Grace Parish in West Babylon put it, "*we* founded this parish," and parishioners were encouraged in this way of thinking by their priests.[41] Father John Leonard of Our Lady of Grace congratulated his parishioners when they broke ground on a school just four years after the parish's founding: "You have to admit that you have come a long way in a short time," he wrote. "I say you—because who else is responsible? You have given blood—in prayers, work, sacrifice, money, and YOURSELVES."[42]

Lay Teachers of Religion

Religious education classes, especially for students in public schools, were one of the very first ministries most new suburban parishes launched. The recruitment and training of the laity as teachers in home-based programs of religious education was a turning point for the laity's involvement in the Church.[43] Lay teachers were also a catalyst for adult education programs aimed at establishing a mature laity capable of understanding and implementing the documents of the Second Vatican Council in what many came to see as "the age of the laity."

Just as a lack of classroom space drove religious education classes into parishioners' homes, so too did an insufficient number of religious sisters drive bustling suburban parishes to seek parishioners as volunteer CCD instructors. Patricia Megale, who later earned a master's of religious education and served as the Diocese of Rockville Centre's associate director of catechesis, recalled how even the confessional became a recruitment space. During Confession, Megale told Fr. Henry Benack of Queen of the Most Holy Rosary Parish in Roosevelt that she felt the need to do more for the parish. "He almost came through the screen at me," she remembered, "because in those days they were taking anybody who could breathe and read and write to teach Religion."[44]

At first priests moderated a parish's religious education program, recruited and trained volunteer teachers, and prepared lesson plans for teachers who had rudimentary knowledge of theology and were unpracticed in teaching. At Maria Regina Parish in Seaford, pastor Fr. James F. Bradley recruited and trained women and men as catechists. "All week long he would spend time writing lessons plans," his associate, Msgr. Robert Emmet Fagan, recalled, because "it took a lot of confidence for people to think they could 'quote' teach religion. They used to say, 'I get more out of it than the children.'" Only as the lay catechists "got more confidence in themselves," could the priest delegate responsibility.[45]

Dioceses quickly recognized the need to more systematically train and support lay teachers of religion, especially as the Second Vatican Council radically reoriented conceptions of the faith and the best means of teaching it. In 1960 Msgr. Joseph F. Lawlor, the director of CCD for the Diocese of Rockville Centre—one of the largest such programs in the country—established a diocesan-wide training program consisting of thirty two-hour training sessions.[46] "A true lay apostolate," Lawlor wrote, "must have the means of training, forming, and developing its members" and the Second Vatican Council required that "teachers be capable of interpreting the Scriptures and the Liturgy in accordance with the most up-to-date findings of Catholics scholars."[47] Contemporary surveys of lay catechists showed that they "recognized their need for help and instruction." As Dolores Antonucci of Blessed Sacrament Parish in Valley Stream put it, "you realize your inadequacies. Without up-to-date training in Christian teaching, I don't know how anyone could manage in the CCD classroom today." Ernesto Oriano, a catechist at Our Holy Redeemer Parish in Freeport, added: "I never seem to stop having to learn. After six years of teaching, I can say every year is just as difficult, or more so, than before."[48]

By 1968 an estimated 6,221 lay teachers and 1,300 religious and seminarians were teaching in the diocese's CCD programs.[49] Monsignor Frederick Schaefer, who succeeded Monsignor Lawlor as diocesan director of CCD in 1965, expanded the teacher-training program from nine, to sixty, and then to 120 centers across the diocese, employing high school teachers with graduate degrees in theology as instructors. "We trained something like 3,000 teachers," Schaefer recalled, with the "intent to make religious education a respectable and acceptable professional program."[50] Indeed, by 1967 St. Aidan Parish in Williston Park became the first parish in the diocese, and one of only a few in the entire region, to hire a full-time professional lay director of CCD. Frank A. Grady, a former teacher, psychologist, and journalist promised that the program's teachers would be given "extensive training and guidance" because quality teachers were the key to a successful program.[51]

When diocesan CCD directors from throughout New York State met in 1970, they too expressed the hope that "professional teacher-training programs" would soon be graduating "paid professional religious teachers."[52] But it is clear that CCD programs continued to rely predominantly on volunteer teachers, the vast majority of whom were women, and that parishes faced increasing difficulty recruiting parishioners to teach CCD. In 1971 the parish magazine of Our Lady of Grace Parish in West Babylon pleaded for 200 volunteer teachers for the 4,000 students in the parish's religious education program. "This is the age of the laity," the magazine implored, "the age when no one can afford to say 'no' if he can possibly say 'yes.'"[53]

Adult Education Programs

Training programs for lay religious education teachers were part of a broader effort to expand the mission of the CCD to include adult education classes and discussion groups and to provide a middle-class and highly educated laity with a mature formation in the faith. Within American Catholicism, such efforts had roots in the various forms of community organizing employed by the Social Action Department (SAD) of the National Catholic Welfare Conference (NCWC). The NCWC, founded in 1917 with a headquarters in the nation's capital, was the first organizing body of the US Catholic bishops. Its standing committees and permanent staff provided an official and unified voice for the bishops through joint statements and congressional testimony.[54] From the 1920s onward, SAD organized conferences, summer institutes, and labor schools on behalf of the NCWC to instruct the laity in the Church's social principles and inspire political action. Given the nation's long tradition of citizen formation, and the popularity of secular adult education programs between 1950 and 1970, diocesan and parochial programs for adult formation were evidence of Catholic participation in and borrowing from American models. The National Opinion Research Center (NORC) at the University of Chicago found that 25 million American adults participated in education programs through 1961 alone, and in 1965 *The Long Island Catholic* argued that "nowhere is this phenomenon more apparent than on Long Island." Fifteen thousand adults took part that year in programs sponsored by the Nassau Association for Public School Adult Education.[55] The following year, in his annual letter to inaugurate the CCD school year, Bishop Walter Kellenberg "called for a greater emphasis on adult education programs" in the diocese, where some 53,000 lay people were already participating in programs of religious education.[56]

Adult education classes were undoubtedly seen as an important means of providing sufficient volunteer teachers for a parish's CCD program. But the push for adult education was not simply utilitarian, and neither was it merely a result of the Second Vatican Council's affirmation of lay ministry. Rather, as Monsignor Schaefer recalled years later, "the sense had been present a long, long time" before Vatican II, that "the extremely high level of education of the people in both Nassau and Suffolk Counties—probably the highest in the country"—required the Church to "present to them an introduction of doctrinal teaching that was equivalent to the educational level they had experienced in other parts of their lives."⁵⁷

Mary Ann Viccora of St. Anne Parish in Floral Park agreed. In 1959, she helped found the New York School of Theology for Laymen at St. Vincent Ferrer High School in New York City. An evening school, taught by college professors, with ten courses in dogmatic and moral theology, social doctrine, catechetics, and other topics, the school was attended by 250 students in its first semester and 400 in its second. "They are all concerned and modern Catholic laymen," Viccora stated. "The school is intended to answer the need of intelligent, inquiring adults—a need which has not been satisfied by the ordinary religious instruction classes or now-and-then, hit-or-miss sermons and lectures."⁵⁸

The Diocese of Rockville Centre ran a similar adult education program in conjunction with Molloy College. Begun by the Diocese of Brooklyn as a social-action school, the scope of the program was broadened in 1957, and in 1963 the Diocese of Rockville Centre's Education Department began administering the program. Approximately 400 men and women, most in their mid-thirties, attended an eight-week session of one-hour weekly classes. Course titles included not only "The Philosophy of St. Thomas Aquinas," and "Christian Marriage," but also "Adolescent Guidance," "How to Give Sex Education to Children," "The Contribution of the Negro to American History," and "The American Theatre—O'Neill to Albee."⁵⁹

This was the only Catholic adult education program on Long Island until St. Aidan Parish in Williston Park and St. Patrick Parish in Glen Cove established their own adult education programs beginning in 1964. Father Martin J. Healey, the pastor of St. Patrick's, explained that the program emerged out of "the desire and need of the intelligent Catholic to understand his faith."⁶⁰ However, the course offerings at St. Patrick's not only included liturgy, scripture, and ecclesiology, but also mathematics, French, and Italian.⁶¹ Over the next several years, numerous parishes across Long Island instituted various forms of adult education including courses in catechesis and doctrine, lectures and speaker series, parent training sessions, Bible studies, and discussion groups.⁶²

Some priests of the diocese, including Fr. Thomas Colgan of St. Raymond Parish in East Rockaway, considered discussion groups "one of the most popular and successful forms of adult education." St. Raymond's founded its Bellarmine Discussion Group in 1961 "to educate the adult laity in religious subjects" and "to develop lay leadership."⁶³ According to Msgr. Henry Reel, such discussion groups "began to flourish after Vatican II" and were essential in helping the laity gain "knowledge of scripture and liturgy" in a time of change.⁶⁴ Parishioners of Our Lady of Loretto Parish in Hempstead expressly organized Vatican II Forums as an opportunity for the "reform and renewal" of their parish.⁶⁵ Even the diocese's newspaper and the parish publications that proliferated in this era were described as an "educational force" and a means of exposing the laity to the implications of the Second Vatican Council.⁶⁶ Father Paul McKeever, onetime editor of *The Long Island Catholic*, described the diocesan paper as "an appendage to the Council" that provided more information about the Council than any other diocesan newspaper in the country.⁶⁷

But by the late 1960s interest in adult education had begun to wane. In a 1966 survey of the laity on parish discussion groups, *The Long Island Catholic* found that participants felt "the intimate atmosphere of a living room" was either "too threatening or simply unappealing," and that it was too difficult to navigate participants' differing political positions.⁶⁸ That challenge could only have increased as the faithful staked out divergent positions on civil rights, the war in Vietnam, and the proscriptions in *Humanae Vitae*. Indeed, in the pivotal year of 1968, parishes across the diocese, including St. Patrick Parish in Huntington, St. Matthew Parish in Dix Hills, St. Luke Parish in Brentwood, and St. Boniface Parish in Elmont, reported rapidly declining participation in adult education. Father Donald Desmond of St. Boniface, however, posited a simpler explanation for the lack of participation: "maybe the average person, who works hard all day, doesn't want to be committed to a lecture series," he suggested.⁶⁹

The Family Apostolates

The quest for a deeper understanding of the faith, for new forms of spirituality, and for different outlets of Christian service, as well as evolutions in parish and family life, led suburban laity to abandon the traditional parish associations that were a remnant of a previous era. When the earliest waves of suburban parishes were established in the late 1940s and early 1950s, forming Holy Name and Rosary Societies was one of the first tasks undertaken and these traditional parish societies flourished.⁷⁰ When St. Frances de Chantal Parish in Wantagh was established in 1952, 150 men immediately formed a Holy Name Society and 200 women organized a Rosary Society.⁷¹ Even long-established parishes, which boomed thanks to postwar suburbanization, found their new young parishioners eager to form associations. St. Anne Parish in Brentwood, established in 1895, saw its Ladies of St. Anne founded in 1950, its Nocturnal Adoration Society founded in 1957, and its chapter of the Knights of Columbus founded in 1959.⁷²

But these associations were single gender, centered on the parish church and hall, and aimed toward perpetuating the faith in a hostile Protestant environment. In the suburbs the idealization of the nuclear family led commuting husbands and stay-at-home wives to seek opportunities to participate in associations together and to prioritize being at home with their families rather than at the parish for a society meeting.[73] Along with the diminishment of pious devotions these changes accelerated the decline of traditional parish associations like the Holy Name Society and the Rosary Society. A 1968 article in *The Long Island Catholic* noted that Holy Name Societies were dying out, but was uncertain if this was "due to unexciting programming, lack of time, or simply that such a society may have become an anachronism."[74]

In their place, new lay associations were born. These new institutions focused on supporting family life, forestalling a family crisis, and providing a small community that might compensate for the loss of extended family connections in the suburbs. Concern for the health of the American family was hardly a postwar novelty but, as sociologist Peter Berger pointed out, by 1959 "a full-blown ideology" of the family permeated American religion and culture.[75] The US Catholic bishops had established a Family Life Bureau as early as 1931, but until 1945 it remained a small research department.[76] A 1943 national survey of parish priests found no parish societies "working exclusively on family issues." By 1958, however, there were more than ten national Catholic organizations "concerned solely with strengthening Catholic family values."[77] Because suburban parishes were overextended and failing to meet the needs of families, these organizations emerged on the periphery of parish life, and because they were focused on marriage and family, they were increasingly led by laypeople eager to exercise authority in the Church. They thus contributed not only to the shift from parish to home but also to a growing expectation of lay leadership in the life of the Church.

The Christian Family Movement (CFM) emerged from small discussion groups organized by active laypeople in Chicago and South Bend in the early 1940s. CFM was founded as a national organization when Pat and Patty Crowley and Burnie and Helene Bauer met at the 1948 Cana Conference. Organized by the laity, and based on small groups of married couples, CFM represented a strikingly different approach to family ministry than the cleric-led and institutional model promoted by the bishops' Family Life Bureau. The conflict between these two forms of leadership, and the widespread growth of CFM throughout the 1950s, is evidence that a "fast-growing group of suburban, middle-class Catholics" was determined to exercise a more active role in the Church.[78]

By the mid-1950s CFM was the most popular association for married couples in the Archdiocese of New York, according to Msgr. George A. Kelly, the director of the New York Family Life Bureau.[79] CFM couples organized "much of the family life activity" that occurred in the archdiocese's parishes including Pre-Cana Conferences for engaged couples, parent workshops, family Communions, and family picnics.[80] In 1960 Bishop Walter Kellenberg told seventy couples at Long Island's first CFM convention that he was "most anxious that CFM expand and grow in the Rockville Centre diocese."[81] Given the success of the movement in the region's suburbs, he had reason to be optimistic. In 1957 there were thirty parishes in the Archdiocese of New York in which CFM was organized: two were in Manhattan, and six were in the Bronx, but the remaining twenty-two chapters were all in the archdiocese's northern suburban counties.[82]

The CFM consisted of groups of four or five couples meeting every two weeks in the home of a member for a three-part meeting guided by an "Inquiry Program" booklet. Based on the Jocist Method pioneered by the Young Christian Worker Movement in Belgium, the meeting progressed from a study of Scripture, and of the Liturgy, to a Social Inquiry in which participants would "Observe, Judge, and Act" on a particular issue in their community.[83] Matthew J. Guerin of West Islip stressed that while CFM included study and discussion, it completed them "with a call to specific action," and on Long Island CFM organized to donate family life books to local libraries; hand out meal prayer cards at local restaurants; assist with parish Pre-Cana programs; lead parish fundraisers; learn Spanish to assist migrant worker families; and visit the homes of Black families to learn about the problems they faced.[84] Committed as they were to applying the Church's social teaching to contemporary problems, Jeremy Bonner has described CFM activists as "the advance guard of the Vatican II generation."[85]

However, as its name implied, the greatest appeal of the CFM, especially in suburbia, was its focus on the family, its ability to provide suburban couples with likeminded friends, and its offer of a "couples apostolate" in a "suburban atmosphere in which men and women spent most of their days apart."[86] A 1956 survey of CFM chaplains attributed the growth of CFM to suburbanites' mobility, desire for community, and lack of an extended family network, as well as "the reduction of parish life" to the celebration of the Sacraments.[87] Dr. George N. Schuster, addressing the thirteenth national CFM convention at the University of Notre Dame, "stressed the historical trend toward the home as the fundamental social unit of the time" as a crucial factor in CFM's growth, and Don Nyreen of St. Agnes Parish in Rockville Centre celebrated CFM as being "the only place [couples] can do anything religious together as a couple."[88]

The Cana Conference, which grew alongside CFM and was an important outlet of action for CFM couples, was aimed more exclusively at marriage education.[89] Cana Conferences met on successive Sunday afternoons for a series of lectures on topics such as how to deal with in-law problems and how to teach children about sex. Pre-Cana Conferences extended this formation to couples preparing to wed. Nationwide, the 1950s were the highwater mark of the Cana Conferences, when nearly every diocese in the country boasted a Cana or Pre-Cana Conference.[90] Cana Conferences were first organized by the Diocese of Brooklyn in Suffolk County in 1946, and by 1952 they had expanded to seventeen regional groups across the four counties of Long Island.[91]

In 1959 Msgr. Gerald J. Ryan, the diocesan director of the Cana Conference, established an executive board of nine married couples for the new Diocese of Rockville Centre. "What impresses me about Cana," Ryan said, "is that it is a movement of lay people for lay people." Board member Dr. Frank Martin concurred, saying, "Cana is a field where the lay person can be developed and utilized in the work of the Church."[92] Over the next five years, Cana experienced a "population explosion," conducting 335 Cana and Pre-Cana Conferences for more than 39,000 people.[93] In 1964 the conferences were restructured "to present a comprehensive picture of married life" rather than addressing select topics. Panels of married couples replaced lectures, and nine weekly sessions were reorganized into three blocs addressing husband-wife relationships, parent-child relationships, and the family's role in society.[94] That year alone, more than 19,000 people attended Cana and Pre-Cana Conferences, an increase of 5,000 from the previous year.[95]

Again, the needs created by demographic change were seen as crucial catalysts of Cana's popularity. Father Walter Imbiorski, the Archdiocese of Chicago's director of Marriage and Family Life Education, argued that family life programs were essential because the extended family networks that urban neighborhoods once provided were gone. Suburban couples were now on their own in a pluralistic and rapidly changing culture to discern "what values to hold on to and how to build internal security."[96] *The Long Island Catholic* added that changing gender and family roles, and the suburbs' "one-family cubicles," left couples "away from family, and utterly dependent upon one another to satisfy their mutual needs." Meanwhile, there was "little available in parish life to help Christian couples grow in their marriage."[97]

The Marriage Encounter movement developed as another extra-parochial opportunity for couples to receive support for marriage and family life. Founded by Fr. Gabriel Calvo in Spain during the 1950s, the movement was

Figure 4.1. James and Madelaine Harper (*center*), the executive secretary couple for Marriage Encounter in the New York area, meet with Joan and Jim Kennedy (*right*) and Edna and Jack Berner (*left*). Source: Antoinette Bosco, "L.I. Couples Say 'Yes' to Encounter," *Long Island Catholic* 9, no. 52 (April 22, 1971): 18.

based on weekend retreats in which three team couples and a priest chaplain helped participating couples to better communicate their emotions and form a true partnership.[98] After attending a Marriage Encounter weekend at the 1967 CFM convention, several couples from Port Washington approached Fr. Charles A. Gallagher, a Jesuit assigned to St. Ignatius Retreat House in Manhasset, to bring Marriage Encounter to Long Island.[99] By the following year, twenty-two weekends had been presented in the New York area, and by 1971 Gallagher and couples in Rockville Centre had become the leaders of the Worldwide Marriage Encounter movement, spreading their ministry across the country and abroad.[100]

Throughout the 1970s dozens of different marriage enrichment programs, both religious and secular, gained popularity in the United States but Worldwide Marriage Encounter was the largest such group. In New York it was "the fastest growing and most praised Christian movement" according to *The Long Island Catholic*. In 1973–74 alone, approximately 21,250 couples from Nassau and Suffolk Counties made the encounter. By 1978 25,000 couples had made a Marriage Encounter in Brooklyn, and some 60,000 couples in the Diocese of Rockville Centre. The movement even developed versions of the encounter for Jewish and Episcopalian couples. A parish journal from Blessed Sacrament Parish in Valley Stream described Marriage Encounter as "a groundswell answer" to the "new and urgent stresses" that threatened the fabric of family life.[101]

Marriage Encounter offered opportunities for lay leadership like CFM and the Cana Conference. But it was unique among marriage apostolates for the emphasis it placed on the relationship between married couples and the priest chaplain. Indeed, Father Gallagher claimed that "the heart of the whole movement is the interplay of the two sacraments of Holy Orders and Matrimony."[102] This was particularly important among suburban Catholics who felt unknown by the priests in their large parish communities. Dr. and Mrs. Joseph Smith, the Long Island contact couple for Marriage Encounter, said that the movement enabled "the priest to develop a deeply personal relationship with people" that was often missing in a parish setting. "The contact increases people's knowledge of the humanness of the priest," Dr. Smith added, "while never diminishing his special role. It creates a bond that I believe was nonexistent between Holy Orders and Matrimony."[103] Marriage Encounter was also said to transform how couples participated in the life of their parish. James and Madelaine Harper of Christ the King Parish in Commack, who served as Marriage Encounter's New York executive secretary team, noted that "instead of husbands being on parish council, the Holy Name, the St. Vincent de Paul Society, and wives being in separate societies, couples do the parish work—together."[104]

The Decline of the Family Apostolates

That the family apostolates were especially successful in suburbia also created problems for the organizations. Father Edward M. Kohler of Chicago, the national chaplain to CFM, noted during a visit to Long Island in 1970 that suburbanites joined CFM because they were looking for friends in their new community. But because suburbia was mostly white and middle class this meant that "hardly any of the 40 million American poor, or blue-collar workers," belonged to CFM.[105] Since Long Island was especially segregated it is no surprise that Fr. William Geary, the moderator of CFM at St. Agnes Parish in Rockville Centre, agreed that, nearly all participating couples were between the ages of thirty-five and forty-five, middle class, and white. He argued that the movement needed to "broaden its base to include a greater number of non-white," young, and low-income couples.[106]

Persistent tensions also emerged within the movement between those who saw CFM as a family movement and those who saw it as a social action movement. National CFM leaders felt lay Catholics should be more active in politics and there was no more pressing issue in the 1960s than race relations. The new inquiry book of 1963 included "discussion of Negro family needs such as housing, education," and employment, and the 1964 inquiry book was entitled *Race and Politics*.[107] For some participants, discussion of civil rights took CFM beyond its proper focus on family life. It also made the movement susceptible to the divisions over civil rights that plagued the nation and with it the Church. Interviewed in 1981 about his tenure in the 1960s as director of the Diocese of Rockville Centre's Family Life Bureau, Msgr. Joseph Lawlor suggested that some CFM chapters "became activist groups" and that departing from a focus on family issues "was the beginning of the end" for CFM.[108] So, too, Patty Crowley, one of the founders of CFM, pointedly stated in 1990 that CFM's attempts to address racism and politics were what had divided the movement and led to its decline.[109]

In 1972 *The Long Island Catholic* declared CFM "a once vital Christian movement now on the wane." Nationwide, CFM membership had peaked in 1963 at 40,000 couples, but by the start of the 1970s its membership was consistently declining and on Long Island only St. Peter Parish in Port Washington and St. Joseph the Worker Parish in East Patchogue had thriving chapters. Father Gerald Murphy, a Jesuit chaplain to the CFM in Port Washington, felt that CFM was "part of a whole number of movements which have seen their day, are fading, and must be replaced by a new direction or something else entirely. Movements which were so strong in the fifties and sixties," he said, "have no strength today."[110]

Others thought that the CFM had fulfilled its purpose by funneling the laity into other apostolates like the Cana Conferences and Marriage Encounter. But Cana Conferences, too, had all but died out by the end of the 1960s, and Pre-Cana Conferences, which survived because there were no adequate alternatives to prepare engaged couples for marriage, were increasingly "viewed with derision and distaste."[111] Couples attending a Pre-Cana Conference at St. Boniface Parish in 1972 resented being made to attend and called the presentations "really boring" and "an insult to our intelligence." Additionally, only five of the sixteen attendees reported that they regularly attended Sunday Mass.[112] The clergy's waning interest in Pre-Cana was said to be a result of priests being too busy, or being reluctant to speak about birth control in light of Pope Paul VI's prohibition against artificial birth control in his 1968 encyclical *Humanae Vitae*.[113] Although Fr. Edward M. Kohler, the CFM national chaplain, insisted in 1970 that birth control "just doesn't come up anymore," it is clear that this silence masked the laity's broad embrace of reproductive technologies and signaled a loss of credibility and authority for the hierarchy and the Church's teaching on family life.[114] As with debates over civil rights, the deepening of divisions within the laity, and between the laity and Church teaching, on gender roles, sexuality, and family planning drove the decline of the family apostolates.

Even Marriage Encounter, which had expansive growth in the 1970s, faced criticisms and found its popularity declining by the end of the decade. Some couples who made a Marriage Encounter complained about the "intensity of the follow-up activities." Although defenders of Marriage Encounter argued that its veteran couples provided much of the labor behind Pre-Cana programs, Lucille and Andrew Buffalino of Huntington Station complained that "the concentration on Encounter leaves you time for practically nothing else." A survey by *The Long Island Catholic* found couples who critiqued the program's "excessive emotionalism," and still others who worried that Marriage Encounter was becoming "an exclusive club," marked by a "messianic flavor."[115] Dr. and Mrs. Joseph Smith were sensitive to these critiques and insisted: "we don't want to be an elite group, we don't want to say this is the only way to have a good marriage."[116] But by 1982 Fr. Edward Hogan of Rockaway Point lamented that Marriage Encounter, which had been "a rage a decade ago," was now "feeble." He proposed a familiar explanation and possible solution: "Many couples cannot afford to go away," he wrote, "so why not give them an alternative and help them make a 'Marriage Encounter at Home.'"[117]

The Rise to Lay Maturity

Even before Vatican II parish religious education programs and the family apostolates had provided the laity with increased opportunities for grassroots leadership of the Church's ministries. In new suburban communities pastors also encouraged the laity to exert leadership and defend the interests of the Church by being involved in local politics, especially public school boards.[118] As the Council progressed, the theology that undergirded the family apostolates helped shape the Council documents on the vocation of the laity.[119] And in the wake of the Council, an acceleration of "laymen and women taking on key responsibilities" in diocesan offices like Catholic Charities, and major institutions such as hospitals, led *The Long Island Catholic* to describe 1967 as "the year of the laity."[120]

Changes to the Mass, however, were the most visible reform of the Council. Here, too, laypeople were given a more active role, serving as commentators, lectors, and extraordinary ministers of Holy Communion. A 1968 editorial in *The Long Island Catholic* cheered these new roles as evidence of the layman "sharing in the priestly function of the Church."[121] To help implement liturgical reform, the Diocesan Liturgical Commission held workshops to train parish liturgical committees. Some participants complained of priests who were "reluctant to take the time and effort to implement liturgical changes," while others warned of pushback or apathy from fellow parishioners. But Louis Tedesco of St. Raphael Parish in East Meadow spoke to the value of the reforms: "I used to think liturgy was the priest's area, and we just stood by and followed his lead," he said. "Now it's clear that we and the priests have to work together to make liturgy a real celebration in the parish."[122]

Even decades later, parishioners reported that the most powerful and personally rewarding leadership role that was opened to them was being able to assist in the distribution of Holy Communion during the Eucharistic Liturgy.[123] According to Catholic belief, the bread and wine used at Mass become the very body and blood of Christ, and prior to the Council the laity could not touch the host or sacred vessels at all. That lay extraordinary ministers of Communion were allowed to hold in their hands the single most important element of Catholic worship was thus an especially apt image of the transfer of power from the clergy to the laity. In May 1971 the Vatican gave the US bishops a one-year indult for select laity to distribute Communion, and the widespread expectation that this approval would be extended was fulfilled.[124] The following year Bishop Kellenberg permitted the practice in the Diocese of Rockville Centre, stipulating that lay people should be selected according to an order of preference: "subdeacons, clerics in minor orders, those who have received tonsure, men religious, women religious, laymen, and laywomen."[125] The diocese commissioned 188 ministers in 15 parishes, of whom 87 were religious sisters, 68 were lay men, 17 were religious brothers, and 16 were lay women.[126]

According to *The Long Island Catholic*, the reaction to extraordinary ministers was "overwhelmingly favorable," and was proof of the laity's increased leadership in the Church. "I am enthusiastic," said William Ryan of St. Rose of Lima Parish in Massapequa, "I feel that it is a further step, even though mostly symbolic, in the direction of greater participation of lay people in the liturgy and the life of the Church." It is striking that the majority of extraordinary ministers were women, despite the fact that laywomen were at the bottom of the diocese's order of precedence. Christine McCoy, an extraordinary minister at St. Gerard Parish in Terryville celebrated this inclusion of women as proof that Jesus "wants women to have a greater share and participation in the Mass."[127] Indeed, throughout the late 1960s and early 1970s, Antoinette Bosco—a wife, mother of six, and staff writer for *The Long*

Island Catholic—narrated in the pages of the diocesan newspaper as well as in *Marriage* magazine, a "quiet revolution" in how laywomen thought of their gender and vocation, and the roles they took up in the family, in the family apostolates, and in the Church.[128]

Parish Councils

An even more celebrated, and less symbolic, attempt to bring the laity into positions of leadership and decision-making was the advent of school boards and parish councils. Father Patrick Shanahan, the superintendent of schools in the Diocese of Rockville Centre, emphasized that in the first fourteen years of the diocese's history, forty new parish schools were built and another forty schools built expansions, and that it was only "right and just" that the laity who funded these efforts had "some voice in the policies" governing those schools.[129] According to Shanahan, the school board's role was to assist the pastor in formulating school policy; evaluating curriculum; planning, operating, and maintaining the school plant and pupil transportation; overseeing teacher development; and preparing the school's annual budget.[130] By the mid-1960s several parishes had established school boards on their own initiative, but in 1968 Kellenberg mandated that all parishes form both a school board and an advisory council by Pentecost Sunday 1969. Guidelines were developed to ensure a collaborative relationship between the two parish bodies.[131] This made Rockville Centre one of only a handful of dioceses across the country that required parishes to have both parish advisory councils and school boards.[132]

In some instances, pastors had welcomed the laity to advise and consult about the development of their parishes from their very establishment, if only through informal means. The widespread growth of parish councils, however, was the result of the Second Vatican Council, and parish histories universally describe the councils as a truly consequential decision to include the laity in decision-making.[133] "All the decrees of the Vatican II Council can be summed up in a few words: let the people participate," declared St. Pius X Parish's twentieth anniversary journal. The authors enthused that the parish council was "a vehicle to establish co-responsibility among the laity, clergy, and religious" and that its message to the people was: "YOU ARE THE CHURCH!"[134] But the initial responses to parish councils also "included much confusion and fear." During open house meetings to prepare parishioners of St. Mary Parish in East Islip for their new parish council, some people "expressed the worry that if laymen 'take over'" it would diminish the status of the priest, and that if laymen were given "freedom" it would undermine the authority of the Church.[135]

Other parishes reported an "inability to stimulate interest among parishioners" in the parish council.[136] Anthony Mansueto, the council chair at St. Matthew Parish in Dix Hills said he was not at all sure a parish council was necessary. Noting that only 118 families out of 1,820 had voted in the council elections, St. Matthew's pastor Fr. Leo J. Goggin, agreed that "there are many who are just not interested in parish councils."[137] Fr. Daniel Potterton, pastor of St. Paul the Apostle Parish in Jericho, wondered if parish councils were expecting too much of lay people "who are, of necessity, so preoccupied with family and jobs. The people do not yet have an appreciation of what it is to run a parish," he said, and "the parish council was imposed on them. If it had been a grassroots movement, we would have had more than a tenth of the parish voting."[138] Others suggested that the laity's lack of interest, and lack of experience in running a parish, led council members to constantly revert "to the old attitude of 'Father knows best.'"[139]

The National Council of Catholic Men (NCCM) had called for parishes to receive several months of instruction before a council was established, and offered to assist dioceses in running workshops for priests and councilors. Through its Religious Education Department, the Diocese of Rockville Centre did run three sets of weekend workshops in 1969 and 1970 for lay presidents of parish councils, school boards, and liturgy committees. But there does not seem to have been any long-term, diocesan-wide program of parish council training as there had been for lay CCD teachers. Richard H. Dement of NCCM lamented to Bishop Walter Kellenberg that the "ultimate success of the councils" was threatened because they had been brought into existence "without rhyme or reason," and only because "Vatican II said they are necessary."[140]

On top of inspiring interest in council elections, parishes were also concerned with making their council represent the geographical, gender, and occupational diversity of the parish.[141] Priests and people debated what methods of electing or appointing council members would best achieve this goal. Assumption of the Blessed Virgin Mary Parish in Centereach, which had the diocese's first fully elected parish council, found that their eighteen members were a cross-section of the parish including a plumber, pharmacist, truck driver, chiropractor, receptionist, and housewife.[142] But John Cooney, the council chairman at St. Rose of Lima Parish in Massapequa, lamented that it was the most popular people from the parish's various societies who were elected, whether they were truly qualified or not. "We're not used to employing all the talent of a parish," council vice chairman Frank Flood added. "There must be many people who never joined existing societies who have a lot to offer."[143]

The greatest concern about the representative quality of parish councils was whether or not young people were adequately represented. In 1968, as parish councils were being formed, 65 percent of Long Island's population was under twenty-five years of age. Because there were so many young people in St. Bernard Parish in Levittown, its council had several young adult members, but very few other parishes had any young councilors and only a handful of councils reserved positions for a youth representative.[144] Even in 1985 only half of the diocese's parish councils reported having a youth member.

Councils seemed to have the greatest success garnering parishioner involvement when they aimed to answer a specific question or solve a particular need, such as painting the parish school or updating the parish census.[145] By far the most pressing concern, common to all suburban religious communities, was the parish's financial security. Councils launched increased giving campaigns and instituted bingo games to improve their parish's short-term financial health. But Fr. Charles A. Ribaudo of St. Rose of Lima Parish in Massapequa argued that long-term questions about how to pay off parish debt and fund parish schools required that councils develop "a philosophy of money in the parish."[146]

Although parish councils were said to represent the promise of lay involvement, many observers recognized that the councils' greatest challenge would be "'to stir the apathetic masses.'" Indeed, some saw parish councils as a "'last hope' for re-sparking people in a parish to move out of passivity." Such high hopes for parish councils were dashed. "We thought people would pack the meetings," said James J. Dermody, a councilor at St. Jude in Mastic Beach, "but that didn't happen." Even in parishes considered to be "forward-moving" and "progressive," many parishioners remained uninterested in the parish council. In 1973 St. Pius X Parish in Plainview, a parish of approximately 1,700 families, reported that at several council meetings "there were not enough members to make a quorum."[147]

Proponents of parish councils agreed that the source of this apathy was that councils lacked real decision-making power—they were entirely advisory to the pastor who maintained ultimate authority in the parish. "The frustration of not being able to make decisions has been our toughest problem," said James Murphy, a parish councilor at St. Anne Parish in Brentwood. "When people are not permitted to act decisively," he said, "they run out of gas and the whole thing dies."[148] Dr. Raymond F. Zambito, a parishioner at St. Gertrude Parish in Bayville and later a founder of the diocese's federation of lay organizations, said that laymen had not achieved co-responsibility because the clergy did not take the laity or their expertise seriously. "The institutional church is dragging its feet," he complained.[149]

Some lay parish councilors felt they were being thwarted by pastors who too frequently vetoed their motions or refused to work with them collaboratively. There were also pastors, including Msgr. Lawrence Ballweg of St. Bernard Parish in Levittown, who were disappointed in the councils and "didn't find them helpful at all," because parishioners saw the council "not as advisory but as an opportunity to tell the pastor that he was doing something wrong."[150] There were, however, parishes that exhibited a good working relationship between council and pastor. "He has met us more than half way," said parish council secretary Billie Williams of Fr. Hugh H. Graham, pastor of St. Rose of Lima Parish in Massapequa.[151] Indeed, in a few parishes, the promise of lay decision-making seemed to be fulfilled. Frank W. Cumminsky, chairman of the parish council at St. Thomas More Parish in Hauppauge called the community "a layman's parish," and the pastor, Fr. Robert J. Kirwin, added that "the people are making decisions and will continue unless any contravene canon law."[152]

A Partisan Divide

The building of postwar parishes, the advent of new lay apostolates, of programs for adult education in the faith, and of new lay associations shaped the promise—expressed in, and advanced by, the Second Vatican Council—that the faithful could have a greater role in the ministry and leadership of the Church. Parish councils were presented by Church leaders, and received by the most committed laypeople, as novel ecclesial structures capable of fulfilling the promise of lay leadership. But parish councils came into existence at precisely the moment when the number of laity participating in parish life and attending Sunday Mass began to decline precipitously.[153] Since at least 1945 Catholic leaders had been calling for greater lay participation in the mission of the Church and complained about apathy among the laity.[154] Such concerns spiked in the late 1960s and 1970s, however, as parishes experienced a drop-off in Mass attendance and a decline in traditional parish societies. The new associations and structures meant to foster lay participation struggled to garner interest and maintain support. Martin H. Work, the executive director of the National Council of Catholic Men, called apathy and indifference "a major concern," and "the number one problem of the laity."[155]

In 1970, when *The Long Island Catholic* attempted to conduct a survey of its 190,000 readers on the subject of lay participation, editors received only 90 responses compared to the usual 300, leading them to quip: "Talk of Apathy Causing More Apathy."[156] The responses that were received helped confirm the widespread belief that divisions within the laity hampered efforts to magnify the laity's voice in Church affairs. These divisions, often described as splitting the laity into "liberal" and "conservative" camps—but also often breaking along levels of education and income—formed over a diversity of issues including civil rights, the war in Vietnam, abortion, birth control, and changes in the Church's liturgy. Most fundamentally, however, the laity was divided between "conservatives" who thought the reforms of Vatican II were too-much too-soon and "liberals" who thought they were not enough, and what these reforms meant for the relationship between the clergy and laity.[157]

In February 1969, Dr. Raymond Zambito, a parishioner at St. Gertrude Parish in Bayville, gathered the leadership of eight lay organizations to establish the Federation of Lay Organizations of the Diocese of Rockville Centre.[158] The federation, which was said to be without precedent in the American Church, aimed to "strengthen the effectiveness" of the lay movements, and advocate for greater inclusion of the laity in Church affairs, all while allowing each group autonomy to pursue their specific mission.[159] But the federation was undermined by differing understandings of the layman's role in the post–Vatican II Church. When one of the federation's member organizations proposed a petition demanding financial transparency from the diocese, the Legion of Mary withdrew from the federation saying that they could not do anything without the direction and support of the bishop and clergy.[160]

The Long Island Association of Laymen (LIAL), established in May 1967 to give the laity a voice in the Church's decision-making, also collapsed after only a few short years.[161] According to LIAL's first president, Thomas Hunter of Syosset, the association was formed by laity "who believed the Church was dragging its heels after Vatican II."[162] James Harper of Christ the King Parish in Commack, the last president of LIAL, added that these laypeople had belonged to CFM and Teams of Our Lady, and some had been on parish councils and faced resistance to reform from their pastors. They hoped that uniting with other laity across the diocese could "do some good and make some further change in the Church."[163] LIAL was launched with grand plans for lay formation programming and committees on ecumenism, social action, parish structures, education, and liturgy.[164] One of its first resolutions even called on Bishop Walter Kellenberg to announce a moratorium on the building of parochial schools until LIAL could more closely study the issue.[165]

But by October 1969 LIAL's meetings were so poorly attended it was clear the organization had no future. Founding members agreed that the suspicions of the clergy undermined any influence the organization might have developed. What LIAL had "offered as loving criticism," Hunter said, the bishop and clergy "too often regarded as hostile confrontation."[166] But Harper added that many of the laity shared this evaluation and reflected that LIAL had "found a lot of resistance from within the laity itself."[167] One laywoman who participated in LIAL meetings as the leader of a constituent organization, commented that LIAL was "not a balanced group" and seemed to be "taking the new role of the laity the wrong way."[168] William Godfrey of St. James, one of LIAL's founding members, added that "LIAL was essentially an organization of college graduates, age 35–45, all with fairly liberal backgrounds. There were no blue-collar workers." LIAL never found a way to unite laity from across generational, ideological, and class divides.[169]

Growing polarization within the laity, which undermined LIAL and the Federation of Lay Organizations, was a widely discussed crisis.[170] An effort launched on Long Island to confront the crisis briefly drew national attention, but it too suffered from a lack of interest and faded quickly. Father Paul C. Driscoll and Therese D. Siller established the Intra-Church Relations Committee (ICRC) in 1965 to encourage dialogue across the Church's ideological divide, modeling it on ecumenical dialogues between Catholics and other religious bodies.[171] The group emerged from discussion groups at Curé of Ars Parish in Merrick and from a report Driscoll had written on "Polarization Within the Church."[172] Driscoll's ten-page report, which argued that the crisis in the Church was "not primarily between clergy and laity but between the liberal and conservative cultures," suggested the formation of speakers' bureaus to host moderated discussions of controversial topics. The report was printed in *Homiletic and Pastoral Review*, circulated to over a thousand Catholic leaders and institutions around the country, and positively reviewed by the editors of *America*.[173] It led to the ICRC sponsoring a newspaper column syndicated in several Catholic newspapers across the country, and to invitations from dioceses and parishes to speak on implementing their model.[174]

Here again, by 1969 the ICRC found that few other intra-church groups had been formed and their own was dwindling. Driscoll surmised that "not everybody who had strong opinions wanted to take part in discussion with people who had other points of view."[175] His colleague, Therese Siller, added that the intra-church movement "tended to vaporize" as the debate over

Figure 4.2. Members of St. Frances de Chantal Parish in Wantagh board a bus to Washington, DC, to protest against abortion in 1970. *Source*: Box 3, Archives of St. Frances de Chantal Parish, Wantagh, NY).

abortion took center stage.[176] For her part, she could not remain neutral or "straddle the fence on an issue like abortion," and she devoted more of her time to the pro-life movement, ultimately running for the New York State Senate and testifying before the US Senate on the issue.[177] In 1972 Driscoll was named the full-time director of the diocese's pro-life office. "This was possibly the most controversial area I could have gotten into," he recalled. "Very few people wanted any dialogue on this particular area."[178]

Conclusion—an Unfulfilled Promise?

In 1984 Bishop John McGann announced a fourteen-member commission to study the effectiveness of parish councils in preparation for revising diocesan guidelines, which had not been updated since they were first written sixteen years earlier.[179] Public hearings, attended by over 150 clergy and lay representatives from 100 parishes, revealed that councils had a good male-female balance, but that only five councils in the diocese had their own operating budgets; only half of councils had a youth representative; more than half spent the majority of their meetings on committee reports; and only a third of councils reported a clear sense of their role or were involved in decision-making. Parish staffs were poorly represented on councils, council communications with the parish-at-large were weak, and councils lacked unity and training. Most fundamentally, attendees "cited more weaknesses than strengths in parish councils."[180]

When a final report was published the following year, the diocesan commission concluded: "all is not well." Pastors saw parish councils as "a necessary evil" and were not sufficiently trained to work effectively with them. The laity professed to understand councils as "a model for collegiality," but in the commission's estimation many lay people seemed "to be asking for the opposite, for a false model based upon the perception that the Church can be a democracy." These faithful therefore perceived that councils could only be "a pretense for consultation, a farce, or a rubber stamp." The commission also surmised that because councils worked according to "the American democratic model," there was not enough "building up of community or living of Christian principles" among council members. Although the commission felt that the reasons for mandating parish councils were still valid, and it recommended that a diocesan office provide councils with training and support, the report stated bluntly that many priests and faithful "would prefer nothing to what they now experience."[181]

Parish councils had clearly not lived up to the hopes and expectations of those who had envisioned them as vehicles of lay leadership in the Church. Parish councils were hobbled from the beginning by disparate understandings of their purpose, apathy among parishioners, and ideological divisions within the laity. Nevertheless, throughout the 1970s, more and more lay people took positions of responsibility in the administration of the Church at both the diocesan and parish levels. The Notre Dame Study of Catholic Parish Life found that the decline in the number of priests and a spirit of reform after Vatican II had resulted in "grassroots reform" that gave the laity "far more real control and responsibility." Laypeople—especially laywomen—the study found, occupied more than 80 percent of all leadership roles and nearly 60 percent of paid positions in the nation's parishes, including as directors of religious education, liturgy, music, and youth ministry.[182] On Long Island, for example, between 1983 and 1987 the parishes of the Diocese of Rockville Centre employed more than 185 religious education coordinators, 54 percent of whom were laypeople, and 95 percent of whom were women.[183]

Additionally, the Notre Dame Study found that there was very little resistance among the faithful to fellow laypeople, including laywomen, taking up new roles in diocesan administration and parish ministry. Although parish councils had not fostered lay leadership as originally envisioned—in part because of divisions within the laity about the right relationship between priests and people—even this failure was not enough to undermine the inexorable rise of laypeople into positions of responsibility within the Church. Such an increased role for the laity in the governance of Church institutions, and in the Church's pastoral ministries, had undoubtedly received validation and encouragement in the documents and spirit of the Second Vatican Council. But it was the rapid expansion of the Church into the postwar suburbs, and the practical and pastoral challenges this posed for parish life, that both increased expectations for, and necessitated, an increased lay role in Church leadership.

FIVE

Suburban Parish Boundaries: Race, Ethnicity, and Mixed Parishes in Suburbia

Just days after Rev. Dr. Martin Luther King Jr. was assassinated in April 1968, Fr. Andrew Connolly, then the principal of Holy Trinity High School in Hicksville, celebrated Palm Sunday Mass at nearby Holy Family Parish. He preached that day about how the death of Doctor King was "the same as the passion of Jesus Christ." Connolly recalled that of the thousand parishioners in the hall "approximately three hundred of them got up to leave." Connolly asked Bishop Kellenberg to reassign him to parish work "or special work in race relations." Although he confessed to being raised in a casually racist Irish American home, Connolly claimed to have worked hard to overcome his prejudices and to have been involved in civil rights work from his teenage years. He was assigned as associate pastor of Our Lady of the Miraculous Medal Parish, in the largely Black community of Wyandanch, and arrived in June 1968 not long after the area had experienced racial rioting.[1]

The tracks of the Long Island Railroad cut Wyandanch in half, cleaving the predominantly white section to the north from the overwhelmingly Black section to the south. Of the 800 to 1,000 families who belonged to Our Lady of the Miraculous Medal Parish, only 80 to 90 were Black. Connolly noticed that white residents of the northern section of the parish—an area called Huntington Hills—actually attended Mass at St. Matthew Parish in Dix Hills. "The pastor simply let it happen," Connolly recalled. But when Connolly was named the parish's administrator in 1972, he announced that parishioners would need his permission to attend Mass in another church. A delegation of the affected parishioners met with Connolly and argued that he was only interested in where they attended Mass because he wanted their money. But he insisted he was only interested in their minds and hearts. "You go up to that church because you don't want to be here," he challenged his parishioners, "because of black and poor" people at Miraculous Medal. "I want you to hear the Gospel," Connolly pleaded. His stipulations, however, went unheeded, indicating that even as the ethnic and territorial definitions of the parish increasingly lost their meaning in the suburban Church the racial boundaries that defined Catholic parishes remained.[2]

Postwar suburbanization helped complete the amalgamation of various ethnically inflected forms of Catholicism into one religiously identified body of American Catholicism, a process that had begun as each ethnic group became further removed from the experience of immigration. In the postwar suburbs laity who had seen themselves as Irish, Polish, or Italian Catholics when they lived in urban ethnic enclaves came increasingly to see themselves simply as Catholic. Parishes established to serve European immigrants shed their ethnic affiliations and the names of new suburban parishes, the feasts and rituals they observed, and the lay associations that animated them were no longer defined by ethnicity. However, because of suburbia's deep racial segregation, newly suburbanized Catholics also increasingly identified themselves as white. Loyal support of the nation during wartime and suburban homeownership in the postwar period bestowed on Italian Catholics in particular status as white Americans, which they had frequently been denied in past generations. Despite the best efforts of Church leaders and some lay activists to support civil rights and parish integration, others among the laity sought to maintain residential segregation and defined the boundaries of their parish through racial exclusivity. Meanwhile, suburbia's comparatively small community of Black Catholics demanded that their Church live up to its teachings on race and racism, and address their unique needs.

Even as the civil rights movement progressed toward its denouement, Latin American immigration to Long Island, which had begun in the 1950s, increased dramatically in the 1970s. The Diocese of Rockville Centre and its parishes wrestled with how best to serve an overwhelmingly Catholic immigrant community that was scattered across Long Island and whose practice of the faith was so closely linked to its language and ethnic culture. Some white Catholics, inspired in part by the Church's revivified commitment to enculturated faith, desired to recover their lost ethnic identity and attempted to revive religious traditions associated with their European heritage and with the urban ethnic neighborhood. The suburban Church was thus forced to grapple anew with how ethnicity should inform religious practice even as parishes struggled to unite faithful from diverse backgrounds—a challenge that has only been amplified in the years since.

Ethnic Parishes on Long Island

In the first decades of the 1900s realtors and city businessmen aggressively developed land around railroad tracks and commuter stations on Long Island, infilling older communities and transforming farm fields into new villages.[3] Newcomers of Irish, German, Polish, and Italian stock swelled the ranks of Long Island's Catholics and the Diocese of Brooklyn worked to establish parishes or missions for each of the communities that popped up near new railroad stations.[4] Although the majority of these new parishes were territorial parishes dominated by Irish Americans, there were several national parishes established including St. Hedwig Parish in Floral Park, organized in 1905. Of the parishioners at St. Hedwig, 75 percent were Polish.[5] But the ethnic group that would become Long Island's largest and most important was Italian Catholics. There were very few Italians on Long Island until, in the 1880s, Italian immigrants began working on the Long Island Railroad and in the local nurseries and sand-mining industry. By the 1920s Italians had established identifiable enclaves in several communities and parishes across Long Island including St. Peter of Alcantara in Port Washington, Our Lady of Good Counsel in Inwood, and St. Anthony of Padua in Rocky Point.[6]

Parishes took differing approaches to serving these Italian immigrants. St. Brigid Parish in Westbury, the oldest parish in Nassau County, was founded in 1856 by Irish immigrants. In the 1880s, when Italian immigrants from Durazzano, Nola, and Saviano arrived to work on the estates and nurseries in the area, the parish made accommodations for these newcomers that undermined any drive to form a separate Italian ethnic parish. Rather than compete to celebrate feasts in honor of each town's respective patron, the pastor suggested that a celebration of Mary would be unifying. Thus began Westbury's Feast of the Assumption in 1910, making it older than even Manhattan's Feast of San Gennaro. Italian immigrants arrived in Glen Cove from Sturno near Naples in the 1880s and 1890s. They attended St. Patrick Parish until they were inspired, by the Polish immigrants who had founded St. Hyacinth Parish, to establish their own national parish. St. Rocco Parish in Glen Cove, founded in 1937, remains "the only truly on-going Italian national parish on Long Island," and even today its Feast of St. Rocco is the largest of its kind on Long Island. When Italians from Emilia-Romagna in northern Italy settled in Copiague, they began worshipping at St. Martin of Tours Parish in Amityville until Our Lady of the Assumption Parish was established in 1929. While technically a territorial not a national parish, Our Lady of the Assumption was considered an Italian parish, with

Italian clergy, parish associations, and feast celebrations.⁷ Similarly, when Italian Americans from New York City first began moving into Patchogue in the 1870s and 1880s they attended the overwhelmingly Irish St. Francis de Sales Parish. In 1922, Saints Felicity and Perpetua Parish was established in the heart of the Italian neighborhood. Although it was technically a territorial parish it was overwhelmingly Italian and in the mid-1920s the name of the parish was changed to Our Lady of Mount Carmel.

These communities remained relatively small until after World War II when New York City's Italian Americans participated in the great exodus to the suburbs. According to US Census data, New York's first-generation Italians remained concentrated in urban areas, but by 1970 47 percent of the metropolitan area's second-generation Italian Americans lived in areas with fewer than 100,000 residents, and 41 percent lived in places with fewer than 50,000 residents.⁸ As a result of this migration, Italians had become the largest single nationality on Long Island by 1970, and by 1980 Italians comprised nearly 25 percent of Long Island's two million residents. Nassau and Suffolk County thus constituted "the largest concentration of people of Italian descent in two contiguous counties outside of Italy."⁹

From Ethnic Parishes to Suburban Parishes

But the move to the suburbs accelerated intermarriage, acculturation, and the decline of ethnicity's importance within American Catholicism. By the 1960s the third generation of Italian Americans was very likely to marry non-Italians, though marriage to a fellow Catholic remained predominant.¹⁰ Data from a 1963 survey showed that 60 percent of third-generation Italian Americans intermarried, and that among the youngest of that generation— those thirty years of age or younger—nearly 70 percent intermarried. The data showed that Italian Catholics chose spouses from Irish, German, Polish, or other Eastern European Catholic backgrounds in percentages consistent with their proportion of the American Catholic population.¹¹ Thus, many commentators, perhaps most famously sociologist Will Herberg, emphasized that while ethnicity's importance was diminished in suburbia, religion remained a crucial marker of social divisions. Catholics, Protestants, and especially Jews increasingly lived in close proximity to one another in suburbia. And yet, intermarriage was still largely interethnic and intrareligious. Catholics, Protestants, and Jews continued to live almost completely different social lives, from grade-school playgrounds to the golf course at the country club.¹²

The diminishment of ethnic difference within the melting pot of American Catholicism was especially evident as Italian Americans accommodated themselves more and more to the Irish form of Catholicism that had long dominated the Church in the United States. Among first-generation Italian immigrants, adult men were suspicious of the clergy, and Mass attendance outside of major holidays, weddings, and funerals was left for the young, the old, and for women. Italian Catholicism was also premised on personal, supernatural relationships with the Madonna and the saints, in whose honor elaborate public *festas* were celebrated. The Irish, however, were deeply loyal to the clergy, whose American ranks they dominated. They were also much stricter in their observance of religious norms, especially the requirement to attend Sunday Mass, and they were strongly supportive of parochial education. The Irish clergy disdained Italian *festas* as a form of quasi-paganism, but these traditions endured thanks to the system of national parishes that allowed immigrants to worship in their own language and with their own traditions.[13]

However, especially after World War II, as each succeeding generation of Italian Americans intermarried and left urban enclaves for the suburbs, they conformed more and more to the Irish norms that marked American Catholicism—a process that some have referred to as "Hibernization."[14] The strong attachment of first-generation Italian Americans to the extended family gave way to the separation of households and the nuclear family that were characteristic of American society in the postwar suburbs.[15] Second- and third-generation Italian Americans attended Sunday Mass and received the sacraments at rates that were similar to those of Irish Americans. Other traditionally Italian religious practices, from the celebration of feast days, the observance of novenas, the lighting of candles before statues, and praying to Mary and the saints rather than to God were all brought in line with Irish patterns of devotion.[16] An especially "significant indicator of 'Hibernization,'" was Italians' increasing support of parochial schools. Prior to World War II many Italian Americans had resisted sending their children to Catholic schools, but began to do so in the 1950s.[17] A 1977 study found that only 15.6 percent of Irish Catholics had never attended a Catholic school, but 61.2 percent of first-generation Italians and 59.6 percent of second-generation Italians had never attended a Catholic school. In the third generation, however, that percentage fell to 34.6 percent.[18]

These changes in ethnicity's influence on religious practice were, unsurprisingly, paralleled by the diminution of ethnicity's centrality to the parish. Even the names of newly established suburban parishes bear out the decrease of ethnic affiliation. Of the sixteen parishes established in the Diocese of Rockville Centre's first fifteen years, none were national parishes, and over a dozen had universally Catholic names with no noticeable ethnic association, including parishes named for the Good Shepherd, Christ the King, Our Lady of Grace, Our Lady Queen of Martyrs, the evangelists Saints Matthew, Mark, and Luke, and the apostles Peter and Paul.

Even previously national parishes, and those territorial parishes that had functioned as ethnic parishes, were transformed by assimilation and suburban expansion into traditional geographic parishes.[19] The 1950s and early 1960s witnessed the decline of Italian ethnicity even in parishes that continued to be dominated by the descendants of Italian immigrants, as the use of Italian in preaching dwindled and *festas* in honor of saints lacked their previous intensity, ceased to perform their previous functions, or were no longer held at all.[20] At Our Lady of the Assumption Parish in Copiague, for example, a significant influx of Polish and Latino immigrants in the 1950s and '60s altered the character of the parish despite second- and third-generation Italian Americans still predominating. Monsignor Anthony De-Laura found that these parishioners had little interest in Italian-language preaching and in 1967, when DeLaura stepped down as the parish's last Italian pastor, it signaled the end of the parish's ethnic era. Although Our Lady of Mount Carmel in Patchogue was founded as a territorial parish in 1922, records show that over 88 percent of the Confirmation class that year was Italian. But by 1951 just 68 percent of the Confirmation class was Italian, and the postwar boom brought even more non-Italians to the area. In 1963 the parish hosted its Feast of Saint Liberata for the last time, and in the mid-1960s a new, larger church was built to accommodate the parish's burgeoning congregation. More than a mile from the heart of the Italian neighborhood, the modern church was deemed to be "in keeping with the automobile-oriented" community it served, and without "the old ethnic flavor."[21] Altogether, Italian and Irish American Catholics, onetime nemeses in the era of the immigrant Church, worked together to build the suburban Church.[22]

Most Catholic pastoral leaders and commentators celebrated this development. Encouraged by the full participation of Catholics in the World War, and by the theological speculation that would fully flower during Vatican II, many Catholic liberals—especially a younger generation of clergy and laity—had come to see the ethnic parish as an obstacle to full engagement in American life and therefore celebrated the collapse of the ethnic ghetto precipitated by suburbanization. Priest-sociologist Andrew Greeley observed that in suburbia Catholics were entering "the ultimate melting pot." Indeed, he said there was "little to distinguish the Catholic suburbanite from his Protestant neighbor," let alone from other Catholics of different ethnic backgrounds. In suburbia the Catholic was finally regarded as "a full-fledged American." The inauguration of John F. Kennedy as president in 1961 and the opening of the Second Vatican Council in 1962 seemed to confirm American Catholicism's emergence from its urban ghetto and its increasingly confident engagement with American politics and culture.[23]

Race, Racism, and Civil Rights in the Suburban Church

While suburban parishes were no longer marked by their ethnic character, they were still defined by racial difference, and suburbanization helped complete the process by which the descendants of European immigrants became "white."[24] Federal policies like the GI Bill, FHA financing requirements, and restrictive covenants made it possible for white ethnics to leave urban enclaves and achieve homeownership in ethnically heterogeneous suburbs, a powerful proof of their inclusion in mainstream white society.[25] But these same policies also excluded Black Americans, ensuring that the suburbs, and therefore the suburban parish, were highly segregated racially.[26] Long Island's postwar development was thus marked by large swaths of all-white communities with only a smattering of "minority pockets," where Black veterans and their families could settle, including Wyandanch, North Amityville, Hempstead, Freeport, and Roosevelt.[27] As late as 1990, two-thirds of Long Island's neighborhoods were less than 1 percent Black and half had no Black residents at all, making Long Island the fifteenth-most segregated metropolitan area in the United States.[28]

The liberal Catholic urbanists and commentators who celebrated the breakup of the ethnic parish, but fretted over the ill effects of suburbanization, never centered white racism in their critiques of suburbia. But they judged that suburbanites had fled the city to absolve themselves of their obligation to serve the needs of urban minorities, and they saw in the civil rights movement an opportunity to advance both a more metropolitan view of the city and the Second Vatican Council's vision for the Church.[29] Dennis Geaney, for example, wrote that Catholic suburbanites were "not concerned with the race problem" and that they had moved "to the suburbs in flight from it."[30]

As Fr. Andrew Connolly's experience at Our Lady of the Miraculous Medal Parish in Wyandanch proved, even in areas where Black and white Catholic suburbanites lived within the same territorial parish, some white Catholics chose the church at which they attended Sunday Mass by virtue of its racial exclusivity. After Our Lady of the Miraculous Medal's establishment in 1936, territory had twice been broken off of its original twenty-eight-square-mile territory to establish new parishes: Ss. Cyril and Methodius Parish in Deer Park in 1956, and Our Lady of Grace Parish in West Babylon in 1962. That left 800 families in Our Lady of the Miraculous Medal and in 1968 there was a rumor in Wyandanch that another parish would be created from the northern, and mainly white, section of the parish. This would "clearly make the Wyandanch parish a Negro mission," worried Andy Wills, president of OLMM's Holy Name Society. "What's really sad is that this is the way most of the white Catholics want it," lamented Mrs. Frank Faivre, another parishioner of OLMM. "Some of my neighbors thought I was crazy to join the Wyandanch Mother's Club," she said; "they said they wouldn't come into Wyandanch. They go elsewhere."[31]

Despite suburbia's stark racial segregation and examples of Catholic racism, there are also numerous examples of suburban laity and clergy being active in civil rights issues. In 1962, five years after the Diocese of Rockville Centre was established, Bishop Walter Kellenberg formed the Catholic Interracial Council of Long Island to encourage collaboration between the races in an effort to combat racism. With the Council still in its infancy, in August 1963, it organized as many as 100 members, including three seminarians and the diocesan vocation director, to join thousands of other Catholics from around the nation in the March on Washington.[32] Althea Gardiner of St. Brigid Parish in Westbury, a member of the Interracial Council and the NAACP, felt that "the wonderful success of the March" showed how all people "could stand together, without bitterness, without hatred, and a spirit of brotherhood." And Thomas Green of West Hempstead stated that "the demonstration gave tremendous meaning" to his faith, and gave him "more spiritual satisfaction" than any "rosary or candlelight service."[33]

Within months of the March, the Council hosted a meeting of over 400 priests and lay leaders from 119 parishes in the diocese to suggest what concrete actions Catholics on Long Island could take "to further interracial justice and understanding." In addition to examining "personal prejudices," the Council encouraged every parish to "establish a committee on housing to stem panic and educate people about real estate values."[34] At its founding, the Council's director, Fr. Francis B. Concannon, had decried the "un-Christ-like racial attitudes, prejudice and misunderstanding" that made "it difficult for members of minority groups to achieve the family betterment" that whites had sought in moving to the suburbs.[35] "No man has the right to expect to retain a racially restricted neighborhood," argued Dennis J. Clark, the Council's executive secretary.[36] Calling open housing a moral issue, the Council worked to disabuse white homeowners of the belief that property values declined when minorities moved into previously all-white neighborhoods.³⁷ Meeting participants also proposed home visitation programs as a means of improving both personal contact between Black and white residents and urban-suburban partnerships. And they suggested that all teachers in the diocese's parochial schools attend a course on Black history and culture and interracial justice.³⁸ These recommendations, focusing on housing, interracial understanding, and education in schools, proved to shape the priorities of the Interracial Council over the following decades.

Most pressingly, when Black families attempting to integrate white neighborhoods were met with racist intimidation and violence, the Catholic Interracial Council, pastors, parishioners, and the diocesan bishop denounced racism and organized support for the victims. In September 1970 Mr. and Mrs. Willy Early were building a $40,000 custom home in all-white Massapequa Gardens when vandals painted hate slogans on the home's foundation and later smashed out all the newly installed windows. Although the Earlys were Lutheran, the area was heavily Catholic, so Mrs. Barbara Roethel of the Nassau County Human Rights Commission—and herself a parishioner of Corpus Christi Parish in Mineola—contacted *Newsday* and *The Long Island Catholic* and asked the Catholic Interracial Council to investigate. The priests at St. Rose of Lima Parish preached about the moral implications of the attack and wrote in the Sunday bulletin that "we as a parish deplore racial bigotry." The parish council then wrote letters of support to the Earlys and to the homebuilder who had agreed to work with them, and parishioners participated in a rally at the property. Monsignor Michael J. McLaughlin of the Interracial Council applauded the priests and parishioners' efforts and the Earlys called the community support "very encouraging."³⁹

Although few if any parishes established housing committees to address racial integration's effects on property values, the Interracial Council sponsored its own events to discuss open housing and, in 1965, cooperated with the President's Committee on Equal Opportunity in Housing to host the nation's first Suburban Fair Housing Conference.⁴⁰ The Council's efforts met with at least some success when, in 1968, parishioners of St. Aidan Parish in Williston Park published a fair housing manifesto in their parish bulletin. "We don't want to attempt to preserve our community as a 'Christian one' or 'white one,'" the notice stated, "we just want nice people, no matter what their religion or color of skin." Noting that Catholics of Irish, Italian, and Polish descent knew well the ill effects of racial and religious double-standards, the statement warned real estate agents not to accept racist listings and threatened: "Do what is right and you will prosper. Do what is wrong and we'll try to put you out of business."⁴¹ Not all of Long Island's Catholic were converted. Noting that New York State had laws preventing discrimination in housing sales, one letter-writer to *The Long Island Catholic* called St. Aidan's manifesto "sanctimonious" and their threat "rather reminiscent of the lynch mobs."[42] And at Blessed Sacrament Parish in Valley Stream, where many parishioners had fled racial change in Brooklyn and "were determined that they were not going to move again," pastor Msgr. Edmond Trench jokingly referred to the Belt Parkway as the Maginot Line: "we had our guns trained to keep the people in Queens in Queens," he said.[43]

The Interracial Council also sponsored home visitation days in which Black and white families met and got to know one another in each other's homes. Mrs. Kathryn Rowcroft helped launch the program with three other women shortly after moving into Our Lady of Lourdes Parish in Malverne. "I'm impatient and sick over discrimination," she said. "You reach a point where, by virtue of your silence, people think you agree with their prejudices. . . . I decided to let everyone know quietly and nicely where we stood on the racial question."[44] The Nassau County program was so successful that Council members in Suffolk County worked to establish an ecumenical Friendship Sunday on the same model.[45]

In order to inculcate the Church's teachings on racial justice in younger generations, the Interracial Council worked with the diocese's high schools, including St. Pius X Seminary in Uniondale and Chaminade High School in Mineola, to form junior chapters of the Council. Members organized panel discussions and book clubs for their fellow students and volunteered to tutor Black elementary school students among other activities.[46] In the wake of the racial riots that had gripped the nation in 1967 and 1968, the Council also worked with the diocesan superintendent of schools to introduce Catholic school principals and teachers to Black history and culture, and to assist them in implementing such lessons in their classrooms. A mandatory, four-week teacher workshop called Re-Education for Mutual Acceptance in the Rockville Centre Diocese (REMARC) was the longtime vision of Mrs. Betty Coles, the Catholic Interracial Council's education chair and a public-school educator, and was believed to be the first of its kind in the nation.[47]

The following year, the Council collaborated with *The Long Island Catholic* newspaper and the diocesan Department of Education to produce a seventeen-week series of bi-weekly articles on Black history that shed light on the current plight of Black Americans. Written by Leroy L. Ramsey, a professor of Black history at Hofstra University and a member of the faculty at Plainview High School, the articles were used as part of a mandatory curriculum in the diocese's seventh- and eighth-grade classrooms. Father Paul E. McKeever, the editor of *The Long Island Catholic*, expressed hope that parents, too, would read the first-of-its-kind series to "correct their own thinking" and to "eliminate the misconceptions, fears, myths, and stereotypes" that plagued interracial relations.[48] *The Long Island Catholic* proudly reported that public schools, universities, public libraries, and the Nassau County Historical Museum all requested the articles for use in their own programs, and teachers in diocesan parochial schools "expressed their enthusiasm for the program." Nearly 90 percent of the diocese's schools reported incorporating the articles into their curricula and principals reported that parental "opposition to the program had been considerably less than expected."[49] Indeed, the newspaper series was deemed so successful that, with financial support from Long Island Lighting Company, the diocesan educational television station produced a Black history television series entitled *Four Hundred Years*, which was also made available to all interested public schools.[50]

Despite these concerted efforts, members of the Interracial Council consistently doubted the effect they were having and were critical of the interracial commitment of the diocese, its priests, and people. In 1969, just eighteen months after Bishop Kellenberg had released a major statement on racial issues, members of the Council had largely negative evaluations of the diocese's response. Monsignor Michael McLaughlin assessed that work was proceeding "as well as could be expected," and Jean Dember, a Black member of the newly formed Diocesan Interracial Affairs Commission, said that its early discussions were "beyond my hopes."[51] But Mrs. Betty Coles, then president of the Catholic Interracial Council, saw no improvement in the coordination of the diocese's interracial efforts. Coles had stated that when she moved to Long Island in 1956, she was "shocked at the prejudice and discrimination" she found, which she thought was "as bad, if not worse than what [she] experienced in the Deep South."[52] Over a decade later, she said, there was a "lack of interest on the part of a large percentage of the clergy and laity," and lamented that the people tapped to lead diocesan "agencies and programs dealing with race" had "no knowledge, no expertise" on the problems of the day.[53] Father Lawrence E. Lucas, a Black priest from Harlem, told the Catholic Interracial Council that such organizations had served their purpose in the 1930s, '40s, and '50s, but that they were "performing no real function in the '70s."[54]

By the time the Council celebrated its tenth anniversary in 1973, the Watergate scandal, the war in Vietnam, and debates over the legality of abortion had come to center stage. The Council's then-president John Walsh acknowledged that membership in the CIC had peaked in the mid-1960s at about 400 but was down to just "50 or 60 active people," and that the home visits program with which the Council had begun, "served a purpose at the time" but had "died out" long ago. He attributed the waning interest in the

Council's activities to a general public apathy, in which people were "withdrawing from reality, staying home, watching TV."[55] By the early 1980s a Council-sponsored discussion on "Racism in Suffolk County" attracted just twenty-five people. Father Andrew Connolly cited this as proof that "people think that there is no longer a problem of racism" despite the fact that "there is a prejudice in most white people."[56] Just a few years earlier, Connolly had critiqued the diocesan presbyterate, suggesting that there were no more than "ten priests in this diocese that are seriously concerned about race."[57]

Our Lady of the Miraculous Medal Parish and Affordable Housing in Wyandanch

As civil rights institutions like the Interracial Council were waning in the late 1960s, activists' attention turned to community organizing to address poverty and systemic inequalities. Father Andrew Connolly's work at Our Lady of the Miraculous Medal Parish in Wyandanch is indicative of this shift in emphasis and revelatory of the centrality of grassroots efforts on the parish level in the Church's attempt to address matters of race and ethnicity, poverty and justice.

Wyandanch is an unincorporated area in Suffolk County's Town of Babylon. After World War II the relatively inexpensive housing in the already "somewhat integrated" area drew an influx of middle-class African Americans who found work in nearby state hospitals and military industries.[58] As Fr. Stephen A. Cuddeback, the founding pastor of Our Lady of the Miraculous Medal Parish recalled, the residents of Wyandanch "wanted to keep the area 'countried,'" however, and opposed the expansion of industry.[59] As a result, Wyandanch lacked job opportunities and had the highest tax rate in the Town of Babylon. As white residents began to move out of Wyandanch, poorer Blacks moved in. Wyandanch's population did not reach 6,000 until 1960, but by 1968 the population had nearly doubled to approximately 11,000 and the Black population increased by 90 percent.

Overtaxed and underresourced, Wyandanch seemed poised for the kind of social unrest plaguing America's cities in the late 1960s. Indeed, in August 1967 violence broke out in Wyandanch as groups of Black young adults smashed windows, overturned cars, set fire to a school auditorium, a VFW post, and an ambulance garage, and hurled bottles and rocks at police and firefighters.[60] *The Long Island Catholic* provided very limited coverage of the riots that consumed the nation's urban areas and made almost no mention of racial disturbances that occurred across Long Island.[61] But the summer after the riots in Wyandanch, the newspaper launched a lengthy series of investigative reports into conditions in the community. "The forces trying to keep Wyandanch cool this summer are not getting the support they need," one young resident worried. Another, Mrs. Betty Wilds, summarized Wyandanch's needs: "We need more shopping areas, better transportation, more jobs, an ambulance that can be used, better health care, more parks that look like parks and not overgrown lots." But the investigative reporters saw few resources the community could marshal to address these needs. "Like other communities on Long Island," they assessed, Wyandanch "has little or no sense of community, no self-government, no real identity, and no central institution to call its own."[62]

The Long Island Catholic was especially concerned with the role religion was playing in Wyandanch's confrontation with "race and poverty problems." The investigation showed that various denominations, and several Catholic organizations, were working to improve social services in the area. The St. Vincent de Paul Society opened a thrift store, sixty students from Holy Family Diocesan High School began a tutoring program, the diocese started a preschool program at Our Lady of the Miraculous Medal Parish, and Good Samaritan Hospital in West Islip collaborated with the Suffolk County Health Department to establish a health clinic in the community. But the reporters' overall evaluation was that religion had "generally failed in Wyandanch," that the churches had been "too parochial," and they had "misread the signs of the times." Citing Vatican II's Constitution on the Church in the Modern World, the editors called for the churches to develop an awareness of the conditions that had created the ghetto and to "join together," ecumenically, to solve Wyandanch's "social and moral problems."[63]

Black residents, too, said that church communities had not been sufficiently active participants in improving Wyandanch. Father John B. Hull, the administrator of Our Lady of the Miraculous Medal Parish, admitted this was "an unfortunate but valid impression." The majority of the parish's 1,000 families were white and were not "malicious or hostile," he said, but lived on the perimeter of Wyandanch and were "not sensitive" to the needs of poorer Black residents. Father Andrew Connolly, then the associate pastor, had hoped for some activism from the parish council but, he bemoaned, "we've done nothing."[64] In fact, Our Lady of the Miraculous Medal Parish was already beginning to address some immediate needs by paying the rent of a local cooperative grocery store, purchasing a station wagon for the Community Action Center, and lending the parish hall for various community gatherings including school board and scout troop meetings. And in the following years, the parish would work to address one of the area's most persistent long-term problems: the need for affordable housing. Our

Lady of the Miraculous Medal Parish was one of the founding members of the Wyandanch Community Development Corporation, which received a $25,000 grant from the Suffolk County Development Corporation for surveys and a master housing plan for Wyandanch.[65]

After several years' planning, the development corporation proposed the building of low-income housing consisting of 182 townhouses and apartments, ranging from one-room efficiencies to five-bedroom units. The complex was planned to house 692 people with 10 percent of the units going to senior citizens, 20 percent to low-income families, and 70 percent to moderate-income families. To be built by a private developer, the project was to receive mortgage assistance from the state Urban Development Corporation and contain its own sewage-treatment plant, laundry facilities, community meeting rooms, and recreation areas.[66]

The Commonwealth Housing Proposal, as the project was called, garnered support from Long Island's religious leaders, including the chief pastor of the Lutheran Church on Long Island. In June 1973 Bishop Walter Kellenberg wrote a public letter to Father Connolly, by then the administrator of Our Lady of the Miraculous Medal and secretary of the Wyandanch Community Development Corporation. Kellenberg called housing "the most critical problem on Long Island" and praised the proposal's "careful planning and close coordination with the Babylon Town Board."[67]

The project's opponents, however, compelled the state legislature to strip the Urban Development Corporation's power to override local zoning laws, which left the proposal's fate in the hands of the Babylon Town Board.[68] The "hastily-formed" Babylon Citizens for Home Rule, and the Wheatley Heights Civic Association, among other groups, warned that the housing development would raise taxes and overcrowd schools. *The Long Island Catholic* decried these arguments as scare tactics, seeing in their opposition "the ugly spectre of racial bigotry."[69] But the Babylon Town Board voted down the proposal arguing, among other things, that single-family homes on the site would generate more tax revenue, that the development would draw more welfare families to Wyandanch, and that so many young families with children would overburden the school district.[70]

A *Long Island Catholic* editorial called the rejection of the proposal a disappointment and judged that the stated reasons for the decision didn't "hold up under scrutiny." Having rejected a grassroots approach, in which Black residents tried to "solve their own problems," the editors said it was now "incumbent on the board to develop its own plan" to solve a housing crisis that would only get worse.[71] In fact, over the following decade, few low-income housing projects met any success on Long Island. The affordable housing crisis became so acute in the 1980s that an estimated 90,000 illegal apartments were created in the basements and attics of Long Island's single-family homes—an illegal market that accounted for one-third of the entire rental market.[72]

Black Catholics in Suburbia

Although Wyandanch was one of the larger African American communities on Long Island, Our Lady of the Miraculous Medal Parish had only eighty to ninety registered Black families in the late 1960s. This highlights the fact that, throughout the postwar period, the number of Black Catholics in Nassau and Suffolk Counties remained small, and they were dispersed throughout Long Island, hampering community-building and the diocese's attempts at ministry to this distinct group. As late as 1980, there were thought to be between 7,500 and 8,000 Black Catholics in the diocese out of a Catholic population of 1.2 million.[73] Mrs. Barbara Horsham-Brathwaite, who would serve as director of the diocesan ministry for Black Catholics, recalled attending Mass for years at Our Lady of Lourdes Parish in Malverne before she met another Black parishioner. "There are so many Masses here on Long Island," she said, "you could go back and forth and never meet everyone in the parish."[74]

In 1980 *The Long Island Catholic* printed a three-part series on the experiences of Black Catholics in the diocese and on their contribution to the local Church. The series revealed both Black Catholics' continued experience of racism in the Church and their sense that things had greatly improved. Interviews reflected praise for individual parishes, critiques of the diocese's overall effort to engage Black Catholics, and decidedly mixed opinions about one of the Church's most important ministries: the parochial school.

Mrs. Horsham-Brithwaite, herself a product of Catholic schooling, celebrated that "the Catholic church has been the easiest, private school system for black people to be educated in," but felt that her urban Catholic school had not prepared her for "communities in the suburbs where people were not used to seeing" Black Catholics.[75] Nathaniel and Marie Watson of Roosevelt were converts from the Baptist denomination, regular volunteers with Marriage Encounter, and their son, Joseph, was the only Black student at St. Pius X Preparatory Seminary in Uniondale. "Everywhere we go people are surprised that black Catholics exist. The days of overt racism are over," they said, and yet they still felt they experienced racism every day and that the Church needed to become "more sensitized to the cultural aspects of black people."[76]

Charles Burns of Lakeview, a retired Nassau County detective, had a son at Chaminade High School in Mineola and a daughter at St. Agnes High School in Rockville Centre. But his three older children had attended public schools because, at the time, the Catholic schools wouldn't admit them. "I guess they felt the parishioners weren't ready," Burns said. "I'm not bitter about it. It was not the time for it. It should have been . . . but in 25 years the Church has become more open to blacks. The Church has come a long way. I feel the Church has grown in every way," he said.[77] However, Mercedes Smallwood of Our Lady of the Miraculous Medal Parish in Wyandanch complained: "I don't feel the Church cares about me. OLMM Parish does and the priests do" but "I don't find love in the Catholic Church." As a member of the Black Catholic Lay Caucus, Smallwood had compiled a list of grievances against the diocese including that CCD materials contained stereotyped caricatures of Black people, and that there were insufficient Black teachers in parish schools. "I'm against Catholic schools," she said. They are places where "whites send their kids . . . because they want to get them away from blacks. You get a better religious education . . . in CCD programs," she argued.[78] Mrs. Sandra Thomas of Wheatley Heights, a social worker and parishioner of Our Lady of the Miraculous Medal Parish in Wyandanch, also praised her parish as "the most unique church" she had ever attended, with "a cross section of wealth and nationalities," and a "nice, warm feeling." But she, too, felt the Church as a whole had "failed to recognize" Black Catholics and rarely mentioned Black saints. The Church "does a lot for the poor," she said, but "helps quietly," and needs instead to "come out as a front runner."[79]

The following year, in 1981, the diocese established a new Office of Ministry for Black Catholics to increase the opportunities for Black lay leadership, to foster religious and priestly vocations among young Black Catholics, and to improve the whole Church's understanding of Black history and culture. Vincent F. A. Golphin, the office's founding director, stressed that Black Catholics tended to be scattered across parishes and therefore lacked "unifying forces." But he hoped that since Black Americans were "anxious to secure the advantages of Catholic education for their children," parochial schools might be a way for the diocese to "become a rapid agent for evolution within the black community."[80]

Hispanic Immigration to the Suburban Church

Catholics on Long Island were, however, increasingly focused on a different challenge, which became more evident in the late 1960s and early 1970s and has since come to define a new era for US Catholicism: the rising tide of immigration from Latin America. Drawn by employment in defense manufacturing industries, Puerto Rican immigrants began arriving on Long Island during World War II, and by the early 1950s were prominent in several communities on Long Island, especially Brentwood, Central Islip, Glen Cove, and Huntington Station.[81] Cuban refugees also arrived on Long Island in sizable numbers throughout the 1960s and totaled more than 5,000 by 1970.[82]

Some of the Church's earliest efforts to serve Spanish-speaking immigrants on Long Island were aimed primarily at improving conditions for migrant farm workers who were, in the late 1960s and early 1970s, living in shacks in Suffolk County. Monsignor James L. Griffin of St. Anthony Parish in East Northport, Sister Maureen Michael of the Dominican Sisters of the Sick and Poor, and laity involved in the Christian Family Movement provided the migrants with Mass, English tutoring, meals, and medical services.[83]

Recognizing the growing trend of Hispanic immigration, Bishop Kellenberg founded a Diocesan Office of the Spanish Apostolate as early as 1968, and shortly thereafter, in 1972, Catholic Charities opened an Office of Spanish Social Services. But from the 1960s until today, most of the responsibility for welcoming and assimilating Spanish-speaking Catholics into the life of the local Church fell to local parishes and pastors. St. Joseph the Worker Parish in East Patchogue began a monthly Spanish Mass in 1969 after recognizing that there were approximately 100 Spanish-speaking families living in the parish. That same year, Our Lady of Loretto Parish in Hempstead began a weekly Spanish Mass and held a dance for Spanish-speaking parishioners that drew several hundred attendees. At St. Patrick's in Glen Cove, the Spanish-speaking parishioners founded their own parish association but encouraged members to also join other parish societies so as to be "fully integrated into the life of the parish."[84]

By far the largest Spanish-speaking community in the diocese was centered in Brentwood, where two parishes spearheaded ministry to Hispanic Catholics. At St. Anne Parish, Spanish-speaking parishioners recruited families for the weekly Spanish Mass, formed a Rosary Apostolate among Puerto Ricans in the parish, and organized the diocese's first Cursillo in 1965. The Cursillo, which was introduced to the United States from Spain in 1957, is a three-day retreat aimed at deepening participants' commitment to the faith and making them active participants in the ministries of their parish. By 1975 some 500 retreatants from sixteen parishes across the diocese had made a Cursillo and Bishop Kellenberg had approved the establishment of a Cursillo House in which weekly meetings were held.[85]

In 1965 the diocese established a new parish in Brentwood, St. Luke's. Within its first year, Fr. Thomas A. Judge estimated that his parish had some 400 Puerto Rican families, which represented nearly 20 percent of the newborn parish, and stated that his "main concern" was "how to bring non-white families into the stream of parish life." The pastor turned a vacant ambulance garage into a Catholic center, recruited three Puerto Rican Sisters of St. Joseph to provide religious education to seventy Spanish-speaking children, and began learning Spanish.[86] "This is all new . . . and we still don't know what to do," Father Judge confessed. "We're trying to show them we're interested, that we care about all of them. We want to get them involved in the parish."[87]

With their motherhouse located in Brentwood, the Sisters of Saint Joseph also became involved in ministry to the Spanish-speaking. They established Operation Northwest in the summer of 1966 with $15,000 in federal funding from President Johnson's War on Poverty to aid poor Black and Puerto Rican grade-schoolers during the summer months, and to assist their parents with literacy. Originally housed in an area public school, the program moved to St. Anne's School the following summer. Enrollment more than doubled to 300 students, who were served by forty nuns working full-time on the program and another twenty-eight nuns who volunteered in their free time.[88]

Perhaps, the longest lasting parochial ministry to Hispanics, Pronto, was founded in 1969 by parishioners of St. Anne Parish to refer Spanish-speaking members of the community to existing social service agencies. "In Puerto Rico, the Church is everything. The first place the people go no matter what the problem is," explained Elizabeth Guanill, the chair of the Pronto committee. "When they come here, the American Church is very different, and they don't know how to approach the Church." With support from the diocesan office of Catholic Charities, Pronto opened in a rented storefront on Pineaire Drive and Fifth Avenue.[89] Three neighboring parishes—St. Luke in Brentwood, St. John of God in Central Islip, and St. Patrick in Bay Shore—joined St. Anne's in sponsoring Pronto both financially and with lay volunteers. Over the ensuing years, Pronto added its own services, including tutoring, transportation, a food pantry, and a thrift shop, and by the early 1980s was serving more than 7,000 families a year.[90]

The flow of Hispanic immigration to Long Island was, however, only then beginning to quicken. Between 1968 and 1972 alone, the New York State Department of Education found that the number of children with Spanish surnames in Nassau County's public schools more than doubled. Hundreds of thousands of refugees from El Salvador arrived in the United

States in the years leading up to that nation's civil war.[91] By 1983 there were an estimated 40,000 Salvadorans on Long Island and by 1987 that number had jumped to 100,000 or more. The vast majority of these refugees were undocumented immigrants from the rural, eastern section of El Salvador, especially La Union and Morazan.[92] With little education and few marketable skills, Salvadoran migrants benefited from changes in Long Island's demographics. An increase in the number of households with two working parents, and a "baby bust" in the 1970s and '80s that led to a decline in the number of young native-born workers, significantly increased the demand for low-wage service industry workers.[93] Altogether, by 1985 Hispanics made up approximately 11 percent of Long Island's population and there were an estimated 175,000 Spanish-speaking Catholics in the diocese.[94] This was, of course, just one small indication of a much broader national trend. The US Catholic Bishops estimate that between 1960 and 2012 growth in the number of Hispanics in the United States accounted for 70 percent of the growth in the US Catholic population.[95]

Hispanic Immigrants in Suburban Parishes

Catholic immigrants of the nineteenth century tended to settle in urban enclaves and were often provided national parishes, with their own priests to serve their spiritual and temporal needs. The Hispanic Catholics who immigrated to Long Island in the 1960s and '70s were, however, scattered throughout Long Island's suburban communities, settling wherever affordable housing could be found.[96] Already, by 1974 some seventeen parishes across Long Island provided at least some services for Spanish-speaking Catholics.[97] Some parishes, like St. Anne's in Brentwood, had been welcoming so many Hispanic Catholics for so long that they approximated a national parish, offering robust ministries in Spanish. Jose and Juanita Diaz had arrived on Long Island from Puerto Rico in 1956 and bought a house in Brentwood in 1962. "St. Anne's has been wonderful for the spiritual needs of the Puerto Rican people," Mrs. Diaz said in 1969. "I have no complaints."[98]

But without the aid of national parishes, the majority of Hispanic Catholic immigrants were made to adjust to American life, and find their place in the American Church, in parishes they shared with a majority white and English-speaking community.[99] These suburban parishes were premised on an Americanized Catholicism that downplayed ethnic expressions in liturgical and pious devotions. Hispanic immigrants' desire to worship in Spanish, and to observe the pious practices and devotions of their homelands, posed new challenges in suburban parishes no longer accustomed to ethnic expressions of Catholicism. As a 1974 *Long Island Catholic* article argued, Hispanics' "feelings about religion are out of kilter with those of most US-born Catholics" and the Catholicism of the post-ethnic suburbs. To the Spanish-speaking Catholic, "religion is devotional" and "there are novenas and rosaries to say, candles to light, and statues to adorn with flowers." The Spanish-speaking "do not want to relinquish their special customs," the article summarized, "they are looking for acceptance and appreciation without absorption."[100] Carlos Figueroa of St. Anne Parish boldly asserted, "it's an injustice to force people who do not understand the language to attend a Mass they don't understand and to listen to a sermon they don't understand."[101]

Those involved in Hispanic ministry in the Dioceses of Rockville Centre assessed that, by the 1970s, progress had been made in "eliminating the terrible sense of alienation experienced by many Spanish-speaking Catholics."[102] But few parishes were said to have achieved a balance between promoting parish unity among English and Spanish-speaking parishioners and preserving the group identity of Hispanic Catholics. "Our goal is to accomplish a blend of all the different elements in the parish while encouraging them to retain their ethnic identity," said Fr. William Murphy, pastor of Our Lady of Loretto Church in Hempstead. "We're trying to grow in community, but we haven't quite accomplished that yet."[103]

Strikingly, few attributed this to deliberate indifference or prejudice. Father Tomaz Gormide, a Brazilian priest assigned to Corpus Christi Parish in Mineola, admitted in 1983 that some Catholics, including priests, objected to helping Salvadoran immigrants because they were illegal aliens.[104] But most people involved in Spanish ministries blamed the dispersion of Hispanics across the diocese, the lack of Spanish-speaking priests, and the fundamental challenge of finding ways to "both meet the special needs of the Spanish-speaking" and integrate them into the broader parish community.[105] Only in 1984 did the Diocese of Rockville Centre undertake a study to identify where Long Island's Spanish-speaking population was concentrated and how to improve pastoral services to those communities.[106] Father John Krane of St. Anne Parish in Brentwood felt the diocese was slow to recognize the needs of Hispanics Catholics, less because of "deliberate indifference" or racism, and more because of the "elusiveness and mobility" that characterized an immigrant group, many of whom were in the country illegally, and all of whom were desperate for housing.[107]

Despite some positive steps, Hispanic Catholics and the priests who ministered to them argued that the diocese and its parishes weren't doing enough to care for Spanish-speaking Catholics. At a gathering of the diocese's Hispanic community, held at St. Brigid Parish in Westbury in 1985, Lydia Rivera said that "the lack of enthusiasm on the part of local priests was causing Hispanics to abandon the Catholic Church and seek recognition in other sects." The 800 attendees recommended that the Church "utilize Hispanic devotions to maintain the faith and participate in Apostolic work" and that priests be made to "study the culture of Hispanic countries so as to respect their customs."[108]

The White Ethnic Revival

While some English-speaking Catholics may simply have rejected Hispanic immigrants' assertion of a right to their traditional forms of religiosity, others took inspiration from it, as well as from the Black pride of the civil rights movement and the Second Vatican Council's appreciation of enculturated expressions of faith. Lamenting that they and their immigrant forbears had been encouraged to abandon "old world" traditions, these laity participated in a "white ethnic revival" of the late 1960s and '70s.[109] At this time, commentators noted a distinct increase in the number of Americans expressing interest in their ethnic heritage—in the language, music, literature, and history of European homelands—even in suburbia where it had been thought that ethnicity was surrendered in favor of identification as a white homeowner. This so-called ethnic revival was evident in the activity of ethnic fraternal associations, in popular interest in genealogical research and travel to ancestral homelands, and even in the rise of scholarly research into ethnicity including through the creation of the Center for Urban Ethnic Affairs and the Center for the Study of American Pluralism.[110] However, experts debated whether or not this truly marked a revival of ethnicity and what had inspired it.

Some scholars, including sociologist Herbert Gans, argued forcefully that there was no ethnic revival, that ethnic assimilation continued apace, and that third-generation Italians, for example, exhibited a merely "symbolic ethnicity." This entirely voluntary embrace of ethnic heritage was confined to private, "leisure time activities such as eating spaghetti, purchasing ancestral collectibles, attending traditional religious festivals, or visiting the native country of one's grandparents."[111] What looked like an ethnic revival, these scholars argued, was evidence of the upward social mobility of third-generation ethnics, and a white backlash against the civil rights movement and the political and social gains of African Americans.[112] White ethnic Americans sought to absolve themselves of privilege, these scholars held, by identifying as members of an immigrant ethnic or religious group which had historically faced discrimination.[113]

Other scholars, including sociologists Nathan Glazer and Daniel Patrick Moynihan, argued that ethnicity had survived the migration to the suburbs and that the ethnic revival was not merely a racist backlash against Black Power. It was, rather, a response to lingering anti-ethnic prejudices in American society and had been inspired by Black, Puerto Rican, and Native American assertions of pride and activism.[114] Unsurprisingly, numerous Catholic intellectuals, including Andrew Greeley and Michael Novak, and activists such as Msgr. Geno Baroni and future US Senator Barbara Mikulski, were leaders of the white-ethnic revival.[115] They repudiated what they called the "'cultural genocide' of the melting pot," and the eagerness of some Catholics for denigrating European Catholic ethnicity and assimilating into American culture.[116] Inspired by the civil rights movement and the Second Vatican Council, these theorists posited that healthy ethnic communities could be a refuge from the upheavals plaguing the Church and nation, and a springboard for a multiracial, multiethnic, working-class coalition.[117]

Between 1971 and 1982 *The Long Island Catholic* published Greeley's weekly syndicated opinion piece, which often addressed issues of ethnicity. From his own survey data Greeley regularly argued that intermarriage and suburbanization had not destroyed ethnic differences, and he praised Black pride as a model for white ethnics, insisting that pluralism and respect for heritage and culture did not inevitably lead to conflict. But Greeley saved his sharpest words for elite liberal Catholics such as Fr. Donald Campion, SJ, the editor of *America* magazine who in 1975 dismissed the focus on white ethnicity as "primitive" and "un-Christian." Greeley claimed that *America* had "jumped on the bandwagon" of what he called "every faddish particularism," from liberation theology to Black, Latino, and Indian power. It was only when ethnic Catholic particularism opposed the "bland, empty, dull universalism of Midtown Manhattan," Greeley complained, that liberal Catholics abandoned their professed love for heterogeneity and pluralism.[118]

On Long Island there was ample evidence of renewed ethnic pride in the 1970s and '80s. In 1975 Holy Trinity High School in Hicksville began hosting annual Oktoberfest celebrations that in 1983 included a Bavarian Folk Mass to mark the 300th anniversary of German immigration to the United States.[119] When the pastor of St. Isidore Parish in Riverhead planned a renovation of the church to celebrate its 75th anniversary in 1977, parishioners complained that he had done so without consulting them. The bishop had to visit the parish to quell their anger and assure them "there was never any intention to demean or interfere with the fine Polish heritage embodied" in their "landmark structure."[120] A few years later, in 1982, Polish Americans at St. Isidore Parish in Riverhead, Our Lady of Poland Church in Southampton, St. Ladislaus Parish in Hempstead, St. Hyacinth Parish in Glen Cove, and Our Lady of Ostrabrama Parish in Cutchogue organized Masses and processions to mark the 600th anniversary of the arrival in Jasna Gora, Poland, of the icon of Our Lady of Czestochowa.[121]

A revival of interest in Italian ethnicity was especially evident in the establishment of Italian *festa* celebrations even in parishes that had never had one before and were never national parishes. In 1971 the Assumption of the Blessed Virgin Mary Parish in Centereach established a three-day "Italian style festa" in honor of St. Joseph including a Mass, procession, food, and music. *The Long Island Catholic* explained that "nostalgically remembering . . . the fervor and frolic of the Italian street feasts," Mrs. Tess DePasquale had convinced her pastor and fellow parishioners to "recapture the aura of bygone religious feasts."[122] But it was also clear that such celebrations no longer functioned the same way they had for first-generation Italian immigrants. The year before, in 1970, Sacred Heart Parish in Island Park began sponsoring a Feast of San Gennaro which, by its fifth year, was attracting between 65,000 and 70,000 visitors.[123] Although the festival was "predominantly Italian in nature," Fr. Harold F. Langley called his parish "a League of Nations" and said that the purpose of the feast was to "develop a spirit of unity" among various local constituencies. Founding chairwoman Phyllis DeSiena oversaw some 500 volunteers "representing a variety of ethnic backgrounds and faiths," and serving not just pizza, sausage and peppers, and Ferrara's Italian cookies, but corn on the cob, hamburgers, and even knishes.[124]

The revival of interest in Italian ethnic heritage also did not translate into greater demand for, or appreciation of, religious services in the Italian language. Priests of the diocese gathered in 1982 to "share their experiences and frustration" in serving the non-English-speaking Italian families in the diocese. They estimated that, thanks to modern-day immigration, there were about 5,000 Italian-speakers in the diocese, including about a thousand parishioners at both St. Rocco in Glen Cove and St. Brigid in Westbury, and about 800 at Our Lady of Grace in West Babylon. Although Our Lady of Grace had a weekly Sunday Mass in Italian, Fr. Walter Tonelotto discovered that religious education and holy hours in Italian had to be organized by Italian-speaking families in their own homes because there was no network of services provided by parishes or the diocese.[125]

Conclusion

Postwar suburbanization diminished the importance of ethnicity and elevated the importance of race as markers of parish boundaries, which made integrating and serving Black Catholics and Hispanic Catholic immigrants more challenging for the suburban Church. Racist policies and practices in real estate and home financing resulted in high levels of racial segregation in suburbia, limiting the overall number of Black Catholics on Long Island and segregating them into smaller enclaves. Already a minority within the American Church, Black Catholics on Long Island struggled to form community among themselves and to garner appreciation from diocesan officials and white Catholics for their particular history and needs.

Throughout the postwar period, suburban Catholic parishes were also premised on an Americanized expression of the faith that diminished ethnic forms of piety and communal celebration. Catholic pastoral leaders abandoned the use of national parishes in favor of integrating various Catholic ethnic groups into territorial parishes. When Latin American immigration to Long Island increased dramatically in the late 1960s, Hispanic Catholics were scattered across the diocese wherever affordable housing could be found. Over time, concentrations of Hispanic Catholics in certain parishes created *de facto* national parishes where Spanish-speaking ministries were robust. But many parishes with a majority white population also had sizable Hispanic populations and ministering to the Spanish-speaking in such mixed parishes proved a significant challenge.

Nationwide, dioceses and parishes today continue to wrestle with the pastoral challenges that immigration, increasing ethnic diversity, and mixed parishes pose. The fact that so many new immigrants now make their first American home in suburbs heightens the challenge to pastoral leaders. However, it also provides scholars with unique opportunities to explore the ways that ethnicity, religion, and assimilation function in suburban communities as opposed to urban contexts, and to uncover commonalities and crucial differences in the stories of successive generations of immigrant Catholics. This much is already clear: just as Catholic immigrants of the nineteenth century made the cities of the Northeast and Midwest the beating heart of American Catholicism, and the postwar generation shifted the epicenter of the Church from cities to suburbs, so too post-1968 waves of Hispanic, Asian, and African immigrants have once again made a sizable portion of American Catholicism an immigrant church, and have increasingly shifted the heart of US Catholicism to the cities and suburbs of the South and West.

SIX

Suburban Catholic Education: Parochial Schools, CCD, and Ecclesiastical Polarization

On September 11, 1966, Our Lady of Grace Parish in West Babylon broke ground for a $1.5-million, twenty-four-room school and convent.[1] The parish had been founded in 1962 when territory and approximately 6,000 families from St. Joseph Parish in Babylon, Our Lady of Perpetual Help Parish in Lindenhurst, and Our Lady of the Miraculous Medal Parish in Wyandanch were broken off to create one of five new parishes erected to mark the Diocese of Rockville Centre's fifth anniversary. The young parish had already dedicated, in June 1965, an award-winning, modernist auditorium-church, designed by parishioner Ralph Mignone, which it planned to use as a gymnasium and cafeteria for its new school once a church was added to the parish plant.[2]

Like so many suburban Catholics, parishioners at Our Lady of Grace were eager for a parish school. Indeed, some of the first parishioners were said to have resented being forced by the diocese to transfer to the newly formed parish from parishes that already had schools. Father John E. Leonard, Our Lady of Grace's pastor, recounted that on his first night in the temporary rectory a mother rang the doorbell to demand, "Father, when are you going to build a school?"[3] As the building was going up, Leonard thanked his parishioners for surpassing the funding drive goal and enthused: "what better way to fulfill our responsibility to our children than to help 'pave the road ahead' through the gentle ministrations of the Sisters who will teach them daily in our school."[4] But then, just two months before the building's June 1968 dedication, Leonard announced that it would not, in fact, be a parochial school but would rather serve as a religious education center for the parish's CCD classes.

Parishioners had assumed that because Leonard's sister, Joan de Lourdes Leonard, was a Sister of St. Joseph, that their pastor would be able to secure

Figure 6.1. Fr. John Leonard, pastor of Our Lady of Grace, and Sr. Dorothy Fowler, CSJ, survey the parish's newly completed school building.
Source: Box 3, Archives of Our Lady of Grace Parish, West Babylon, NY.

twenty sisters to teach in the new parish school. They had also been told during the fundraising campaign that the children of volunteers and donors would receive first priority for admission. But only four sisters proved available for assignment to the parish, and the hiring of a lay faculty would have meant increased tuition costs. Even more fundamentally, the impressively large school still had capacity for only 1,200 students, just 20 percent of the 6,400 children who were eligible for admission.[5] "It is impossible to accept everyone," Leonard said, "How do you choose?"[6] And so, after conferring with "trustees, the clergy, and several parishioners," Leonard sought the bishop's approval to open the new building as a religious education center.[7] Our Lady of Grace became the third parish in the diocese to choose having a religious education center over a parish school.[8]

This was just one of the first signs that even amid a postwar schoolbuilding boom, suburbanization was undermining the parochial school's privileged place in American Catholicism and transforming conceptions of how the faith should be passed down to the next generation.[9] The 1950s and early 1960s are remembered as the heyday of the American Catholic school and conjure images of bishops breaking ground for or dedicating new parochial schools weekly, and young habited sisters presiding over classrooms overflowing with uniformed students. The surfeit of 1950s institutional buildings dotting the American Catholic landscape today—and now requiring expensive deferred maintenance—testifies that those were indeed boom years for Catholic schools. Yet even as dioceses built dozens of new parish schools in the 1950s and 1960s, they simply could not keep up with demographic expansion in the suburbs and parents' demands for Catholic schools. The long-held dream of educating every Catholic child in a parochial school slipped further and further from reach. There were never enough religious sisters to fully staff the suburbs' new parochial schools, and rising educational costs, including the salaries that had to be paid to an increasing number of lay teachers, drove up parish schools' tuition. In addition, alongside a school, suburban parishes had to provide a CCD program for the exponentially larger number of parish children who attended public schools.

Such rising costs led many suburban parishes established in the late 1950s and early 1960s to forgo opening a parochial school entirely even when they could afford to build a school building. Instead, they chose to operate religious education centers to provide CCD instruction for all their young people. In many ways, this represented the triumph of parochial schools' critics who had argued that a separate Catholic educational system was both unaffordable and undesirable, and that CCD programs could provide comparable or even superior faith formation. In the 1970s and '80s, as demographic change and continuously rising tuition costs drove down parochial school enrollments, parents who still desired Catholic education for their children were pitted against bishops in debates over the closure of schools. With increasing percentages of Catholic children in afterschool religious education programs, debates also arose about how successful such programs were at forming youth in the practice of the faith, especially absent the support of a Catholic subculture. These debates not only revealed the limits of the laity's influence on Church decision-making, but they also became entwined with contemporaneous debates about the interpretation of Vatican II and the morality of abortion, and thus reflected and fueled polarization within the Church. Altogether, postwar suburbanization's effects on Catholic education remain some of the most pressing challenges confronting American Catholicism to this day.

The Demand for Catholic Schools

In the 1840s and 1850s both nativist anti-Catholicism and a Catholic spirit of exceptionalism led American Catholics to create a network of parallel institutions to defend against both persecution and assimilation. By far the most important of these institutions was the parochial school, which was the principal means of educating and socializing young Catholics in the faith.[10] The American bishops were so convinced that no ministry of the Church was as effective as the parish school in transmitting the faith to the next generation that in 1850 Archbishop John Hughes of New York argued the time had come "to build the schoolhouse first and the church afterward." But it was in the child-centered postwar suburbs that the parochial school became the center of parish life more than ever before.[11] Stories of suburban Catholics who purchased homes to be near a parochial school, or who begged their pastors to open a school, are legion. Andrew Greeley lamented that too many suburban parishioners were "only too quick" to complain that their pastor hadn't built or expanded a parochial school quickly enough.[12]

Why were these parents so insistent that their children have a Catholic school education? Writing in 1964 Fr. Daniel E. Fagan, a faculty member at St. Pius X Seminary and a weekend associate at St. Pius X Parish in Plainview, said that "the basic answer lies in the fact that the American public school system has never been able to provide what Catholics consider a complete education."[13] When they were asked, Catholic parents said much the same. In April 1959, when Our Holy Redeemer School in Freeport announced that it would have to restrict the size of its classes, 300 parents camped out in 40-degree temperatures and 20–30 mph winds to register their children for one of the 100 available spaces. Sister Clare Therese, the school's principal, called the vigil an "edifying tribute to Catholic education." Two men—both members of the parish and fathers of five waiting to register their sons—explained why they were so intent on placing their children in a Catholic school. Bill Sheering, a graduate of a Catholic high school and college, explained that he "didn't believe in the progressive education taught in the public schools," and said that he wanted his children "to have discipline and learn the three Rs." Joseph Byrne added: "I consider the learning of religion of utmost importance and the released-time program (of the public schools) is not sufficient. I want all my children educated in a Catholic atmosphere."[14] For these parents, one hour per week of religious instruction in a CCD program could never replace the holistic formation they expected their children to receive if they were suffused in a Catholic school environment.

Such overwhelming demand for parochial schools marked the early years of the postwar suburban parishes. Between 1945 and 1949 the number of families in St. Aidan Parish in Williston Park more than doubled

Figure 6.2. Opening day of St. Frances de Chantal School, 1956.
Source: Box 3, Archives of St. Frances de Chantal Parish, Wantagh, NY.

from 700 to 1,600. Soaring building costs and the death of a pastor delayed the parish's dream of building a school, but when Fr. Raymond Clark was named pastor in 1947 he "was under pressure to erect a parish school." In 1949 St. Aidan's was the first parish in the Diocese of Brooklyn to receive permission to build a school since the end of World War II. The building fund's goal of $150,000 was surpassed in a month and in the fall of 1950 a school accommodating 1,000 children was dedicated. The school was so quickly overcrowded that in 1955 a second school was built so that the total enrollment of St. Aidan's topped 1,600 students.[15] That same year, St. Brigid Parish in Westbury built a new $900,000 building for its parish school, which had been founded in 1915. Although the building had room for 900 students, "due to the constant influx of new families," overflow classes had to be held in the parish hall for the school's 1,200 students, and still some 1,500 children remained in CCD.[16]

This pattern of demand continued when the Diocese of Rockville Centre was established in 1957. At that time, fifty of the diocese's parishes had more than 400 baptisms a year, with a few celebrating as many as 900 baptisms a year. As the diocese's first superintendent of schools Msgr. Edgar

McCarren noted, "this meant that every year, at the age of six, there was a solid phalanx of 400 or more kids coming up wanting to get into school. If you had a Catholic school, and you had a large one with three classrooms on the first-grade level, and you could put 50 kids in each class, you could take 150 of the 300 or 400" children who would apply.[17] At St. Ignatius Loyola Parish in Hicksville, Msgr. Lawrence Ballweg remembered there being one classroom with 100 children in first grade, but that there were still "people who couldn't get their kids into Catholic school" and who were unhappy because "they felt we should be able to care for all of them."[18]

The Catholic School Building Boom

The parishes in the best position to provide families with the possibility of a Catholic education were long-established parishes, some of which already had small parochial schools. In the early 1950s many parishes that had been founded in the first half of the century either expanded their preexisting school buildings or established a school for the first time. Sacred Heart Parish in Cutchogue and Corpus Christi Parish in Mineola, for example, were both established in 1901 and built parish schools in 1950 and 1954, respectively. St. Barnabas the Apostle Parish in Bellmore, founded in 1912, opened its school in 1932, and in 1954 completed a school expansion that accommodated 900 students.[19] So, too, St. William the Abbot Parish, established in 1928 in Seaford, opened its school in 1954, and St. Anne Parish, Garden City, which was established in 1929, opened a school in 1951.

However, the parishes established in Nassau and Suffolk Counties between the end of World War II and the erection of the Diocese of Rockville Centre in 1957 were frequently unable to open a parish school for a decade or more. And this, despite the fact that the Diocese of Brooklyn's Building Commission stated that the building of a parish school "should take first place in all planning of new parishes with the church the last item of construction."[20] St. Martha Parish in Uniondale, for example, was founded in 1949 and grew from under 500 parishioners to more than 4,500 parishioners in its first ten years. The parish built and paid for a $350,000 church for 700 congregants in 1953, before it opened a $950,000 school with fourteen classrooms in 1957. The parish then added six more classrooms in 1959 to bring the school's enrollment to 1,000 students.[21]

Founded in 1951, Holy Family Parish in Hicksville had 2,280 families with 3,444 children when its first census was conducted in 1952. In the fall of 1953 the parish dedicated a rectory and convent, as well as a chapel for 300, with a connected multipurpose auditorium that allowed

Table 6.1 Parishes and Parochial Schools in Nassau and Suffolk Counties, 1945–1957

Parish Established	Parish (County)	School Opened
1948	Our Lady of Fatima, Manorhaven (N)	-
	St. Anthony of Padua, Rocky Point (S)	-
	St. Bernard, Levittown (N)	1962
	St. Margaret of Scotland, Selden (S)	-
	St. Sylvester, Medford (S)	-
1949	St. James, Setauket (S)	-
	St. Jude, Mastic Beach (S)	-
	St. Martha, Uniondale (N)	1957
1950	Blessed Sacrament, Valley Stream (N)	1957
	St. Therese of Lisieux, Montauk (S)	1959
1951	Holy Family, Hicksville (N)	1960
	St. Anthony of Padua, East Northport (S)	-
	St. James, Seaford (N)	1962
	St. Vincent de Paul, Elmont (N)	1961
1952	Sacred Heart, N. Merrick (N)	1959
	St. Edward the Confessor, Syosset (N)	1961
	St. Frances de Chantal, Wantagh (N)	1956
	St. Patrick, Smithtown (S)	1966
	St. Rose of Lima, Massapequa (N)	1960
1953	Our Lady of Mercy, Hicksville (N)	1962
	St. Frances Cabrini, Coram (S)	-
1955	Assumption of the Blessed Virgin Mary, Centereach (S)	CCD Center, 1971
	Maria Regina, Seaford (N)	1962
	Our Lady of Lourdes, Massapequa Park (N)	1962
	St. Joseph the Worker, East Patchogue (S)	1960
	St. Pius X, Plainview (N)	1959
1956	Our Lady of Lourdes, West Islip (S)	1965
	SS. Cyril and Methodius, Deer Park (S)	1962

Note: N = Nassau County; S = Suffolk County

for an additional 700 seats at Sunday Mass and classroom space for religious education during the week. "Many of the parents were already thinking 'Catholic school' for their growing offspring," a parish journal records, "but Holy Family School was several years in the future." Not until 1957 did the parish purchase land from the Hicksville School District and begin planning a sixteen-classroom school. Fundraising efforts were so successful, however, that even before construction began eight classrooms were added to the project, which was completed in September 1960.[22] Overall, the diocese's school-building efforts were impressive. The diocese inherited approximately seventy parochial elementary schools, educating nearly 47,000 students, when it was established in 1957 and the diocese added four new schools in its first year.[23] Between 1957 and 1962, twenty-six new elementary schools were built and expansions were made at thirty-eight more grade schools, resulting in the addition of some 40,000 desks in the diocese's first five years.[24]

Bishop Kellenberg also launched the diocese's single-largest building campaign to address the need for more Catholic high schools. In the 1920s and '30s, many urban dioceses had increased the number of their Catholic high schools as secondary education became more universal. As the number of young people seeking a Catholic high school education rose even higher in the postwar years, these dioceses found the need to expand further. During Archbishop Molloy's tenure as bishop of Brooklyn, from 1922 to 1956, twelve private and diocesan high schools were opened in Brooklyn and Queens, but in 1960 his successor, Bishop Bryan J. McEntegart, was compelled to launch a $37-million campaign to build six additional diocesan high schools. Between 1957 and 1968 enrollment in the Catholic high schools of Brooklyn and Queens rose from 11,563 to 22,867.[25] Similarly, during Cardinal Spellman's tenure as archbishop of New York, from 1939 to 1967, the number of high schools in the archdiocese rose from seventy-five to ninety-nine and their enrollment increased fourfold from 12,187 students to 50,037.[26]

When the Diocese of Rockville Centre was established in 1957, there were thirteen private Catholic high schools in Nassau and Suffolk Counties, almost all of them operated by religious orders. Within the first two years of the diocese's existence, the pastors of Holy Family Parish in Hicksville, St. William the Abbot Parish in Seaford, St. Joseph Parish in Babylon, St. Barnabas Parish in Bellmore, and St. Frances de Chantal Parish in Wantagh all approached Bishop Kellenberg for permission to build parochial high schools. These requests were strong proof of the need for more Catholic high schools on Long Island, but they were all denied as the diocese was envisioning a more comprehensive approach akin to the high school campaign undertaken in the Diocese of Brooklyn.[27]

On March 12, 1963, Kellenberg proposed, and all the pastors of the diocese "overwhelmingly approved," a plan for the Diocese of Rockville Centre to build four regional diocesan high schools—two in Nassau and two in Suffolk County—each able to accommodate 2,400 students.[28] In September of that year, the diocese launched a funding drive in which 35,000 lay volunteers solicited pledges from 225,000 households. Monsignor Henry Reel recalls that the drive was "met with wide approval and enthusiastic support," proving the laity's unquestionable commitment to Catholic education, and providing "a very unifying experience" for the still young diocese.[29] Over 17,000 faithful attended the drive's kick-off celebration at Roosevelt Raceway and *The Long Island Catholic* published near weekly updates on

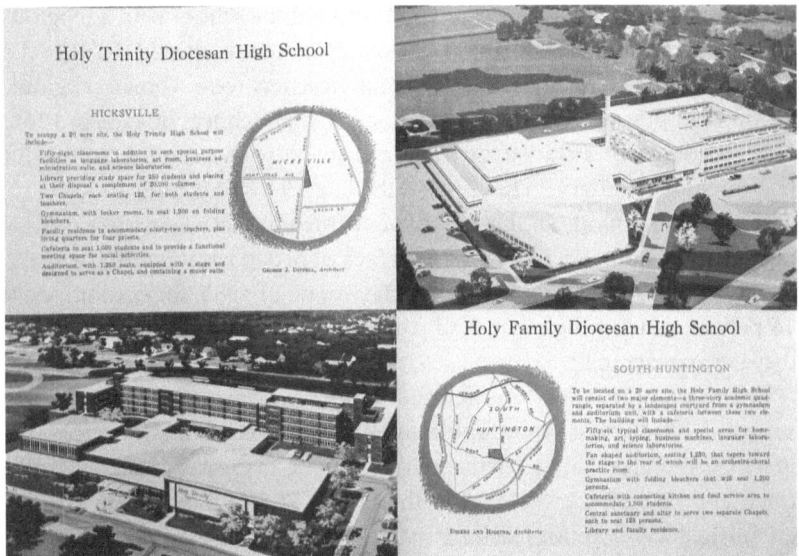

Figure 6.3. Campaign brochure showing two of the Diocese of Rockville Centre's four proposed high schools, 1963. *Source*: Box 131, Folder: HS Campaign, Chancellor's Collection, Subject Files, ADRVC.

the drive's progress, celebrating parishes that reached and exceeded their pledge goal.[30] St. Paul the Apostle Parish in Jericho boasted that parishioners pledged 60 percent more than their parish goal and even in 1971 the fiftieth anniversary journal of Our Lady of Victory Parish in Floral Park proudly recalled the fact that the parish exceeded their assessed goal of $250,000 by $70,000.[31] Thus the diocesan campaign's overall pledge goal was reached in just nine months, instead of the three years that had been anticipated, and nearly $25 million was ultimately raised.[32] By 1966 all four high schools—Holy Trinity in Hicksville, Maria Regina in Uniondale, Holy Family in South Huntington, and St. John the Baptist in West Islip—were welcoming their first freshman classes, which boosted the total number of students in the diocese's Catholic high schools by more than 25 percent to just over 12,000 students.[33]

Critiques of the Parochial School

This postwar building boom—like the American Catholic educational system itself—was premised on the presence of consecrated religious, especially religious sisters, who not only taught virtually for free but also ensured the quality of religious instruction and suffused the school with a religious atmosphere. When the Diocese of Rockville Centre was erected, 1,071 of the diocese's 1,300 elementary and secondary teachers were women religious, brothers, or priests.[34] When the four diocesan high schools opened in 1966, each school's staff included approximately two dozen sisters from two different religious orders.[35] However, in the late 1940s and early 1950s there had been concerns about the quality of instruction that sisters were providing in secular subjects because of their lack of pedagogical training and the unwieldy number of children in each classroom. In 1955, for example, only 16 percent of teaching sisters had completed three years of college before they began teaching.[36]

Intent on proving the excellence of Catholic schools, the hierarchy and superiors of religious communities developed Sister Formation programs in which young teaching sisters received training in the subjects they would teach and in pedagogy.[37] In 1955 the Sisters of St. Joseph of Brentwood established a college for teaching sisters—the first four-year college of any kind in Suffolk County—under the direction of Sr. Mary Meany, CSJ, a national leader in the Sister Formation movement.[38] A decade later, the Sisters of St. Dominic in Amityville founded St. Albert the Great College, as a branch of Molloy College in Rockville Centre, to prepare their sisters for the classroom.[39] The nationwide effort to improve the training of teaching sisters paid dividends: by 1964, 80 percent of sisters only began teaching after having finished at least three years of college studies.[40]

Spawned by concerns over the quality of teaching in suburban parochial schools, Sister Formation programs in turn had a profound impact on the religious women who participated in them. These programs exposed participating nuns to the most recent developments in theology, and to members of other religious communities, and were thereby an important catalyst for the reform of religious life sanctioned by the Second Vatican Council. In turn, however, the revolutionary changes that the 1960s brought to religious life would also lead to the closure of Sister Formation programs. As the number of young women entering religious life declined, the percentage of postulants who already had college degrees rose, and as sisters moved away from teaching to other ministries, the Sister Formation programs shuttered. Long Island's Brentwood College closed in 1971 after having educated 491 sisters for classroom teaching.[41]

Concern for the quality of classroom instruction also led Catholic schools to begin limiting class size. In some instances, parochial schools had classes of seventy or eighty students. In a 1982 interview Msgr. Edgar McCarren recalled having been "one of the first Catholic School

Figure 6.4. The 3B and 4B classroom in St. Anne School, April 1946. *Source*: Archives of St. Anne Parish, Brentwood, NY.

Superintendents in the country to set a limit on the number of children in Catholic schools," though he admitted he used fire safety, not pedagogy, as his excuse in order to undercut potential complaints from parents.[42] A year after a 1958 fire killed ninety-two students and three teaching sisters at Our Lady of the Angels School in Chicago, Bishop Kellenberg announced that class sizes throughout the Diocese of Rockville Centre would be limited to fifty students.[43]

While class limits improved teacher-student ratios, they compounded the shortage of available desks in Catholic schools and of religious sisters for faculties. Religious orders had never been able to fully meet the demands for teaching sisters that the suburban expansion of Catholic schools had placed on them. While vocations to women's religious life increased by 21 percent between 1945 and 1950 the number of students in parochial schools increased by 200 percent.[44] From the very beginning of the suburban boom, lay teachers were recruited to fill out the staffs of parochial schools. This need only grew as the number of parochial schools and students outstripped even the growing number of sisters in the 1960s.[45] Already by 1962 lay teachers in the Diocese of Rockville Centre comprised

35 percent of the school system's staff, and in the academic year 1967–68—the year of the highest student enrollment in Long Island's Catholic schools—only 1,500 of the nearly 2,500 teachers were religious.[46]

In turn, the necessity of paying lay faculty drove up Catholic schools' tuition demands, as did inflation, and increases in other educational costs including specialized facilities and equipment like science labs and audiovisual technologies. The expense of building and operating parochial schools was a major element of critics' arguments against a separate Catholic educational system. This argument was bolstered by the fact that suburban Catholic parents also faced the financial strain of ever-increasing property taxes. Between 1950 and 1960, property taxes in Nassau and Suffolk Counties increased by 469 percent, from $31.7 million to $180.4 million, in large part because of public school districts' need to expand their facilities.[47]

The argument against parochial schools, however, wasn't solely about financing. In 1964 the critique of and nationwide debate over Catholic schools hit a high point when a Catholic housewife and mother of five boys, Mary Perkins Ryan, published *Are Parochial Schools the Answer?* and decidedly answered in the negative. As a *Long Island Catholic* article summarized, Ryan "proposed that Catholic schools be abolished," because she felt "superior spiritual formation" could be provided for "more Catholic children in programs held outside schools."[48] Even if it were possible for every Catholic child to attend a parish school, Ryan said, "I am not convinced that attendance at a Catholic school would be the best way of preparing a young person for Catholic living in today's world." Parochial schools were "a sheltered, even a hothouse" environment that did not prepare students for the "prevailing secular atmosphere" in which they would live and be called to spread the Gospel. Freed from the financial burdens of a parochial school, parishes, pastors, and parents could "act more fully as responsible members of the community."[49] That same year, Fr. Barry McGannon, SJ, concurred and suggested in *Christian Wisdom and Christian Formation* that parochial school buildings become schools of religion to "compliment rather than compete with" public schools.[50]

Religious Education Centers

Such proposals essentially aimed to extend to all Catholic youth an arrangement that had existed to provide religious instruction for public school students since the early twentieth century. Catholic leaders, while encouraging the expansion of parochial schools, also supported the creation of release time programs that dismissed public school students early to receive instruction in their faith.[51] New York first proposed release time programs in 1917 and implemented them in 1923. Governor Herbert Lehman expanded the program in 1940 and the number of students in New York City's release time classes grew from 3,000 in 1941 to 105,467 a decade later, and some 80 percent of these students were Catholic. When the US Supreme Court ruled in *McCollum v. Board of Education* (1948) that such religion classes could not be held in tax-funded school buildings, New York City's program was deemed safe because its classes took place away from public school grounds, and indeed four years later, in *Zorach v. Clauson* (1952), the justices upheld New York's program in a 6-to-3 decision.[52]

Release time and CCD programs in Long Island's suburban parishes were incredibly large.[53] In 1963 Ss. Cyril and Methodius School in Deer Park enrolled 1,000 students, but the parish had 6,200 children in its CCD program.[54] St. Anne's School in Brentwood educated 1,100 students in 1966, but the parish's CCD program taught 4,000 students, including 700 first communicants who were instructed by 100 volunteer teachers.[55] The pastor of St. Ignatius Loyola Parish in Hicksville reported in 1969 that his CCD program enrolled over 3,000 and was still growing.[56] In fact, when Msgr. Joseph Lawlor, the first diocesan director of religious education, attended national meetings he found that other dioceses didn't have as many total CCD students as there were in just one of Long Island's largest parishes.[57] As Msgr. Frederick Schaefer, who replaced Lawlor in 1965 noted, there was always a 2-to-1 ratio of CCD students to parochial school students in the diocese. And yet, Schaefer admitted that the Church focused its personnel and financial resources on parish schools. Throughout his decade in diocesan education, Schaefer said he had to fight the mentality "that the children in public schools were less Catholic" than those in parish schools, and he worked to redirect resources and recruit and train teachers for religious education programs.[58]

Whereas nineteen of the twenty-eight parishes established on Long Island between 1945 and 1957—and all but one of the fifteen parishes founded in Nassau County in that era—ultimately did build a parochial school, by the time the Diocese of Rockville Centre was establishing its first wave of new parishes in the late 1950s and early 1960s, an entirely different approach to Catholic education had taken hold. Of the twenty-one parishes founded after the diocese's erection in 1957 only one—Christ the King Parish in Commack—ever opened a parochial school. Both Holy Name of Jesus Parish in Woodbury, founded in 1962, and St. Luke Parish in Brentwood, established in 1965, announced plans to build schools and yet never did.[59] This dearth of school-building in the Diocese of Rockville Centre presaged

Table 6.2 Parishes and Parochial Schools Founded on Long Island after 1957

Parish Established	Parish (County)	School Opened
1959	Christ the King, Commack (S)	1963
1959	St. Gertrude, Bayville (N)	-
1962	St. Paul the Apostle, Jericho (N)	-
1962	Holy Name of Jesus, Woodbury (N)	-
1962	Our Lady of Grace, West Babylon (S)	CCD Center
1962	St. Peter the Apostle, N. Great River (S)	CCD Center
1962	St. Elizabeth, Melville (S)	CCD Center
1965	St. Matthew, Dix Hills (S)	CCD Center
1965	St. Luke, Brentwood (S)	CCD Center
1966	Our Lady Queen of Martyrs, Centerport (S)	-
1966	St. Francis of Assisi, Greenlawn (S)	-
1967	St. Thomas More, Hauppauge (S)	CCD Center
1968	St. Gerard Majella, Terryville (S)	-
1970	Good Shepherd, Hollbrook (S)	-
1971	St. Louis de Montfort, Sound Beach (S)	-
1973	St. Mark, Shoreham (S)	-
1987	Our Lady of Hope, Carle Place (N)	-
1988	Resurrection, Farmingville (S)	-
1988	St. Elizabeth Ann Seton, Ronkonkoma (S)	-
1988	Holy Cross, Nesconset (S)	-
1996	Ss. Peter and Paul, Manorville (S)	-

Note: N = Nassau County; S = Suffolk County

a nationwide trend in which "almost no Catholic schools were built in the United States from the mid-1960s to almost 1990."[60]

Some of the Long Island parishes which never opened a school may not have been able to finance a building. But in the late 1960s and early 1970s, six of the parishes founded after 1957, and several older parishes, constructed purpose-built religious education centers or all-purpose buildings with classrooms for their CCD programs. Under the direction of Msgr. James L. Griffin, Immaculate Conception Parish in Westhampton Beach became the first parish in the diocese to decide, in 1967, to build a catechetical center.[61] In September of that same year, an "overwhelming majority" of parishioners at St. Elizabeth Parish in Melville voted to build a convent and a one-story, ten-classroom religious education center instead of a school. Our Lady of the Assumption Parish in Copiague built a twelve-classroom catechetical center in 1971, and that same year Assumption of the Blessed Virgin Mary Parish in Centereach built a two-floor, ten-classroom religious education center with a kitchen, library, and an all-purpose room.[62]

This indicates that the principal reason most parishes did not open a parish school was not the inability to finance construction of a building. As early as 1963 the national trade journal *Catholic Property Administration* had published a series of articles on the growing phenomenon of religious education centers, their benefits, and their specific building requirements indicating that suburban parishes had the resources to build.[63] Rather, pastors and parishioners worried about a lack of teaching sisters, the higher tuitions needed to pay a lay faculty, the impossibility of accommodating all of the parish's youth, and the challenge of choosing who could attend. Father Arthur J. Kane, the pastor of Immaculate Conception Parish in Westhampton Beach, pointed to the "extremely heavy financial burden" of operating a parish school as one reason for his parishioners' vote and added that the "excellence" of the area's public schools also affected parents' decision.[64] Monsignor Russell J. Neighbor, the director of the National Center of CCD, highlighted similar reasons when he noted, in 1968, that fifty dioceses across the country had begun operating 250 religious education centers and predicted that their spread was inevitable.[65]

Father John Leonard, too, cited these reasons when he decided that same year to open the planned twenty-four-room parochial school at Our Lady of Grace Parish as a religious education center. Parishioners' reactions to his decision show that not all Catholic parents accepted religious education centers as adequate replacements of parochial schools. Shortly after Leonard's announcements, he described parishioners' reactions as excellent. "The day after we made the announcement," he said, "I received some 25 letters in the mail . . . each letter contained words of congratulations. There was not one unsatisfactory comment in the batch," he declared.[66] But parish histories and interviews with parishioners universally tell a different tale. The decision "caused grief and aggravation to all" and was "a controversy that would remain with the parish for several years to come," recalled the parish's twenty-fifth anniversary journal.[67] Another parish history states that "there were feelings of betrayal, bitterness, and resentment among parishioners," some of whom began attending other parishes or "discontinued their financial support" of Our Lady of Grace.[68] Articles in the parish's monthly magazine, *Our Parish*, indicate that even years later parents continued to ask when the building would "become a REAL school."[69] And Leonard himself seemed to admit there was significant displeasure with his decision, when he wrote of a fictional parishioner in a letter to his parish:

> Mrs. Brown is a little disconcerted about her parish school. In fact it is not even called a parochial school but rather a Catechetical Center and/or a Center for Religious Education. Her boy is not to be bathed in his religion. Rather he is to receive it in vitamin-form, once a week—while at the same time taking advantage of all the facilities of the public school system which his parish could

not possibly afford to supply. In this one weekly session of religious instruction he will be grounded in the fundamentals of his faith in proportion to his age and powers of comprehension. During the rest of the week, Mrs. Brown (and maybe even Mr. Brown) will discuss with him what he has learned and help him put that learning into practice. And we guarantee John Brown will grow up in his faith in exact proportion as Mr. and Mrs. Brown cooperate in making certain he attend his vitamin-like instructions and show him by their example that there is a goal beyond this life worth living for.[70]

Lay Faculties and Rising Costs

Father Leonard's inability to recruit sufficient teaching sisters for a parochial school reflected the rapidly changing demographics of the American nun.[71] Between 1948 and 1957 34,448 women entered religious life and in the early 1960s some 7,000 women entered religious life each year.[72] Beginning in the late 1960s the number of religious women in the United States declined precipitously from a height of 181,421 sisters in 1966 to 102,504 sisters in 1990.[73] Between 1966 and 1976 alone, the number of women religious in the United States declined by 28 percent, a change reflecting both an unprecedented number of departures from religious life in the wake of Vatican II reforms and societal changes offering women other opportunities, and a concurrent decline in the number of new vocations.[74] Over that same timeframe, the number of women entering religious life declined by 81 percent.[75]

Additionally, among the women religious who remained, an increasing number ventured into ministries beyond education, especially among minorities and the urban poor, in part because some sisters had come to see suburban parochial schools as elitist and racist. Between 1965 and 1983 the number of sisters engaged in teaching ministry in the Diocese of Rockville Centre thus declined by 57 percent from 1,433 to 616 sisters.[76] Religious orders increasingly struggled to maintain their commitments to staff parochial schools, and when those schools had to pay additional lay teachers, parishes struggled to finance them.[77] In 1970 the Dominican Sisters of Amityville undertook an evaluation of all the schools they staffed in order to retrench. Although the sisters did not publicize the metrics they employed, parishioners at Curé of Ars Parish in Merrick were told that the criteria included the school's finances and enrollment, the condition of the physical plant, the attitude of parishioners toward the school, and the quality of relations with the parish's priests. Curé of Ars School had 671 students, seven sisters, eleven lay teachers, and a $110,000 deficit when the Dominican Sisters announced they were withdrawing. The principal, Sr. Rita Anne, warned that, "we were the first but there will be others."

Some parishioners wondered if a "Catholic atmosphere" could be maintained in a school staffed exclusively by laypeople. Andrew Greeley had found in a small 1969 survey for the National Council of Catholic Men (NCCM) that only 13 percent of Catholics thought a parochial school had to be staffed by sisters to maintain its Catholic character.[78] But some parents resented when religious orders "abandoned" their children's school and no longer thought the extra expense of parochial school tuition was worth it.[79] Others thought the sisters' departure could be "a blessing in disguise" precisely because area Catholics might become more involved in the public school system and work to improve afterschool religious education for all the parish's children.

In the case of Curé of Ars Parish in Merrick, its school remained open with a lay faculty and continued to operate until 1992 when it became part of a regional Catholic school.[80] So, too, when the Immaculate Heart of Mary Sisters (IHM) of Scranton left St. Philip and St. James School in St. James in 1970, the school remained open with a fully lay staff. The parish was conducting an experiment, the pastor said, to "explore the whole concept of what a parochial school is" and whether it is "possible for lay Christians to provide a Christian education for children in a school system."[81] Although "some parents moved their kids out and put them in the public or neighboring parochial schools," and there was a financial deficit at first, the school survived and remains open today. At St. Joseph's School in Kings Park, however, the departure of the Amityville Dominicans in 1970 led to a decline in enrollment by 1972 from 672 students to 432 students and the school was closed.

Rockville Centre, like dioceses across the country, was increasingly dependent on lay teachers, and on Long Island these teachers sought better pay and benefits by organizing a teachers' union. Father Andrew Connolly, once principal of Holy Trinity Diocesan High School in Hicksville, recalls advising lay faculty members to unionize because the diocese would otherwise try to pay them as little as possible.[82] After lay teachers in the four diocesan high schools did unionize in 1970, Fr. Patrick Shanahan, the superintendent of schools from 1969 to 1975 referred to the union as "one of the heartaches of the school system." Although Shanahan felt the union's requests were fair, the diocese's resources could not meet their demands, and he felt unionization created an adversarial relationship that did "not help to build up the spirit of the Catholic schools."[83]

In 1976, after a one-day walkout, a strike was narrowly avoided when bargaining led to agreement on a one-year contract.[84] But the following year, the union's demands for increased pay and equal seniority to religious teachers led to a six-week strike. The four schools remained open, staffed by religious and nonunion lay teachers, but after the fifth week of the strike the diocese threatened to hire replacement workers and the union filed a grievance for unfair labor practices.[85] The following week a contract was signed that increased salaries and benefits, lowered class sizes, and established uniform policies for tenure and grievances.[86]

Five years later, in September 1981, 235 lay high school teachers were again on strike demanding salary increases amid 10 percent inflation. Again, the four schools remained open during the eight-week strike, but Bishop John McGann drew criticism for union busting when he hired replacement teachers. Later that fall, the 1,204 lay teachers in the diocese's eighty-four elementary schools voted against unionization 703 votes to 429.[87] "We are delighted with the results," said then–Superintendent of Schools Dr. Hugh Carroll, and numerous principals, pastors, and presidents of parents' associations agreed, fearing that increased salary costs would have forced even more school closures.[88]

Enrollment Declines and School Closures

As the number of lay teachers and tuition costs rose, enrollment in Catholic schools declined. From the end of World War II through the mid-1960s enrollments in America's parochial schools had consistently increased each year. In 1965 the Church educated nearly 4.5 million students, some 47 percent of Catholic children. But in just three years' time, seemingly without warning, enrollments in parochial schools fell to 3.9 million students, under 40 percent of all Catholic youth.[89] In the 1968–69 school year, numerous dioceses recorded significant one-year enrollment drops. This downturn was especially evident in urban areas but even in the suburbs, where parental demand for parochial education had been high despite limited space, many more parents began sending their children to public schools.[90] On Long Island parochial school enrollment had grown from 47,000 students in 1957 to 78,900 in 1968, which proved to be the highwater mark. Enrollments declined steadily for the next decade, falling to just 35,000 by 1976. At Holy Name of Mary Parish in Valley Stream, for example, twelve classrooms were added to the school in 1963 and there were 1,000 students enrolled in 1967. But just five years later, in 1972, enrollment had plummeted to under 700 students.[91]

The dramatic decline in parochial school enrollments in the late 1960s is almost certainly related to upheavals in the American economy. Robert M.

Collins has argued that 1968 "marked the beginning of an awkward transition from the postwar boom to a new era of economic stagnation cum inflation," or stagflation. Although often overshadowed by the year's tumultuous political and social events, 1968 saw inflation and consumer prices shoot up and President Lyndon Johnson pass a temporary 10 percent surcharge on corporate and individual income taxes.[92] In March *Time* magazine explored how "soaring costs of construction and plant maintenance, more expensive training aids and equipment, and a doubling of teachers' salaries" over the previous decade had created a vexing fiscal crisis for Catholic schools nationwide. As parochial school systems raised tuition "to the limit of parental tolerance and beyond," they were "caught in a viciously accelerating cycle," *Time* stated. Parents who decided they couldn't afford both taxes and parochial school tuition transferred their children to public schools, "increasing the tax burden as well as the cost per pupil for those remaining in parochial schools."[93]

The sudden drop in parochial school enrollments forced many dioceses to close schools that were draining limited parish and diocesan resources.[94] In 1968 637 parochial schools closed nationwide, and another 400 closed in 1970.[95] Catholic educators, meanwhile, sought reforms that might save parochial schools. Father Neil G. McCluskey, SJ, argued that the parish-run school was an anachronism that had to give way to regional schools under diocesan control and funded by a kind of school tax, paid not just by school parents, but by every member of the diocese.[96] Russell Shaw and Fr. C. Albert Koob of the National Catholic Education Association (NCEA) also suggested that parish schools be consolidated into regional schools and that they "be less child-centered," increasing their offerings for "other segments of the Christian community."[97] But few if any dioceses embraced such revolutionary changes and many parochial schools continued to teeter on the brink of closure.

At St. Anthony Parish in Oceanside, which opened its school in 1961, a rise in the number of lay teachers increased the financial burden on the parish and resulted in the need to borrow $15,000 from the diocese. When just a decade later, in 1971, the Blauvelt Dominican Sisters announced that they were withdrawing from the school entirely, plans were initially made to hire additional lay teachers. But given the financial strain this would place on the already indebted parish, the diocese closed the school. A parish history summarized that "as much as the building of the school had been a unifying influence, its closing was a divisive one," and parishioners resented "the adamant stand taken by the Chancery."[98] Schools that did not close required increased subsidies from parish coffers. Parish council minutes from

St. Frances de Chantal Parish in Wantagh indicate that in 1977 70 percent of the parish's annual budget went to subsidize the parish school, although only 10 percent of the parish's families had children in the school.[99]

With few opportunities for cost cutting, pastors and school boards were left to fight for increased enrollments by promoting the benefits of a Catholic school. At St. Pius X Parish in Plainview, parishioner and school board member Russell David wrote in the parish magazine in 1973 that he was astonished by how often people questioned the need for the parish's school. When he arrived at the parish in 1965 he was frequently told that he "couldn't count on the school opening in September," and eight years later he still heard frequent rumors about the school's closing. David thought it sad that parents let such gossip discourage them from enrolling their children and reminded them that while public schools had removed American flags, Bibles, the Pledge of Allegiance, and prayer from the classroom, the parochial school still taught "that there is a meaning to life, a purpose, a goal."[100] The school board at St. Pius X stressed that parochial schools were worth the sacrifice of time and money, and highlighted the school's strengths, including its small class sizes, highly qualified staff, strong community spirit, and its support of "spiritual development," which the board called "the one characteristic that makes a parochial school unique."[101]

A Crisis of Faith Formation

The decline in parochial school enrollment meant that an ever-greater number of Catholic youths received their instruction in the faith through CCD programs or religious education centers. But the faith formation offered by these institutions became the subject of debate within the American Church, especially in the wake of the Second Vatican Council. Catechetical centers had been embraced by liberal critics of parochial schools not only as an expedient in the face of rising costs and an insufficient number of parochial school desks, but also as a more authentic and effective means of religious formation. Their advent was also accompanied by a wholesale rethinking of how religious education should be conducted, at whom it should be aimed, and who should do the teaching.

Proponents of the new catechetical centers charged that even the CCD or release time model of religious education aimed to pass on the faith simply by exposing schoolchildren to religious sisters once a week. "Our CCD is doing a tremendous job, but is one hour a week enough?" asked the editors of Our Lady of Grace's *Our Parish* magazine in 1966, two years before its new school building would open as a catechetical center. "Anyone who

Suburban Catholic Education / 175

has watched our sex-inovated [*sic*] TV commercials and shows must answer, 'NO,'" the lay editors argued.¹⁰²

These same critics argued that religious education should be centered in the home and that parents should be the primary educators. The handful of sisters who came to work at Our Lady of Grace Parish's catechetical center therefore concentrated "more on families than on children in classrooms" and stressed adult education to ensure that parents were prepared to serve as their children's primary educators. But even at Our Lady of Grace, which boasted the diocese's most robust catechetical center, it was not evident that

Figure 6.5. Sister Ann Higgins, CSJ, visits with Mrs. McAuley as part of the Home Visitation Program at St. Bernard Parish in Levittown. Sister Ann taught religious education at St. Bernard's from 1970 to 1978 and was Parish Home Visitor from 1973 to 1978. From 1986 to 1989 she also visited homes for Our Lady of Grace's catechetical center in West Babylon. *Source*: Carol Speranza, "Visiting Sister Adds Her Own Personal Touch to Parish Life," *Long Island Catholic* 12, no. 38 (January 31, 1974): 2.

many Catholic parents embraced this new model of religious education. In 1970 parents there were given the option to teach their own child or send them to a class taught by a volunteer catechist. Only 160 first-graders were taught at home by their parents, but nearly 400 received religious instruction from a catechist.[103] Thus, even in parishes with catechetical centers, the religious instruction of youth essentially functioned like longstanding CCD and release time programs.

What is more, the way that the faith was taught in such programs changed throughout the 1960s and 1970s as catechists employed new methods of instruction that they saw as inspired by Vatican II and necessitated by a rapidly changing world. Sister Dorothy Fowler, one of the directors of Our Lady of Grace's catechetical center, stated that "in an evolutionary world," in which "we know that man is limitless," the approach to "learning about God, life, and faith" needed to evolve also. "We begin with man now . . . with man's own experience, not God," Fowler explained.[104] Lorraine Smith, a volunteer teacher at Our Lady of Grace's catechetical center, defended this new model of catechesis, arguing that teachers couldn't spoon-feed students as they had in the past. It was good, she held, "to disagree, to discuss, to debate" the faith because "the Church is God's people." However, Smith admitted to hearing parishioners complain about "the liberal teachers" who taught at the Center.[105] Sue McRedmon, a parishioner at St. Pius X Parish in Plainview, railed against the new catechesis, warning that the Church was "facing a radical destruction of the transmission of the Catholic faith." Religion teachers were spreading doubt instead of faith, she argued, because they stressed the need to question the Church's teaching. She urged parents to pray that their children's CCD teachers might resist "the deplorable disintegration taking place in the Church."[106]

Criticism of CCD programs and catechetical centers was by no means limited to a handful of disgruntled parents. In fact, there was near universal consensus among the clergy and even many diocesan officials that, compared to parochial schools, religious education programs were woefully insufficient in inculcating children in the practice of the faith. Andrew Greeley had long argued that CCD programs were "not a functional alternative to Catholic schools," and that "the romance of certain liberal Catholic writers with CCD" was rooted solely in their "ideological objections to Catholic schools."[107] In 1969 Greeley found that 74 percent of Catholics felt that CCD wasn't doing a good job.[108] Writing in his weekly syndicated column, Greeley emphatically stated that religious education programs did not "even begin to be an adequate substitute for Catholic schools—much less the superior replacement that some of the righteous CCD enthusiasts of the 1960s thought it would be." Although his 1976 study, *Catholic Schools in a Declining Church*, had shown that CCD produced "very little if any effect on those who have participated in it," Greeley suggested that such programs were a "guilt reducer" for bishops and pastors who were "too lazy to raise the money" to keep parochial schools open, and for parents who thought "a bigger car is more important than parochial school tuition."[109] In 1972, even Mary Perkins Ryan, who had argued that parochial schools should be replaced with afterschool catechetical programs, wrote that concerns about the state of religious education were "becoming increasingly urgent." She confessed that she had been "astonishingly naïve" to suggest, as she had in 1964, that the Liturgy "could become by itself the chief means of Christian education for individuals and communities."[110] Such assessments marked a drastic shift from the euphoria of the 1950s suburban building boom and the optimism surrounding religious education in the 1960s.

While not ascribing blame as Greeley had, many priests of the Diocese of Rockville Centre strongly agreed that there was "simply no substitute for the Catholic school." Interviewed in the 1980s about their ministry during the first two decades of the diocese's history, they lamented that CCD programs had failed to pass on the faith the way that parochial schools had for so long, and they predicted grave consequences for the long-term vitality of the Church. A religious education program "of hourly religion classes for approximately twenty-five weeks per year" was simply not enough, Msgr. John Bennett said. As a result, second-graders in Catholic schools knew more about religion than sixth-graders in CCD, Msgr. George Graham assessed. Father Patrick Shanahan summarized: "in terms of knowing the Faith, the Catholic school student has it all over the non-Catholic school student." The fact that "fewer and fewer children are going to Catholic schools is going to cause a great crisis for the Church," Bishop Emil Wcela warned; "I see it already." Like so many of the priests interviewed, Wcela referenced Andrew Greeley's scholarship while stating his conviction that "when young people drift away from the Church . . . if they have gone to Catholic schools, many of them will come back to the Church" when they marry and have children. But "the people who have had religious education only are not likely to return." The crucial point was not so much the weak instruction in the tenants of the faith as it was CCD's inability to replicate the community formed in a parochial school.[111]

After years of studying and promoting the Catholic school system, Greeley was convinced that like the Catholic neighborhood of which it was once a part, parochial schools had "produced a substantial impact on the educational, political, moral, religious, sexual, and financial behavior of its students," but that it had been "abandoned at the height of its success. Historians of the future," he predicted, "can marvel at how foolish we were to give up because of a loss of nerve and a loss of faith what have been our best resources. Catholics schools, after all," he wrote, "were the answer."[112]

High School Closures

Monsignor James F. Coffey served as the first rector of St. Pius X Preparatory Seminary which had been the first major building project of the newly established Diocese of Rockville Centre. Interviewed in 1981, Coffey articulated how the history of the seminary paralleled that of the diocese itself. "The development of that seminary," he suggested, "says a lot about the history of this diocese. That seminary was inaugurated in 1958 and the mood of the Diocese was one of euphoria," Coffey continued:

> We were living at a time when World War II veterans were now raising young families, new homes were being built all over this suburban Diocese, young families were crowding the churches, begging for places in the schools, fighting for chairs where there weren't any. Nothing except euphoria was visible on the horizon in 1958.

But such euphoria was short-lived. "That mood changed during the 1960s," Coffey said, "both in our social world and in our political world, in the American world, and certainly in the world of the church."[113] St. Pius's enrollments, in its early years, increased from 106 students in its opening year of 1958 to 415 students in 1962. But the number of graduates who continued their studies for priesthood and were ordained was disappointing. Of the original 106 students only five were ordained twelve years later, and a 1975 study showed that only one-third of graduates even continued on to the major seminary. Enrollment was just 288 in 1969 and fell even further, to just 186 students in 1983. Between 1980 and 1983 only 18 of the 288 young men who graduated from St. Pius elected to enter the major seminary.[114]

The four high schools built by the Diocese of Rockville Centre in the early 1960s similarly reflected the development of the diocese itself. The highly successful 1963 funding drive to build the schools had been an important point of pride and source of unity for the still-young diocese and, in the words of Monsignor Henry Reel, "a beautiful commitment to Catholic education was unquestionable throughout the entire procedure." But as Reel later lamented, this "tremendous enthusiasm and commitment" was "in stark contrast" to the struggles that the high schools faced throughout their existence.[115] Emblematic as they were of the diocese's heady days of expansion, the subsequent history of the high schools and seminary, the decision to close them, and the laity's reaction to the closures helps illuminate how postwar suburbanization had transformed American Catholicism.

On December 5, 1983, Bishop John R. McGann announced that, at the end of the academic year, two of Rockville Centre's four diocesan high schools, opened in 1966, would close and St. Pius X Preparatory Seminary would also cease operations. Holy Trinity High School in Hicksville and St. John the Baptist High School in West Islip would continue to be owned and operated by the diocese. Maria Regina High School in Uniondale, however, would be closed and its building leased to St. Agnes Cathedral High School, which would move from its location in Rockville Centre. Holy Family High School in South Huntington would also be closed, and its building would become the new home of St. Anthony's High School, formerly of Smithtown. McGann explained that the high schools were being closed because they were underenrolled and were facing continuous financial deficits. St. Agnes, which was operated by the Cathedral Parish, and St. Francis, which was owned by the Franciscans, stood on better fiscal footing but their aging facilities were in need of expensive maintenance and upgrades.[116] In his letter to members of the diocese, McGann said he made the announcement with "enthusiasm and with a vision for the future" and made no mention of any sadness that the closures might cause among the faithful.[117]

The four high schools had been a serious financial drain on the diocese since their inception in 1966. As early as 1971 low enrollments, a decline in the number of teaching sisters, and negotiations with the lay teachers' union led to a budget crisis that threatened to close the schools. That year alone, the schools were employing forty-one more lay teachers than they had the year before, and the number of religious sisters teaching in the schools would only drop further. Paying higher salaries for lay teachers meant that schools had to charge higher rates of tuition and that more families requested financial assistance.[118] It also meant that more parents who were squeezed by mortgage payments and exorbitant property taxes, impressed by the quality of local public schools, or disappointed in the quality of religious instruction without religious sisters on the faculty, simply chose not to pay for Catholic schooling at all.

Although the four high schools had each been built to accommodate 2,400 students, only St. John the Baptist ever reached maximum capacity, enrolling 2,439 students in 1977–78 before shrinking to a little over 2,380 students in the early 1980s. Holy Trinity hit its peak enrollment of 2,205 in

1973–74 and then declined to an average of 1,650 in the early 1980s. But Holy Family's largest enrollment was just over 2,000 in its opening year and declined to 1,164 in what became its final year. Maria Regina enrolled 2,055 students in 1972–73 and just 1,290 in 1982–83. The schools' low enrollments, combined with rising costs, resulted in operating deficits that required the diocese to provide significant subsidies. Between 1966 and 1983, the diocese contributed $13,120,624 to the four schools: Holy Trinity and St. John the Baptist, which remained open, were given $2,750,581 and $1,847,602 respectively, and Maria Regina and Holy Family, which ultimately closed, received $3,190,792 and $5,331,649, respectively.[119]

Throughout the 1970s, the future of the high schools was studied and discussed by different diocesan entities and various options for restructuring the schools and limiting the diocese's liability were proposed, but little action was taken. In the spring of 1976, once more facing the possible closure of all four schools, Bishop Kellenberg and the Diocesan Consultors gave unanimous support to establishing the schools as separate and independent corporations owned by lay boards of trustees rather than the diocese. But when Kellenberg retired later that year, and Bishop McGann replaced him, that decision was seemingly postponed as McGann asked the schools' principals and boards to discuss the possibility of closing, merging, or turning over the schools to lay administration. In 1978 the Diocesan Consultors approved the continuation of subsidies for a period of three years, at the end of which time lay boards would be established to own and operate each school. But because of turnover in the administration of the Diocesan Education Office, no progress was made in preparing for such a transition, and all four principals opposed the plan anyway, preferring that the schools remain under diocesan control.[120] In February 1982 the Diocesan Senate of Priests unanimously passed a recommendation that all four schools be passed to lay boards, but the principals remained opposed to the plan. And in the fall of 1983, the Senate of Priests and the Board of Consultors voted in support of McGann's proposal to shutter two of the schools.[121]

McGann's decision to close St. Pius X high school seminary represented the demise of the first institution built by the new diocese and the failure of Bishop Kellenberg's dream for a fountain of priestly vocations. It was, however, consistent with a nationwide trend for minor seminaries. In the twenty-five years since St. Pius X's founding, so much had changed in the broader culture and within the Church that parents and even seminary faculties doubted whether it was appropriate for high school–aged boys to be training for the priesthood.[122] The relative lack of an outcry against this part of McGann's announcement, and the tendency of critics to frame the closure of St. Pius X simply as a loss of yet more high school desks, indicates that St. Pius X had not lived up to Bishop Kellenberg's hopes for a seminary and had come to be seen as just another of the diocese's high schools.

Whatever the schools' troubles, the decision to close them was "a very painful time," according to Monsignor John F. Bennett who, in 1983, served as secretary to Bishop McGann. "The protest of the people was overwhelming," Bennett recalled, and within a few days of McGann's announcement the diocese had received over 650 letters and telegrams opposing the closures.[123] An editorial in the *New York Daily News* captured the tenor of the protests to come. Columnist Michael Hanrahan argued that it was the clergy who had taught Catholic parents of their obligation to raise their children in the faith, and that Catholic schools were the proven means of accomplishing that goal. But now, contrary to the spirit of Vatican II, Bishop McGann was cavalierly dismissing the concerns of those faithful who had supported Catholic education for so long. "One might think that you have to be suffering, underprivileged, or in some dire need to gain consideration by the local hierarchy," Hanrahan sniped.[124]

The thrust of Hanrahan's argument was telling. Postwar suburbanization had empowered the laity to see themselves as deserving of a voice in the Church's decision-making processes. Suburban Catholics had enthusiastically helped build new parishes and schools from the ground up and they believed their time, effort, and financial contributions had earned them a say in their development. The Second Vatican Council only confirmed that the lay faithful were called to contribute their expertise to build up the Church and properly apply its teaching to the modern world. Although the laity of the diocese lacked the power to overturn McGann's decision, that they felt free to so sharply critique him indicates how radically the balance of power between clergy and laity had shifted. And the rhetoric they employed not only confirmed their newfound understanding of how decision-making should occur in the Church, it also revealed how the Church was increasingly divided into conservative and liberal factions.

Parents from the high schools slated for closure, and other concerned members of the diocese, formed the Coalition for Catholic Education to fight the decision and took out advertisements in local newspapers. Over 4,000 people attended a protest rally on January 13, 1984, at the Nassau Coliseum at which speakers critiqued both the decision-making process and the bishop's rationale. They argued that in a post-conciliar Church the laity had a right to participate in Church decision-making and they encouraged attendees to withhold donations and refrain from volunteering in their parishes until the closures were reversed. One of the speakers, Edward

Walsh from Maria Regina High School, said that parents had been "used and tricked" by the diocese. They had been full partners in the building of the schools, in fundraising, and in increasing the schools' enrollment, but they were not consulted about the closures, and the bishop had thereby "written a primer, a guide book, on how not to close schools."[125] Daniel J. Gorman, president of the coalition, similarly complained that McGann was "treating the laity . . . like children," and that the faithful had "invested too much time and money into the Catholic school system for that kind of hypocrisy."[126] A reporter for the conservative Catholic weekly *The Wanderer* went so far as to suggest that McGann's lack of consultation was proof that the post-conciliar "Church of subsidiarity, collegiality, community, and co-responsibility" was in fact "a few Church bureaucrats" who insisted that the faithful "either abandon the teachings of Roman Catholicism or shut up."[127]

McGann did receive public support from some clergy and laity who argued that the demographic realities of Long Island and the fiscal realities of the diocese necessitated a consolidation of high schools.[128] The public-school districts of Long Island were also experiencing a decline in enrollments because of the "Baby Bust" of the late 1960s and early 1970s. In 1984 public school enrollments in Nassau and Suffolk Counties were estimated to have fallen by a third in just the prior ten to fifteen years, from 700,000 to 464,000 students, and a number of schools had been closed or consolidated.[129] McGann's supporters also pointed out that all of the students currently enrolled in the diocese's Catholic high schools could still be accommodated in the reorganized schools, and indeed, the vast majority of underclass students at the closed and merged schools re-enrolled for the next academic year.[130] But key members of the clergy also confirmed that McGann's decision had not been made with especially broad consultation. Father Francis Thomas Keenan, SM, the provincial superior of the Marianists who ran Chaminade High School in Mineola, spoke at the parents' protest rally and wrote McGann that his decision had been made unilaterally and was therefore "totally unexpected by all the people who had to live with it."[131] Father Donald Desmond, who served as principal of Maria Regina High School for its last seven years, complained to Dr. Hugh Carroll, the superintendent of schools, that he "was simply informed" of the decision to close the schools despite Carroll's public insistence that Desmond had been a part of the decision-making process.[132]

Monsignor Daniel S. Hamilton, editor of *The Long Island Catholic*, went even further in suggestions he made regarding how to address the fallout from the decision. Writing to Fr. Charles W. Swiger, of the Office of Research and Planning, Hamilton evaluated that very few people were privy to the bishops' deliberations, including the priests and religious of the diocese, and that the major constituencies affected by the changes were totally unaware they were coming. Although he admitted there were some plausible explanations for this lack of consultation, Hamilton stressed that it was "very difficult in the present Church atmosphere, to render such explanations convincing." There had been studies done on the effectiveness of the preparatory seminary, for example, and yet they had never been made public. "Today it is expected that studies like these will be published or otherwise aired publicly," Hamilton argued.[133] McGann's personal secretary, Monsignor Bennett, added in his memo to Father Swiger that "the text of the Bishop's announcement might have included" some words of "concern for those affected by this decision."[134] These internal critiques of the diocese's lack of transparency, and of the bishop's lack of pastoral concern for the suffering of the faithful, sadly prefigure the complaints made nationwide in the decades that followed as the Church in the United States endured waves of parish and school closures and devastating revelations of priestly sexual abuse and episcopal cover-ups.[135]

For his part, Bishop McGann admitted that he "took a calculated risk" by not involving parents in his decision to close the high schools. McGann explained that several years earlier he had spoken to parents about the schools' enrollments and deficits and was "accused of sowing seeds of doubt about the schools' future." He therefore decided that "no matter what we did there would be a problem."[136] Because he was convinced that ownership by independent lay boards would not have saved the schools, he went ahead with the closures. The Vatican's Apostolic Delegate to the United States, having received letters of complaint from laity of the diocese, inquired with McGann about his decision-making process and his assessment of the public reaction. McGann told Archbishop Pio Laghi that "secrecy was vital to the integrity of the institutions in question" and that "a public process would have created an ongoing controversy." The bishop argued that the objections were from a vocal minority and predicted "an abatement of the initial opposition and a gradual acceptance of the inevitability of some change."[137]

Conclusion

McGann's prediction of gradual acceptance proved prescient, but his dismissal of critics as a vocal minority may also reflect the fact that the debate over the closures was being filtered through the lens of liberal–conservative conflict within the Church. McGann was likely convinced that his critics were conservative Catholics inclined to criticize him for what they perceived

Figure 6.6. Bettie Franks (*left*) and Gail and Ralph Lopez (*right*) of East Meadow are among the 4,000 Long Islanders to attend a rally in Nassau Coliseum protesting the closing of three diocesan high schools. *Source: Newsday* ©1984 *Newsday*. All rights reserved. Used under license.

to be his liberal tendencies. Although the Coalition for Catholic Education argued that the laity had the right to participate in Church decision-making—an argument typically perceived as liberal in orientation—many of its leading voices railed against McGann for being too liberal and employed politically conservative rhetoric and images to advocate for the high schools' survival.

Daniel J. Gorman, the coalition's president, explicitly tied the high schools' troubles to a liberal interpretation of the Second Vatican Council. "The principals at Holy Family and Maria Regina," Gorman claimed, had gotten "all caught up with the excesses of the way Vatican II was interpreted and so the schools got a bad reputation as a result of that attendance plunged." Although these "innovative principals" had been replaced with "solid Catholic priests," by then the schools' decline could merely be "held in check." In Gorman's estimation St. John the Baptist High School had been "very strict about its specifically Catholic identity" and this explained how it was able to keep enrollment at capacity. Mary Tracy, of the New York Interstate Committee for Clergy and Laity, added much broader critiques of McGann's administration, complaining that he condoned liturgical abuse, welcomed liberal speakers at the seminary, supported sex education in parochial schools, and was apparently "too busy lecturing [President Ronald] Reagan about El Salvador" to save Catholic schools.[138]

Later that same year, Catholic divisions over abortion would take center stage in American politics. Mario Cuomo, the Catholic governor of New York, would give a highly contentious defense of his pro-choice politics in a speech at the University of Notre Dame. And Rep. Geraldine Ferraro of Queens, also a Catholic, would become the Democratic nominee for vice president and face rebuke from John Cardinal O'Connor, the archbishop of New York, for her pro-choice position. But on Long Island the abortion debates then beginning to rile American Catholicism were being contextualized within the longstanding debate over the necessity and viability of Catholic schools. A reporter covering the Coalition for Catholic Education's protest rally for the liberal Catholic weekly *National Catholic Reporter* spotted a bumper sticker in the parking lot that read: "Catholic Education Has a Right to Life."[139]

SEVEN

Politics in Catholic Suburbia: State Funding, School Prayer, and Political Realignment

When Fr. John Leonard announced in June 1968 that Our Lady of Grace Parish's brand-new school building would serve as a catechetical center, not a parochial school, he was responding to the demographic and financial realities of the suburban Church. Our Lady of Grace could not afford to build a school large enough to accommodate every child in the booming parish, religious orders of sisters could not provide sufficient numbers of teachers to staff parochial schools, and parents could not afford to pay the increased tuition needed to fund a lay faculty, especially when they were already paying suburban mortgages and property taxes.

Catholic educators recognized that these same economic factors also undercut parents' desire to place their children in parochial schools. Dr. Hugh Carroll, who served as superintendent of schools for the Diocese of Rockville Centre from 1980 to 1989, and Catholic leaders like him had long been quick to admit that Long Island had "some of the finest school systems in the country." With parents paying high property taxes to support public schools, Carroll knew Catholic leaders had "to make some hefty arguments" to convince them to also pay tuition to send their children to a Catholic school.[1] Priests of the diocese were united in their assessment that "taxes are the main burden the people face," as Msgr. Charles Swiger put it, and the Catholic press and laity were vocal in their critique of exorbitant taxes.[2] Not long after Our Lady of Grace Parish decided not to open a parochial school, in a 1971 article entitled, "Can We Afford Our Schools? No!!" Barbara Maertz wrote in Our Lady of Grace's *Our Parish* magazine: "School budgets are going higher and higher, property taxes are soaring and a solution is nowhere in sight. A complete revolt seems just a few years away."[3]

Voter revolts against soaring tax rates had already erupted in the years immediately prior to Maertz's article, and in less than a decade, Long Island's Catholic voters would help animate the so-called Reagan Revolution. In the wake of Ronald Reagan's election, pundits and historians alike focused foremost on the role of evangelicals and the Sun Belt South in the rise of conservatism throughout the postwar period. When discussing the Catholic voters who moved to the right in the period, those same commentators stressed the role played by racial backlash and opposition to abortion in driving Catholic voters into the Republican camp.[4]

But from the very beginning of the suburban boom in the late 1940s, there was speculation that first-time suburban homeowners, including the many Catholics fleeing New York's five boroughs, might become Republicans in suburbia. Many Catholic voters were in fact drawn toward conservative politics from the 1940s through the 1980s, but less so by the politics of racial backlash or anti-abortion politics than by the demographic and economic pressures in suburbia. For Catholic voters these particularly suburban pressures were also filtered through a set of religious concerns, especially surrounding the education of children and the protection of the nuclear family.

The fiscal crisis that threatened Catholic schools, in large part because of suburbanization, led New York's Catholic bishops to redouble their efforts to obtain state aid for nonpublic schools. But the defeat of a 1967 referendum to revise the state constitution showed that New York's Catholic voters ultimately prioritized tax relief and local control over obtaining state aid for nonpublic schools, indicated their increasing dissatisfaction with New Deal liberalism, and signaled their openness to conservative political positions. Meanwhile, it was Catholic parents on Long Island, attempting to secure religion's place in their children's public schools, who drove the era's Supreme Court decisions on church-state relations. Such political activism also highlights how Catholics and Jews, who were both suburbanizing and asserting their rights in a pluralistic America at the same time, took very different approaches to matters of church and state.[5] The methods employed by Catholic parents in these debates also foreshadowed the conservative coalition-building role that Catholics would play in the gathering culture wars. Finally, the divergent political priorities of the bishops and the laity, and divisions within the laity itself, illuminate how suburbanization had eliminated an important aspect of Catholic separatism. No longer could American Catholics be assumed to be a Democratic monolith.[6] They had, rather, become emblematic of the suburban swing voter and of the nation's increasing political polarization.

Nassau County Politics

The Catholics who flocked to the postwar suburban developments of Long Island became residents of a county with a long history of Republican dominance. From Nassau County's founding at the turn of the twentieth century, its politics had been marked by fear of the influence of New York City and its Democratic machine. In 1898 the county was created when the towns of Hempstead, North Hempstead, and Oyster Bay withdrew from Queens County as it was about to be annexed into New York City.[7] And in the decades before World War II, G. Wilbur Doughty, and his nephew J. Russell Sprague, successively built a powerful Republican machine premised on protecting Nassau County from Tammany Hall. Sprague oversaw the passage of the Nassau Charter in 1936 and was elected the county's first executive in 1938, a position he was reelected to four times until his retirement in 1952.[8] During Sprague's reign, *The New Republic* called Nassau "the most Republican county of the United States" and the Nassau GOP exercised considerable influence on the national party.[9]

After World War II Long Island's population swelled with veterans and their families. Between 1948 and 1952 alone, Nassau County's population increased by 65 percent. Sprague and Nassau's GOP establishment worried that these new suburbanites—especially Catholic transplants from New York's outer boroughs—would maintain their allegiance to the Democratic Party.[10] In fact, roughly half of Nassau's newly registered voters between 1945 and 1961 chose to enroll as Democrats. Republicans' registration advantage in Nassau County was cut from 5-to-1 to less than 2-to-1, and both major parties became competitive in the county. But Republicans still outnumbered Democrats by 200,000 voters and the moderate Republican machine was largely able to maintain its power.[11]

That the Nassau County GOP was not wiped out by the influx of urban Democratic voters indicates that some number of the new arrivals were, in fact, Republicans and many others became so when they moved to Long Island. As with the Democratic machine in New York City, new suburbanites discovered that belonging to the party in power paid dividends in patronage jobs.[12] And at the height of the Cold War consensus, the two major parties were also not sharply divided, especially in New York where a moderate Republicanism reigned. Where the parties differed most was on taxes. Suburban homeownership and some of the highest property taxes in the nation, drove some Long Islanders to the GOP, which strove to lower those taxes.[13] Under Sprague's leadership, the Nassau GOP also sustained its longstanding alliance with the building trades and defense workers, reached out to public-sector unionists, and captured the loyalty of the county's largest ethnic group by tapping Italian Americans for elected office and party leadership positions.[14]

Republican control of Long Island was not uncontested, however. In statewide elections throughout the 1950s and '60s, voters in Nassau County often split their tickets and political corruption and internecine power struggles hampered the GOP.[15] This resulted in Democrats being elected to county executive positions. H. Lee Dennison was elected Suffolk's first county executive in 1959. Eugene H. Nickerson was the first Democrat to secure Nassau's executive office in 1961, by a margin of 6,500 votes, and was reelected in 1964 and 1967. But the GOP maintained control of the counties' other offices and voter registration remained in Republicans' favor.[16] Nassau County Democrats never capitalized on Nickerson's victories, failing to build a patronage machine, and through the 1960s were increasingly divided by national issues like civil rights, women's rights, and the Vietnam War.[17] By 1970 the GOP was back in power in Nassau County and a new party chairman, Joseph Margiotta, reaffirmed the party's position as the defender of suburban life and solidified the party's ties to the building trades and the public sector unions. His own "personal leanings towards conservatism" prepared the party to adjust to shifting political winds as debates over school busing, housing, taxes, and abortion increased conservatism's appeal to suburban voters.[18]

Religion in Public Schools

For Catholic voters who moved to Long Island's postwar suburbs, education quickly became a crucial issue driving them toward conservative politics. That so many of Long Island's Catholic parents chose, or were forced by overcrowding and financial strain, to send their children to public schools in the late 1950s and 1960s led them to be active in political and legal debates about the funding and operation of public schools. Such debates highlight how different religious traditions shaped postwar politics, especially around education and church-state relations. While both Catholics and Jews were suburbanizing at this time, and both were fighting for "the recognition of America's religious pluralism," they held very different visions of what that should look like in practice.[19]

Suburban migration had been reshaping Long Island's religious landscape and overcrowding its public schools throughout the 1950s. By 1959 23.2 percent of Nassau County residents attended Roman Catholic churches, 17.7 percent belonged to Protestant churches, and 15.8 percent had joined Jewish synagogues.[20] Public school funding and the place of religion in public schools became flashpoints between these Catholic and Jewish suburbanites. Levittown's earliest residents reported that within the first few years of the community's existence, debates over education pitted well-educated Jewish liberals, who overwhelmingly sent their children to public schools and supported progressive education and higher taxes to fund those schools, against conservative blue-collar Catholics, who supported their own parochial school system and fought for moral training and discipline in public schools, lower taxes, and state aid to nonpublic schools.[21]

Brooklyn's diocesan newspaper, *The Tablet*, which covered all of Long Island until 1962, frequently editorialized against what it saw as needlessly high taxes driven by extravagant spending on school construction projects. In 1957 William R. Donaldson, the vice president of the Suffolk Taxpayers Association ripped the "nothing is too good for our children philosophy" which led to "deluxe new schools" and drove parents from "joyful elation in their new homes" to "a state of quiet desperation" as they tried to "conserve enough of a cushion to meet next month's payment on the mortgage and taxes."[22] In an article reprinted from *Reader's Digest*, Holman Harvey of Pleasantville lamented that amid a critical shortage of classroom space, funds were being "lavished on facilities befitting an exclusive club," and said "the waste of taxpayers' money in school building is fantastic."[23] *The Tablet*'s editors crowed when a study by New York's State Commissioner of Education, Dr. James E. Allen Jr., concurred that school construction costs were inflated because some district authorities desired a "monument" for their town.[24] And the editors applauded voters in West Hempstead who were "willing to finance what was needed but couldn't afford to be extra fancy." In the Herricks Union Free School District, where a huge influx of new residents in the late 1950s caused the overcrowding of schools and necessitated the use of double shifts, proposals for two new junior high schools were repeatedly voted down with voters staking out positions along religious lines.[25] Only in 1958 did voters in the district approve a $2,050,000 bond issue for a new junior high school after rejecting the previous year's proposal because it cost 45 percent more and "included too many frills."[26]

At the same time, Long Island's Catholic parents and voters were involved in public debates about the presence of religion and prayer in public schools. In May 1956 three lay Catholics—Salvatore Gangi, Gerald King, and Edward Doyle—were elected to the school board in Levittown. The "Catholic Slate," as they were called, attacked their non-Catholic incumbents for raising taxes and contributing to the godlessness of Levittown's public schools. In September they permitted a principal in the school district to write a letter to parents encouraging them to provide their children with "some religious training in the church of his choice" so as to instill "the principles of honesty, obedience, truthfulness, and respect for authority." During the holiday season that school year, Jewish parents complained that one of Levittown's public celebrations included children singing overtly Christian songs. Catholic school board members were accused of being "deliberately provocative by injecting religion" into the delicate public matter of education, and near riots erupted at school board meetings. The next May voters removed the board's Catholic majority, but similar controversies occurred in Hyde Park, as well as in New Jersey, Illinois, Texas, and California.[27]

Also in 1956, the New Hyde Park School District proposed posting an "interdenominational version of the Ten Commandments in every public school classroom" in an attempt to "fight the twin evils of communism and juvenile delinquency."[28] When two supporters of the plan were elected to the school board, *The Tablet* argued that the proposal had been "backed by the overwhelming majority of the taxpayers."[29] But State Commissioner of Education Allen ruled against the proposal, leading Dr. Frank E. Picciano, the president of New Hyde Park's school board and later president of the Diocese of Rockville Centre's Diocesan School Board, to accuse him of being anti-Catholic. Picciano also decried the loss of local control and urged voters to write elected officials in support of a State Assembly bill reversing Allen's decision.[30]

Later that year, public pressure forced school boards in Plainview, Valley Stream, and East Islip to back down from proposals to ban the word "Christmas" and traditional holiday celebrations from public school classrooms. *The Tablet* saw the proposals as part of a secularization campaign being waged by "left-wingers, secularists, materialists, and atheists," including the American Civil Liberties Union, the American Jewish Congress, and Protestants and Other Americans United for the Separation of Church and State (POAU). The editors cited a 1952 statement from the US bishops that warned of a strategy to "secularize completely the public school and then to claim for it a total monopoly of education." In East Islip, Fr. John F. Brennan of St. Mary Parish joined other Christian clergyman, the American Legion, the Chamber of Commerce, and the Islip *Press Herald* and *Town Crier* newspapers in publicly protesting the proposal and celebrating the board's decision to rescind it.[31] Meanwhile, in New Hyde Park, Frank Picciano and the public school board drew fire for barring discussion and celebration of Hanukkah while Christmas celebrations were allowed to continue.[32]

The most significant conflict, however, was over prayer in public schools. Throughout the nineteenth and early twentieth centuries, America's Catholic bishops had opposed Bible reading and prayer in public schools because these schools were dominated by Protestants. The bishops feared that Catholic children in public schools, who were not allowed to use Catholic Bibles, would fall victim to proselytization. But, as Kathleen Holscher has shown, in the late 1940s the Cold War made Catholic leaders more concerned that secularism, especially in schools, would make America vulnerable to Communism. In the mid-1950s, for the first time, the US bishops proposed that Bible reading in public schools was in fact constitutional, and in 1954 the Knights of Columbus succeeded in lobbying Congress to add the phrase "under God" to the Pledge of Allegiance students across the country said every morning. Meanwhile, religious reforms were also transforming the way Catholics thought about the Scriptures. From the 1940s through the 1960s, Catholic pastoral leaders increasingly promoted Bible reading among the laity, and in the wake of the Second Vatican Council the Church would sanction cooperation with non-Catholics in the production of Bibles and in interdenominational prayer.[33]

Like debates about public school financing, positions on religion in Long Island's public-school classrooms broke down along denominational lines.[34] In November 1951 the New York Board of Regents unanimously adopted a prayer for use at the opening of the school day in public schools across the state.[35] The nondenominational prayer and a new moral values curriculum were seen as antidotes to juvenile delinquency, which had spiked in the preceding years. However, at the objection of Jewish parents, the prayer was removed from public schools in New York City, and by 1955 only 17 percent of the state's 900 school districts used the prayer. On Long Island, only six of the sixty-one school districts employed the Regents Prayer, including Bethpage, Carle Place, Glen Cove, Levittown, New Hyde Park, and Port Washington.[36]

Long Island's Catholic parents, however, were leading advocates of the Regents Prayer. In July 1956 Mary Harte, the vice president of the Herricks School Board, proposed using the Regents Prayer in the district's schools, which until that time had taken no action on the prayer. Harte was a mother of three and a devout parishioner of St. Aidan Parish in Williston Park, "an older, all-white, blue-collar Catholic neighborhood." Her pastor, Fr. Alfred Loewe, had urged her to use her position to promote religion in the public schools to which so many of her fellow parishioners sent their children because they could not afford parochial school tuition. The board voted down the proposal 3–2, but when new school board elections were held two Catholics—William Vitale Jr. and Anne Birch—were elected, and Philip Fried became the board's only Jewish member. On July 8, 1958, the board approved the use of the Regents Prayer throughout the district. Nearly 20 percent of families in the district "formally endorsed the prayer," with letters to the board running 200 to 1 in favor of the prayer. But support again broke down along religious lines, with the signatories of petitions and the civic associations backing use of the prayer coming from overwhelmingly Catholic neighborhoods.[37] When teachers Michael Carbone and Scot Finegan, who were both lapsed Catholics, opposed the use of the prayer, their Catholic students reported them to Fr. Charles Bermingham of St. Aidan Parish.[38]

Opposition to the prayer inspired Lawrence Roth, an avowed Communist of Jewish lineage, to approach the New York Civil Liberties Union (NYCLU), which hired thirty-four-year-old lawyer William Butler, a non-practicing Catholic with three priest-uncles, to represent Roth against the school district. Roth and Butler recruited other parents to join the suit as plaintiffs by placing advertisements in local newspapers, prompting the editors of *The Tablet* to comment that this proved there was a "lack of opposition." In reality, opposition to the prayer had been growing but the heat of controversy also drove potential complainants away. The final list of plaintiffs contained just five people, all of whom were of Jewish descent, including Roth's neighbor, Steven Engel, whose name was ultimately lent to the case.[39]

In August 1959 a judge of the State Supreme Court ruled that the Regents Prayer was constitutional so long as it was not made mandatory, and a five-judge panel of the Appellate Division unanimously upheld this decision in October 1960.[40] As the case was appealed to the US Supreme Court, a third party was admitted to the suit that enjoyed the backing of Catholic leaders. Comprised of sixteen parents, including seven Protestants, five Catholics, three Jews, and one parent of no faith, the party argued that if the prayer were outlawed their children's constitutional rights would be infringed. When the US Supreme Court heard *Engel v. Vitale*, the gallery was filled with nuns and seminarians, but their prayers weren't answered. On June 25, 1962, the majority declared the Regents Prayer unconstitutional, and public school prayer "wholly inconsistent with the Establishment Clause."[41] The following year, in its *Abington v. Schempp* decision, the court would go a step further declaring that Bible reading in public schools was also unconstitutional.

Reactions to *Engel* were swift and severe. While President John F. Kennedy called for the decision to be respected, *America* magazine called it "quite literally a stupid decision . . . a decision that spits in the face of our history, our tradition, and our heritage as a religious people."[42] The editors of *The Tablet* called it "preposterous" and sarcastically suggested that readers refuse to pay their taxes since "In God We Trust" was printed on their money.[43] Catholic bishops across the country also critiqued the decision. Cardinal Spellman warned that the decision struck "at the heart of the Godly tradition in which America's children have for so long been raised," and Bishop Kellenberg confessed astonishment that "the leading juridical figures" in the nation could be so "confused concerning the 'establishment of religion' and religion itself."[44] A Gallup poll found that 80 percent of the nation's parents approved of religious observances in public schools, and defenders of school prayer argued that the court's decision was narrow and specifically forbade the Regents Prayer only because it was composed by agents of the state.[45] On Long Island, the Baldwin School District therefore began using a prayer composed by a voluntary agency, schools in New Hyde Park used the fourth stanza of "America," and schools in Levittown and Lindenhurst used a section of the Declaration of Independence. School districts in Hicksville, Merrick, Malverne, Oyster Bay, Oceanside, Lawrence, East Norwich, East Meadow, West Hempstead, West Babylon, Patchogue, Rockville Centre and Glen Cove adopted moments of silent meditation at the start of the school day.[46]

Supporters of the decision, however, sought to broaden its application with POAU and the ACLU, calling for a reconsideration of the 1947 *Everson* case that had permitted taxpayer-funded bus transportation for non–public school students.[47] Orthodox Jewish and especially Catholic leaders reasonably feared that the *Engel* ruling threatened their chances of obtaining government aid for religious schools. Editors of *The Tablet* therefore argued that efforts should be made to see the decision overturned just as the Supreme Court's 8-to-1 decision in *McCollum v. Board of Education* (1948), which ruled release time programs unconstitutional, was effectively reversed by *Zorach v. Clauson* (1952).[48]

A nationwide effort was launched to pass a constitutional amendment permitting prayer in public schools and Frank Becker, a Catholic and the Republican congressman for Nassau County, led the campaign. Becker lamented the *Engel* ruling, stating: "This is not the first tragic decision of this court, but I would say it is the most tragic in the history of the United States."[49] Dan Reehill, a Catholic firefighter, and one of the Long Island parents who petitioned the court in favor of the Regents Prayer, vowed to back the constitutional amendment to overturn *Engel* and blamed the nation's bishops for being insufficiently vocal prior to the court's decision.[50] Becker's proposed amendment led to "one of the largest correspondence campaigns in congressional history." Between December 1963 and July 1964, some 13,000 letters on religion in public schools were sent to the House Judiciary Committee. *Christian Century* declared that the volume of mail indicated that the "so-called prayer amendment" was "of greater importance than the civil rights bill" to many citizens.[51]

The letter campaign revealed the importance of women in the debate over public education, as letters from mothers dominated both the pro- and anti-amendment camps. Conservative women, including many Catholics, wrote to support prayer in schools as a defense of home and family. They framed their arguments not as a strategy of the Cold War, but as a determination to halt "the brainwashing of their children" by secular and liberal educators, and as a remedy for juvenile delinquency and crime. Among these women was Phyllis Schlafly, who would rise to prominence in the New Right in the 1970s as she led opposition to the Equal Rights Amendment. Like many conservative women, Schlafly got her start in politics fighting school board battles against what she perceived to be secularist pedagogues.[52]

The fight over Becker's school prayer amendment also foreshadowed what sociologist Robert Wuthnow has called the "restructuring" of American religion, and presaged the formation of the Religious Right.[53] Protestants and Catholics were both internally divided over the constitutionality of prayer in public schools. Although Catholic bishops were united in their criticism of the *Engel* and *Abington* decisions, they were not especially vocal in advocating for the Becker amendment. Letters to the House Judiciary Committee and a survey of Catholic periodicals indicated that Catholic laity were also divided over the decisions.[54] Catholic conservatives thus began to recognize that they had more in common, politically, with conservative Protestants than they had with liberal Catholics and, absent the backing of the hierarchy, became open to a more populist politics.[55] Thus a full decade before *Roe v. Wade* (1973) legalized abortion, the Long Island-based battle over prayer in public schools modeled both the conservative and interreligious coalition building, and the legislative tactics, that conservative Catholics would employ in later battles of the culture war.[56]

State Funding for Parochial Schools

If the Catholic bishops of New York were not as active as they could have been in the campaign to protect prayer in public schools, it was because they were expending considerable energy ensuring the survival of their parochial schools. By the late 1960s the financial status of Catholic schools had become dire. In 1967 there were no new Catholic elementary schools opened in the Archdiocese of New York for the first time since World War II, and in the Diocese of Brooklyn, for the first time in its history, the diocese had "no school construction plans whatsoever on its drawing boards." Even more ominously, the high schools of the archdiocese were operating at a $1.8-million deficit, and the combined deficit of both dioceses' high schools was estimated at $3.3 million.⁵⁷ In the Diocese of Rockville Centre, the four diocesan high schools that opened in 1966 operated at a deficit from their inception and "became an almost insoluble financial problem" for the diocese.⁵⁸

Catholic educational leaders had long been convinced that to solve parochial schools' financial crisis they needed to secure government aid for non-public schools. The bishops saw the *Engel* and *Abington* decisions as an opportunity to paint the public schools as bastions of godlessness and to thereby strengthen their push for federal aid to parochial schools.⁵⁹ But they more often made their case by arguing that Catholic schools saved the taxpayers millions of dollars.⁶⁰ Even the comptroller of New York City, Lazarus Joseph, estimated in 1953 that the parochial schools of the Archdiocese of New York and the Diocese of Brooklyn saved the city $425 million in buildings and $110 million in annual maintenance and operation costs by educating children who would otherwise have to be provided for by public schools.⁶¹

Catholic lobbying efforts were stymied, however, by a ban on taxpayers' money supporting religious organizations. Inspired by a proposed amendment to the US Constitution, suggested by President Ulysses S. Grant and sponsored by Republican congressman James G. Blaine of Maine in 1875, the State of New York had adopted a revised state Constitution in 1894, which contained article XI, section 3, forbidding state aid to church-related schools.⁶² In 1938 this so-called Blaine Amendment was modified to allow state funding that supported the "health and welfare" of students in non-public schools, including bus transportation, school lunches, and health services.⁶³ In 1959, when the Burnt Hills School District refused to fund bus transportation for students at two Catholic schools, arguing that it violated church-state separation, the State Board of Education intervened and the State Supreme Court ruled that it was constitutional for the state to provide transportation as a matter of health and welfare.⁶⁴ That same year, State Senator Edward J. Speno (Republican of Nassau County) and Assemblyman William C. Brennan (Democrat of Queens) proposed legislation that made public transportation for all schools mandatory, thereby eliminating an onerous requirement for non–public school parents to appear before the school board personally and annually to request transportation for their child.⁶⁵ The bill was finally passed and signed into law by Gov. Nelson Rockefeller in 1960.⁶⁶ By 1965 Senator Speno had also joined in sponsoring legislation to provide textbooks to students at all public and nonpublic schools. The bill was overwhelmingly approved the following year on the principal that the benefit was being granted by the state to the individual student, not to the school.⁶⁷

Having obtained state funding for bus transportation and textbooks, Catholic educators hoped that the child benefit theory would also assist them in fully repealing the state's Blaine Amendment.[68] Catholic schools were still in desperate need of financial relief, as they did not receive state assistance for their largest expenditures: the construction of facilities, the purchase of classroom equipment, and teachers' salaries. Blaine was, at the very least, an important "symbolic impediment" to such aid.[69] But because of how the legislature and courts had altered the application of the Blaine Amendment, and because full repeal was still a controversial issue, legislators left the hot-button issue to a state constitutional convention that was approved by voters in 1967.[70]

The Repeal of the Blaine Amendment

American Catholics in the late 1960s were divided over the war in Vietnam, birth control, and the implementation of Vatican II. They broadly agreed, however, that public aid should be made available to parochial schools. Politicians from both parties, whether they were Catholic or not, appealed to Catholic voters by supporting Blaine repeal.[71] The bishops of New York's eight dioceses led the charge to repeal Blaine through the New York State Catholic Conference (NYSCC), their lobbying office in Albany, and through cooperation with Citizens for Educational Freedom (CEF), a nationwide nonsectarian organization with some 250,000 members who lobbied for state and federal aid to nonpublic schools.[72] NYSCC and CEF questioned candidates running to be delegates to the constitutional convention and backed those who supported repeal. Democrats won control of the convention with 102 delegates to the Republicans' 84 delegates but, despite being the central issue of the convention, repeal was the only issue the two parties agreed upon.[73] Both Anthony Travia, a Democrat from Brooklyn and the New York State Assembly speaker, and Earl W. Brydges, a Republican from Niagara Falls and the majority leader in the state senate, were Roman Catholics committed to repeal of Blaine and they led their respective parties in the convention.[74]

During the convention, CEF so successfully mobilized supporters of repeal that delegates' mail ran "approximately three to one in favor of repeal," and CEF was therefore able to obtain pledges to repeal Blaine from 67 percent of the delegates.[75] Support for repeal did, however, break down along religious lines with the majority of Catholic delegates in favor of repeal and the majority of Protestant and Jewish delegates in favor of retaining Blaine.[76] The effort to save Blaine was led by Rev. Donald S. Harrington, a minister of the Unitarian Universalist Community Church in New York City and the state chairman of the Liberal Party. The Catholic media paid close attention to any anti-Catholic rhetoric deployed by Blaine proponents and was especially happy to call attention to Protestant and Jewish voices favoring repeal.[77] Harrington achieved the backing of only 25 Democrats, 20 Republicans, and 3 Liberals in the convention, and repeal prevailed with 70 Democrats, 58 Republicans, and 2 Conservatives voting to strike Blaine from the new constitution.[78]

Despite agreeing on Blaine's repeal, Travia and Brydges differed on how the draft constitution should be presented to the people of the state for approval: either as a single charter or in a series of propositions. Father Patrick Shanahan, the superintendent of Catholic schools in the Diocese of Rockville Centre, recalled how the NYSCC's "initial strategy" had been "to get the Blaine Amendment separated from the rest of the Constitution" so that the people could simply vote on the repeal of Blaine. Shanahan recognized that many of the convention's alterations to the constitution "were very contrary to a republican philosophy that local government should have as much power as it could." He warned Bishop Kellenberg that if Blaine repeal was not separated from the rest of the constitution, the whole charter would "go down 4-to-1 on the Island."[79]

Because Earl Brydges supported the repeal of Blaine, but rejected much of the rest of the charter, he proposed a "separate items" presentation.[80] Republicans were critical of charter provisions that would have made the state responsible for all welfare and court costs throughout the state. Abe Seldin, a Republican delegate from New Hyde Park, warned that this would "decimate villages and towns" as Long Islanders had known them, and Joseph F. Carlino, a Republican delegate from Long Beach, argued that this would lead to "the ultimate abolition of local government units below the county level."[81] For his part, Travia supported the charter's liberal provisions in their entirety and backed a "package deal" in which the people would vote the whole charter up or down. Travia was able to win Cardinal Spellman and his point man on Blaine repeal, Msgr. George A. Kelly, over to this position and achieved a narrow victory for his approach at the convention.[82]

As attention turned to the referendum, opponents of repeal mobilized to defeat the charter. The Committee for Public Education and Religious Liberty (PEARL), which claimed 10 million members nationwide, attacked the charter for violating the separation of church and state. The United Parents Association and the United Federation of Teachers suggested that if the charter was passed the public school system would collapse as only the poorest and most troubled students would remain in public schools. They also claimed that racial integration would be undermined as white students fled public schools for private and religious schools. Finally, repeal opponents threatened that providing state funding for nonpublic schools would cost the state an additional $1 billion a year, requiring massive tax increases.[83]

Monsignor Edgar P. McCarren, who in addition to serving as the secretary of education for the Diocese of Rockville Centre was also director of the Research Institute for Catholic Education, published articles in the Catholic press bolstering the repeal effort and the new constitution to which it was wed. McCarren attempted to debunk claims that the new constitution would cause a major increase in state spending. To the contrary, because "parochial schools were facing extinction for economic reasons," he argued that the state could either pay part of non–public school costs now, or pay for all students' costs when parochial schools were shuttered and they were forced into public schools.[84] Approximately 200,000 of the state's poorest students, he also noted, were in parochial schools in New York City at tremendous savings to the public.[85]

McCarren also hit back at claims that parochial schools were "havens of segregation," insisting that parochial schools were, rather, "instruments of integration." He pointed to surveys indicating that devotion to parochial schools slowed "the flight of whites from changing neighborhoods" and resulted in parochial-school populations that were more integrated than even the neighborhoods surrounding them.[86] Against claims that the mere existence of religious schools encouraged divisiveness, McCarren cited studies showing that graduates of Catholic schools were just as likely as public school graduates to "have Protestant friends, to be involved in civic activities, to be respectful of civil liberties, to be open-minded, and to be tolerant of others."[87]

Perhaps most importantly, McCarren attempted to argue that the proposed charter would actually aid the suburban taxpayer. It was true, McCarren admitted, that "the basic economic thrust of the new Constitution" was "to help the cities." And he defended this aim by reminding his suburban readers of the race riots that had torn through the nation's cities that summer of 1967. "There are many people in the suburbs," he lamented, "who do not believe that the problems of the city are their problems." But the new charter, McCarren argued, shifted "the burden of taxation from the small property owner to the wealthy and more affluent" because it financed welfare costs not at the local level, where Medicaid alone threatened to "break the back financially of every county in the state," but at the state level, where corporations and the wealthy could be made to share the burden with local taxpayers.[88]

The Catholic press, which had closely followed the effort to repeal Blaine for years, also covered the constitutional convention closely and editorialized in favor of the proposed charter. *The Long Island Catholic* became the first religious publication to ever win a top award from the National Newspaper Association when it earned a third-place prize for community service for its coverage of the constitutional convention.[89] The editors of *The Long Island* Catholic, writing in support of the new charter, called fears of its costs "grossly overstated," and celebrated its Bill of Rights, which had won the backing of the convention's African American delegates.[90] *The Catholic News* advocated the charter's approval by publishing a special section the week of the referendum outlining the benefits of the charter's provisions and calling it a "sound, progressive, and humane" document.[91] Meanwhile, *The New York Times* defended the Blaine Amendment and, along with almost all of the city's daily newspapers, advised readers to reject the proposed state constitution.[92]

It was Msgr. George A. Kelly and CEF, however, who truly led the Church's Blaine repeal campaign. Kelly arranged for parishioners to receive pro-charter pamphlets and hear pro-repeal sermons at church, encouraged the laity to exert pressure on elected officials, and produced short films featuring pro-repeal politicians that were sent by closed-circuit television to parishes across the state.[93] In the weeks leading up to the referendum, Kelly and the CEF hosted a "Fairness to Children" rally at Madison Square Garden to promote the charter. Fifteen thousand attendees heard speeches from Sen. Eugene J. McCarthy of Minnesota, the Catholic and antiwar Democrat who just weeks later, on November 30, 1967, would announce his candidacy for the Democratic nomination for president against incumbent Lyndon B. Johnson. Other speakers included the president of Fordham University, Fr. Robert I. Gannon, SJ; Republican State Senator Edward Speno of Nassau County; George Meany, president of the AFL-CIO; Bishop Fulton Sheen of Rochester; and Francis Cardinal Spellman.[94]

All these lobbying efforts cost upwards of $2 million, but they may ultimately have proven counterproductive. Some of Kelly's advertisements were deemed manipulative and misleading, and both the campaign's magnitude and its bare-knuckled tactics were thought to be unseemly for the Church.[95] From the start, the constitutional convention had failed "to capture genuine public interest or esteem" and as the referendum approached it increasingly appeared as if the charter was heading for defeat.[96] It was also clear that not all of the state's bishops were in support of Cardinal Spellman's approach to charter revision. Only three of the state's eight bishops released public statements in support of the charter, and on Long Island Bishop Kellenberg instructed his priests not to preach in support or condemnation of the charter.[97] Instead, Fr. Patrick Shanahan and Fr. Robert Emmet Fagan, the newly appointed director of community research and development for the Diocese of Rockville Centre, ran forums in parishes across the diocese to inform the faithful about the pros and cons of the charter's proposals.[98]

Kellenberg and his priest advisors had been disappointed with the cardinal's decision to support Anthony Travia's "package deal" approach to the charter referendum and feared that this doomed the effort for Blaine repeal. "Msgr. George A. Kelly from the Archdiocese was a good friend of Tony Travia," Fr. Patrick Shanahan recalled years later, "and I guess Travia sold him a bill of goods." Shanahan also felt that the archdiocese's decision to fund television commercials in support of the charter through CEF was "a dishonest approach" and he "forced a bit of a confrontation" on their content. Meanwhile, Spellman and Sen. Robert F. Kennedy of New York were pressuring Kellenberg to publicly support the new constitution.[99] But, as Monsignor Fagan summarized in a 1981 interview, Kellenberg didn't believe he could "tell people how to vote" and preferred instead to "leave it to the people to vote their conscience." As a result, Fagan said, parishioners who favored the Blaine repeal said that they were "out to close the schools," and the faithful who opposed the new charter imagined that the bishop would "tell people the Sunday before the election to vote yes." In the end, however, Fagan recalled that only one parish in the diocese handed out pamphlets advocating passage of the charter.[100]

Parsing an Election Defeat

On November 7, 1967, voters across New York State roundly rejected the proposed constitution by a margin of 3 to 1.[101] The charter was defeated in all of the state's counties and in all of the city's five boroughs, including Queens and Staten Island, which *The New York Times* noted had large suburban Catholic populations. In the Bronx, only two of the twelve Assembly Districts voted in favor of the charter: the largely Puerto Rican 77th in the South Bronx, and the heavily African American 78th in Crotona Park. But "the strongly Catholic 80th District in Parkchester and Throgs Neck . . . voted against the constitution 19,239 to 18,949."[102] On Long Island, where Catholics made up almost 50 percent of the population, the constitution failed in Nassau County by a vote of 95,919 to 399,891 and in Suffolk by a vote of 53,470 to 198,863. "In two heavily Catholic election districts in Suffolk," the 8th in Smithtown and the 65th in Babylon, "the constitution was turned down by substantial margins."[103]

Explanations for the charter's defeat varied widely. Many commentators blamed Anthony Travia's miscalculation in taking an all-or-nothing approach to the referendum.[104] Leo Pfeffer, special counsel to the American Jewish Congress, which had opposed the charter, said that the vote could not "be explained by anything other than the public's desire to retain Blaine" and defend the separation of church and state. Noting that voters had also narrowly passed a $2.5-billion transportation bond issue, Pfeffer argued that the charter's defeat was "based on principle and not the pocketbook."[105] Writing to the editors of *The Long Island Catholic*, Audrey L. J. Smart of Franklin Square, an independent voter and mother of parochial school students, stated that she opposed the charter because she felt it wrong for public funds to support private schools.[106]

Father Robert Emmet Fagan, however, blamed pushback from Catholic voters against the Church's tactics during the constitutional convention. Fagan suggested that charter revision was the first major political campaign that the Church had engaged in after Vatican II and that "it came through loud and clear" that the faithful were saying: "you don't tell us—laymen—how to vote."[107] Editorials in *The Long Island Catholic* concurred and, without naming him, questioned Cardinal Spellman's dominance of the Church's political activism. "Who speaks for THE Catholic Church in New York State," the editors asked, and "what can be done to restructure the New York State Catholic Committee so that it reflects more grassroots Catholic opinion?"[108] Other articles critiqued the Church for employing a preconciliar-style "power play" that undermined years of ecumenical dialogue and gave the impression that the Church cared only about state funding for parochial schools and not other crucial social issues.[109]

Letters to the editor of *The Long Island Catholic* echoed these sentiments. While saluting Bishop Kellenberg's restraint, members of the nascent Long Island Association of Laymen deplored the "Tammany-type battle waged by many Church officials" and asked how many laymen had been consulted by bishops and clergy who then "presumed to go into the public forum and speak in the name of our entire Church." Joseph J. Hynes, of the Hempstead Town Conservative Committee, also commended Bishop Kellenberg for his "relatively neutral position," but dismissed CEF as a "front for the clergy," and celebrated voters' recognition that state aid would bring with it state control.[110]

Others rejected this analysis, defending both the constitution and the hierarchy's support for it.[111] Leonard W. Belter of Manhasset insisted in a letter to *The Long Island Catholic* that Catholics need not apologize for strenuously fighting to remove "a piece of Victorian bigotry" from the state constitution.

He also presciently wondered if the bishops' critics would have the Church stand mute as the legislature moved on to debate a new abortion bill, or if they would "speak out with clarity and conviction and perhaps with a measure of passion."[112] Father Joseph M. Sullivan of Brooklyn added that those who called for more grassroots input into the Church's lobbying efforts, and for greater focus on issues of social justice, ignored the fact that the whole constitution was a matter of justice. The bishops who backed the charter, he said, "far outdistanced the general membership" of the Church "on issues of racial justice, such as housing, integration, welfare, and education."[113]

A consensus emerged, however, that the principal issue behind the charter's defeat was the fear that it would increase taxes and undermine local control, two especially suburban concerns. State Republicans highlighted that the constitution was "designed to benefit New York City at the expense of the suburbs" and successfully painted the charter as "a high-tax document."[114] Even before Election Day Anthony Travia warned that if the charter were defeated it would be because of "the wild charges" that it would "cause an increase in taxes and cost millions of dollars for direct aid to private schools." Immediately after the election, *The New York Times* surmised that voters were mindful of "many issues other than the proposal to allow aid to parochial schools," and noted that districts with "large Catholic but also tax-conscious homeowner populations" resoundingly rejected the charter. Voters had "accepted as fact," *The Catholic News* said, that the constitution would "bring a huge increase in taxes," and they "emphatically questioned" the shift in the tax burden that the charter represented. *The Long Island Catholic* summarized that "more and more experts are convinced taxes played a bigger part than anyone will want to admit" and revealed that even an unidentified spokesman for PEARL confessed that the "anti-tax" vote killed the charter. *The Long Island Catholic* cited Jeremiah Buckley, the national executive director of CEF, who said that "the majority voted their pocketbooks," and quoted Father McCarren, who, echoing Andrew Greeley's critique of suburbia, claimed that "Catholic bigotry against people on welfare," and not opposition to the repeal of Blaine, had doomed the charter.[115]

Within a month of the charter's defeat Cardinal Spellman was dead and so, too, was the effort to repeal the Blaine Amendment.[116] Early in 1968 repeal was proposed in the state legislature but the NYSCC asked for a delay until the US Supreme Court had decided the constitutionality of textbook loan programs to nonpublic schools. Although the Court ruled favorably on the programs' constitutionality in June 1968, repeal efforts were further delayed in 1969 because legislators feared the debate would negatively impact that year's New York City mayoral race. Repeal was also considered in 1971 but was never seriously taken up again.[117]

The charter's defeat was said to signal the death of "the concept of a 'Catholic vote.'" Writing in *New York Newsday*, Bernie Bookbinder noted that despite the Church's campaign in support of the constitution, the faithful rejected the charter because "Catholics vote as taxpayers, as city dwellers, as farmers, or whatever, not just as Catholics."[118] It does seem that increased taxes weighed more heavily in Catholic voters' minds than the possibility of state aid for parochial schools. But as Andrew Greeley wrote as late as 1978, support for Catholic schools was "almost the only thing about which there had not been a decline in American Catholicism" in the fifteen years from 1963 to 1978. Greeley found that three-quarters of American Catholics supported "the continued existence" of parochial schools and supported state aid to those schools.[119] New York's suburban Catholic voters may have prioritized taxes and local control over Blaine repeal, but they may well have believed that state aid for nonpublic schools could be achieved through the legislature, separately from the matter of the constitution.

The vote on the draft constitution also came amid a wave of tax revolts by middle-class voters, on Long Island and across the nation, who were angered by rising school costs.[120] In the spring of 1967 forty-three Long Island school budgets for the 1967–68 school year were initially voted down by taxpayers compared with eighteen the year before. A member of the Nassau County school board assessed that voters were "carefully scrutinizing the budgets" and warned that school districts were "in for rougher times ahead."[121] Voters across Long Island faced an average increase of 16 percent in school taxes that year. For the first time in a decade, districts anticipated only a small increase in enrollment and little construction costs, but increasing budgets were needed to offset teachers' demands for higher pay. "I want to see how much they can cut without hurting the children," Mrs. Nita Ackers told *The New York Times* after voting against the Hicksville Board of Education's third proposed budget. "I voted against as a form of protest against higher taxes," Mrs. Theresa Fisher said.[122]

In the wake of such pressures, Catholic school officials warned that a decrease in Catholic school enrollments would drive public school costs even higher. In February 1969 the New York State Council of Catholic School Superintendents announced that enrollment in the state's Catholic schools had declined by more than 25,000 students that year alone, and by nearly 59,000 over the preceding five years. While a declining birth rate accounted for some of this decline, the council singled out ever-rising tuition costs for greater blame. The cost to taxpayers for public schools to absorb these students was said to be $29.5 million, leading *Time* magazine to call parochial schools "a bargain for society." Even Governor Rockefeller said parents paying taxes and parochial school tuition deserved "a sincere debt of gratitude from all of us in the state."[123]

Richard Nixon and Catholic Political Realignment

Long Island Catholics' fight over religion in public schools and over state funding for parochial schools, and their support of suburban tax revolts, was the leading edge of a national political trend in which American Catholic voters displayed increasing disaffection with the New Deal coalition and openness to conservative politics. Catholics' fierce anticommunism, and Dwight D. Eisenhower's personal popularity, had drawn some Catholic voters to the right as early as the elections of 1948 and 1952. In 1960 78 percent of American Catholics voted for the Irish Catholic Democrat, John F. Kennedy, but even this was below the 80 percent of the Catholic vote that Al Smith had secured in 1928. For many working- and middle-class Catholics, Kennedy—who, it was noted, had never attended a Catholic school—was more Boston Brahmin than one of their own. Thanks to Richard Nixon's strong anticommunist credentials, he won a number of New York City's Catholic neighborhoods and, on Long Island, won 55 percent of votes in Babylon, 57 percent of votes in Smithtown, and 53 percent of votes in Oyster Bay—all heavily Catholic areas.[124]

With Sen. Barry Goldwater of Arizona atop the Republican ticket in 1964, Democrat Lyndon B. Johnson won both Nassau and Suffolk Counties despite Republicans' significant registration advantage.[125] And yet, the rightward movement of Long Island's Catholic voters was still evident. Whereas statewide, Goldwater received just 32.3 percent of the vote, in largely Catholic sections of Long Island he polled well ahead of his state total, receiving 43 percent of votes in Babylon, 45 percent of votes in Smithtown, and 42 percent of votes in Oyster Bay.

Four years later, Catholic movement to the right was once again most evident on Long Island. Although he lost the 1968 presidential election, Democrat Hubert Humphrey won 59 percent of the nation's Catholic vote, with Republican Richard Nixon receiving 33 percent, and third-party candidate George Wallace receiving 8 percent. But in Catholic-dominated areas of Long Island, Nixon received 62 percent of votes in Babylon, 65 percent in Smithtown, and 57 percent in Oyster Bay.[126]

Evaluating the results of the 1968 elections, many Democrats surmised that their increasing inability to hold Catholic voters within the New Deal coalition was due to racial backlash.[127] As discussed in chapter 5, scholars and pundits in the late 1960s were focusing their attention on white ethnics and, as Joshua Zeitz has written, in politics the term was used to represent voters from various religions, nationalities, and income brackets, "whose principal connection seemed to be their resentment of black radicalism and the welfare state." Working-class Catholics, especially the descendants of Italian and Eastern European immigrants, made up a significant percentage of the demographic. As Zeitz has shown, by the 1960s New York City had become a more difficult place for such white ethnics. From the 1940s to the late 1960s blue-collar jobs evaporated as industry moved to the Sunbelt. At the same time, the Great Migration increased the city's Black population, and racial discrimination in housing and employment drove a spike in "violent crime rates, welfare dependency, and neighborhood decay."[128]

But the ethnic revival of the late 1960s and 1970s and the Catholic revolt from the New Deal coalition were not principally driven by race consciousness or anti-Black racism. National polls had long revealed that American Catholics held consistently more liberal positions on race relations than all other whites except Jews. That George Wallace's share of the 1968 Catholic vote was less than half his share of the total vote also indicates that race was not the central factor for Catholic voters. Even in 1970, after the height of Black urban protest, a Harris poll taken for the National Urban League found that Polish, Irish, and Italian ethnics were less likely than other white Americans to "harbor anti-black attitudes." Racial backlash simply "does not provide the explanation of lasting changes in Catholic voting patterns." Rather, the overriding concern of white ethnics and their advocates was economic, as inflation and tax increases, including New York's institution of a citywide personal income tax in 1966, cut into the savings and income of working-class whites.[129]

Suburban Catholics on Long Island shared these economic concerns. Just weeks after the assassination of Dr. Martin Luther King Jr. in April 1968, Lillian S. Curley of Rockville Centre wrote *The Long Island Catholic* to respond to a previous letter critiquing the white racism and inaction of the Church. While acknowledging the "grave sins of discrimination" and calling for zeal in addressing "root social problems," Curley insisted it was "time to stop using the white middle class as a whipping boy or a scapegoat for all our social ills." She noted that "only one generation removed from the ghetto themselves," working- and middle-class whites contributed "the vast billions of dollars" in taxes which supported the welfare system and various government poverty programs.[130] A year later, in August 1969, Mary White of Carle Place wrote *The Long Island Catholic* in support of lowering interest rates on student loans, which had climbed from 3 to 7 percent that year. She noted that these loans were made to students whose middle-class families pay "the highest taxes, get no relief funds or government subsidies, no free food . . . and who usually has a husband who works two jobs or a wife who must work outside the home." Theirs, White wrote, is "truly a voice crying in the wilderness."[131] And in an April 1971 lecture to the Rosary-Altar Society of St. Rose of Lima Parish in Massapequa, historian Salvatore LaGumina quoted a *New York Times* article to lament that urban ethnics paid "the bill for every major government program" but were "virtually ignored in the funding of programs and services," and then "stereotyped as a racist" and "made fun of because he likes the flag."[132]

Throughout his first term, Nixon made a concerted effort to win over white ethnic and Catholic voters, many of whom may have appreciated his strong anticommunist credentials and law-and-order rhetoric. The May 1970 Hard Hat Riot, in which construction workers attacked college students and hippies on the streets of Lower Manhattan, convinced Nixon that blue-collar white ethnics could provide him much-needed support amid anti–Vietnam War protests.[133] As the election of 1972 approached, Norman Podhoretz, the editor of *Commentary*, predicted that "just as black assertion set the climate" for the politics of the 1960s, "a comparable Catholic, white ethnic assertion" would dominate the 1970s.[134] Nixon advisors Charles Colson, Roy Morey, and Pat Buchanan, himself a Catholic, supported cultivating Catholic leaders in crucial northeastern states. Morey, however, argued that Catholic voters would be more responsive to appeals based on ethnicity, as well as general social, cultural, and economic issues, rather than religion.[135]

Even as the war in Vietnam raged, Nixon and various Republican advisors deemed that the most important issue for courting Catholic voters was the acute financial crisis facing Catholic education, brought on by suburbanization, the decline in religious vocations, and rising educational costs. In 1960 Nixon had supported government aid to Catholic schools—while John Kennedy had not—but the debate remained focused on the state and local levels. As federal aid to education expanded throughout the 1960s, Catholic schools lost out on federal funding that benefited only the public schools with whom they were increasingly competing.[136] Meanwhile, the Republican Party shifted the basis of their appeal to Catholic voters from an emphasis on anticommunism to a focus on education. In 1968 the party's platform called for federal education programs to benefit students in nonpublic schools, arguing that such programs could be made constitutional if the payments were made directly to families rather than being funneled through state agencies.¹³⁷ During his first administration, President Nixon met with New York's Terence Cardinal Cooke in April 1969 and January 1972 and in both meetings funding for Catholic schools was a principal concern.¹³⁸

Nixon advisor Roy Morey worried that appealing to Catholics on school funding was a risky proposition since more than twice as many Catholic children attended public schools than attended parochial schools. Additionally, pressing aid for parochial schools risked alienating some Protestant voters and public-school teachers, among others. An August 1972 Gallup poll showed that among all voters, 43 percent said they would be more inclined to support a candidate who advocated aid for nonpublic schools and 42 percent said they would be less inclined. But the very same poll showed that 70 percent of Catholic voters would be more inclined to vote for a candidate favoring non–public school aid, and only 21 percent would be less inclined.¹³⁹

With encouragement from Pat Buchanan, Nixon campaigned for reelection on his support of funding for parochial schools including in speeches before a convention of the Knights of Columbus in August 1971 and the National Catholic Education Association in April 1972.¹⁴⁰ "In your fight to save your schools, you can count on my support," Nixon told the Knights. And at the 1972 Republican National Convention, the party platform stressed that "non-public schools, both church oriented and non-sectarian" played an "indispensable role" in the nation and stated Nixon's "determination to help halt the accelerating trend of non-public school closures."¹⁴¹

In campaign ads in *The Long Island Catholic*, Nixon hit hard on the theme of aid for parochial schools, heading off any criticism that he had failed to deliver on the issue in his first term. "You're bothered by the fact that every day one more private or parochial school closes," the ad began. "So is President Nixon." The ad summarized Nixon's opposition to busing and his support of tax credits for parents of parochial school students. "America needs her non-public schools. Those non-public schools need help. . . . We must and will find ways to provide that help," Nixon was quoted as saying. The problem, the ad warned, was finding a form of aid that Congress would approve and the Supreme Court would deem constitutional. But to find such a solution required "a man in the White House" who wanted to find it. "President Nixon is that man," the ad concluded.¹⁴²

Nixon won reelection handily in 1972 with 61 percent of the popular vote. Although Sen. George McGovern had selected John F. Kennedy's Catholic brother-in-law, Sargent Shriver, as his running mate, and 60 percent of Catholic voters were registered Democrats, Nixon secured 59 percent of the

Catholic vote, a significant increase from his 1968 tally, and a new record high for a Republican candidate. Nixon cut deeply into Democrats' white ethnic constituency, increasing his share of the Irish, Italian, and Jewish votes by nearly 20 percent from his 1968 numbers.[143] As he had in 1968, Nixon polled even better than his national tallies in New York. According to exit polls, Nixon won 58 percent of the nation's Italian vote, but earned 68 percent of New York's Italian vote and came within just 80,000 votes of carrying New York City.[144]

Abortion Politics and the Election of 1976

Nixon's appeal to Catholic voters in 1972 also included his opposition to abortion. Journalist Theodore White, covering the Nixon campaign, noted that the president wrote a letter to Terence Cardinal Cooke of New York joining him in opposing New York State's legalization of abortion. But in 1972 "abortion was a peripheral issue," in the presidential campaign. It was only in 1976, the first election after the US Supreme Court legalized abortion nationwide with its January 1973 *Roe v. Wade* decision, that abortion played a more central role in a presidential election, and even then abortion failed to mobilize evangelical voters until 1980.[145]

In New York, however, the fight over abortion was already reshaping politics and once again lay Catholics in the suburbs of Long Island were at the forefront of the debate. Stacey Taranto has shown how Catholic housewives on Long Island were central to the founding of the New York State Right to Life Party and to the conservative takeover of the New York State Republican Party, once the bastion of moderate Rockefeller Republicanism. For these women, the postwar suburban ideal conformed to their religious convictions regarding the traditional family, which amid the Cold War they also saw as a bulwark against the spread of Communism.[146] They were brought to political activism through their involvement in parish organizations that were established to fulfill Vatican II's call for more robust lay leadership. Jane Gilroy, for example, became involved in electoral politics through Curé of Ars Parish in Merrick, which she and her husband joined in the early 1960s. The parish's newly ordained associate pastor, Fr. Paul Driscoll, organized parishioners into various dialogue groups, including the Intra-Church Relations Committee and a mothers group centered on debates over the New York State Legislature's attempts to legalize abortion. After New York legalized abortion, these women founded the New York State Right to Life Party in 1970 and launched an ultimately unsuccessful petition drive to place Gilroy on the ballot in that year's election for governor.

These female Catholic activists were motivated by what they perceived to be threats not only to the very life of the unborn child, but also to traditional family life. In the late 1970s, these same concerns drove Catholic activist Phyllis Schlafly to found the Eagle Forum, and conservative evangelical Beverly LaHaye to found Concerned Women for America, two national political lobbying organizations aimed at rallying women in opposition to the Equal Rights Amendment.[147] Social conservatives like Schlafly, who as has been noted got her start fighting for religion in public schools, saw the ERA as "antifamily, antichildren, and pro-abortion," and as an attempt by radical feminists to advance gay rights and undermine the obligation of men to financially support mothers and children.[148] Meanwhile, throughout the 1970s, the platform and the candidates endorsed by the Democratic Party were being transformed by the McGovern-Frazier Commission. Its invitation to feminists and various minority-rights groups to have more say in party affairs pushed the party beyond traditional economic and labor concerns to advocacy of the ERA and abortion rights.[149]

Catholic women on Long Island, like many Catholic voters, began to feel as if the Democratic Party was abandoning them. But in New York, the Republican Party was also controlled by a liberal faction headed by Gov. Nelson Rockefeller who signed legislation legalizing abortion in the state in 1970. Conservatives were so marginal in the state GOP that some members had broken away in 1962 to establish a Conservative Party. But in the mid-1970s, conservative Republican Party bosses like Joseph Margiotta of Nassau County began to tap into the grassroots political organizations that pro-life and antifeminist women had established.[150]

In the 1976 presidential election both Jimmy Carter and Gerald Ford strenuously courted Catholic voters and the US Catholic bishops, for whom abortion was a central concern. Although Gerald Ford's record on abortion was mixed, Ronald Reagan's supporters at the 1976 Republican National Convention assured that the party's platform called for a constitutional amendment to ban abortion, in stark contrast with the Democratic Party. Both candidates met with then-Archbishop Joseph Bernardin of Cincinnati, president of the National Conference of Catholic Bishops, to discuss abortion policy. In public statements after their meetings, the bishops called Carter's position a "disappointment" and left their meeting with Ford "encouraged" but not "totally satisfied."[151]

Unable to win the bishops' approval of his abortion stance, Carter appealed to Catholic voters' concerns about threats to ethnic tradition, family life, neighborhoods, and parochial schools. Calling ethnic heritage "the living fiber that holds America together," Carter declared in a *Long Island*

Catholic campaign ad: "I intend to see it preserved." He pledged, too, that he would have "no more urgent priority" than the support and strengthening of the American family. Carter's ad also worried that "the right of millions of low and middle income Americans to choose a religious education for their children" was under threat. Carter declared: "I am firmly committed to conducting a systematic and continuing search for constitutionally acceptable methods for providing aid to parents whose children attend non segregated private schools."[152] Andrew Greeley, for one, was unconvinced. He argued that Catholics should fear a Carter presidency because Carter's "resolute refusal to say a single good word about Catholic schools" smacked of "hard backed bigotry."[153]

Ford's campaign ads also touted the importance of neighborhoods and highlighted the president's fight against big government in favor of "local control." The ads reminded voters that Ford deemed abortion "morally wrong" and backed a constitutional amendment "allowing each state to pass its own laws" on abortion. But the ads framed abortion, and the legalization of contraceptives, principally as undermining "the authority of parents" and dealing a "serious blow to the very fiber of the family unit."[154]

Local control and parental choice were also the contexts in which Ford's ads discussed education, which was by far the most prominent issue addressed. Educational quality, the ads argued, was improved by "more local control of local schools" and was imperiled by "the kind of federal interference" that had resulted in "the forced busing of children." The ads assured Catholic voters that Ford appreciated the financial sacrifice made by parents with children in parochial schools, and the fact that these schools lessened the financial burden on public schools and taxpayers. Ford, therefore, strongly supported tax-credit assistance for parents with children in parochial schools and rejected Carter's statement in favor of "the taxation of church properties other than the church building itself."[155]

Public opinion polls late in the campaign showed that Ford's support for tax relief for parents of parochial school students had helped narrow the gap with Carter.[156] Ultimately, however, amid the fallout from Watergate, Carter won the election and the American Catholic vote with 57 percent of ballots to Ford's 42 percent. Still, Ford surpassed the Catholic tallies achieved by the Republican nominees in 1960, 1964, and 1968, and on Long Island Ford won both Nassau and Suffolk Counties. This was a strong indication that the days of the Catholic Democratic monolith had passed, and that Nixon's inroads with Catholic voters were not an aberration. But 1976 also indicated that Catholic voters were willing to split their ballots, becoming classic swing voters rather than reliable conservatives.[157] New York's 1976 Senate race highlights that fact and makes clear the relative importance of issues like abortion and nonpublic school funding to suburban Catholic voters.

In the 1976 New York primaries, Daniel Patrick Moynihan—the Catholic social scientist, political advisor, and diplomat—ran against Rep. Bella Abzug for the Democratic nomination for US Senate.[158] In a *Long Island Catholic* campaign ad, Moynihan touted his otherwise undefined "vote against abortion" and his "insistence on inserting aid to parochial schools in the platform of the Democratic Party."[159] Subsequent letters to the editor critiqued the advertisement because it misrepresented Moynihan's pro-choice position and *Long Island Catholic* editors apologized for approving an ad that gave a "false impression."[160] Still, Moynihan ran ahead of Abzug in New York City and the Long Island suburbs, securing victory by fewer than 10,000 votes, to take on incumbent Republican senator James Buckley in the general election.[161] In campaign ads, Buckley proposed a "check list" for "thinking Catholics" that highlighted his sponsorship of a pro-life constitutional amendment and Moynihan's pro-choice opposition to the bill.[162] In the wake of New York City's near bankruptcy and Buckley's delayed support for a federal bailout, Moynihan defeated the conservative incumbent, even besting Carter's numbers in Catholic neighborhoods.[163]

True to his word, the following year Moynihan joined Republican senator Bob Packwood of Oregon in proposing the Tuition Tax Credit Act, which would have allowed parents to deduct up to $500 of the tuition they paid for their children's nonpublic schooling.[164] Despite garnering twenty-six Republican and twenty-four Democrat co-sponsors in the Senate, a version of the bill passing the House of Representatives, and polling data showing that two-thirds of Americans favored such tuition tax credits, President Carter threated to veto the legislation on constitutional grounds and the bill foundered.[165] Moynihan scored the subtle anti-Catholicism of the bill's opponents, Carter's failure to fulfill his campaign pledge to help save Catholic schools, and the ill effects on middle class taxpayers. "Middle-income Americans have come to feel a genuine grievance over this matter," Moynihan wrote. "These parents pay most of the taxes in America and get relatively few of the social services."[166]

The Reagan Revolution

Carter's victory in 1976 was framed as evidence of evangelical Christianity's rising political involvement and influence.[167] Although it was initially unclear to which political party the evangelical bloc would gravitate, debates around moral issues, family values, and race relations ultimately drove evangelicals to an alliance with the Republican Party.[168] Catholics had dominated pro-life politics from their inception in the late 1960s, and as late as 1980 some 70 percent of the National Right to Life Committee was Catholic.[169] But opposition to the ERA and abortion grew among evangelicals as Christian Right leaders like Jerry Falwell, who founded Moral Majority in 1979, framed these positions as a defense of motherhood and forged a coalition with conservative Catholics in defense of the "traditional family" and "family values."[170] Evangelicals' conversion to pro-life advocacy came as the Republican Party solidified its opposition to abortion and the ERA. By 1980 conservative women like Phyllis Schlafly had linked their movement to the Religious Right and exerted their influence in the Republican Party to strip support of the ERA from the platform and to ensure the GOP was unambiguous in its support of a right-to-life amendment to the constitution.[171]

Ronald Reagan was late in coming to the pro-life position, having signed legislation in 1967 as governor of California that legalized abortion in the state. His selection of George H. W. Bush as his running mate also unsettled pro-life advocates as Bush opposed abortion but had been a supporter of Planned Parenthood and did not favor a human life amendment. Reagan's opposition to abortion was sufficient to appeal to evangelicals and conservative Catholics, but it is also clear that abortion was not the decisive issue in the 1980 election. An October 1980 Gallup poll found that pro-life voters split evenly between Carter and Reagan, with 33 percent of Carter's backers and 32 percent of Reagan's supporters favoring a ban on abortion.[172]

But Reagan's appeal to the suburban Catholic women who had launched the pro-life movement—and to Catholic voters more generally—was not limited to his direct opposition to abortion and the ERA. Throughout the 1970s a downturn in the economy and the pressures of suburban economics compelled these women to support conservative politics because they feared that soaring property taxes would compel women to work outside the home, thereby undermining the traditional family life they sought to defend. This was an especially pressing concern in Nassau County where property owners paid the highest taxes of any county in the country, 60 percent of which went to fund public schools.[173] So, too, was the plight of parochial schools especially in light of Carter's unkept promises. Indeed, in appealing to Catholic voters, Reagan "more often emphasized his support for tuition tax credits for parents of students in private schools" than he did his opposition to abortion.[174]

Winning the support of New York's suburban taxpayers was especially important given that the four suburban counties surrounding New York City accounted for one-quarter of all votes in the state by 1980.[175] Throughout the postwar period, the influence of New York's suburbs had been growing along with their population. In 1950 the four downstate suburban counties of Nassau, Suffolk, Westchester, and Rockland accounted for just 12 percent of the statewide vote compared to New York City's 48 percent. But by 1966 the suburbs' share had risen to 20 percent and the city's had dropped to 40 percent. In 1980 Nassau County had 1.4 million residents, and if it were a city, it would have been the nation's fifth largest. For the first time in the state's history, Nassau County registered the largest number of votes, unseating the urban counties of Kings (Brooklyn) and Queens, and together the four suburban counties accounted for 25 percent of the entire statewide vote. Catholics were an especially important segment of this suburban bloc, comprising up to 50 percent of the population in New York's four suburban counties.[176] Thanks in part to the white ethnic revival, there remained vestiges of ethnic politics as well: Italian Americans were power players as the single largest ethnic group in the state and some 20 percent of the electorate.[177]

Emblematic of these trends, was the Republican candidate for New York's US Senate seat in 1980, Alfonse D'Amato. From the working-class South Shore town of Island Park, D'Amato was a forty-three-year-old, second-generation Italian American who had worked his way up through the Nassau County Republican machine to serve as Town Supervisor of Hempstead, the nation's largest town with 800,000 residents. Although his opponents accused him of corruption and racism, D'Amato had built a reputation as a savvy politician who, in collaboration with Joseph M. Margiotta the GOP chairman of Nassau County, ran one of the most powerful and effective political machines in the nation.[178]

D'Amato saw in the death of Nelson Rockefeller, in January 1979, a symbol of the demise of the Liberal Republicanism he had championed. To D'Amato's eyes, Long Island's GOP was now dominated by Catholic voters who "had abandoned the Democratic Party when they left the confines of the city" and were "fed up with welfare, taxes, and the social experimentation of a drifting, post-McGovern Democratic Party."[179] Sensing an opportunity, D'Amato challenged incumbent US Senator Jacob Javitz, another Liberal Republican icon who had been in office for twenty-four years, for the GOP nomination. Described by the press as "an authentic suburbanite voice at a time when the suburbs" were "gaining influence," D'Amato appealed to suburban frustrations over inflation, taxes, and crime.[180] "The middle class was trampled during the 1970s," D'Amato would later recall. "We would speak for them, fight for them."[181] Securing endorsements from the Right to Life Party and the Conservative Party, D'Amato defeated Javits thanks to decisive victories in Long Island's middle-class suburbs, including Floral Park, Uniondale, and East Meadow, which gave him "majorities of 2 to 1 and 3 to 1."[182]

In a three-way race against Democrat Elizabeth Holtzman, and Jacob Javitz running on the Liberal Party line, Al D'Amato eked out a slim victory in the general election. Holtzman won nearly two-thirds of the state's Jewish vote and would have won the election if Javitz, who garnered just 11 percent of the vote, had dropped out of the race. D'Amato found strong support among Italians and pro-life voters, and his victory was described as "a microcosm of Ronald Reagan's more impressive showing nationwide," in that he won by capturing the densely populated suburbs and polling well among blue-collar union voters.[183]

At the top of the ticket Ronald Reagan won New York State by 2.67 percent because his margins of victory in Nassau and Suffolk Counties were larger than any of Carter's victories in any county other than Manhattan. Reagan captured 55.9 percent of votes in Nassau and 57 percent of votes in Suffolk. He made particular inroads among ethnic voters, securing the Irish vote in every large state, including New York, and winning 57 percent of New York's Italian vote.[184] Reagan also won over New York's pro-life voters. Although the Right to Life Party had been founded in Nassau County, and its nominee Ellen McCormack was from Merrick, she won only 27,829 votes in the state, just one-fifth of the party's tally in the 1978 gubernatorial race.[185] Whereas in 1976 57 percent of New York Catholics voted for Jimmy Carter, in 1980 he won only 44 percent of the state's Catholic vote, with Reagan securing 47 percent. Reagan and D'Amato both won over suburban, middle-class, Catholic voters "by marrying pro-family issues to economic ones," pledging to lower taxes, limit government overreach, provide financial support to parochial schools, and enact a human life amendment.[186]

Nationwide, polls by Gallup and CBS found that Reagan won between 47 and 50 percent of the Catholic vote, making 1980 another election in which a plurality of Catholics voted for the Republican candidate as they had in 1956 and 1972. The Reagan Revolution of 1980 marked what pollster Richard Wirthlin called a "rolling realignment" of Catholic voters. After the disruption of Watergate, Catholic voters resumed their movement out of the New Deal coalition—a transition that was driven in large part by the migration of Catholics to the postwar suburbs.[187] Exit polling would indicate that Reagan owed his victory even more to white evangelicals who accounted for nearly two-thirds of his votes, and in the decades to come evangelical voters would prove to be a more reliably conservative voting bloc. The departure of Catholic voters from the New Deal coalition made them swing voters rather than staunch conservatives.[188] In New York, for example, Catholic voters backed Reagan and D'Amato in 1980, but also supported Daniel Patrick Moynihan's reelection in 1982—an election he won with 65 percent of the vote.[189]

Throughout his first term, Reagan continued to court Catholic voters by appointing several Catholics to high-level positions in his administration, and by naming an official ambassador to the Vatican. In August 1982 Reagan addressed a gathering of the US bishops and the Knights of Columbus in Hartford, Connecticut, and once again highlighted his opposition to abortion, his support for tax credits for families with children in Catholic schools, and his backing of a constitutional amendment to allow prayer in public schools. In 1984 Reagan was reelected with 55 percent of the Catholic vote, an improvement even upon Nixon's record success in 1972.[190]

Conclusion—Political Polarization

The conservative takeover of New York's Republican Party that was launched by suburban Catholic women in the late 1960s was complete by the 1990s. At that time a Marist Institute survey of New York voters found that 51.6 percent of New York Republicans were Catholic, and 49 percent called themselves conservative. And this transformation was seen as "a metaphor for the party's fortunes nationwide." As one longtime Republican strategist summarized in 1992, "The Republican Party is a suburban, blue-collar party now. We used to be a progressive Protestant party. Now we're a conservative Catholic party."[191]

As Catholics proved more and more comfortable voting for Republicans, liberal Catholics fretted that the Catholic constituency was being co-opted by the New Right and abandoning the Church's social teaching. As early as 1971 sisters from various religious orders established Network, a social justice lobby to call attention to issues such as human rights, nuclear disarmament, and health care, which they felt were being ignored by Catholics' focus on aid for parochial schools and abortion. Sister Carol Coston, OP, Network's executive director, warned in 1980 that Catholics' burgeoning alliance with evangelicals and the New Right was "potentially dangerous" as its focus on abortion "risked defeat of the overall social justice agenda."[192] By the early 1990s, with political polarization within the Church increasing, liberal Catholics like Notre Dame theologian Rev. Richard McBrien and *Commonweal* editor Margaret O'Brien Steinfels fretted that conservatives were repositioning the Catholic center so that liberals were about to "fall off the map."[193]

But although conservative Catholic voters opposed abortion and backed candidates endorsed by Religious Right organizations, such as the Christian Coalition or Focus on the Family, they also proved hesitant to join such organizations and maintained "a somewhat distinctive identity within the Christian right."[194] Indeed, unlike evangelical Protestants, who became reliable Republican voters after the Reagan Revolution, American Catholic voters' openness to conservatism resulted in the bifurcation of the once monolithic Catholic voting bloc. Catholics became "the ultimate swing voters," with 40 percent reliably voting for Republicans, 40 percent reliably voting for Democrats, and the remainder voting for either party.[195] In this sense, the Catholic voting bloc ceased to exist and suburbanization can be said to have launched the realignment of Catholic voters, which completed their assimilation into the American mainstream, "for whom partisanship plays a greater role in shaping political behavior than group affiliation."[196]

The political polarization that split American Catholics left and right also drove a wedge between lay Catholics and their bishops. As many Catholic voters moved to the right throughout the 1970s and '80s, a new cohort of US bishops replaced a Cold War generation and shifted the American Church's priorities to the left. In 1970, even as politicians from both parties began to pay more attention to white ethnic voters, the US bishops announced that they would disband their Task Force on Urban Problems. And during the Reagan administrations, the bishops downplayed their quest for government aid to parochial schools and restrictions on abortion, in favor of advocating for liberal economic reforms and nuclear prohibition. But the bishops' pastoral letters on these topics had limited, if any, influence on Reagan and they failed to win over the majority of lay Catholics. As presidential advisor Edwin Meese noted in 1984, "the shepherds don't always reflect the views of their flocks." Indeed, a 1986 Lilly Foundation study found that only 39 percent of US Catholics even believed it appropriate for the bishops to make public statements on nuclear weapons and economic policy. By 1992 Cardinal Joseph Bernardin of Chicago was forced to concede that the bishops were "not in the same ballpark as our people."[197] That division would only increase in subsequent decades as American Catholics felt free to dissent from various moral, pastoral, and political positions advocated by the bishops and as revelations of clergy sexual abuse and episcopal cover-up decimated the bishops' moral authority.

Epilogue:
The Suburban Church and Religious Disaffiliation

In the early 1970s, in his weekly syndicated newspaper column, Andrew Greeley began sounding the alarm about survey results that found steep declines in Sunday Mass attendance and a rise in the number of Americans who were raised Catholic but no longer identified themselves as such—a process referred to as disaffiliation. "Something dramatic and not a little frightening is happening in the American Catholic Church," Greeley wrote.[1] Several priests of the Diocese of Rockville Centre disagreed. "We have maintained the same Mass attendance for the past four years," said Fr. Robert Kirwin, pastor of St. Thomas More Church in Hauppauge. And Fr. John Gorman, pastor of St. Lawrence in Sayville stated bluntly: "I tend to disagree with Father Greeley. I have seen no marked drop off in mass attendance."[2] But not every priest was unconcerned. Paulist Father John B. Sheerin, CSP, confessed in his own weekly column that Greeley's survey did "uncover a drop in Catholic Church attendance that is worthy of far more concern than most Catholics had given it."[3]

In fact, after a decade of increases in the late 1940s and 1950s, the number of American Catholics attending Mass on Sunday had peaked at an astonishing 74 percent in 1958, the year after the Diocese of Rockville Centre became the nation's first suburban diocese.[4] That number slowly but steadily declined in subsequent years, and in the late 1970s Greeley continued to forewarn and excoriate the bishops he felt were doing nothing to stem the tide. "The erosion of religious practice among American Catholics continues and there is no sign of it bottoming out," Greeley wrote in 1975.[5] And in 1978 he found that "the deterioration in American Catholic devotional practice" was continuing, and added that it was "now taken for granted" by Church leaders who "still did nothing."[6] According to data compiled by the Center for Applied Research in the Apostolate (CARA), the percentage of

American Catholics who attended Mass every week dropped from 55 percent in 1970, to 42 percent in 1980, 32 percent in 1990, 30 percent in 2000, 24 percent in 2010, to just 17 percent in 2020.[7]

In the 1960s and '70s, even amid the steady decline in Sunday Mass attendance, the numbers of people who were raised Catholic but later disaffiliated from the Church were actually a source of some hope. In 1965 about 14 percent of those who said they were raised Catholic reported being something other than Catholic. But this rate of disaffiliation was considerably better than that of other denominations, including the 18 percent for Baptists, 35 percent for Lutherans, and 43 percent for Methodists.[8] And the rate of Catholics leaving the Church held fairly steady, with Andrew Greeley reporting 16 percent Catholic disaffiliation in 1979.[9] But beginning in the 1990s, the number of disaffiliated Catholics rose considerably along with the number of Americans who claimed to have no religion at all—the "nones." Today, more than a third of Americans who were raised Catholic "no longer see themselves as such. And over half of *those*, amounting to almost one in five out of everyone who says they were raised Catholic," now say they have no religion. Among US Catholics born since 1970, "a Catholic upbringing has produced twice as many nones as it has weekly Mass-going Catholics."[10]

Altogether such sobering statistics prove that in the era of the suburban Church the children, grandchildren, and great-grandchildren of the postwar generation who pioneered suburban parishes have participated less and less in the life of faith. Over time, the rates at which they have attended Mass, had their marriages blessed and their children baptized, and sent their children to parochial schools have all declined. Sociologists of religion who have studied this phenomenon have begun to explore a web of interrelated reasons for why the Boomer generation of Catholics, their children, and grandchildren have ceased practicing the faith in ever-increasing numbers. Although there are divergent opinions about the relative importance of various causes, it is clear today that the Church is reaping "seeds sown decades before, as Stephen Bullivant has put it."[11] And many of the most plausible explanations for the declines are deeply connected to changes in American Catholicism wrought by postwar suburbanization and its attendant social transformations.

As this study has argued, Catholic migration to the suburbs broke down the walls of the urban Catholic ghetto which had "reinforced participation and identification with the Church."[12] Whereas in the old neighborhoods, much of social and familial life revolved around religion and the parish church, in the suburbs, parishes "no longer held the default monopoly over parishioners' time and social life." As with the consumer goods that filled new suburban homes, the ambient culture of suburbia—which by the 1960s and '70s was increasingly at odds with the Church on matters of marriage, sex, and family—offered so many things to organize one's life around other than religion, that the life of faith became one more commodity to choose, or not.[13]

Although newly suburbanized Catholics tried mightily to replicate the institutional and associational infrastructure they had known in their urban parishes, they were hampered by financial constraints, a shortage of priests and religious sisters, political divisions within the Church, and even the spatial arrangement of suburbia. Sunday Masses in drive-in theaters, school auditoriums, and modernist churches lacked both the sense of community and the sense of the sacred that many of the faithful sought. Especially after Vatican II, the Mass itself became a point of contention between those preferring more traditional or more experimental forms of worship.[14] Even at the highpoint of vocations, the number of religious sisters was insufficient to staff the needed number of parochial schools. But then, in the late 1960s and early 1970s, a wave of defections from religious life and the evaporation of new recruits created a true vocations crisis. In the space of three years, between 1969 and 1972, the three largest orders of teaching sisters in the Diocese of Rockville Centre saw 121 sisters retire, 119 die, 444 leave religious life, and only 41 women enter the convent.[15] Editors at *The Long Island Catholic* feared that the collapse of religious vocations "marked a decline in religious convictions in our Catholic families," and expressed "the haunting fear" that the vocation crisis was "a clear sign of declining vitality in the Church."[16]

This contributed not only to staffing and financial crises for parochial schools but to a crisis in confidence regarding the centrality of Catholic schools to the task of inculcating the faith in the next generation. Parishes stopped building new Catholic schools, dioceses closed or consolidated existing schools, and enrollments in Catholic schools declined. Between 1964 and 1969 the number of Catholic school students in New York State declined by nearly 60,000, and nationwide between 1970 and 1985 the number of parochial school students dropped by 32 percent, a decrease of almost 1.5 million children.[17] In the decades after the Second Vatican Council, as more and more Catholic youth received religious formation in weekly CCD classes, the quality of instruction in such programs was frequently deemed inadequate. Forays into novel theology and experiments in pedagogical methods left a whole generation of Catholic youth less knowledgeable about the tenets and practices of the faith and less likely to maintain it especially in the face of an increasingly pluralistic society.[18]

The Church's inability to provide sufficient Catholic schools for rapidly expanding suburbs spawned Catholic political activism demanding state funding for nonpublic schools and, at the same time, political activism that defended religion and prayer in public schools. The tactics employed, and ecumenical alliances forged, in the 1960s during legal battles over prayer in schools informed efforts in the 1970s and 1980s to combat liberalized abortion laws. Thus, the fight for school prayer can be seen as an early skirmish in the culture wars that engulfed the nation in the coming decades as cultural and political debates over "divorce, abortion, homosexuality, and women's equality" became more contentious.[19] Studies of religious disaffiliation indicate that many who have stopped participating in religious community have been turned off by what they perceive to be the political agendas of religious leaders.[20] This is especially true among millennials—those born between 1991 and 1996—who make up the largest bloc of "nones" and were raised in a culture in which traditional Catholic positions on culture war issues were portrayed as retrograde.[21]

Finally, recent surveys of religious disaffiliation reveal that scandals in the Church—especially the sexual abuse of minors by priests and religious and the cover-up of these crimes by Church authorities—have helped drive an increase in those leaving the Church.[22] Although the effects of the clergy abuse scandals on religious disaffiliation were first evident in the early 1990s and grew exponentially in the early 2000s, the instances of abuse and cover-up span the entire postwar period and were highest in earlier decades.[23] In early 2002 a series of reports by *The Boston Globe*'s Spotlight Team brought national attention to clergy sexual abuse, to the Church's reassignment of accused priests, and its failure to report allegations to authorities.[24] After the United States Conference of Catholic Bishops commissioned a study in 2004, researchers at the John Jay College of Criminal Justice and CARA determined that the number of reported cases of clergy sexual abuse of minors was highest between 1960 and 1984. Incidents of abuse "increased steadily from the mid-1960s through the late 1970s," were in "sharp decline by 1985," and "remain low" today.[25] Even as more incidents of abuse have been reported in subsequent years, this statistical concentration of cases in the mid-1960s to the mid-1980s has held true.[26]

The majority of sexual abuse cases in the United States thus occurred during the very years at the heart of this study. Such abuse was not the focus of this research and at no point did any archival record of an accusation or any evidence of cover-up emerge. Still, at least one of the priests cited in this study, Fr. Andrew L. Millar, was subsequently convicted of sexually abusing a minor in 2000.[27] In 2020, the Diocese of Rockville Centre announced that it would file for Chapter 11 bankruptcy protection after more than 200 lawsuits were filed against it alleging sexual abuse by clergy. The diocese released the names of 101 accused priests, and victims' advocacy organizations published a list of an additional 46 priests accused of abuse in Nassau or Suffolk County, including when the counties were part of the Diocese of Brooklyn.[28] With New York State's lifting of the statute of limitations for lawsuits claiming child sexual abuse, the number of claimants against the diocese rose to 600. Despite a proposal that would provide victims with a settlement of between $185 and $200 million, negotiations between the diocese and its creditors remain stalled.[29]

Scholars are only now beginning to grapple with the history of clergy sexual abuse and how to integrate it into the broader history of twentieth-century American Catholicism.[30] Whatever they uncover about the contours and causes of the crisis, it is already clear that the Church's postwar boom years also contained horrors whose full effects would only be appreciated in later decades. This is an especially tragic and extreme example of one of the key ironies of this book: that even as the postwar move to the suburbs was marked by the optimism and excitement of proliferating parishes and schools and of classrooms, seminaries, and convents bursting at the seams, suburbanization was undermining the structures that had sustained the vibrant Catholic world of the "immigrant Church." In opening an entirely new era for the Church, suburbanization sowed seeds that would ultimately erode the vitality of the Church in the early postwar period.[31] Today, even as the Church grapples with the continued fallout from the sexual abuse crisis, rising disaffiliation, and the challenge of integrating and serving sizable new waves of working-class immigrants from Latin America, it is still wrestling with, and largely defined by, the challenges first posed by the collapse of the Catholic ghetto and the spread of crabgrass Catholicism.

ACKNOWLEDGMENTS

This book began at Columbia University, where Ira Katznelson was one of the first people to welcome me to campus. Even as the focus of my research was shifting considerably—and as the university called upon him to serve as interim provost—Ira always found time to check in with me, put me at ease, and push my project forward with his incisive questions. Rebecca Kobrin believed in the possibilities of this project—and my ability to pull it off—long before I did and always provided kind encouragement when it was needed most. Although I didn't write about my native Staten Island as he had hoped, Kenneth T. Jackson enthusiastically embraced this project as a unique contribution to the study of suburbia. I'm grateful that he allowed this book's title to serve as a tribute to his magisterial work *Crabgrass Frontier*. Courtney Bender offered insightful comments on my writing and, in generously discussing her own research, reminded me of the excitement of academic discovery. This book was inspired by questions Tom Sugrue posed in an essay on postwar American Catholicism, and I am deeply grateful for his generous and helpful feedback.

Throughout my time at Columbia, Eric Foner, Mae Ngai, David Greenberg, Elizabeth Blackmar, and the late Alan Brinkley thoughtfully inquired about my research, read drafts of my work, and encouraged my development as a teacher. As a member of Columbia University's Seminar on the City, I was privileged to meet a group of distinguished urban scholars who welcomed me as one of their own and taught me much about the field. It was a particular pleasure to work so closely with the seminar's chair, Lisa Keller, and to be the beneficiary of her wise counsel and unstinting generosity.

Prior to my time at Columbia, Lesley Woodcock Tentler, Timothy Meagher, and Michael Kimmage of the Catholic University of America helped direct my first forays into research with tremendous expertise and kindness.

I was also welcomed into a wonderful community of historians including Wesley Bush, Ryan Carpenter, Vanessa Corcoran, Aaron Gies, Tommy Patteson, Seth and Mary Smith, and Julie Yarwood. When I arrived on Morningside Heights, George Aumoithe, Nick Juravich, Jason Resnikoff, Pollyanna Rhee, and Ian Shin made me feel most welcome and showed me the ropes. I couldn't have asked for better colleagues than Lindsey Dayton, Michael Kideckel, Kathryn Lasdow, AJ Murphy, Jack Neubauer, and Micah McElroy. Michael Glass generously shared research from his superb project on Long Island's suburbs—undertaken at Princeton University—which taught me a great deal about my own. Most of all, David Allen, Eric Herschthal, and Benjamin Serby commiserated and celebrated with me, inspired me to think more deeply and to work harder, and helped me solve all the world's problems while savoring the charms of the world's greatest city. Their friendship is ample reward for the trials and tribulations of research and writing.

This book was finished at the University of Notre Dame, where my formation as an historian began. As an undergraduate and a seminarian I had the privilege of learning from eminent religious historians Scott Appleby, Timothy Matovina, John McGreevy, and Mark Noll, who have remained generous mentors through the years. I was also glad to meet then–doctoral students Kirk Farney and Michael Skaggs, whose friendship and prayerful encouragement have followed me since. When my time at Columbia ended, Kathleen Sprows Cummings welcomed me as a postdoctoral fellow at the Cushwa Center for the Study of American Catholicism, which has been a true intellectual home for me for more than two decades. Even amid the trials of the academy during COVID-19, Philip Byers, Rose Luminiello, MaDonna Noak, Jacqueline Willy Romero, Shane Ulbrich, and I shared work, forged friendships, and found ways to laugh.

It is a rare privilege indeed to be able to return, as a member of the faculty, to the department that first nurtured my passion for history as an undergraduate major. I'm deeply grateful for the opportunity to collaborate with, and be mentored by, such an excellent group of scholars and teachers. In particular, the members of the Colloquium on Religion in American History—including Colin Barr, Peter Cajka, Darren Dochuk, Linda Przybyszewski, Sarah Shortall, Thomas Tweed, and a host of stellar graduate students—provided helpful feedback on drafts of this project. So, too, I have benefited from the comments of panelists, commentators, and participants at workshops and conferences hosted by the American Catholic History Association, the Columbia University Seminar on Religion in America, the Fitzgerald Institute for Real Estate, the Society for US Intellectual History, and the Urban History Association. It is a terrific honor that this book found a home with the University of Chicago Press's superb Historical Studies of Urban America series, and I am deeply grateful to Tim Mennel, Andrea Blatz, Tim Gilfoyle, and the anonymous readers of the manuscript for all of their advice, encouragement, and support. Thanks to Kate Blackmer for her expertise in creating the book's maps.

Throughout the duration of this project I have been assisted by generous financial support from the Sacred Heart Institute of the Archdiocese of New York and the Dioceses of Brooklyn and Rockville Centre, and the Institute for Scholarship in the Liberal Arts in the College of Arts and Letters at the University of Notre Dame; through summer research grants from the Cushwa Center for the Study of American Catholicism and the American Catholic Historical Association; through the Schoff Fund at the University Seminars of Columbia University; and through a Mohler Research Grant from the American Catholic History Research Center at the Catholic University of America. I was also honored to be the recipient of the 2019 John Tracy Ellis Dissertation Award from the American Catholic Historical Association and the 2020 Bancroft Dissertation Award from Columbia University.

This book would not have been possible without the expert assistance of numerous archivists, including Maria Mazzenga, William John Shepherd, and Shane MacDonald at the Catholic University of America's American Catholic History Research Center; Sarah L. Patterson at the Archives of the Archdiocese of Cincinnati; Julie Motyka at the Archives of the Archdiocese of Indianapolis; David Crum and Rick Kenney of the Catholic War Veterans of America; Kevin Cawley and Joseph Smith at the University of Notre Dame Archives; William Fliss and Amy Cary at Marquette University Archives; Michael J. O'Connor at Hofstra University Special Collections; Sr. Margaret Kavanagh, OP, at the Sisters of St. Dominic of Amityville's Queen of the Rosary Archives and Heritage Center; Virginia Dowd at the Sisters of St. Joseph of Brentwood Archives; and Betsy Johnson at the Sisters of Mercy Heritage Center in Belmont, North Carolina. Katie Feighery at the Archives of the Archdiocese of New York and Joseph Coen at the Archives of the Diocese of Brooklyn hosted me for extended research visits and steered me to important finds. Sister Maryanne Fitzgerald, SC, chancellor of the Diocese of Rockville Centre, was instrumental in facilitating much of my research in the archives and parishes of Long Island. I spent several months working in the archives of the Diocese of Rockville Centre, where Krista Ammirati and Elyse Hayes provided invaluable assistance. During that time, now-Archbishop Richard Henning graciously allowed me to reside at Immaculate Conception Seminary, and along with Fathers Walter Kedjierski, Greg Rannazzisi, and Sean Davidson shared edifying conversations that were a welcome reprieve from research.

One of the most enjoyable aspects of my research was visiting suburban parishes and speaking with founding-era parishioners. They are far too many to thank all by name, but I am grateful to Fr. Stanislaw Wadowski at St. Anne Parish in Brentwood; Fr. Ralph Sommer of St. Bernard Parish in Levittown; Fr. Gregory Cappuccino of St. Frances de Chantal Parish in Wantagh; Fr. John Derasmo of St. James Parish in Seaford; Fr. Cristobal Martin of St. Luke Parish in Brentwood; Msgr. Vincent Rush of Our Lady of Grace Parish in West Babylon; Fr. Thomas M. Fusco of Our Lady of Victory Parish in Floral Park; Fr. Valentine Rebello of St. Pius X Parish in Plainview; and Fr. Kenneth Zach of St. Rose of Lima Parish in Massapequa for generously facilitating these visits, and to their parishioners who shared their stories.

Over the past decade I have had the pleasure of residing and assisting at two parishes as a priest-in-residence. I thank the parishioners of Little Flower Parish in Bethesda, Maryland, and Holy Trinity Parish on Manhattan's Upper West Side for their many kindnesses. With characteristic pastoral tact, Monsignors Peter Vaghi, William Kane, Thomas Leonard, and Thomas Sandi, and Fathers George Stuart, Mark Ivany, Anthony Lickteig, and Gary Mead supported me with priestly fraternity while never asking too frequently how my writing was going. I am grateful, too, for the support of my religious community, the Congregation of Holy Cross, and especially Fr. Wilson D. Miscamble, CSC, and Fr. Walter Jenkins, CSC, for sharing their wise counsel and good humor through thick and thin. I finished this book while serving as priest-in-residence of Stanford Hall at the University of Notre Dame. I will be forever grateful to Fr. Christopher Brennan, CSC, and all the "Griffins" of Stanford Hall for the opportunity to share life and faith with them, and for their encouragement of this project.

Across the years I have been lucky to make friends who have become family to me, especially Kevin and Jeanette Haley, Ken and Julie Hallenius, Josh and Stacey Noem, Steve and Maureen Blaha, Scott Cullen, Patrick D'Onofrio, Brenda Greiner, Erin and John Infranca, Linda Kueter, Tiffany and Dave Reidy, Alan Trammel, and Joseph Palmer. They have all given more to me and this book than they likely realize or than I could ever repay. I am profoundly blessed to have loving and supportive aunts and uncles, and cousins—too numerous to mention—who are very dear friends. They have kept abreast of my progress and eagerly anticipated this book's publication. I hope it makes them proud. Finally, there has never been any gift greater than the love of my family: my brother and sister-in-law, Matthew and Christine; my niece and goddaughter, Aria Rose; my nephew, Dean Richard; and my parents, Richard and Andrea, to whom this book is dedicated. Words cannot express my gratitude and love for them all.

APPENDIX

Note: All demographic data for the Diocese of Rockville Centre is from *The Official Catholic Directory* published annually by P. J. Kenedy and Sons of New Providence, NJ. Demographic data for the Diocese of Rockville Centre first appears in *The Official Catholic Directory* in 1958, a year after the diocese's erection. Prior to 1958, the statistical data for Nassau and Suffolk Counties was included in *The Official Catholic Directory*'s entries for the Diocese of Brooklyn. I have approximated annual statistical data for the number of priests, teaching sisters, parochial elementary school students, and parochial and diocesan high school students in the two Long Island counties between 1945 and 1957 by compiling the data available from individual parish and school reports contained in the entries for the Diocese of Brooklyn through those years.

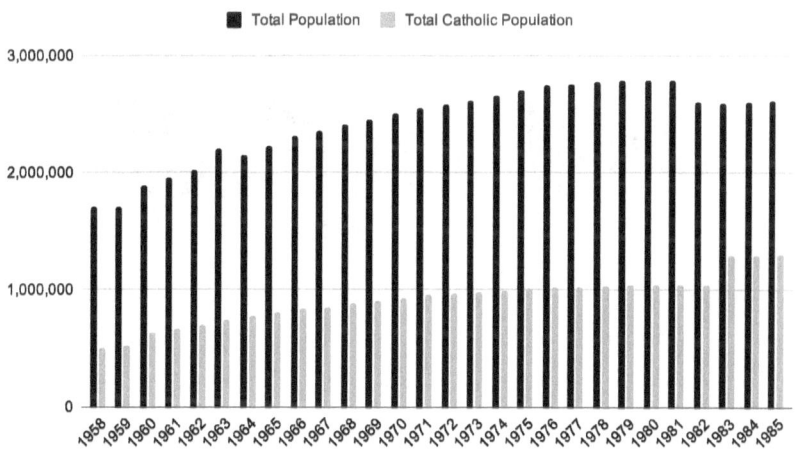

Population of the Diocese of Rockville Centre, 1958–1985

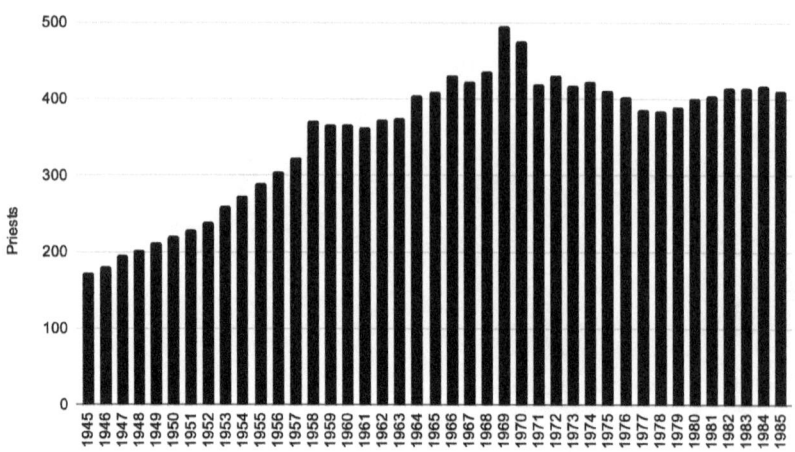

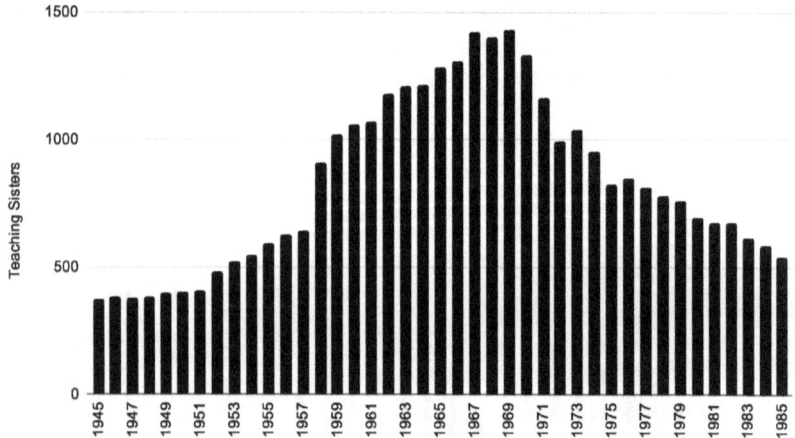

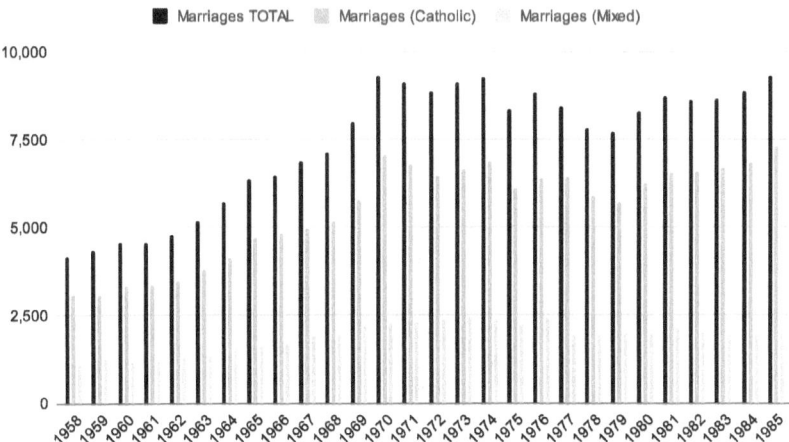

Marriages in the Diocese of Rockville Centre, 1958–1985

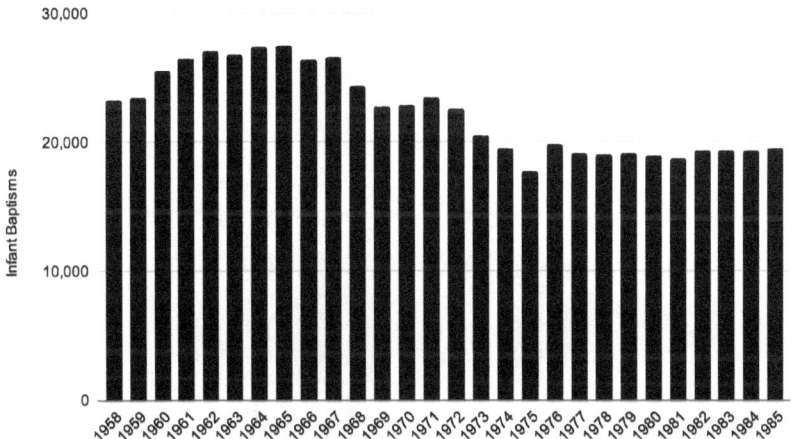

Infant Baptisms in the Diocese of Rockville Centre, 1958–1985

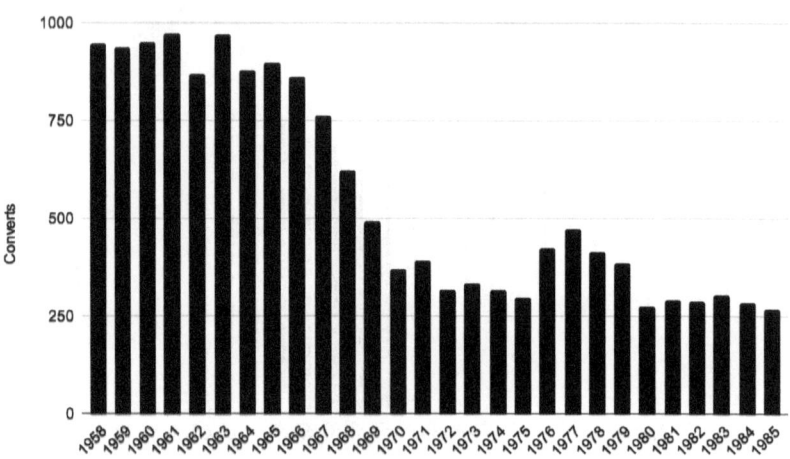

Converts in the Diocese of Rockville Centre, 1958–1985

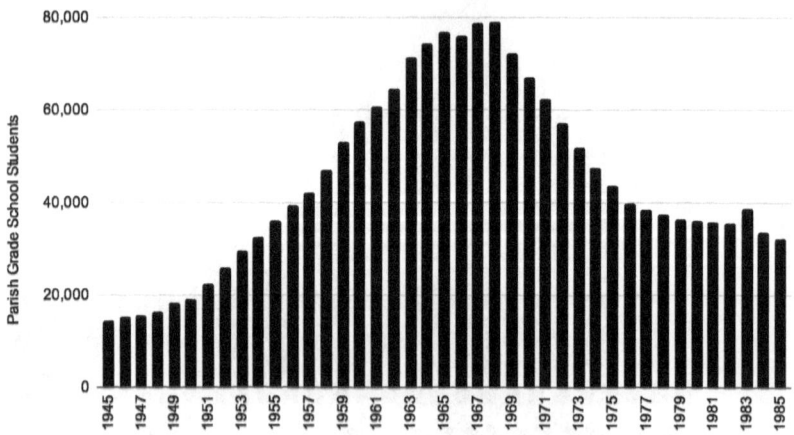

Grade School Students in Nassau & Suffolk Counties, 1945–1985

Diocesan H.S. Students in Nassau & Suffolk Counties, 1945–1985

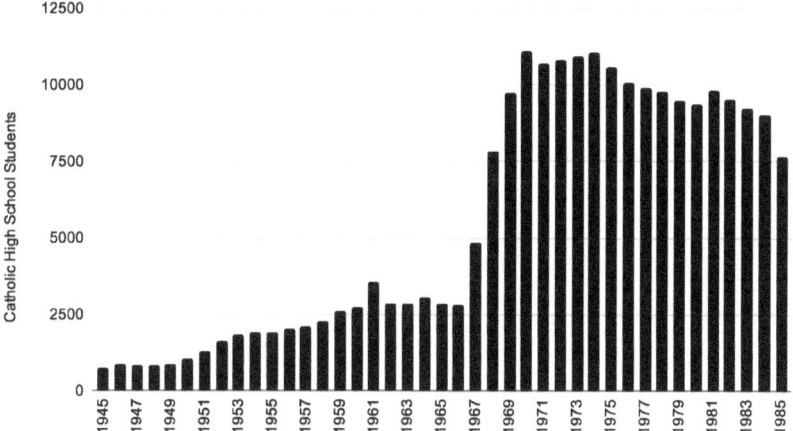

Elementary, High School, and Total Students in CCD in the Diocese of Rockville Centre, 1958–1985

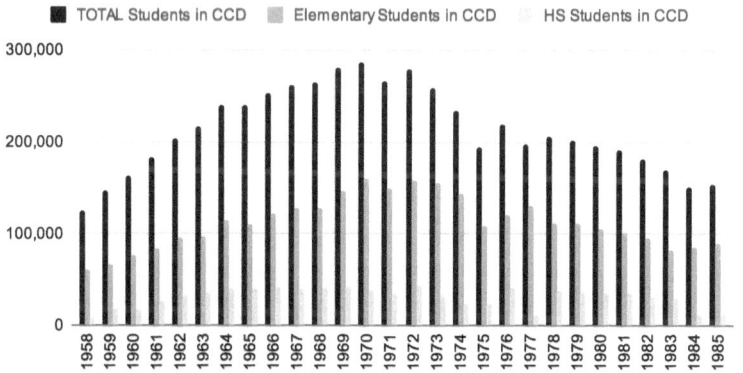

NOTES

INTRODUCTION
1. Portions of this book were first published in Stephen M. Koeth, CSC, "Crabgrass Catholicism: U.S. Catholics and the Historiography of Postwar Suburbia," *US Catholic Historian* 37, no. 4 (Fall 2019): 1–27, Copyright © [2019] The Catholic University of America Press. For the history of Ss. Cyril and Methodius Parish, I relied on "Parish History," found at http://www.sscyrilandmethodius.org/Parish-Information/Parish-History (since replaced with https://sscmdp.org/); *Saint Cyril and Saint Methodius Church: Deer Park, Long Island, New York* (Assorted Parish Journals file, Archives of the Diocese of Rockville Centre [ADRVC]); "Four Buildings Dedicated in Day," *Long Island Catholic* 2, no. 11 (July 11, 1963): 1; "From This . . . Came That," *Long Island Catholic* 3, no. 10 (July 2, 1964): 11. A "parish plant" is the entire complex of buildings making up the parish, usually including the church, school, rectory, and convent, and in urban contexts often covering the better part of a city block.
2. "Deer Park, N.Y.: A Suffolk Hamlet of Modest Homes," *New York Times*, March 7, 1999, 3; "Deer Park," in *The Encyclopedia of New York State*, ed. Peter Eisenstadt, Laura-Eve Moss, and Carole F. Huxley (Syracuse, NY: Syracuse University Press, 2005), 442; "Deer Park," Town of Babylon official website, https://www.townofbabylon.com/280/Deer-Park.
3. "From This . . . Came That," 11.
4. "Parish History," http://www.sscyrilandmethodius.org/Parish-Information/Parish-History; "Four Buildings Dedicated in Day," 1; *Saint Cyril and Saint Methodius Church: Deer Park, Long Island, New York*.
5. *Saint Cyril and Saint Methodius Church: Deer Park, Long Island, New York*; "Four Buildings Dedicated in Day," 1.
6. "From This . . . Came That," 11.
7. Jay P. Dolan, *The Immigrant Church: New York's Irish and German Catholics, 1815–1865* (Baltimore: Johns Hopkins University Press, 1975).
8. Patrick W. Carey, *Catholics in America: A History* (New York: Sheed and Ward, 2008), 93.
9. John T. McGreevy, *Parish Boundaries: The Catholic Encounter with Race in the Twentieth-Century Urban North* (Chicago: University of Chicago Press, 1996), 80.
10. James O'Toole, *The Faithful: A History of Catholics in America* (Cambridge, MA: Belknap Press of Harvard University Press, 2008), 193. The story "was the same on

the opposite side of the country. Anaheim, California, just south of Los Angeles, had one parish in 1945, but three of them in 1960; Van Nuys, in the San Fernando Valley, had a single parish in 1945, but four of them in 1960, and three of these had schools with a total of 2300 pupils."

11. Thomas J. Sugrue, "The Catholic Encounter with the 1960s," in *Catholics in the American Century: Recasting Narratives of U.S. History*, ed. R. Scott Appleby and Kathleen Sprows Cummings (Ithaca, NY: Cornell University Press, 2012), 70. In the conclusion to his study of religion's flourishing in late nineteenth- and twentieth-century New York, Jon Butler provides an initial survey of how Catholicism did and did not change in the first years of Long Island's suburban boom: *God in Gotham: The Miracle of Religion in Modern Manhattan* (New York: Oxford University Press, 2020).

12. Dolan, *The Immigrant Church*, 9–10.

13. For a sampling of population statistics, see "Diocese Is Nation's 5th Largest," *Long Island Catholic* 3, no. 1 (April 30, 1964): 2; "Diocese Has 3rd Largest Gain," *Long Island Catholic* 4, no. 1 (April 29, 1965): 1.

14. Kathleen Sprows Cummings, Timothy Matovina, and Robert A. Orsi, eds., *Catholics in the Vatican II Era: Local Histories of a Global Event* (New York: Cambridge University Press, 2017), xv.

15. Cummings, Matovina, and Orsi, *Catholics in the Vatican II Era*, xvii.

16. Nathan Glazer and Daniel Patrick Moynihan, "Ethnicity," in *The Fontana Dictionary of Modern Thought*, 2nd ed., ed. Alan Bullock, Oliver Stallybrass, and Stephen Trombley (London: Fontana Press, 1988), 285.

17. Kenneth T. Jackson, *Crabgrass Frontier: The Suburbanization of the United States* (New York: Oxford University Press, 1985). Jackson credits his mentor, Richard C. Wade of the University of Chicago, with coining the term "crabgrass frontier," which recalls the title of Wade's own masterwork, *The Urban Frontier: Pioneer Life in Early Pittsburgh, Cincinnati, Lexington, Louisville, and St. Louis* (Chicago: University of Chicago Press, 1964).

18. Kevin M. Kruse and Thomas J. Sugrue, eds., *The New Suburban History* (Chicago: University of Chicago Press, 2006), 3. For examples of the "new suburban history," see Becky Nicolaides, *My Blue Heaven: Life and Politics in the Working-Class Suburbs of Los Angeles, 1920–1965* (Chicago: University of Chicago Press, 2002); Andrew Wiese, *Places of Their Own: African American Suburbanization in the Twentieth Century* (Chicago: University of Chicago Press, 2004). See also Robert Self, *American Babylon: Race and the Struggle for Postwar Oakland* (Princeton, NJ: Princeton University Press, 2003); Kevin Kruse, *White Flight: Atlanta and the Making of Modern Conservatism* (Princeton, NJ: Princeton University Press, 2005); Matthew D. Lassiter, *The Silent Majority: Suburban Politics in the Sunbelt South* (Princeton, NJ: Princeton University Press, 2006).

19. For suburbia and consumer culture, see Lizabeth Cohen, *A Consumer's Republic: The Politics of Mass Consumption in Postwar America* (New York: Alfred A. Knopf, 2003); Curtis Miner, "Pink Houses for Little Boxes: The Evolution of 1950s Kitchen Designs in Levittown," in *Second Suburb: Levittown, Pennsylvania*, ed. Dianne Harris (Pittsburgh: University of Pittsburgh Press, 2010), 278. For the lives of suburban women, see Elaine Tyler May, *Homeward Bound: American Families in the Cold War Era* (New York: Basic Books, 1988); Stacey Taranto, *Kitchen Table Politics: Conservative Women and Family Values in New York* (Philadelphia: University of Pennsylvania Press, 2017). For the environmental movement in suburbia, see Christopher Sellers, "Suburban Nature, Class, and Environmentalism in Levittown," in Harris, *Second Suburb*, 282.

20. Michelle Nickerson, "Beyond Smog, Sprawl, and Asphalt: Developments in the Not-So-New Suburban History," *Journal of Urban History* 4, no. 1 (2015): 171–80. Among

the influential collections of essays Nickerson surveys are Dianne Harris, ed., *Second Suburb: Levittown, Pennsylvania* (Pittsburgh: University of Pittsburgh Press, 2010); Kruse and Sugrue, eds., *The New Suburban History;* and Becky M. Nicolaides and Andrew Wiese, eds., *The Suburban Reader* (New York: Routledge, 2006). A few prominent exceptions have focused on the American Jewish experience of suburbia; see Debra Dash Moore, *To the Golden Cities: Pursuing the American Jewish Dream in Miami and L.A.* (New York: The Free Press, 1994); Etan Diamond, *And I Will Dwell in Their Midst: Orthodox Jews in Suburbia* (Chapel Hill: University of North Carolina Press, 2000); Lila Corwin Berman, *Metropolitan Jews: Politics, Race, and Religion in Postwar Detroit* (Chicago: University of Chicago Press, 2015).

21. See, for example, Mark S. Massa, SJ, *The American Catholic Revolution: How the '60s Changed the Church Forever* (New York: Oxford University Press, 2010); O'Toole, *The Faithful;* James P. McCartin, *Prayers of the Faithful: The Shifting Spiritual Life of American Catholics* (Cambridge, MA: Harvard University Press, 2010); Mary Ellen O'Donnell, *Ingrained Habits: Growing Up Catholic in Mid-Twentieth-Century America* (Washington, DC: Catholic University of America Press, 2018).
22. Andrew M. Greeley, *The Church and the Suburbs* (New York: Sheed and Ward, 1959).
23. Gerald Gamm, *Urban Exodus: Why the Jews Left Boston and the Catholics Stayed* (Cambridge, MA: Harvard University Press, 1999); McGreevy, *Parish Boundaries.*
24. R. Scott Appleby, "Forgotten Americans?," in Appleby and Cummings, *Catholics in the American Century,* 158.
25. Kruse and Sugrue, *The New Suburban History,* 1.
26. See Steve Bruce, *The Rise and Fall of the New Christian Right: Conservative Protestant Politics in America 1978–1988* (Oxford: Clarendon Press, 1988); William Martin, *With God on Our Side: The Rise of the Religious Right in America* (New York: Broadway Books, 1996); Lisa McGirr, *Suburban Warriors: The Origins of the New American Right* (Princeton, NJ: Princeton University Press, 2001); Lassiter, *The Silent Majority;* Steven P. Miller, *Billy Graham and the Rise of the Republican South* (Philadelphia: University of Pennsylvania Press, 2009); Daniel K. Williams, *God's Own Party: The Making of the Christian Right* (New York: Oxford University Press, 2010); Michelle Nickerson, *Mothers of Conservatism: Women and the Postwar Right* (Princeton, NJ: Princeton University Press, 2012); Darren Dochuk, *From Biblebelt to Sunbelt: Plain-Folk Religion, Grassroots Politics, and the Rise of Evangelical Conservatism* (New York: Norton, 2012).
27. See Jonathan Rieder, *Canarsie: The Jews and Italians of Brooklyn Against Liberalism* (Cambridge, MA: Harvard University Press, 1985); Kenneth D. Durr, *Behind the Backlash: White Working-Class Politics in Baltimore, 1940–1980* (Chapel Hill: University of North Carolina Press, 2003); Joshua M. Zeitz, *White Ethnic New York: Jews, Catholics, and the Shaping of Postwar Politics* (Chapel Hill: University of North Carolina Press, 2007); Neil J. Young, *We Gather Together: The Religious Right and the Problem of Interfaith Politics* (New York: Oxford University Press, 2016); Taranto, *Kitchen Table Politics.*
28. John Barry Ryan and Caitlin Milazzo provide evidence that suburbanization, not abortion politics, is primarily responsible for the political realignment of American Catholicism: "The South, the Suburbs, and the Vatican Too: Explaining Partisan Change Among Catholics," *Political Behavior* 37 (2015): 441–63.
29. The voluminous historiography on the demise of New Deal liberalism, includes Alan Brinkley, *The End of Reform: New Deal Liberalism in Recession and War* (New York: Vintage, 1996); Alan Brinkley, *Liberalism and Its Discontents* (Cambridge, MA: Harvard University Press, 1998); Steve Fraser and Gary Gerstle, *The Rise and Fall of the New Deal Order, 1930–1980* (Princeton, NJ: Princeton University Press, 1989); Judith

Stein, *Pivotal Decade: How the United States Traded Factories for Finance in the Seventies* (New Haven, CT: Yale University Press, 2010); Alonzo L. Hamby, *Liberalism and Its Challengers: From F.D.R. to Bush* (New York: Oxford University Press, 1992).

30. For more on the culture wars see James Davidson Hunter, *Culture Wars: The Struggle to Define America* (New York: Basic Books, 1991); Andrew Hartman, *A War for the Soul of America: A History of the Culture Wars* (Chicago: University of Chicago Press, 2015).

31. This new scholarship attempts to move beyond both a close reading of the Council's documents, and the debate over whether the Council was fundamentally in continuity with or a rupture from the past. For more on that interpretive debate, see John W. O'Malley, *Vatican II: Did Anything Happen?* (New York: Continuum, 2007); Matthew L. Lamb and Matthew Levering, *Vatican II: Renewal Within Tradition* (New York: Oxford University Press, 2008); Massimo Faggioli, *Vatican II: The Battle for Meaning* (New York: Paulist Press, 2012); Jeremy Bonner, Christopher D. Denny, and Mary Beth Fraser Connolly, eds., *Empowering the People of God: Catholic Action Before and After Vatican II* (New York: Fordham University Press, 2014); Joseph P. Chinnici, *American Catholicism Transformed: From the Cold War Through the Council* (New York: Oxford University Press, 2021).

32. Cummings, Matovina, and Orsi, *Catholics in the Vatican II Era*; Lucas Van Rimpay, Sam Miglarese, and David A. Morgan, eds., *The Long Shadow of Vatican II: Living Faith and Negotiating Authority Since the Second Vatican Council* (Chapel Hill: University of North Carolina Press, 2015).

33. Gerald P. Fogarty, "The Parish and Community in American Catholic History," *US Catholic Historian* 4, nos. 3/4 (1985): 257.

34. Will Herberg, *Protestant, Catholic, Jew: An Essay in American Religious Sociology*, rev. ed. (Chicago: University of Chicago Press, 1983), 157–58. Herberg argues that the "ethnic amalgamation" of the suburbs had helped create a "new type of American Catholic." For changes to public devotions, see O'Toole, *The Faithful*, 222–23; Timothy Kelly, *The Transformation of American Catholicism: The Pittsburgh Laity and the Second Vatican Council, 1950–1972* (Notre Dame, IN: University of Notre Dame Press, 2009), 55–59; and Timothy Kelly, "Suburbanization and the Decline of Catholic Public Ritual in Pittsburgh," *Journal of Social History* 28, no. 2 (Winter 1994): 311–30.

CHAPTER ONE

1. Muriel Reno, "Life in a Housing Project Is Fun," *America* 82, no. 83 (March 11, 1950): 663.
2. Harry Schlegel, "Town and Country: Take Mine. I'm All for the City," *The Sign* 34, no. 12 (July 1955): 34; Art Smith, "Town and Country: Give Me a Little House in the Country," *The Sign* 34, no. 12 (July 1955): 34.
3. Milton Lomask, "Your Stake in Public Housing," *The Sign* 34, no. 12 (July 1955): 16.
4. John T. McGreevy, *Catholicism: A Global History from the French Revolution to Pope Francis* (New York: W. W. Norton, 2022).
5. Patrick W. Carey, *Catholics in America: A History* (New York: Sheed and Ward, 2004), 30. The newly erected Diocese of New York originally covered the entirety of the state and seven counties in northeastern New Jersey: Sussex, Bergen, Morris, Essex, Somerset, Middlesex, and Monmouth.
6. David S. Bovée, *The Church and the Land: The National Catholic Rural Life Conference and American Society, 1923–2007* (Washington, DC: Catholic University of America Press, 2010), 1; Brian Mitchell, ed., *Building the American Catholic City—Parishes and Institutions* (New York: Garland, 1988), vi; and see Oscar Handlin, *The Uprooted: The*

Epic Story of the Great Migrations that Made the American People (New York: Grosset and Dunlap, 1951). For summaries of the ten largest European immigrant communities within American Catholicism, see Jay P. Dolan, *The American Catholic Experience: A History from Colonial Times to the Present* (Notre Dame, IN: University of Notre Dame Press, 1992), 127–39.

7. Bovée, *The Church and the Land*, 5–7; and see Ray Allen Billington, *The Protestant Crusade, 1800–1860: A Study in the Origins of American Nativism* (New York: Macmillan, 1938); and Gerald Shaughnessy, *Has the Immigrant Kept the Faith? A Study of Immigration and Catholic Growth in the United States, 1790–1920* (New York: Macmillan, 1925). Shaughnessy's 1925 statistical study proved that the "leakage" of immigrants from the Church had, in fact, been negligible.
8. Bovée, *The Church and the Land*, 10; and see Robert D. Cross, "The Changing Image of the City Among American Catholics," *Catholic Historical Review* 48, no. 1 (April 1962): 37; Henry J. Browne, "Archbishop Hughes and Western Colonization," *Catholic Historical Review*, 36, no. 3 (October 1950): 257–85.
9. Bovée, *The Church and the Land*, 8–9, 24; Edward S. Shapiro, "Catholic Agrarian Thought and the New Deal," *Catholic Historical Review* 65, no. 4 (October 1979): 586.
10. Bovée, *The Church and the Land*, 10; Cross, "The Changing Image of the City Among American Catholics," 37. For more on Catholic colonization societies, see Sr. Mary Gilbert Kelly, *Catholic Immigration Colonization Projects, 1815–1860* (New York: United States Catholic Historical Society, 1939); Browne, "Archbishop Hughes and Western Colonization," 257–85; James P. Shannon, *Catholic Colonization on the Western Frontier* (New Haven, CT: Yale University Press, 1957).
11. Cross, "The Changing Image of the City Among American Catholics," 34–36.
12. Timothy Michael Dolan, *"Some Seed Fell on Good Ground": The Life of Edwin V. O'Hara* (Washington, DC: Catholic University of America Press, 1992), 3, 11–14, 28, 41–46, 53, 74, 84, 91; and Bovée, *The Church and the Land*, 40, 48.
13. Jeffrey D. Marlett, *Saving the Heartland: Catholic Missionaries in Rural America, 1920–1960* (DeKalb: Northern Illinois University Press, 2002), 12; Dolan, *"Some Seed Fell on Good Ground,"* 85 and 92. For more on the Catholic Extension Society, see James P. Gaffey, *Francis Clement Kelley and the American Catholic Dream* (Bensenville, IL: Heritage Foundation, 1980). For more on the Central Verein, and its founder Frederick Kenkel, see Philip Gleason, *The Conservative Reformers: German-American Catholics and the Social Order* (Notre Dame, IN: University of Notre Dame Press, 1968). For more on the Catholic Worker Movement see Mel Piehl, *Breaking Bread: The Catholic Worker and the Origin of Catholic Radicalism in America* (Philadelphia: Temple University Press, 1982). For more on the Grail Movement see Alden V. Brown, *The Grail Movement and American Catholicism, 1940–1975* (Notre Dame, IN: University of Notre Dame Press, 1989). For more on the NCRLC's collaborators see Christopher Hamlin and John T. McGreevy, "The Greening of America, Catholic Style, 1930–1950," *Environmental History*, 11, no. 3 (July 2006): 464–99; and Jeffrey Marlett, "Harvesting an Overlooked Freedom: The Anti-Urban Vision of American Catholic Agrarianism, 1920–1950," *US Catholic Historian* 16, no. 4 (Fall 1998): 88–108.
14. Bovée, *The Church and the Land*, 59, 60, 149; and see Hamlin and McGreevy, "The Greening of America, Catholic Style," 486.
15. Bovée, *The Church and the Land*, 143, 168; Marlett, *Saving the Heartland*, 11; and Dolan, *"Some Seed Fell on Good Ground,"* 87 and 96. Membership in the Conference grew from 560 members in 1929, to approximately 1,000 in 1932, to nearly 2,400 by 1940, and to over 10,000 by 1958. The Conference's publications included

St. Isidore's Plow, which became *Catholic Rural Life* in 1925, *Landward, Land and Home,* and *The Christian Farmer*.

16. Jay P. Dolan, *The Immigrant Church: New York's Irish and German Catholics, 1815–1865* (Baltimore: Johns Hopkins University Press, 1975), 26, 20–21; Joseph J. Casino, "From Sanctuary to Involvement: A History of the Catholic Parish in the Northeast," in *American Catholic Parish: A History from 1850 to the Present*, ed. Jay P. Dolan (New York: Paulist Press, 1987), 3, 48. See also Herbert J. Gans, *The Urban Villagers: Group and Class in the Life of Italian-Americans* (New York: Free Press, 1965); For more on the interrelation of the Catholic parish and the urban neighborhood, see Benjamin Looker, *A Nation of Neighborhoods: Imagining Cities, Communities, and Democracy in Postwar America* (Chicago: University of Chicago Press, 2015), 262.
17. Mitchell, *Building the American Catholic City*, v.
18. Eileen McMahon, *What Parish Are You From?: A Chicago Irish Community and Race Relations* (Lexington: University Press of Kentucky, 1996).
19. Dolan, *The Immigrant Church*, 60, 100, 4; and see Timothy Meagher, ed., *Urban American Catholicism: The Culture and Identity of the American Catholic People* (New York: Garland, 1988), iii.
20. Casino, "From Sanctuary to Involvement," 25; Dolan, *The Immigrant Church*, 149–51. For more on the development of parish missions, see Jay P. Dolan, *Catholic Revivalism, 1830–1900* (Notre Dame, IN: University of Notre Dame Press, 1978).
21. Dolan, *The Immigrant Church*, 56; Casino, "From Sanctuary to Involvement," 14–15; and see Msgr. Florence D. Cohalan, *A Popular History of the Archdiocese of New York* (Yonkers, NY: United States Catholic Historical Society, 1983), 75, 88–89.
22. Mitchell, *Building the American Catholic City*, v. Martin Marty provides a helpful explication of the term and defense of its use in "The Catholic Ghetto and All the Other Ghettos," *Catholic Historical Review* 68, no. 2 (April 1982): 185–205.
23. James O'Toole, *The Faithful: A History of Catholics in America* (Cambridge, MA: Belknap Press of Harvard University Press, 2008), 104.
24. Joseph G. Mannard, "'Our Dear Houses Are Here, There + Every Where': The Convent Revolution in Antebellum America," *American Catholic Studies* 128, no. 2 (Summer 2017): 8; Margaret M. McGuinness, *Called to Serve: A History of Nuns in America* (New York: New York University Press, 2013), 61.
25. Dolan, *The Immigrant Church*, 100; Casino, "From Sanctuary to Involvement," 22, 23.
26. Dolan, *The Immigrant Church*, 65; Casino, "From Sanctuary to Involvement," 24, 31.
27. Casino, "From Sanctuary to Involvement," 17–18; Dolan, *The Immigrant Church*, 88–89, 162–64. For more on the history of trusteeism in the American Church, see Patrick W. Carey, *People, Priests, and Prelates: Ecclesiastic Democracy and the Tensions of Trusteeism* (Notre Dame, IN: University of Notre Dame Press, 1987).
28. Dolan, *The Immigrant Church*, 76–78, 128–29; Mitchell, *Building the American Catholic City*, iv.
29. Casino, "From Sanctuary to Involvement," 37, 40.
30. Casino, "From Sanctuary to Involvement," 50, 53.
31. Meagher, *Urban American Catholicism*, iv; and see Robert A. Orsi, *The Madonna of 115th Street: Faith and Community in Italian Harlem, 1880–1950* (New Haven, CT: Yale University Press, 1985).
32. Casino, "From Sanctuary to Involvement," 48–50, 54–55.
33. Casino, "From Sanctuary to Involvement," 38, 61.
34. Casino, "From Sanctuary to Involvement," 66, 67; Jay P. Dolan, "American Catholics in a Changing Society: Parish and Ministry, 1930 to the Present," in *Transforming*

Parish Ministry: The Changing Roles of Catholic Clergy, Laity, and Women Religious, ed. Jay P. Dolan (New York: Crossroads, 1989), 288. In New York only one new national parish was founded in these years: St. Ann's Italian Parish in Yonkers.
35. Meagher, *Urban American Catholicism*, ix. For more on the changing relationship between ethnic Catholics in New York, see Paul Moses, *An Unlikely Union: The Love-Hate Story of New York's Irish and Italians* (New York: New York University Press, 2015).
36. Casino, "From Sanctuary to Involvement," 69–70.
37. Meagher, *Urban American Catholicism*, v, viii.
38. Casino, "From Sanctuary to Involvement," 68. For more on the history of popular devotions in this era see Ann Taves, *The Household of Faith: Roman Catholic Devotions in Mid-Nineteenth-Century America* (Notre Dame, IN: University of Notre Dame Press, 1986); McCartin, *Prayers of the Faithful*, 10–41.
39. Jeremy Bonner, Christopher D. Denny, and Mary Beth Fraser Connolly, eds., *Empowering the People of God: Catholic Action Before and After Vatican II* (New York: Fordham University Press, 2014), 2–3, 22–23; Gerd-Rainer Horn, "Catholic Action: A Twentieth-Century Social Movement (1920s–1930s)," in Horn, *Western European Liberation Theology: The First Wave (1924–1959)* (New York: Oxford University Press, 2008), 5–53.
40. For background on Virgil Michel and on the history of the liturgical movement in the United States, see Paul Marx, *Virgil Michel and the Liturgical Movement* (Collegeville, MN: Liturgical Press, 1957); R. William Franklin and Robert Spaeth, *Virgil Michel: American Catholic* (Collegeville, MN: Liturgical Press, 1988); Robert Tuzik, "The Contribution of Msgr. Reynold Hillenbrand (1905–1979) to the Liturgical Movement in the United States: Influences and Development" (PhD diss., University of Notre Dame, 1989); and Keith F. Pecklers, SJ, *The Unread Vision: The Liturgical Movement in the United States of America—1926–1955* (Collegeville, MN: Liturgical Press, 1998).
41. Dolan, *"Some Seed Fell on Good Ground,"* 98; and see Marlett, *Saving the Heartland*, 7; Bovée, *The Church and the Land*, 104. The word "rogation" comes from *rogo* meaning "to ask." Rogation Days occurred on April 25, the Feast of St. Mark, and on the Monday, Tuesday, and Wednesday before the Feast of Ascension Thursday. Rogation days were a time of prayer, fasting, abstinence, the singing of litanies, Masses, and the blessing of crops. Often, rural communities also made a procession around the boundaries of the parish, which was referred to as the "beating of the bounds."
42. Casino, "From Sanctuary to Involvement," 68.
43. Bonner, Denny, and Connolly, *Empowering the People of God*, 3.
44. Jackson, *Crabgrass Frontier*, 20.
45. Michael H. Ebner, "Re-Reading Suburban America: Urban Population Deconcentration, 1810–1980," *American Quarterly* 37, no. 3 (1985): 372. See Jackson, *Crabgrass Frontier*, 25–32, for more on Brooklyn's rise as "the first commuter suburb."
46. Thomas J. Shelley, *The History of the Archdiocese of New York* (Strasbourg: Éditions du Signe, 1999), 534.
47. Cohalan, *A Popular History of the Archdiocese of New York*, 71–72. For more on the history of the Archdiocese of New York, see Shelley, *The History of the Archdiocese of New York*; Terry Golway, ed., *Catholics in New York: Society, Culture, and Politics, 1808–1946* (New York: Fordham University Press, 2008).
48. Jackson, *Crabgrass Frontier*, 175–76.
49. Shelley, *The History of the Archdiocese of New York*, 535.
50. Fact sheet from Archdiocesan Archives and Library, AANY, St. Joseph's Seminary, Yonkers, New York; Shelley, *The History of the Archdiocese of New York*, 535, 553.

51. Jackson, *Crabgrass Frontier*, 196, 198; Ebner, "Re-Reading Suburban America," 379. For more on redlining see Richard Rothstein, *The Color of Law: A Forgotten History of How Our Government Segregated America* (New York: Norton, 2017); LaDale C. Winling and Todd M. Michney, "The Roots of Redlining: Academic, Governmental, and Professional Networks in the Making of the New Deal Lending Regime," *Journal of American History* 108, no. 1 (June 2021): 42–69.
52. Barton J. Bernstein, "Reluctance and Resistance: Wilson Wyatt and Veterans' Housing in the Truman Administration," *Register of the Kentucky Historical Society* 65, no. 1 (January 1967): 47–66; Jackson, *Crabgrass Frontier*, 232–33; Leo Egan, "American Housing," *The Sign* 25, no. 11 (June 1946): 23.
53. Robert F. Wagner Jr., "CWV Housing Policy," *Catholic War Veteran* 11, no. 8 (April 1948): 6, in the National Archives of the Catholic War Veterans of the United States of America, Queens, NY. And see Jackson, *Crabgrass Frontier*, 232.
54. "Cushing: Housing Problem Is Vital, Situation Intolerable," *The Tablet* 40, no. 15 (June 5, 1948): 5.
55. National Catholic Welfare Conference, "Christian Family" (Washington, DC, November 21, 1949), in *Our Bishops Speak: National Pastorals and Annual Statements of the Hierarchy of the United States; Resolutions of Episcopal Committees and Communications of the Administrative Board of the National Welfare Conference, 1919–1951*, ed. Raphael M. Huber (Milwaukee, WI: Bruce, 1952).
56. For more on Msgr. John O'Grady, and especially his work with Catholic Charities, see Thomas W. Tifft, "Toward A More Humane Social Policy: The Work and Influence of Monsignor John O'Grady" (PhD diss., Catholic University of America, 1979); Timothy L. McDonnell, SJ, *The Wagner Housing Act: A Case Study of the Legislative Process* (Chicago: Loyola University Press, 1957); Dorothy M. Brown and Elizabeth McKeown, *The Poor Belong to Us: Catholic Charities and American Welfare* (Cambridge, MA: Harvard University Press, 1997); Donald P. Gavin, *The National Conference of Catholic Charities* (Milwaukee, WI: Catholic Life Publications, 1962), 138–39; Bryan J. Hehir, ed., *Catholic Charities USA: 100 Years at the Intersection of Charity and Justice* (Collegeville, MN: Liturgical Press, 2010).
57. Tifft, "Toward A More Humane Social Policy," 368, 377, 385. O'Grady testified on housing matters before congressional committees and subcommittees numerous times between 1948 and 1952. These statements are all found in John O'Grady Papers, Collection 366, Box 29, Folder 4: Speeches on Housing, 1948–1952, American Catholic History Research Center and University Archives (ACUA), Washington, DC.
58. Tifft, "Toward A More Humane Social Policy," 377, 399–400; John O'Grady, "The New Housing Bill," *Catholic Charities Review* (December 1945): 258–60; statement to the American Legion National Housing Committee, November 4, 1946, John O'Grady Papers, Collection 366, Box 29, Folder 4: Speeches on Housing, 1948–1952, ACUA.
59. Tifft, "Toward A More Humane Social Policy," 377, 394, 415.
60. "Action on Housing," *America* 74, no. 12 (December 22, 1945): 324; "Housing for the People," *America* 74, no. 1 (October 6, 1945): 15–16; "Houses for Veterans," *America* 74, no. 23 (March 9, 1946): 585–86; "U.S. Housing Policy," *America* 74, no. 16 (January 19, 1946): 434.
61. David L. O'Connor, "'For God, Country, and Home': The Origin and Growth of the Catholic War Veterans of the USA, 1935–1957," *Long Island Historical Journal* 11, no. 1 (Fall 1999): 31.

62. Donald F. Crosby, SJ, *God, Church and Flag: Senator Joseph R. McCarthy and the Catholic Church, 1950–1957* (Chapel Hill: University of North Carolina Press, 1978), 190; and O'Connor, "For God, Country, and Home," 35.
63. Crosby, *God, Church and Flag*, 190; and O'Connor, "For God, Country, and Home," 35.
64. Robert F. Wagner Jr., "Washington Housing Rally," *Catholic War Veteran* 11, no. 8 (April 1948): 2, found in the National Archives of the Catholic War Veterans of the United States of America, Queens, NY.
65. "Building Ignores Large Families," *The Tablet* 42, no. 20 (July 8, 1950): 5. *The Tablet* noted that "almost 1,700,000 families with two or more children" had an annual income of $3,000–$4,000 and therefore needed "family-size houses and apartments with three to four bedrooms and sale prices of $6000 to $10,000 or rents of $55 to $80 a month." But FHA figures showed that only 25 percent of rental units with three bedrooms or more rented for under $80 and 37 percent of housing with three or more bedrooms rented for over $100. See also Egan, "American Housing," 23.
66. "Public Housing Scored as Inadequate for Families," *The Tablet* 41, no. 23 (July 30, 1949): 1.
67. William J. Gibbons, "The Moral Issue in Housing," *America* 74, no. 26 (March 30, 1946): 652–53.
68. See Leslie Woodcock Tentler, *Catholics and Contraception: An American History* (Ithaca, NY: Cornell University Press, 2004).
69. Richard Hofstadter popularized and defined the term "agrarian myth" in *The Age of Reform: From Bryan to F.D.R.* (New York: Knopf, 1955), 23.
70. Luigi Ligutti, "Cities Kill," *Commonweal* 32, no. 15 (August 2, 1940): 300–301; see Msgr. Luigi G. Ligutti and Fr. John C. Rawe, SJ, *Rural Roads to Security: America's Third Struggle for Freedom* (Milwaukee, WI: Bruce Publishing, 1940), the "summa of Catholic agrarianism," according to Marlett, *Saving the Heartland*, 51.
71. "Catholics and Rural Life," *Catholic News* 60, no. 12 (November 17, 1945): 10. See also "Our Catholic Population," *Catholic News* 62, no. 30 (March 20, 1948): 14.
72. Hamlin and McGreevy, "The Greening of America, Catholic Style," 470; Bovée, *The Church and the Land*, 184–85. See also "Bishop Urges Blending Industry and Farming in Post-War Plans," *Catholic News* 59, no. 9 (October 28, 1944): 9; "Bishop Griffin Urges Return to Rural Life," *Catholic News* 59, no. 12 (November 18, 1944): 1.
73. Hamlin and McGreevy, "The Greening of America, Catholic Style," 470.
74. Ligutti and Rawe, *Rural Roads to Security*, 150.
75. Walter John Marx, "Beating the Housing Shortage," *The Sign* 27, no. 3 (October 1947): 33–35.
76. "Build Your Own Home," letter to the editor, *America* 82, no. 3 (October 22, 1949): ii. Hill recommended Ed Robinson, *The "Have-More" Plan for a Little Land, a Lot of Living* (New York: Macmillan, 1947); Emerson Hynes, *Seven Keys to a Christian Home* (Des Moines, IA: National Catholic Rural Life Conference, 1949).
77. William F. Kelly, "Catholic Interest in Rural Life Work," *The Tablet* 42, no. 36 (October 28, 1950): 12. Kelly was detailing his attendance at the 28th annual NCLRC convention in Bellville, Illinois. The newspaper of the Diocese of Brooklyn, *The Tablet*, is not to be confused with the British Catholic journal of the same name; see Patrick McNamara, "'Catholic Journalism with Its Sleeves Rolled Up': Patrick F. Scanlan and the Brooklyn *Tablet*, 1917–1968," *U.S. Catholic Historian* 25, no. 3 (Summer 2007): 87–107.
78. Interview with James O'Gara, "The Church and the Farmer," *Sign* 36, no. 12 (July 1957): 13.

79. Bovée, *The Church and the Land*, 84.
80. Cross, "The Changing Image of the City Among American Catholics," 38; Bovée, *The Church and the Land*, 360.
81. Hamlin and McGreevy, "The Greening of America, Catholic Style," 487.
82. Bovée, *The Church and the Land*, 168.
83. "U.S. Housing Policy," 434.
84. "Home-Owning Americans," *America* 84, no. 24 (March 17, 1951): 686; "Growth of Home Ownership," *America* 90, no. 2 (October 10, 1953): 32.
85. "Home-Builders Needed Says Cardinal Cushing," *The Tablet* 46, no. 16 (June 6, 1953): 16.
86. James Bernard Kelley, "Homes for Families: A Housing-Shortage Victim Paints a Realistic Picture," *America* 81, no. 25 (September 24, 1949): 665–66; "Birth-Control Housing," *America* 87, no. 8 (May 24, 1952): 220.
87. Andrew M. Greeley, *The Church and the Suburbs* (New York: Sheed and Ward, 1959), 6–8, 10.
88. Neil P. Hurley, SJ, "New Patterns in American Commuting," *Social Order* 8, no. 7 (September 1958): 344. See also Neil P. Hurley, SJ, "The Church in Suburbia," *America* 98, no. 7 (November 16, 1957): 195.
89. Dennis Clark, "The Church in the Suburbs," *Social Order* 5, no. 1 (January 1955): 26; Donald R. Campion and Dennis Clark, "So You're Moving to Suburbia," *America* 95, no. 3 (April 21, 1956): 80; Robert G. Howes, *The Church and the Change: An Initial Study of the Role of the Roman Catholic Church in the Changing American Community* (Boston: St. Paul Editions, 1961), 78–80.
90. Greeley, *The Church and the Suburbs*, 26; Andrew M. Greeley, *What a Modern Catholic Believes about the Church* (Chicago: The Thomas More Association, 1972), 20.
91. Dennis Clark, "Race and Your Family," *America* 96, no. 23 (March 9, 1957): 642; see also John T. McGreevy, *Parish Boundaries: The Catholic Encounter with Race in the Twentieth-Century Urban North* (Chicago: University of Chicago Press, 1996). The New York Catholic Interracial Council, founded in 1934 by Fr. John LaFarge, SJ, was the first of forty such councils across the country aimed at eradicating racism by combatting ignorance. From the 1930s through the 1960s, LaFarge and the Interracial Councils were principally responsible for increasing American Catholic awareness of racial issues; see David W. Southern, *John LaFarge and the Limits of Catholic Interracialism, 1911–1963* (Baton Rouge: Louisiana State University Press, 1996).
92. Greeley, *The Church and the Suburbs*, 10 and 11; Eli Lederhendler, *New York Jews and the Decline of Urban Ethnicity, 1950–1970* (Syracuse, NY: Syracuse University Press, 2001), 148–49.
93. Greeley, *The Church and the Suburbs*, 10 and 11; Eli Lederhendler, *New York Jews and the Decline of Urban Ethnicity, 1950–1970* (Syracuse, NY: Syracuse University Press, 2001), 148–49; Joshua M. Zeitz, *White Ethnic New York: Jews, Catholics, and the Shaping of Postwar Politics* (Chapel Hill: University of North Carolina Press, 2007), 152.
94. Jackson, *Crabgrass Frontier*, 205; Lederhendler, *New York Jews and the Decline of Urban Ethnicity*, 149; Sarah J. Mahler, *American Dreaming: Immigrant Life on the Margins* (Princeton, NJ: Princeton University Press, 1995), 109–10; Bernie Bookbinder, *Long Island: People and Places, Past and Present* (New York: Harry N. Abrams, 1998), 219; Richard Polenberg, *One Nation Divisible: Class, Race, and Ethnicity in the United States Since 1938* (New York: Penguin, 1980), 134.
95. Looker, *A Nation of Neighborhoods*, 262, citing Andrew Greeley's April 1977 "Address to the National Catholic Educational Association" in San Francisco; also 261.

96. John Tracy Ellis, "American Catholics and the Intellectual Life," *Thought* 30 (1955): 351–88.
97. Looker, *A Nation of Neighborhoods*, 264.
98. Bovée, *The Church and the Land*, 84; Cross, "The Changing Image of the City Among American Catholics," 51, 44–45; and see Michael Johns, *Moment of Grace: The American City in the 1950s* (Berkeley: University of California Press, 2003).
99. Gibson Winter, *The Suburban Captivity of the Churches: An Analysis of Protestant Responsibility in the Expanding Metropolis* (Garden City, NY: Doubleday, 1961), 28–29. Winter's provocative title is a reference to Martin Luther's 1520 treatise, *The Babylonian Captivity of the Church*, which argued that papal absolutism had distorted the biblical conception of the sacraments, making them tools to coerce and control the faithful.
100. Harvey Cox, *The Secular City: Secularization and Urbanization in Theological Perspective* (New York: Macmillan, 1965). The Protestant turn to the city is evident in Lee, *The Church and the Exploding Metropolis*.
101. Harvey Cox, "On Columns and Cities," *Commonweal* 85, no. 9 (November 4, 1966): 135; and see Cox, *The Secular City*, 40–43; Harvey Cox, "Beyond Bonhoeffer?" *Commonweal* 82, no. 21 (September 17, 1965): 653–57. Catherine R. Osborne, *American Catholics and the Church of Tomorrow: Building Churches for the Future, 1925–1975* (Chicago: University of Chicago Press, 2018), 159–60; and Looker, *A Nation of Neighborhoods*, 270. See also Harvey Cox, "Facing the Secular," *Commonweal* 79, no. 21 (February 21, 1964): 619–22.
102. Second Vatican Council, "*Gaudium et Spes*: Pastoral Constitution on the Church in the Modern World," in *Vatican II: Constitutions, Decrees, Declarations*, ed. Austin Flannery, OP (Northport, NY: Costello Publishing, 1996), 165; Osborne, *American Catholics and the Church of Tomorrow*, 159. By 1966, both *Christianity and Crisis* and *Commonweal* had published symposia on Cox's book, Daniel Callahan had edited a collection of critical reviews, essays, and responses from Cox entitled *The Secular City Debate*, and *Commonweal* had hired Cox as a regular columnist. See "The Secular City," *Commonweal* 83, no. 6 (November 12, 1965): 181–90; and Daniel Callahan, *The Secular City Debate* (New York: Macmillan, 1966).
103. Osborne, *American Catholics and the Church of Tomorrow*, 153. For more on the urban crisis, see Thomas J. Sugrue, *The Origins of the Urban Crisis: Race and Inequality in Postwar Detroit* (Princeton, NJ: Princeton University Press, 1996); Robert Self, *American Babylon: Race and the Struggle for Postwar Oakland* (Princeton, NJ: Princeton University Press, 2003).
104. In New York summer immersion programs funded by the Office of Economic Opportunity brought religious sisters into the city to serve poor children. In 1965 28 religious communities ran 39 ministry sites and in 1966, 40 religious communities sent 270 nuns and 50 brothers to summer urban ministry. In 1967 a separate program called Operation Challenge brought 43 sisters from 25 orders to live, pray, and work together in nine Manhattan centers dedicated to catechizing urban youth. See "Summer Programs for Inner City Communities," *Catholic News* 81, no. 29 (July 21, 1966). 1, 3, 11; "Nuns Share Ideas in Unique Community Experiment Part of Summer in the City," *Catholic News* 81, no. 30 (July 28, 1966): 1; "Brings Sisters of Challenge to the Tenements," *Catholic News* 82, no. 34 (August 24, 1967): 1.
105. Amy Koehlinger, *The New Nuns: Racial Justice and Religious Reform in the 1960s* (Cambridge, MA: Harvard University Press, 2007), 11, 40, 138. Koehlinger explores how religious sisters were reassigned to staff new parochial schools in burgeoning Catholic suburbs (10, 41); how these sisters saw suburban Catholics as racist and privileged

(11, 40); and how their experiences of ministry among the urban poor fueled their critique of suburbia and their sense that urban ministry was more in line with the demands of the Second Vatican Council and their own call to religious life (212–13). Diocesan newspapers approvingly covered the efforts of religious women to serve in the inner city and to develop interest in urban issues among suburbanites: "Nuns Role: At 'Heart' of the Problem Areas," *Long Island Catholic* 3, no. 48 (March 25, 1965): 4; "Nuns Live in Harlem Slum, Undergo 'Shock Treatment,'" *Long Island Catholic* 4, no. 20 (September 9, 1965): 15; "Summer Project Aims at New York Poverty," *Long Island Catholic* 4, no. 23 (May 13, 1965): 3; "Valley Stream Class Hears of Bedford-Stuyvesant," *Long Island Catholic* 4, no. 34 (December 16, 1965): 3.

106. Looker, *A Nation of Neighborhoods*, 265; and see McGreevy, *Parish Boundaries*; Matthew J. Cressler, *Authentically Black and Truly Catholic: The Rise of Black Catholicism in the Great Migration* (New York: New York University Press, 2017).

107. Looker, *A Nation of Neighborhoods*, 266, 261. For more on the period's significant changes in Catholic symbols and practice, see Massa, *The American Catholic Revolution*, 15–28; McCartin, *Prayers of the Faithful*, 100–138; James M. O'Toole, ed., *Habits of Devotion: Catholic Religious Practice in Twentieth-Century America* (Ithaca, NY: Cornell University Press, 2004).

108. Looker, *A Nation of Neighborhoods*, 261–62. For more on the white ethnic revival, see Thomas J. Sugrue and John D. Skrentny, "The White Ethnic Strategy," in *Rightward Bound*, ed. Bruce J. Schulman and Julian E. Zelizer (Cambridge, MA: Harvard University Press, 2008), 171–92; Andrew M. Greeley, *Why Can't They Be Like Us? America's White Ethnic Groups* (New York: E. P. Dutton, 1971); Nathan Glazer and Daniel Patrick Moynihan, *Beyond the Melting Pot: The Negroes, Puerto Ricans, Jews, Italians, and Irish of New York City* (Cambridge, MA: Harvard University Press, 1970); Jonathan Rieder, *Canarsie: The Jews and Italians of Brooklyn Against Liberalism* (Cambridge, MA: Harvard University Press, 1985); Zeitz, *White Ethnic New York*; "The Troubled White American: A Special Report on the White Majority," *Newsweek*, October 6, 1969, 29; Matthew Frye Jacobson, *Roots Too: White Ethnic Revival in Post–Civil Rights America* (Cambridge, MA: Harvard University Press, 2008).

109. Looker, *A Nation of Neighborhoods*, 262, 266–67, 268: in particular, they referenced the Vatican Council's defense of the individual's "inherent right to culture," and cited Pope Paul VI's 1971 apostolic letter *A Call to Action*, which "lamented the 'new loneliness' of the contemporary metropolis."

110. Looker, *A Nation of Neighborhoods*, 270–71; and see Daniel T. Rodgers, *Age of Fracture* (Cambridge, MA: Harvard University Press, 2011), 126. Novak added that the "suburban lifestyle" left people "restless and unsatisfied" (Michael Novak, *The Rise of the Unmeltable Ethnics* [New York: Macmillan, 1972], 39). For more on Novak, see Patrick Allitt, *Catholic Intellectuals and Conservative Politics in America, 1950–1985* (Ithaca, NY: Cornell University Press, 1993), 243–88, especially 272–73.

111. Looker, *A Nation of Neighborhoods*, 279–80; John A. Kromkowski and John David Kromkowski, "An American Catholic Perspective on Urban Neighborhoods: The Lens of Monsignor Geno C. Baroni and the Legacy of the Neighborhood Movement," *American Journal of Economics and Sociology* 71, no. 4 (October 2012): 1102–7.

For more on Msgr. Geno Baroni see Lawrence O'Rourke, *Geno: The Life and Mission of Geno Baroni* (New York: Paulist Press, 1991); Gene Halus, "Monsignor Geno Baroni and the Politics of Ethnicity, 1960–1984," *US Catholic Historian* 25, no. 4 (Fall 2007): 133–59; Robert Bauman, "'Kind of a Secular Sacrament': Father Geno Baroni,

Monsignor John J. Egan, and the Catholic War on Poverty," *Catholic Historical Review* 99, no. 2 (April 2013): 298–317.
112. Greeley's early sociological research on educational attainment and career choice among Catholics argued that the children of immigrants had been highly successful: Andrew M. Greeley, *Religion and Career: A Study of College Graduates* (New York: Sheed and Ward, 1963); Andrew M. Greeley and Peter H. Rossi, *The Education of Catholic Americans* (Chicago: Aldine, 1966).
113. Looker, *A Nation of Neighborhoods*, 275–76 citing Andrew Greeley's April 1977 "Address to the National Catholic Educational Association" in San Francisco; William C. McCready and Andrew M. Greeley, "The End of American Catholicism?," *America* 127, no. 13 (October 28, 1972): 337–38. It is worth noting that in Greeley's construction, Catholic suburbanites would have been part of the grassroots opposition to "downtown" Catholic elites and their theological and political concerns.
114. Shapiro argues convincingly that "suburbia has reflected the continuing commitment of most Americans to an updated 'agrarian myth' and to the thesis that cities are nice places to visit but not to inhabit" ("Catholic Agrarian Thought and the New Deal," 598–99).
115. "Where Shall We Live?," *The Tablet* 50, no. 28 (August 24, 1957): 9.

CHAPTER TWO

1. George Dugan, "Kellenberg Gets Possession of See," *New York Times*, May 27, 1957, 25; "Prelate Greeted by His Faithful," *The Tablet* 50, no. 16 (June 1, 1957): 1; see also "Bishop Kellenberg to Enter His Diocese Sunday," *The Tablet* 50, no. 15 (May 25, 1957): 1.
2. "Throng at Mass of Installation," *The Tablet* 50, no. 16 (June 1, 1957): 1. The archbishops present were William D. O'Brien of Chicago, John F. O'Hara, CSC, of Philadelphia, and Patrick A. O'Boyle of Washington, DC. Bishops from as far away as the Bahamas, British Columbia, and Korea were also in attendance.
3. Msgr. William J. McKenna, "Greetings of the Clergy to Bishop Kellenberg," *The Tablet* 50, no. 17 (June 8, 1957): 20.
4. McKenna, "Greetings of the Clergy to Bishop Kellenberg," 20.
5. Jenni Buhr, "Levittown as a Utopian Community," in *Long Island: The Suburban Experience*, ed. Barbara Kelly (Interlaken, NY: Heart of the Lakes Publishing, 1990), 68–69, 70–71. By the end of the 1930s the Levitts had successfully built and sold 2,800 Tudor Revival–style homes in their Strathmore communities.
6. Buhr, "Levittown as a Utopian Community," 69; Jackson, *Crabgrass Frontier*, 234; Edward Smits, *Nassau Suburbia USA*, rev. ed. (Garden City, NY: Doubleday, 1990), 189; and see Boyden Sparkes, "They'll Build Neighborhoods, Not Houses," *Saturday Evening Post* 217, no. 18 (October 28, 1944): 11; "2,000 $60 Rentals Due in L.I. Project," *Newsday*, May 7, 1947, 1.
7. Lynne Matarrese, *The History of Levittown, New York* (New York: Levittown Historical Society, 1997), 38, 195; Smits, *Nassau Suburbia USA*, 195.
8. Smits, *Nassau Suburbia USA*, 189; Buhr, "Levittown as a Utopian Community," 70.
9. Jackson, *Crabgrass Frontier*, 235–36.
10. Paul Goldberger, "Design Notebook," *New York Times*, April 2, 1981, C1, cited in Jackson, *Crabgrass Frontier*, 235.
11. Buhr, "Levittown as a Utopian Community," 70; and see Smits, *Nassau Suburbia USA*, 189, and Jackson, *Crabgrass Frontier*, 235.

12. Jackson, *Crabgrass Frontier*, 235; Smits, *Nassau Suburbia USA*, 194-95.
13. Smits, *Nassau Suburbia USA*, 196-97. For maps of Nassau and Suffolk Counties see appendices.
14. Richard L. Forstall, ed., "Population of Counties by Decennial Census: 1900-1990," Population Division of the US Bureau of the Census, Washington, DC, 1995, https://www.census.gov/population/cencounts/ny190090.txt; and see Smits, *Nassau Suburbia USA*, 198.
15. Smits, *Nassau Suburbia USA*, 198.
16. Forstall, "Population of Counties by Decennial Census"; and see Smits, *Nassau Suburbia USA*, 198.
17. Michael H. Ebner, "Re-Reading Suburban America: Urban Population Deconcentration, 1810-1980," *American Quarterly* 37, no. 3 (1985): 380; R. Alba, *Italian Americans: Into the Twilight of Ethnicity* (Englewood Cliffs, NJ: Prentice-Hall, 1985), 88; Michael B. Katz, "What Is a US City?" in *Why Don't American Cities Burn?*, (Philadelphia: University of Pennsylvania Press, 2012): 28.
18. Campbell Gibson, *Population of the 100 Largest Cities and Other Urban Places in the United States: 1790 to 1990* (Washington, DC: Population Division of the U.S. Bureau of the Census, 1998); and see Msgr. Florence D. Cohalan, *A Popular History of the Archdiocese of New York* (Yonkers, NY: United States Catholic Historical Society, 1983), 296.
19. Thomas J. Shelley, *The History of the Archdiocese of New York* (Strasbourg: Éditions du Signe, 1999), 558. During the 1950s, while many of New York's urban parishes were being emptied of white parishioners, the city experienced an influx of migrants from Puerto Rico. These changes within New York's urban parishes are beyond the scope of this study, but for more on the Puerto Rican Catholic presence in New York, see Jay P. Dolan and Jaime R. Vidal, eds., *Puerto Rican and Cuban Catholics in the U.S., 1900–1965* (Notre Dame, IN: University of Notre Dame Press, 1994); Ana Maria Diaz-Stevens, *Oxcart Catholicism on Fifth Avenue: The Impact of the Puerto Rican Migration upon the Archdiocese of New York* (Notre Dame, IN: University of Notre Dame Press, 1993); Joseph P. Fitzpatrick, SJ, *The Stranger Is Our Own: Reflections on the Journey of Puerto Rican Migrants* (New York: Sheed and Ward, 1997).
20. Forstall, "Population of Counties by Decennial Census"; and see Taranto, *Kitchen Table Politics*, 20.
21. Smits, *Nassau Suburbia USA*, 202.
22. Alba, *Italian Americans*, 88.
23. William B. Prendergast, *The Catholic Voter in American Politics: The Passing of the Democratic Monolith* (Washington, DC: Georgetown University Press, 1999), 8.
24. Prendergast, *The Catholic Voter in American Politics*, 8.
25. Cohalan, *A Popular History of the Archdiocese of New York*, 296. See also "Westchester's Catholic Population Totals 261,000, One-Third of Population," *Catholic News* 75, no. 24 (June 18, 1960): 15.
26. Shelley, *The History of the Archdiocese of New York*, 558.
27. Smits, *Nassau Suburbia USA*, 200.
28. McGreevy, *Parish Boundaries*, 85.
29. "The Dream House," *Catholic News* 74, Staten Island Edition, August 23, 1958, 1. In 1952 St. Bernadette Parish in Dyker Heights, Brooklyn had similarly built and raffled off a fully furnished ranch-style house valued at $40,000; "St. Bernadette's Model Ranch Type Gift Home, Monster Bazaar, Feb. 21, 1953," *The Tablet* 45, no. 33 (October 4, 1952): 8.

30. "Wanamaker's New Village of Vision," *The Tablet* 39, no. 15 (June 7, 1947): 9.
31. Even in the spring of 1960, when the Diocese of Brooklyn purchased property in the rapidly developing Bergen Beach section of Brooklyn, a developer admitted that, despite the diocese's preferring not to make the purchase public yet, he had been informing prospective buyers that a church would be built in the area; March 30, 1960 and June 17, 1960, memos from Secretary of Diocesan Projects, memos to Bishop Bryan McEntegart, March 30 and June 17, 1960, in Box 3, Folder: St. Bernard, BK, Bishops Office Papers, Archives of the Diocese of Brooklyn.
32. Jay M. Price, *Temples for a Modern God: Religious Architecture in Postwar America* (New York: Oxford University Press, 2013), 55–56; and see Gretchen Buggeln, *The Suburban Church: Modernism and Community in Postwar America* (Minneapolis: University of Minnesota Press, 2015); "Private School and Church Building Remain at Record Levels," *Catholic News* 68, no. 48 (July 17, 1954): 15; "Church Building in Nation Will Set Record This Year," *Catholic News* 69, no. 48 (July 2, 1955): 24.
33. "Catholic Population Growth Doubling National Average," *Catholic News* 75, no. 36 (September 17, 1960): 3.
34. "Church in U.S. Plans Construction to Cost Ten Billion in Decade—NY Leads Construction," *Catholic News* 62, no. 44 (June 26, 1948): 1; and see Price, *Temples for a Modern God*, 92. In 1947 Spellman had pledged to the New York Building Congress that he would spend $25 million in construction work in the archdiocese within a year as a stimulus to the postwar recovery, including the new Archbishop Stepinac High School in suburban White Plains. See "Cardinal Exceeds His Pledge of Projects Costing $25,000,000," *Catholic News* 62, no. 34 (April 17, 1948): 1.
35. "U.S. Catholic Construction in 1959 Billion 750 Million," *Catholic News* 74, no. 10 (March 7, 1959): 2.
36. Cohalan, *A Popular History of the Archdiocese of New York*, 340–47, 359; *The Official Catholic Directory of 1960* (New York: P. J. Kenedy and Sons, 1960), 189.
37. John K. Sharp, *History of the Diocese of Brooklyn, 1853–1953: The Catholic Church on Long Island*, vol. 2 (New York: Fordham University Press, 1954), 188–89.
38. Kathryn Johnson, "A Question of Authority: Friction in the Catholic Family Life Movement, 1948–1962," *Catholic Historical Review* 86, no. 2 (April 2000): 217–41.
39. Kathleen Gavigan, "The Rise and Fall of Parish Cohesiveness in Philadelphia," *Records of the American Catholic Historical Society* 86, no. 1 (March 1, 1974): 107.
40. Price, *Temples for a Modern God*, 81. *Church Property Administration* began publishing in 1936 and in 1957 changed its name to *Catholic Property Administration*. In 1964 it was absorbed by *Catholic Market*, which had begun publishing the year before. *Catholic Building and Maintenance* began publishing in 1949 and changed its name to *Catholic Institutional Management* in 1968. In part, these changes represent the tapering of the postwar church-building boom and a shift from new construction to facilities administration and maintenance.
41. For an excellent summary of court cases from across the country that dealt with suburban zoning and religious institutions, see Paul Brindel, "Zoning Out Religious Institutions," *Notre Dame Lawyer* 32, no. 4 (August 1957): 627; Paul Brindel, "Keep That School Out!" *Voice of St. Jude* (February 1958): 6–7.
42. George E. Reed, "Zoning Legislation Affecting Church Schools," *Catholic Property Administration* 25, no. 7 (September/October 1961): 68.
43. "Zoning Law Cannot Exclude Churches and Schools, State High Court Says," *Catholic News* 70, no. 51 (July 21, 1956): 1; and see Arthur L. H. Street, "Diocese Wins Zoning Suit," *Church Property Administration* 21, no. 1 (January–February 1957): 96. The

court's opinion also noted that similar decisions had been made in other zoning cases in Arizona, Illinois, Indiana, Nevada, Ohio, and Texas.
44. Gibson, "Population of the 100 Largest Cities."
45. See Msgr. George A. Kelly, letter to Archbishop Justin Rigali, April 3, 1994, E-23, Folder 17, AANY; Msgr. George A. Kelly, letter to John Cardinal O'Connor, March 26, 1995, and John Cardinal O'Connor, letter to Msgr. George A. Kelly, March 30, 1995, E-34, Folder 30, AANY.
46. Warren Steibel, *Cardinal Spellman: The Man* (New York: Appleton-Century, 1966). During a joint interview in 1966 with the director of archdiocesan building campaigns, Msgr. Leonard Hunt, Cardinal Spellman asked his colleague: "Are you suggesting another diocese?"
47. Msgr. Joseph P. Christopher, letter to Msgr. Florence D. Cohalan, February 25, 1954, S/B-15, Folder 6, AANY. In April 1951 Thomas E. Molloy, Bishop of Brooklyn, was made Archbishop *ad personam* by Pope Pius XII as a personal honor to Molloy without the Diocese of Brooklyn being elevated to the status of archdiocese. See Sr. Joan de Lourdes Leonard, CSJ, *Richly Blessed: The Diocese of Rockville Centre, 1957–1990* (Marceline, MO: Walsworth Publishing, 1991), 2. This was done only after Adeodato Cardinal Piazza of the Vatican's Sacred Consistorial Congregation wrote Cardinal Spellman for his endorsement of the honor (Francis Cardinal Spellman, letter to Adeodate Giovanni Cardinal, March 27, 1951, S/D-12, Folder 5, AANY).
48. John Cooney, *American Pope: The Life and Times of Francis Cardinal Spellman* (New York: Times Books, 1984), 124, 250, suggests some of the reasons for the bad blood between Spellman and Molloy.
49. Msgr. Anthony Savastano, interview by Rev. William Koenig, March 11, 2004, transcript, p. 13, Box 1603, Oral History Project Collection, ADRVC.
50. Spellman's official biographer, Rev. Robert I. Gannon, SJ, attributes the proposed trade to Cardinal Hayes and also indicates that in 1938, a year prior to Hayes's death and Spellman's ascension to New York, there was a rumor that a new diocese would be created for Nassau and Suffolk Counties and that Spellman would be made its bishop; Gannon, *The Cardinal Spellman Story* (Garden City, NY: Doubleday, 1962). The histories of both the Archdiocese of New York and the Diocese of Brooklyn attribute the Queens/Staten Island trade proposal to Spellman, and Msgr. George A. Kelly specifically dates the proposal to 1939, when Spellman was named Archbishop of New York. See Cohalan, *A Popular History of the Archdiocese of New York*, 313; The Diocese of Brooklyn, *Diocese of Immigrants: The Brooklyn Catholic Experience, 1853–2003* (Strasbourg, France: Éditions du Signe, 2004), 107; and Msgr. George Kelly, letter to Cardinal John O'Connor, March 26, 1995, Box E-34, Folder 30, AANY.
51. Bishop James J. Daly, interview by Sr. Joan de Lourdes Leonard, CSJ, September 11, 1981 (hereafter Daly interview), transcript, p. 28, Box 106, Sr. Joan de Lourdes Leonard Collection (hereafter Leonard Collection), ADRVC.
52. The Diocese of Brooklyn, *Diocese of Immigrants*, 107; Msgr. Edmond Trench, interview by Sr. Joan de Lourdes Leonard, CSJ, September 22, 1981 (hereafter Trench interview), transcript, p. 2, Box 106, Leonard Collection, ADRVC.
53. Leonard, *Richly Blessed*, 9.
54. Daly interview, 27.
55. Cooney, *American Pope*, 248–49. See also Gannon, *The Cardinal Spellman Story*, 144–45.

56. George Dugan, "Pope Divides Brooklyn Diocese; Creates a New Long Island See," *New York Times*, April 19, 1957, 1; Leonard, *Richly Blessed*, 7, 22; Diocese of Brooklyn, *Diocese of Immigrants*, 119.
57. Msgr. James F. Coffey, interview by Sr. Joan de Lourdes Leonard, CSJ, August 7, 1981, transcript, p. 1, Box 226, Leonard Collection, ADRVC.
58. Diocese of Brooklyn, *Diocese of Immigrants*, 119–20.
59. Bishop James J. Daly stated in a 1981 interview: "Everyone agrees it was Spellman who made sure it was McEntegart and Bishop Kellenberg and I don't think anyone would dispute that"; Daly interview, 26.
60. "Address of His Eminence, Francis Cardinal Spellman, at the Luncheon Following the Installation of Bishop Walter P. Kellenberg as First Bishop of Rockville Centre, May 27, 1957," Box S/A-18, Folder 11, AANY.
61. Cohalan, *A Popular History of the Archdiocese of New York*, 313. The Vatican decree establishing the Diocese of Rockville Centre specifically mentions that Spellman was consulted about the division and gave his approval: See translation of the decrees of establishment in Box 4, Folder 215, Canon Law Subject Files, Chancery Office Collection, ADB.
62. Msgr. Joseph P. Christopher, letters to Msgr. Florence D. Cohalan, February 19 and 25, 1957, S/B-12, Folder 5, AANY.
63. Fr. Paul McKeever, interview by Sr. Joan de Lourdes Leonard, CSJ, July 8, 1982, transcript, p. 18, Box 226, Leonard Collection, ADRVC. There were, however, even a decade after the division in the mid-1960s disagreements about the number of seminarians the Diocese of Brooklyn could send to the diocesan seminary, Immaculate Conception, which had been built in 1926 by the Diocese of Brooklyn but was located in Huntington, Long Island and was therefore transferred to the control of the Diocese of Rockville Centre.
64. Bishop Bryan McEntegart, letter to Francis Cardinal Spellman, September 25, 1957, Box S/D-12, Folder 5, AANY.
65. Msgr. James P. King, Chancellor of the Diocese of Brooklyn, letter to Msgr. Joseph J. Podhajski, Chancellor of the Diocese of Grand Rapids, July 30, 1973, Box 4, Folder 215, Canon Law Subject Files, Chancery Office Collection, ADB. Msgr. Podhajski had likely written for Brooklyn's advice on how to handle the division of diocesan assets because in 1970 Pope Paul VI had divided the Diocese of Grand Rapids to create the new dioceses of Gaylord and Kalamazoo.
66. Daly interview, 4.
67. See translation of the decrees of establishment in Box 4, Folder 215, Canon Law Subject Files, Chancery Office Collection, ADB.
68. Leonard, *Richly Blessed*, 12.
69. James G. Murray, "The See of Rockville Centre," *Catholic Market* 3, no. 4 (September–October 1964): 42. For more on the history of Rockville Centre, see Preston R. Bassett and Arthur L. Hodges, *The History of Rockville Centre* (Uniondale, NY: Salisbury Printers, 1969); Marilyn Nunes Devlin, *A Brief History of Rockville Centre: The Heritage and History of a Village* (Charleston, SC: The History Press, 2011).
70. Murray, "The See of Rockville Centre," 44; Trench interview, 3. See also Leonard, *Richly Blessed*, 14.
71. Murray, "The See of Rockville Centre," 58; Leonard, *Richly Blessed*, 15.
72. Leonard, *Richly Blessed*, 13–14, 15; "Scenes at Installation in Rockville Centre," *The Tablet*, 50, no. 16 (June 1, 1957): 13. Quealy was a close friend of George Cardinal

Mundelein of Chicago—a former auxiliary bishop of Brooklyn who had family in Rockville Centre—and had made the acquaintance of Pope Pius XII when the then-cardinal Eugenio Pacelli visited Long Island in 1936.

73. Joan Kelly and Adam Z. Horvath, "Bishop's Achievement Recalled," *Newsday*, January 13, 1986, 6.
74. Leonard, *Richly Blessed*, 19, 20–21, 22; and see "Business-Trained Bishop: Walter Philip Kellenberg," *New York Times*, May 28, 1957, 25' "First Rockville Centre Shepherd," *The Tablet*, 50, no. 11 (April 17, 1957); "Bishop Kellenberg," *Long Island Catholic* 1, no. 1 (May 3, 1962): 5.
75. Leonard, *Richly Blessed*, 11. Msgr. Thomas Shelley has noted that "for several years prior to 1957, the Diocese of Brooklyn reported a Catholic population of 1,497,598" and that "after the loss of 497,855 Catholics to the new Diocese of Rockville Centre, Brooklyn reported a Catholic population of 1,429,174, a decrease of only 68,424 Catholics." Shelley suggests "it is hard to resist the suspicion that Brooklyn was deliberately underestimating its Catholic population in order to forestall a division of the diocese." See Thomas J. Shelley, "Keeping the Immigrant Church Catholic: Some Reflections on Dr. John Butler's Lecture," *US Catholic Historian*, 22, no. 2, Urbanism and American Religion (Spring 2004): 79 n. 30.
76. "Diocesan Growth Is 3 Times U.S.," *Long Island Catholic* 2, no. 1 (May 2, 1963): 1. For more, see "Diocese Is Now 13th Largest in Nation," *Long Island Catholic* 1, no. 1 (May 3, 1962): 1A.
77. "Diocesan Growth Is 3 Times U.S.," 1. For more population statistics for the Diocese of Rockville Centre, see demographic charts in the appendix. By way of comparison, in 1963, the archdioceses with more than one million Catholics were Chicago (2,293,900), Boston (1,733,620), New York (1,704,350), Philadelphia (1,263,625), Newark (1,512,311), Detroit (1,429,670), and Los Angeles (1,477,408). The top seven largest dioceses were Brooklyn (1,503,628), Hartford (738,302), Pittsburgh (906,928), Cleveland (834,367), Rockville Centre (735,165), Trenton (538,130), and Providence (525,274).
78. Taranto, *Kitchen Table Politics*, 39.
79. "DRVC Population Numbers," *Long Island Catholic* 9, no. 4 (May 28, 1970): 11. For more, see "Diocese Is Nation's 5th Largest," *Long Island Catholic* 3, no. 1 (April 30, 1964): 2; "Diocese Has 3rd Largest Gain," *Long Island Catholic* 4, no. 1 (April 29, 1965): 1; "Diocese 4th Largest; Grows by 30,141 in Year," *Long Island Catholic* 5, no. 4 (May 19, 1966): 24; "Diocese Is One of Six Showing Population Rise," *Long Island Catholic* 6, no. 52 (April 25, 1968): 18; "Catholic Statistics Published by Kennedy Group," *Long Island Catholic* 8, no. 2 (May 8, 1969): 18.
80. "Catholic Population on LI Increases," *Long Island Catholic* 11, no. 8 (June 22, 1972): 10. For more, see "Diocese Membership Rises by 28,180," *Long Island Catholic* 10, no. 4 (May 27, 1971): 8. Brooklyn had diminished in size through the 1960s but remained the nation's largest diocese with 1,491,273 Catholics. Rockville Centre followed with 954,577.
81. "LI Catholic Population Double National Average," *Long Island Catholic* 21, no. 9 (June 24, 1982): 1. For more, see "Catholic Population on LI Nears One-Million Mark," *Long Island Catholic* 12, no. 3 (May 24, 1973): 3; "Catholic Population on Rise in Nassau," *Long Island Catholic* 14, no. 7 (June 12, 1975): 2; "Topping a Million," *Long Island Catholic* 14, no. 43 (March 4, 1975): 6; "Catholic Population Increases," *Long Island Catholic* 19, no. 5 (May 29, 1980): 8; "US Catholic Population Over the 5 Million Mark," *Long Island Catholic* 20, no. 5 (May 28, 1981): 2; "Shifts in Catholic

Population," *Long Island Catholic* 21, no. 7 (June 10, 1982): 1; "Rockville Centre Is Second Largest Diocese," *Long Island Catholic* 22, no. 17 (August 18, 1983): 2.
82. Leonard, *Richly Blessed*, 60; Butler, *God in Gotham*, 215, 223.
83. Leonard, *Richly Blessed*, 60, 63, 75, 110, 112, 115.
84. Dennis J. Geaney, "Social Action in America," *Commonweal* 66, no. 21 (August 23, 1957): 514; Neil P. Hurley, SJ, "The Church in Suburbia," *America* 98, no. 7 (November 16, 1957): 194.
85. Murray, "The See of Rockville Centre," 42; Robert A. Graham, SJ, "Great Diocese Divided," *America* 97, no. 5 (May 4, 1957): 155.
86. On the 1950s religious revival, see Robert S. Ellwood, *The Fifties Spiritual Marketplace: American Religion in a Decade of Conflict* (New Brunswick, NJ: Rutgers University Press, 1997). For the "suburban captivity" of the church, see Winter, *The Suburban Captivity of the Churches*; and James Hudnut-Beumler, *Looking for God in the Suburbs: The Religion of the American Dream and Its Critics, 1945–1965* (New Brunswick, NJ: Rutgers University Press, 1994).
87. See Joseph H. Fichter, SJ, *Theological Studies* 21, no. 2 (January 1, 1960): 173–74. Joseph F. Scheuer, CPPS, *American Catholic Sociological Review* 21, no. 2 (Summer 1960): 173.
88. See Andrew M. Greeley, "Suburbia: A New Way of Life," *The Sign* 37, no. 6 (January 1958): 11; "The Catholic Suburbanite," *The Sign* 37, no. 7 (February 1958): 30; "Religious Revival: Fact or Fiction?" *Sign* 37, no. 12 (July 1958): 25; "The Suburban Novel," *Catholic World* 187, no. 1122 (September 1958): 428; "The Changing City," *Catholic World* 188, no. 1128 (March 1959): 481; "Conformity or Community," *Sign* 38, no. 12 (July 1959): 18; "The Suburban Parish," *Commonweal* 70, no. 22 (September 25, 1959): 537–39; "The Urban Parish Under a Microscope," *Social Order* 9, no. 7 (September 1959): 335; "Organization Man: Hope for a Halo," *Sign* 39, no. 3 (October 1959): 48; "City Life and the Churches," *America* 103, no. 22 (August 27, 1960): 573–74; "Book Review: Suburbia Revisited," *Social Order* 11, no. 8 (October 1961): 371; "The Church as 'New Community,'" *Sign* 48, no. 4 (November 1968): 27.
89. Dennis Clark, "The Church in the Suburbs," *Social Order* 5, no. 1 (January 1955): 27; Andrew M. Greeley, *The Church and the Suburbs* (New York: Sheed and Ward, 1959), 63, 69; Hurley, "The Church in Suburbia," 194.
90. Greeley, *The Church and the Suburbs*, 33, 52, 53, 63–64, and see Hurley, "The Church in Suburbia," 195.
91. Greeley, *The Church and the Suburbs*, 54–56, 65; Hurley, "The Church in Suburbia," 196, 198, 199.
92. Greeley, *The Church and the Suburbs*, 57; John L. Thomas, SJ, "'Value Ghetto' for Families," *The Tablet* 52, no. 37 (October 24, 1959): 24.
93. Greeley, *The Church and the Suburbs*, 66, 69; Hurley, "The Church in Suburbia," 196; O'Gara, "The Catholic as Citizen," Box 2 Folder 8, UNDA COGA.
94. See Dennis Clark, "Humanizing the City," *Social Order* 6, no. 9 (November 1956): 420. James O'Gara, "Catholics in Suburbia and Catholic Social Thought," n.d., Box 2 Folder 14, UNDA COGA.
95. Greeley, "The Church in the Suburbs: Some Afterthoughts," 7, 8–10; Andrew Greeley, "A New Urbanity," *New City* 5, no. 10 (October 1967): 5–8.
96. Greeley, *The Church and the Suburbs*, xv; Andrew Greeley, "The Church in the Suburbs: Some Afterthoughts," *New City* 6, no. 4 (April 1968): 7.
97. For an introduction to Phyllis McGinley (1905–78) and her work, see Lewis Doyle, "The Poems of Phyllis McGinley," *America* (December 18, 1954): 320–22; Kay

Sullivan, "From Suburbs to Saints: Phyllis McGinley," *Catholic World*, September 1957, 420–25; "Life with a Poet: The Lady from Larchmont," *Newsweek*, September 26, 1960, 120–22; David McCord, "She Speaks a Language of Delight," *Saturday Review*, December 9, 1960, 32; "The Telltale Hearth," *Time* 85, no. 12 (June 18, 1965). Scholarly work on McGinley and her poetry's place in feminist debate, includes Nancy Walker, "Humor and Gender Roles: The 'Funny' Feminism of the Post World War II Suburbs," *American Quarterly* 37, no. 1 (Spring 1985): 98–113; Megan Anne Leroy, "Writing the Mean: Phyllis McGinley and American Domesticity" (MA thesis, University of Florida, 2007); and, especially, Jo Gill, *The Poetics of the American Suburbs* (New York: Palgrave Macmillan, 2013). McGinley's neighbors in Larchmont, biographer Marie Killilea and playwright and humorist Jean Kerr, are two additional examples. Among Killilea's publications see *Karen* (New York: Prentice-Hall, 1952); *With Love from Karen* (New York: Prentice-Hall, 1963). Jean Kerr published essays in *Ladies' Home Journal, Saturday Evening Post, Good Housekeeping, Suburbia Today, Esquire*, and *Vogue*. Her publications also include *Please Don't Eat the Daises* (Garden City, NY: Doubleday, 1957), which rose to number 1 on the *New York Times* Best Seller List for nonfiction on February 2, 1958, and remained in the top 10 for forty-eight weeks; and *The Snake Has All the Lines* (Garden City, NY: Doubleday, 1960).
98. Phyllis McGinley, *A Short Walk from the Station* (New York: Viking Press, 1951), 22. McGinley's introductory essay was originally published as: "Suburbia: Of Thee I Sing," *Harper's*, December 1949, 79, and also appeared in her collection *Province of the Heart* (New York: Dell, 1959), 121 McGinley, *Sixpence in Her Shoes* (New York: Macmillan, 1964).
99. Antoinette Bosco, "Image of 'Happy Housewife' a Fraud?" *Long Island Catholic* 2, no. 32 (December 5, 1963): 9. When Betty Friedan appeared at Roslyn, Long Island's Temple Beth Shalom in 1963, the *Long Island Catholic* reported that the audience gave more applause to a critical questioner than they did to Friedan.
100. Paul Brindel, "A Pox on Suburbia," *Voice of St. Jude* 22, no. 12 (April 1957): 7; "The Suburbs Talk Back," *Voice of St. Jude* (August 1957): 6–8, 32; Joyce Sentner Daly, "I Like Suburbia," *Long Island Catholic* 3, no. 1 (April 30, 1964): 4. Daly resided in Darien, Connecticut, and her essay was originally published in *Country Beautiful Magazine* in 1963. The *Long Island Catholic* also reprinted "Is Suburban Living Crazy?" a defense of suburbia written by "a suburban housewife" and originally published in *Reign of the Sacred Heart* and *Family Digest* magazines; "Is Suburban Living Crazy?," *Long Island Catholic*, no. 7 (August 30, 1962). For more on the development of conscience language in the 1960s see Peter Cajka, *Follow Your Conscience: The Catholic Church and the Spirit of the Sixties* (Chicago: University of Chicago Press, 2021).
101. Despite the slight variance in their initial meanings, the terms "metropolis," "megalopolis," and "cosmopolis" were, used interchangeably. See Robert Lee, ed., *The Church and the Exploding Metropolis* (Richmond, VA: John Knox Press, 1965), 22.
102. J. John Palen, *The Suburbs* (New York: McGraw-Hill, 1995), 90.
103. Countless commentaries in this period unquestionably referred to the suburbs as the future of the Church. See, for example, Msgr. Raymond T. Bosler, "Suburbia and the Church in Revolution," 1969, 1, Box 1, Folder 3, Msgr. Raymond T. Bosler Papers, Collection 015, Archives of the Archdiocese of Indianapolis, The Catholic Center, Indianapolis, IN.
104. Greeley, *The Church and the Suburbs*, xvii, and 57, 192.

105. Dorothy M. Dohen, "The Urban Crisis from the Perspective of the Sociology of Religion," 9, an unpublished paper for the *Symposium on Metropolis* sponsored by the Catholic Theological Society, the USCC's Urban Task Force, and the Social Theology Department of CARA in Washington, DC, May 1–3, 1970, Box 194, Folder 1, Collection 129, ACUA.

CHAPTER THREE

1. *St. Anne Parish's 75th Anniversary Journal*, pp. 17, 22, Box 187, Folder 3, Parish Journals, Chancellor's Collection, ADRVC; *St. Anne Parish's 80th Anniversary Journal*, Archives of St. Anne Parish, Brentwood, NY; Jack Ehrlich and Virginia Sheward, "Drive-In Church Debut Draws 2,000 to Mass; It's the 1st in NY Area," *Newsday*, June 27, 1955, 7; "Drive-In Church Proves Popular in Brentwood," *The Tablet* (July 16, 1955); Antoinette Bosco, "A Profile of St. Anne's: Brentwood's Bustling Parish," *Long Island Catholic* 4, no. 23 (September 30, 1965): 2.
2. See Andrew Greeley, *The Catholic Imagination* (Berkeley: University of California Press, 2001). For more on the relationship between place, space, and the sacred, see Thomas A. Tweed, "Space," *Material Religion* 7, no. 1 (2011): 116–23; Thomas A. Tweed, "Afterward: Narrating Catholic History," in *Crossings and Dwellings: Restored Jesuits, Women Religious, American Experience, 1814–2014*, ed. Kyle B. Roberts and Stephen R. Schloesser (Leiden: Brill, 2017), 725–31; and Osborne, *American Catholics and the Church of Tomorrow*, 36, 141, 223.
3. Timothy J. Gilfoyle, "Michael Katz on Place and Space in Urban History," *Journal of Urban History* 41, no. 4 (July 2015): 574.
4. James O'Toole, *The Faithful: A History of Catholics in America* (Cambridge, MA: Belknap Press of Harvard University Press, 2008), 222–23.
5. *St. Ignatius of Loyola 125th Anniversary Journal, 1872–1983*, pp. 3–10, Box 903, Parish Journals, Bishops Office Collection, ADRVC.
6. Lynne Matarrese, *The History of Levittown, New York* (New York: Levittown Historical Society, 1997), 50; Leonard, *Richly Blessed*, 10, citing an essay on St. Ignatius Loyola Parish by Fr. John H. Wissler.
7. Matarrese, *The History of Levittown*, 50.
8. *St. Ignatius of Loyola 125th Anniversary Journal*, 10.
9. Butler, *God in Gotham*, 224.
10. *St. Martha Parish 25th Anniversary Journal, 1949–1975*, pp. 9, 12, 16, 18–19, Box 618, Seminary Library Collection, ADRVC.
11. *Dedication of St. Frances de Chantal Church, 1987*, Box 6, Item 45, Archives of St. Frances de Chantal Parish, Wantagh, NY.
12. *Our Lady of Mercy Church Dedication Journal, 1957*, Box 163B, Parish Files, Chancellor's Collection, ADRVC. In 1947 the *Levittown Eagle* printed requests from residents—including Mr. and Mrs. H. Larken of 60 Dogwood Lane and Mr. and Mrs. Richard Gremillot of 61 Valley Road—for transportation to Sunday Mass; see "Request Church Transportation," *Island Trees Eagle* 1, no. 2 (November 27, 1947): 4; "Need Cars for Sunday Masses," *Island Trees Eagle* 1, no. 4 (December 11, 1947): 5.
13. *Our Lady of Mercy Church Dedication Journal*.
14. *Our Lady of Grace 50th Anniversary Journal*, Archives of Our Lady of Grace Parish, West Babylon, NY.
15. Robert Moses, letter to Bishop Molloy, September 5, 1947, Box 1, Folder 4, Bishop Molloy Correspondence, 1931–1951, ADB. Moses wrote to follow up on a previous

meeting to discuss "the subject of planning and changes in the Long Island area" and to suggest advisors who could help the diocese "in anticipating future problems" as rapid growth affected "transportation, residence, recreation, business, industry, and shipping."

16. See memo of July 8, 1959, in Box 26, St. Pius X Folder 1, Bishops Office Collection, ADB.
17. "First Mass in New Parish in Tent," *The Tablet* 54, no. 29 (August 29, 1961): 1; and see Secretary of Diocesan Projects, memos to Bishop McEntegart, February 15 and June 17, 1960, and May 1, 1961, Box 3, Folder St. Bernard, BK, Bishops Office Collection, ADB.
18. *St. Martha Parish 25th Anniversary Journal, 1949–1975*, 4.
19. For one example of many, see Bishop Walter Kellenberg, letter to Fr. Jeremiah McLaughlin, January 7, 1970, Box 163B, Folder: St. Joseph, Hewlett, Parish Files, Chancellor's Office, ADRVC.
20. Bishop McEntegart, letter to Fr. Kenny, June 29, 1961, Box 3, Folder St. Bernard, BK, Bishops Office Collection, ADB.
21. Fr. Joseph J. Tschantz of St. Gerard Majella Parish, Hollis, letter to Bishop McEntegart, July 3, 1961, Box 3, Folder St. Bernard, BK, Bishops Office Collection, ADB.
22. Bishop Bryan McEntegart, letter to Fr. Rosario Pitrone, June 29, 1961, Box 8, Folder St. Jude BK, Bishops Office Collection, ADB.
23. Bishop Francis Mugavero, letter to Fr. William A. O'Leary, April 25, 1972, Box 8, Folder St. Laurence BK, Bishops Office Collection, ADB.
24. Bishop Bryan McEntegart, letter to Father Jolley, of St. Columba Parish, Marine Park, Brooklyn, June 19, 1967, Box 4, Folder St. Columba BK, Bishops Office Collection, ADB.
25. Fr. John E. Steinmuller of St. Barbara Parish, letter to Bishop Bryan McEntegart, June 28, 1961, Box 8, Folder St. Jude, BK, Bishops Office Collection, ADB.
26. Msgr. Edmond Trench, interview by Sr. Joan de Lourdes Leonard, CSJ, September 22, 1981, transcript, p. 10–11, Box 106, File Edmond Trench, Sr. Joan De Lourdes Leonard Collection (hereafter Leonard Collection), ADRVC.
27. William F. Whelan, "A Brief Look at the History and Development of the Our Lady of Grace Roman Catholic Church, West Babylon, New York," unpublished ca. 1985, pp. 13, 15, Archives of Our Lady of Grace Parish, West Babylon, NY. In 1966 Our Lady of Grace raffled off a Cadillac and the seller of the winning ticket also won a Ford Mustang.
28. Msgr. Lawrence Ballweg, interview by Sr. Joan de Lourdes Leonard, CSJ, n.d. (ca. August 1981), transcript, pp. 3–6, Box 226, Sr. Joan De Lourdes Leonard Collection, ADRVC.
29. *St. Martha Parish 25th Anniversary Journal*, 12, 16.
30. *St. Martha Parish 10th Anniversary Journal, 1949–1959*, Box 163A, Parish Files, Chancellor's Collection, ADRVC.
31. "Five New Parishes Answer Growth Challenges," *Long Island Catholic* 1, no. 8 (June 21, 1963): 1.
32. Building Commission of the Board of Consultors, minutes for November 30, 1951, and June 10, 1955, Binder 4: January 5, 1951–December 18, 1953, and Binder 5: January 8, 1954–December 13, 1957, Diocesan Buildings and Property Office—Building Commission and Board of Consultors Minutes, ADB.
33. Bishop Emil Wcela, interview by Edward Thompson, February 10, 2004, transcript, p. 16, Box 1603, File Emil Wcela, Oral History Project Collection, ADRVC; Bishop Emil

Wcela, interview by Sr. Joan de Lourdes Leonard, CSJ, September 23, 1981, transcript, pp. 2-3, Box 106, File Emil Wcela, Sr. Joan de Lourdes Leonard Collection, ADRVC.
34. Msgr. Anthony Savastano, interview by Fr. William Koenig, March 11, 2004 (hereafter Savastano interview), transcript, pp. 14-15, Box 1603, File Anthony Savastano, Oral History Project Collection, ADRVC.
35. Butler, *God in Gotham*, 217.
36. "First Mass at Middle Village Parish Our Lady of Hope," *The Tablet* 53, no. 22 (July 9, 1960): 1; "Snow Collapses Tent-Church, Our Lady of Hope, Middle Village," *The Tablet* 54, no. 1 (February 11, 1961): 1.
37. Fr. Patrick J. Kenny, letter to Bishop Bryan McEntegart, August 21, 1961, Box 3, Folder St. Bernard BK, Bishops Office Collection, ADB.
38. "Masses of Christmas Past," *Long Island Catholic* 6, no. 34 (December 21, 1967): 11.
39. *St. Frances de Chantal 50th Anniversary Journal, 1952-2002*, pp. 2, 34, Box 7, Item 5, Archives of St. Frances de Chantal Parish, Wantagh, NY; and see Building Commission of the Board of Consultors, minutes for February 8, 1952, Binder 4: January 5, 1951-December 18, 1953, Diocesan Buildings and Property Office—Building Commission and Board of Consultors Minutes, ADB.
40. *Holy Family Parish 25th Anniversary Journal, 1951-1976*, Box 163B, Chancellor's Collection, Parish Files, ADRVC; Wcela, interview by Leonard, 2.
41. Helen T. Butler, *Our Lady of Grace Parish: The Story about a Community of Faith, Hope, and Love* (Tappan, NY: Custombook, 1987), Archives of Our Lady of Grace Parish, West Babylon, NY.
42. *St. Paul the Apostle Church Dedication Journal, 1968*, Box 158, Chancellor's Collection, ADRVC; *St. Rose of Lima 20th Anniversary Journal, 1952-1972*, Box 158, Parish Files, Chancellor's Collection, ADRVC; "Masses of Christmas Past," 11.
43. *Blessed Sacrament Parish 25th Anniversary Journal, 1950-1975*, Box 616, Seminary Library Collection, ADRVC; "Masses of Christmas Past," 11; *St. Pius X Parish 10th Anniversary Journal, 1955-1965*, Archives of St. Pius X Parish, Plainview, NY.
44. *Holy Family Parish 25th Anniversary Journal*, Chancellor's Parish Files, ADRVC; Savastano interview, 14; *St. Paul the Apostle Parish Church Dedication Journal, 1968*; Butler, *Our Lady of Grace: The Story about a Community of Faith, Hope, and Love*; *St. Matthew Parish Church Dedication Journal, 1968*, Box 903, Parish Journals, Bishops Office Collection, ADRVC; *St. Francis of Assisi Parish Church Dedication Journal, 1971*, p. 13, Box 617, Seminary Library Collection, ADRVC.
45. *Holy Family Parish 25th Anniversary Journal*; "First Mass in St. Jude Parish," *The Tablet* 54, no. 23 (July 15, 1961): 1; "Mass Celebrated in Theatre," *Long Island Catholic* 3, no. 45 (March 4, 1965): 12.
46. Savastano interview, 15.
47. Kenneth T. Jackson, *Crabgrass Frontier: The Suburbanization of the United States* (New York: Oxford University Press, 1985), 246-47, 255. "Drive-In Church," *Newsweek* 40, no. 27 (December 29, 1952): 63.
48. Megan Garber, "Reel Faith: How the Drive-In Movie Theater Helped Create the Megachurch," *The Atlantic*, June 8, 2012.
49. Erica Robles-Anderson, "The Crystal Cathedral: Architecture for Mediated Congregation," *Public Culture* 24, no. 3 (October 2012): 577-99. In 2012 the Crystal Cathedral was purchased by the Roman Catholic Diocese of Orange, which renovated the structure and rededicated it in 2019 as Christ Cathedral. See Derrick Bryson and Neil Vigdor, "For an Extravagant California Church, a Conversion: Televangelism

to Catholicism," *New York Times*, July 19, 2019, A18. Among some Catholic architects and liturgical theologians, the purchase of the cathedral was criticized because the layout of the structure was deemed unsuitable to the Catholic Mass; see Joan Frawley Desmond, "The Crystal Cathedral Becomes Christ Cathedral," *National Catholic Register*, August 19, 2013, https://www.ncregister.com/daily-news/the-crystal-cathedral-becomes-christ-cathedral.

50. *St. Anne Parish's 80th Anniversary Journal.*
51. Gregory Florentino, interview with the author, October 4, 2017, at St. Anne Parish, Brentwood, NY.
52. Maureen Fitzgerald, "Lost at the Drive-In," in *Faith and the Historian: Catholic Perspectives*, ed. Nick Salvatore (Urbana: University of Illinois Press, 2007), 148–49.
53. Fitzgerald, "Lost at the Drive-In," 148–49.
54. "Meeting the Religious Needs of Our Day," *Long Island Catholic* 2, no. 20 (September 12, 1963): 13.
55. *Sacred Heart Parish History, 1938–1975*, Box 903, Parish Journals, Bishops Office Collection, ADRVC.
56. *Our Lady of Mercy Church Dedication Journal.*
57. Wcela, interview by Thompson, 17.
58. Msgr. Robert Emmet Fagan, interview by Sr. Joan de Lourdes Leonard, CSJ, September 4, 1981, transcript, p. 4, Box 226, Sr. Joan de Lourdes Leonard Collection, ADRVC.
59. Savastano interview, 16.
60. Butler, *Our Lady of Grace: The Story about a Community of Faith, Hope, and Love*; Whelan, "A Brief Look at the History and Development of the Our Lady of Grace Roman Catholic Church," 11; "Meeting the Religious Needs of Our Day," 13.
61. *St. Francis of Assisi Parish Church Dedication Journal*, 17; and see Donald Thorman, "Parents Are Also Educators," *Act* 11, no. 4 (March 1958): 8.
62. See Greeley, *The Catholic Imagination*; Elizabeth Kuhns, *The Habit: A History of the Clothing of Catholic Nuns* (New York: Doubleday, 2003); Sally Dwyer-McNulty, *Common Threads: A Cultural History of Clothing in American Catholicism* (Chapel Hill: University of North Carolina Press, 2014).
63. *St. Frances de Chantal Parish 50th Anniversary Journal*, 31; "Renovations and Innovations Add Modern Style to Pre-Cana," *Long Island Catholic* 10, no. 48 (March 30, 1972): 3; Carol Speranza, "Cana, Pre-Cana Offer New Format," *Long Island Catholic* 12, no. 21 (September 17, 1973): 8; Joe and Nancy Massaro, "In Home Pre-Cana Program," *The Victorian* 3, no. 7 (June 1978): 4–5.
64. Msgr. Thomas Hartman, interview by Sr. Joan de Lourdes Leonard, CSJ, September 12, 1988, transcript, p. 3, Box 226, Joan de Lourdes Leonard Collection, ADRVC.
65. Emerson Hynes, *Seven Keys to a Christian Home* (Des Moines, IA: National Catholic Rural Life Conference, 1949), 50, emphasis in the original.
66. Katharine E. Harmon, *There Were Also Many Women There: Lay Women in the Liturgical Movement in the United States, 1926–1959* (Collegeville, MN: Liturgical Press, 2013), 242–45 and 287–98; Butler, *God in Gotham*, 226.
67. *St. Pius X Parish 25th Anniversary Journal, 1955–1980*, Archives of St. Pius X Parish, Plainview, NY.
68. *Our Parish* 1, no. 5 (August 1966): 13, and 1, no. 6 (September 1966): 8.
69. Timothy Kelly, *The Transformation of American Catholicism: The Pittsburgh Laity and the Second Vatican Council, 1950–1972* (Notre Dame, IN: University of Notre Dame Press, 2009), 55–59.

70. For examples, see "Holy Name Rally Attracts 60,000 at Ebbets Field," *The Tablet* 44, no. 14 (May 26, 1951): 1; "Over 76,000 Throng Polo Grounds for Family Rosary Rally," *Catholic News* 67, no. 9 (October 18, 1952): 1.
71. "Kellenberg to Lead Rosary Rally," *Long Island Catholic* 8, no. 22 (September 25, 1969): 1; "Rosary Rally Attracts 5,000," *Long Island Catholic* 16, no. 23 (October 6, 1977): 1.
72. McCartin, *Prayers of the Faithful*, 74, 105; Kathryn Ann Johnson, "The Home Is a Little Church: Gender, Culture, and Authority in American Catholicism, 1940–1962," diss., University of Pennsylvania, 1997, 129, 148, 197, 199.
73. Richard Gribble, CSC, *American Apostle of the Family Rosary: The Life of Patrick J. Peyton, CSC* (New York: Crossroads Publishing, 2005); "Family Rosary on Television," *The Tablet* 42, no. 8 (April 15, 1950): 14.
74. "Children Take Up Block Rosary in Jamaica," *The Tablet* 44, no. 3 (March 10, 1951): 12.
75. "Schedule of Block Rosary Arranged in Orange County," *Catholic News* 74, Orange County Edition (September 30, 1958): 1; *St. Pius X Parish 25th Anniversary Journal*; "When Neighbors Pray Together," *Long Island Catholic* 4, no. 15 (August 5, 1965): 4.
76. "Rosary Chain Adds Links," *Long Island Catholic* 2, no. 2 (May 9, 1963): 2.
77. "Retreats More Popular with Men than Women," *Long Island Catholic* 1, no. 32 (December 6, 1962): 11.
78. For more on Sheen, see Mark S. Massa, *Catholics and American Culture: Fulton Sheen, Dorothy Day, and the Notre Dame Football Team* (New York: Herder and Herder, 1999).
79. "Plan Living Room Retreats, Catholic Hour Programs on TV," *The Tablet* 46, no. 2 (February 28, 1953): 5.
80. "A Do-it-Yourself Retreat," *Long Island Catholic* 1, no. 6 (June 7, 1962): 9; Jean Kelleher, *Halo for a Housewife* (New York: Bruce Publishing, 1962).
81. "Home Retreats in Happauge Offer an Awareness of God," *Long Island Catholic* 12, no. 36 (January 17, 1974): 13.
82. Liz O'Connor, "At Home Retreats Are Right at Home on Long Island," *Long Island Catholic* 15, no. 49 (April 7, 1977): 1; O'Connor, "At Home Retreats," *Long Island Catholic* 13, no. 31 (December 5, 1974): 4; O'Connor, "At Home Retreats Goes International," *Long Island Catholic* 18, no. 2 (May 10, 1979): 2.
83. O'Connor, "At Home Retreats Are Right at Home on Long Island," 1.
84. Rev. Robert E. Lauder, "At Home Retreats," *Long Island Catholic* 22, no. 11 (July 7, 1983): 7.
85. "At Home Retreats," letters, *Long Island Catholic* 22, no. 13 (July 21, 1983): 6.
86. McCartin, *Prayers of the Faithful*, 116–17.
87. Antoinette Bosco, "Home Masses in Brentwood," *Long Island Catholic* 6, no. 17 (August 24, 1967): 4; Wcela, interview by Thompson, 31. At St. Joseph Parish in Hewlett, where sixty home Masses were celebrated as part of a month-long parish renewal program in October 1969, it was also found that "home Masses attract people who might not attend the traditional church mission"; "Home Masses Highlight Parish Renewal in Hewlett," *Long Island Catholic* 8, no. 23 (October 2, 1969): 3.
88. "Bishop Authorizes Home Masses in All Parishes," *Long Island Catholic* 6, no. 18 (August 31, 1967): 1. The bishops of Rochester, Detroit, Milwaukee, Cleveland, Atlanta, and Oklahoma City were the only other bishops who had given diocesan-wide approval to home Masses at that time. The only restrictions Kellenberg placed on the celebration of home Masses were that they had to be approved by the pastor; could not be said on a Sunday or Holy Day of Obligation; had to follow liturgical law and include a homily; had to involve more than two families, unless the Mass was being

said in the home of a sick person; and could not be said more than once in three months in the same home.
89. *St. Pius X Parish 25th Anniversary Journal.*
90. Msgr. John Alesandro, interview by Sr. Joan de Lourdes Leonard, CSJ, n.d., transcript, p. 6, Box 226, Joan de Lourdes Leonard Collection, ADRVC; "East Islip Teens Have Mass in the Home," *Long Island Catholic* 6, no. 25 (October 19, 1967): 4.
91. "Home Missions in Future," *Long Island Catholic* 6, nos. 35–36 (December 28, 1967–January 4, 1968): 4.
92. "Islanders Enthused by Home Masses," *Long Island Catholic* 7, no. 18 (August 29, 1968): 13.
93. Rev. James B. Richter, "Living Room Liturgies: Community at Home Masses," *Long Island Catholic* 7, no. 18 (August 29, 1968): 1.
94. "Mass at Home?" *Act* 21, no. 8 (October 1968): 6.
95. Dorothy Klemm, "Home Mass Program Less Popular Than Expected?" *Long Island Catholic* 9, no. 15 (August 13, 1970): 1.
96. Mark Kurlansky, *1968: The Year that Rocked the World* (New York: Random House, 2005).
97. Kurlansky, *1968*; *Our Parish* (September 1968): 11.
98. *Our Parish* (April 1971): 9. Children in Immaculate Conception Parish in Westhampton Beach were also offered the opportunity to receive their First Communion as part of a home Mass: "CCD Center Where Parish Does Its Thing," *Long Island Catholic* 7, no. 42 (February 13, 1969): 3.
99. Antoinette Bosco, "Armchair Replaces Pulpit in Parish Missions," *Long Island Catholic* 6, nos. 35–36 (December 28, 1967–January 4, 1968): 4; Bosco, "Suffolk Parish Takes Mission into Living Rooms," *Long Island Catholic* 6, no. 5 (June 1, 1967): 4.
100. "Christian Renewal Program in Manorhaven Parish," *Long Island Catholic* 6, no. 48 (March 28, 1968): 3.
101. Carol Speranza, "Westbury Parish Starts Plan to Revitalize Parish Life," *Long Island Catholic* 10, no. 5 (June 3, 1971): 1.
102. "St. Gerard Parish Mission Gives New Vision of Parish Community," *Long Island Catholic* 10, no. 33 (December 16, 1971): 4.
103. Greeley, *The Church and the Suburbs*, 69, 130.
104. Antoinette Bosco, "Uniting City and Suburb," *Long Island Catholic* 7, no. 43 (February 20, 1969): 4.
105. Jay P. Dolan, "American Catholics in a Changing Society: Parish and Ministry, 1930 to the Present," in *Transforming Parish Ministry: The Changing Roles of Catholic Clergy, Laity, and Women Religious*, ed. Jay Dolan (New York: Crossroad, 1989), 310.
106. Nickerson, "Beyond Smog, Sprawl, and Asphalt," 171.
107. "Welcome," *Long Island Catholic* 6, no. 9 (June 29, 1967): 4.
108. "Acquaintances Become a Community in Experiment in Brentwood," *Long Island Catholic* 6, nos. 13–14 (July 27–August 3, 1967): 12.
109. "Active Role of the Layman," *Long Island Catholic* 1, no. 1 (May 3, 1962): 24–26.
110. "Catholic, Protestant Laity Plan Living Room Dialogues," *Long Island Catholic* 4, no. 31 (November 25, 1965): 3; and see William B. Greenspun, CSP, and William A. Norgren, *Living Room Dialogues: A Guide for Lay Discussion* (Glen Rock, NJ: Paulist Press, 1965).
111. "How Ecumenical Work Can Be Carried Out in Parish," *Long Island Catholic* 5, no. 2 (May 5, 1966): 10.
112. Paul G. Crowley, "Jesuit Ecumenism in Three Acts: Lessons from the Life of Robert McAfee Brown," in Roberts and Schloesser, *Crossings and Dwellings*, 693–725.

113. "Nassau Home Aid Service to Begin," *The Tablet* 41, no. 39 (November 19, 1949): 7 ; "More Poor Aided in Nassau County," *The Tablet* 44, no. 2 (March 3, 1951): 2. The number of total cases in the county rose from 367 to 589 and 88 of those were emergency homemaker cases.
114. Antoinette Bosco, "When Trouble Shakes Suburbia's Home Scene," *Long Island Catholic* 2, no. 46 (March 12, 1964): 6; "Family Service Unit Has More Interviews," *Long Island Catholic* 2, no. 51 (April 16, 1964): 3; Antoinette Bosco, "Marriage Counseling," *Long Island Catholic* 2, no. 50 (April 9, 1964): 6.
115. William Goddard, "Home Get-Together Programs," *Long Island Catholic* 3, no. 9 (June 25, 1964): 5.
116. "Home Visit Day," *Long Island Catholic* 4, no. 3 (May 13, 1965): 15; Antoinette Bosco, "Home Visit Day Scheduled Nov. 14 in Nassau," *Long Island Catholic* 4, no. 27 (October 28, 1965): 4.
117. Bosco, "Uniting City and Suburb," 4; "New Group to Help Slum Children Get 2 Weeks in Suburbs," *New York Times*, June 6, 1969, 45; "Suburbia Program Resumes," *Long Island Catholic* 7, no. 30 (November 21, 1968): 20; *St. Francis of Assisi Parish Church Dedication Journal*, 19; Antoinette Bosco, "It's Spelled C-a-m-e-l-o-t to Kids from Brooklyn," *Long Island Catholic* 9, no. 13 (July 30, 1970): 1.
118. In 1989 Jay Dolan referred to the "filling station mentality" of suburban parishes in his essay, "American Catholics in a Changing Society: Parish and Ministry, 1930 to the Present," but the basic metaphor had been employed throughout that period to raise concerns about lay investment in parish community; Dolan, *Transforming Parish Ministry*, 289.
119. Antoinette Bosco, "The Challenges of Change in the Parish: Are Laity Prepared for New Role?" *Long Island Catholic* 7, no. 7 (June 13, 1968): 15.
120. Pat and Patty Crowley, "Introduction," to Bernard Lyons, *Programs for Parish Councils: An Action Manual* (Techny, IL: Divine Word Publications, 1969).
121. Robert D. Putnam, *Bowling Alone: The Collapse and Revival of American Community* (New York: Simon and Schuster, 2000).
122. Fr. John Cervini, interview by Edward Thompson, February 21, 2004, transcript, p. 19, Box 1672, Oral History Project Collection, ADRVC.
123. Bosco, "The Challenges of Change in the Parish," 15.
124. "St. Bernard's Unites Via 2 Approaches," *Long Island Catholic* 8, nos. 35–36 (December 25, 1969–January 1, 1970): 1.
125. Fr. William Donovan, interview by Sr. Joan de Lourdes Leonard, n.d., transcript, pp. 7–10, 16, Box 226, Oral Histories, Joan de Lourdes Leonard Collection, ADRVC.
126. "Legion of Mary in Diocese Goes Into Marketplace," *Long Island Catholic* 5, no. 47 (March 30, 1967): 13; "Legion's Book Borrow Brings Religion to the Shopping Mall," *Long Island Catholic* 17, no. 44 (March 8, 1979): 1; "Shopping Mall Ministers Find Problem: Laden Youth," *Long Island Catholic* 9, no. 9 (July 2, 1970): 4; "Smithhaven Mall Ministries," *Long Island Catholic* 9, no. 42 (February 11, 1971): 9; "Smithhaven Mall Ecumenical Ministries," *Long Island Catholic* 12, no. 47 (April 4, 1974): 16.
127. Leonard, *Richly Blessed*, 67; "Bishop McGann Using TV for Evangelization," *Long Island Catholic* 18, no. 43 (February 28, 1980): 1; "TeLIcommunity to Provide Local Broadcast Services," *Long Island Catholic* 19, no. 3 (May 15, 1980): 3; "Plans Made for Church Satellite TV," *Long Island Catholic* 20, no. 9 (June 25, 1981): 10; "Catholic TV Network Founded, Diocese to Participate," *Long Island Catholic* 20, no. 31 (November 26, 1981): 4.

128. Joseph J. Casino, "From Sanctuary to Involvement: A History of the Catholic Parish in the Northeast," in *American Catholic Parish: A History from 1850 to the Present*, ed. Jay P. Dolan (New York: Paulist Press, 1987), 91–92.
129. "Priest No Longer Has Absolute Authority in Parish," *Long Island Catholic* 23, no. 37 (January 10, 1985): 5; Jim Castelli and Joseph Gremillion, eds., *The Emerging Parish: The Notre Dame Study of Catholic Life Since Vatican II* (San Francisco: Harper and Row, 1987), 131, 201–2.
130. *Diocese of Rockville Centre Quinquennial Report, 1969–1973* (Rockville Centre, NY: Diocese of Rockville Centre, 1973), chap. 3, Box 278, Sr. Joan de Lourdes Leonard Collection, ADRVC; *Diocese of Rockville Centre Quinquennial Report, 1978–1982* (Rockville Centre, NY: Diocese of Rockville Centre, 1982), IV (5).
131. *Diocese of Rockville Centre Quinquennial Report, 1978–1982*, II (2) and XI (6); "Diocese Launches Come Home for Christmas Campaign," *Long Island Catholic* 21, no. 27 (October 28, 1962): 8.
132. McGreevy, *Parish Boundaries*, 264.
133. See Lydia Saad, "Catholics' Church Attendance Resumes Downward Slide," *Gallup News*, April 9, 2018, https://news.gallup.com/poll/232226/church-attendance-among-catholics-resumes-downward-slide.aspx; Frank Newport, "Americans, Including Catholics, Say Birth Control Is Morally Okay," *Gallup News*, May 22, 2012, https://news.gallup.com/poll/154799/americans-including-catholics-say-birth-control-morally.aspx; Newport, "Catholics Similar to Mainstream on Abortion, Stem Cells," *Gallup News*, March 30, 2009, https://news.gallup.com/poll/117154/catholics-similar-mainstream-abortion-stem-cells.aspx.

CHAPTER FOUR

1. "Community Built Parish," *Long Island Catholic* 7, no. 23 (October 3, 1968): 1; "Priests Have Opinions, but It's People Who Make New St. Gerard's Parish Go," *Long Island Catholic* 8, no. 9 (June 26, 1969): 1.
2. "Community Built Parish," 1.
3. A plethora of articles and books published at this time declared the emergence of a mature laity, many of them written by prominent laymen in the Catholic press who lived in the suburbs of New York, including James O'Gara, ed., *Layman in the Church* (New York: Herder and Herder, 1962); Donald Thorman, *The Emerging Layman: The Role of the Catholic Layman in America* (Garden City, NY: Doubleday, 1962); and Daniel Callahan, *The Mind of the Catholic Layman* (New York: Scribner's Sons, 1963).
4. Donald R. Campion and Dennis Clark, "So You're Moving to Suburbia," *America* 95, no. 3 (April 21, 1956): 82.
5. Antoinette Bosco, "CFM: The Name of the Game Is Involvement," *Long Island Catholic* 5, no. 37 (January 19, 1967): 4. Father John Berkery, the director of the lay apostolate for the Diocese of Rockville Centre stated that groups like Christian Family Movement (CFM), Young Christian Workers (YCW), and Young Christian Students (YCS), which predated the Council, "actually contributed to the statement of the Decree on the Laity."
6. "Number of Priests Growing but Not as Fast as Number of Catholics," *Catholic News* 67, no. 32 (March 28, 1953): 18.
7. Bishop John R. McGann, a priest of the Diocese of Rockville Centre who served as an auxiliary bishop to Walter Kellenberg and replaced him as Bishop of Rockville Centre in 1976, put the number of priests in the diocese in 1957 at 371; "Brief History of the Diocese of Rockville Centre," March 6, 1970, Box 106, Folder: Msgr. Charles Swiger,

Sr. Joan de Lourdes Leonard Collection (hereafter Leonard Collection), ADRVC. See appendices for a chart detailing the number of priests in the diocese.
8. For an extended explication of what made "A Plum Parish," see the first chapter of Rev. John Foster, *A Requiem for a Parish* (Westminster, MD: Newman Press, 1962), 3–10.
9. Msgr. Edmond Trench, interview by Sr. Joan de Lourdes Leonard, CSJ, September 22, 1981, transcript, p. 5, Box 106, File Edmond Trench, Leonard Collection, ADRVC.
10. Fr. John Carmody, interview by Sr. Joan de Lourdes Leonard, CSJ, July 25, 1988, transcript, p. 4, Box 226, Leonard Collection, ADRVC.
11. "Kellenberg Opens Prep Seminary," *The Tablet* 51, no. 32 (September 20, 1958): 8; Leonard, *Richly Blessed*, 47–50; "St. Pius X Seminary," *Long Island Catholic* 1, no. 1 (May 3, 1962): 21.
12. "Kellenberg Opens Prep Seminary," 8.
13. "St. Pius X Seminary," 21; "Rockville Centre Prep Seminary Blessed Sunday," *The Tablet* 54, no. 31 (September 9, 1961): 1, 3.
14. "Priest Shortage in Diocese Emphasized by New Figures," *Long Island Catholic* 1, no. 2 (May 10, 1962): 1.
15. "LI Diocese First See to Study Priest Distribution," *Long Island Catholic* 6, no. 30 (November 23, 1967): 10.
16. Msgr. Edmond Trench, interview by Sr. Joan de Lourdes Leonard, CSJ, August 7, 1981, transcript, p. 7, Box 226, Leonard Collection, ADRVC.
17. Bishop Emil Wcela, interview by Edward Thompson, February 10, 2004, transcript, p. 17, Box 1603, Oral History Project Collection, ADRVC.
18. Msgr. Robert Emmet Fagan, interview by Sr. Joan de Lourdes Leonard, CSJ, September 4, 1981 (hereafter Fagan interview), transcript, p. 3, Box 226, Leonard Collection, ADRVC.
19. Msgr. Josiah G. Chatham, "Your Assignment: Build a Suburban Parish," *Homiletic and Pastoral Review* 56, no. 3 (December 1955): 217–23.
20. *St. Martha Parish 25th Anniversary Journal, 1949–1975*, p. 4, Box 618, Seminary Library Collection, ADRVC.
21. "Provide Parish Leadership," *Long Island Catholic* 16, no. 23 (October 6, 1977): 14.
22. Greeley, *The Church and the Suburbs*, 68–69.
23. "Talk about Apathy Causing More Apathy—or So It Seems," *Long Island Catholic* 9, no. 6 (June 11, 1970): 1.
24. Benjamin Looker, *A Nation of Neighborhoods: Imagining Cities, Communities, and Democracy in Postwar America* (Chicago: University of Chicago Press, 2015), 265; David J. Endres, *Many Tongues, One Faith: A History of Franciscan Parish Life in the United States* (Oceanside, CA: Academy of American Franciscan History, 2018), 120.
25. "Laity's Impact on Priests," *Long Island Catholic* 10, no. 1 (May 6, 1971): 11.
26. Fr. Andrew L. Millar, "Ask Father," *Our Parish* 1, no. 8 (January 1974): 2, Archives of Our Lady of Grace Parish, West Babylon, NY.
27. *The Official Catholic Directory of 1969* (New York: P. J. Kenedy and Sons, Publishers, 1969), 705; *The Official Catholic Directory of 1977* (New York: P. J. Kenedy and Sons, Publishers, 1977), 749.
28. John L. Allen Jr., "If Catholicism Were a Corporation, We Wouldn't Distribute Priests Like This," *Crux Now* (July 2, 2024), https://angelusnews.com/voices/allen-redistribute-priests/.
29. "Shortage of Priests Limits Diocese," *Long Island Catholic* 16, no. 25 (October 20, 1977): 1.

30. "Foreign Priests," anonymous letter, *Long Island Catholic* 23, no. 18 (August 24, 1984): 6.
31. Fr. Peter J. Pflomm, "Foreign Priests," letter, *Long Island Catholic* 23, no. 19 (August 30, 1984): 6.
32. Fr. Francis X. McQuade, of St. Hugh Parish in Huntington Station, "Positive Contributions of Foreign Priests," letter, *Long Island Catholic* 23, no. 20 (September 6, 1984): 6; and see Florence Lonette Graffeo of Garden City, "Unforgettable Lessons," letter, *Long Island Catholic* 23, no. 20 (September 6, 1984): 6; Catherine Costello of Lake Grove, "Foreign Priests," letter, *Long Island Catholic* 23, no. 21 (September 13, 1984): 6.
33. *St. Anne Parish's 100th Anniversary Journal*, Archives of St. Anne Parish, Brentwood, NY.
34. Wcela, interview by Thompson, pp. 16–17; Wcela, interview by Sr. Joan de Lourdes Leonard, CSJ, September 23, 1981, transcript, pp. 2–3, Box 106, Leonard Collection, File Emil Wcela, ADRVC.
35. Wcela, interview by Leonard, 2–3.
36. *Blessed Sacrament Parish 25th Anniversary Journal, 1950–1975*, Box 616, Seminary Library Collection, ADRVC.
37. *Holy Family Parish 25th Anniversary Journal, 1951–1976*, Box 163B, Chancellor's Collection, Parish Files, ADRVC.
38. Campion and Clark, "So You're Moving to Suburbia," 82.
39. William F. Whelan, "A Brief Look at the History and Development of the Our Lady of Grace Roman Catholic Church, West Babylon, New York," unpublished, ca. 1985, pp. 13, 15, Archives of Our Lady of Grace Parish, West Babylon, NY.
40. "Pioneering Parish on Firm Foundation," *Long Island Catholic* 4, no. 31 (November 25, 1965): 11; *St. Paul the Apostle Church Dedication Journal, 1968*, Box 158, Chancellor's Collection, ADRVC; "It Doesn't Take Too Long Before a Parish Grows and Prospers," *Long Island Catholic* 4, no. 9 (June 24, 1965): 2.
41. Mrs. Ann Matuza Sessa, interview by the author, July 22, 2017 (hereafter Sessa interview), Our Lady of Grace Parish, West Babylon NY.
42. Fr. J. E. Leonard, "A Day to Remember," *Our Parish* 1, no. 6 (September 1966): 2, Archives of Our Lady of Grace Parish, West Babylon, NY.
43. For a history of catechesis in the United States, see Charles J. Carmody, "The Roman Catholic Catechesis in the United States, 1784–1930: A Study of Its Theory, Development, and Materials" (PhD diss., Loyola University of Chicago, 1975).
44. Mrs. Patricia Megale, interview by Sr. Joan de Lourdes Leonard, CSJ, September 20, 1988, transcript, Box 106, Leonard Collection, ADRVC. Among parishioners I interviewed, Mrs. Ann Matuza Sessa, a founding member of Our Lady of Grace Parish in West Babylon, and Dr. Maryann Rietschlin of St. Pius X Parish in Plainview confirmed that they received very little training before they began teaching CCD; Sessa interview, and Rietschlin, interview with the author, August 3, 2017, St. Pius X Parish, Plainview, NY.
45. Fagan interview, 2.
46. Leonard, *Richly Blessed*, 96; "Training Course Planned by CCD," *Long Island Catholic* 1, no. 38 (January 17, 1963): 1. See also "Confraternity Plans Course of Teachers," *Long Island Catholic* 2, no. 37 (January 9, 1964): 2; "CCD in Diocese Expands Teacher Training," *Long Island Catholic* 5, no. 21 (September 22, 1966): 5.
47. Msgr. Joseph F. Lawlor, "The CCD Is an Apostolate," *Long Island Catholic* 2, no. 43 (February 20, 1964): 11.

48. Antoinette Bosco, "I Never Seem to Stop Having to Learn," *Long Island Catholic* 5, no. 38 (January 26, 1967): 4.
49. "500 LI Catechists to Get Citations; Represents Increase of 275 in Year," *Long Island Catholic* 7, no. 4 (May 23, 1968): 5.
50. Msgr. Frederick Schaefer, interview by Sr. Joan de Lourdes Leonard, CSJ, June 14, 1982 (hereafter Schaefer interview),, transcript, p. 7, Box 106, Leonard Collection, ADRVC.
51. "First in Diocese: Layman to Run Parish CCD," *Long Island Catholic* 6, no. 18 (August 31, 1967): 1. When Grady left within a year for a job with the Twenty-Third Publications firm in Fort Wayne, Indiana, he was replaced by Peter Molloy, a twenty-five-year-old layman with a master's degree in theology; "St. Aidan's Parish New CCD Director," *Long Island Catholic* 7, no. 12 (July 18, 1968): 1.
52. "Proper Training of CCD Teachers a Problem," *Long Island Catholic* 8, no. 48 (April 2, 1970): 15.
53. Sister Dorothy Fowler, "An Open Letter to Members of Our Lady of Grace Parish," *Our Parish* (March 1971): 4, Archives of Our Lady of Grace Parish, West Babylon, NY.
54. For more on the history of the NCWC see Douglas Slawson, *The Foundation and First Decade of the National Catholic Welfare Council* (Washington, DC: Catholic University of America Press, 1992); Joseph McShane, *Sufficiently Radical: Catholicism, Progressivism, and the Bishops' Program of 1919* (Washington, DC: Catholic University of America Press, 1986); Timothy A. Byrnes, *Catholic Bishops in American Politics* (Princeton, NJ: Princeton University Press, 1991); Camilla J. Kari, *Public Witness: The Pastoral Letters of the American Catholic Bishops* (Collegeville, MN: Liturgical Press, 2004); Michael Werner, *Changing Witness: Catholic Bishops and Public Policy, 1917–1994* (Grand Rapids, MI: Eerdmans, 1995). For more on the legendary directors of SAD, Msgr. John A. Ryan and Msgr. George G. Higgins, see Francis L. Broderick, *The Right Reverend New Dealer* (New York: Sheed and Ward, 1963); John J. O'Brien, *George G. Higgins and the Quest for Worker Justice: The Evolution of Catholic Social Thought in America* (Lanham: Rowman and Littlefield, 2005).
55. "25 Million in Adult Classes," *Long Island Catholic* 3, no. 44 (February 25, 1965): 12.
56. "Bishop Kellenberg Urges More Adult CCD Programs," *Long Island Catholic* 5, no. 20 (September 15, 1966): 1.
57. Schaefer interview, 7.
58. Antoinette Bosco, "Theology for the Layman," *Long Island Catholic* 2, no. 37 (January 9, 1964): 6.
59. "Adults to Attend Education Classes," *Long Island Catholic* 2, no. 39 (January 23, 1964): 1; "Adult Education Courses Begin at Malloy College," *Long Island Catholic* 3, no. 41 (February 4, 1965): 1.
60. "Parishes Establishes First Adult Education Programs," *Long Island Catholic* 3, no. 24 (October 8, 1964): 1.
61. "Adult Courses Planned," *Long Island Catholic* 3, no. 24 (October 8, 1964): 2; "2 Parishes Sponsor Courses for Adults," *Long Island Catholic* 3, no. 44 (February 25, 1965): 12.
62. Antoinette Bosco, "Adults Need to Be Challenged by CCD," *Long Island Catholic* 5, no. 17 (August 18, 1966): 7; "People Want to Learn More of Their Religion," *Long Island Catholic* 3, no. 44 (February 25, 1965): 12; "Adult Education Courses Emphasized by Parishes," *Long Island Catholic* 6, no. 22 (September 28, 1967): 39; "Adult Education in Spotlight for CCD Year," *Long Island Catholic* 7, no. 22 (September 26, 1968): 20.

63. "God in the Home," *Long Island Catholic* 1, no. 9 (June 28, 1962): 9.
64. Msgr. Henry Reel, interview by Edward McCormack, n.d., transcript, p. 8, Box 106, Leonard Collection, ADRVC.
65. *Our Lady of Loretto Centennial Parish Journal, 1870–1970*, pp. 20–21, Box 618, Seminary Library Collection, ADRVC.
66. "25 Million in Adult Classes," 12; Bosco, "Adults Need to Be Challenged by CCD," 7. Parishes with robust newspapers or magazines included *St. Aidan's Quarterly*, St. Aidan Parish in Williston Park; *Vox Pacis*, Our Lady of Peace Parish in Lynbrook; *The Redemptor*, Our Holy Redeemer Parish in Freeport; *The Crusade*, St. Mary Parish in East Islip; *The Helmsman*, St. Raymond Parish in Lynbrook; *The Echo*, St. Hugh Parish in Huntington Station; *The Sentinel*, St. Joseph Parish in Ronkonkoma; *The Paracletian*, Holy Spirit Parish in New Hyde Park; *All in the Parish*, St. Anthony of Padua Parish in East Northport; *Our Parish*, Our Lady of Victory Parish in Floral Park; *Parish Billboard*, St. Brigid Parish in Westbury; *The Works of St. Joseph the Worker*, St. Joseph the Worker Parish in East Patchogue; *St. Patrick's Parish News*, St. Patrick Parish in Huntington; and *Notre Dame News and Views*, Notre Dame Parish in New Hyde Park.
67. Fr. Paul McKeever, interview by Sr. Joan de Lourdes Leonard, CSJ, July 8, 1982, transcript, pp. 10, 18, Box 226, Leonard Collection, ADRVC.
68. Antoinette Bosco, "Discussion Groups for Adults," *Long Island Catholic* 5, no. 18 (September 1, 1966): 4.
69. Antoinette Bosco, "CCD: An Effort to Aid the Adult Christian Insights," *Long Island Catholic* 7, no. 22 (September 26, 1968): 20.
70. Butler, *God in Gotham*, 224.
71. *Church Dedication Journal, 1987*, Box 6, Item 45, Archives of St. Frances de Chantal Parish, Wantagh, NY.
72. *St. Anne's 75th Anniversary Journal*, Box 187, Folder 3, Chancellor's Collection, Parish Files, ADRVC.
73. Timothy Kelly, *The Transformation of American Catholicism: The Pittsburgh Laity and the Second Vatican Council, 1950–1972* (Notre Dame, IN: University of Notre Dame Press, 2009), 55–59. Studies of gender and family in the postwar period include Elaine Tyler May, *Homeward Bound: American Families in the Cold War Era* (New York: Basic Books, 1988); Joanne Meyerwitz, *Not June Cleaver: Women and Gender in Postwar America, 1945–1960* (Philadelphia: Temple University Press, 1994); Robert O. Self, *All in the Family: The Realignment of American Democracy Since the 1960s* (New York: Hill and Wang, 2012).
74. Antoinette Bosco, "The Challenges of Change in the Parish: Are Laity Prepared for New Role?" *Long Island Catholic* 7, no. 7 (June 13, 1968): 15.
75. Peter L. Berger, "The Second Children's Crusade," *Christian Century* 76, no. 48 (December 2, 1959): 1399, cited in Jeffrey M. Burns, *American Catholics and the Family Crisis, 1930–1962: An Ideological and Organizational Response* (New York: Garland, 1988), 1.
76. Msgr. George A. Kelly, "The Church Looks to Married Couples, Part Two," *The Tablet* 54, no. 52 (February 3, 1962): 12. Important Catholic studies of the family from this time include Edgar Schmiedler, *Marriage and the Family: A Text for a Course on Marriage and the Family for Use in Catholic Schools* (New York: McGraw-Hill, 1946); John J. Kane, *Marriage and the Family: A Catholic Approach* (New York: Dryden Press, 1952); Fr. John L. Thomas, SJ, *The American Catholic Family* (Englewood Cliffs, NJ: Prentice-Hall, 1956); and Walter Imbiorski, *The New Cana Manual* (Chicago: Delaney Publications, 1957).

77. Kathryn Johnson, "A Question of Authority: Friction in the Catholic Family Life Movement, 1948–1962," *Catholic Historical Review* 86, no. 2 (April 2000): 218.
78. Johnson, "A Question of Authority," 218.
79. "CFM Purposes Outlined by Priests," *Catholic News* 73, no. 51 (December 20, 1958): 19.
80. "CFM Is Organized in 30 Parishes," *Catholic News* 72, no. 19 (May 11, 1957): 11.
81. "CFM of LI Has First Convention," *The Tablet* 53, no. 35 (October 8, 1960): 3.
82. "CFM Is Organized in 30 Parishes," 11. By the following year, the CFM was in fifty of the archdiocese's parishes; George Gent, "Programs on Family Life Thriving Here," *Catholic News* 73, no. 22 (May 31, 1958): 2.
83. "A Family Group in Action," *Long Island Catholic* 1, no. 22 (September 27, 1962): 13. The Jocist Method was developed by Joseph Cardijn, who founded the Young Christian Workers movement in Belgium in 1925. The term "Jocist" derives from the French acronym, JOC, or *Jeunesse ouvrière chrétienne*. For more, see Mary Irene Zotti, *A Time of Awakening: The Young Christian Worker Story in the United States, 1938–1970* (Chicago: Loyola University Press, 1991); Susan Whitney, *Mobilizing Youth: Communists and Catholics in Interwar France* (Durham, NC: Duke University Press, 2009).
84. "Defense of CFM," letter, *The Tablet* 54, no. 4 (March 4, 1961): 6; "Inquiry Program," letter, *Long Island Catholic* 1, no. 22 (September 27, 1962): 13.
85. Jeremy Bonner, "Who Will Guard the Guardians?: Church Government and the Ecclesiology of the People of God, 1965–1969," in *Empowering the People of God: Catholic Action Before and After Vatican II*, ed. Jeremy Bonner, Christopher D. Denny, and Mary Beth Fraser Connolly (New York: Fordham University Press, 2014), 230.
86. Johnson, "A Question of Authority," 224.
87. Burns, *American Catholics and the Family Crisis*, 329, citing Dennis Geaney, "CFM in Perspective," *Act* 9, no. 11 (1956): 8.
88. "Christian Family Move Wins President's Praise," *Long Island Catholic* 2, no. 18 (August 29, 1963): 2; "Christian Family Movement," *Long Island Catholic* 1, no. 22 (September 27, 1962): 13.
89. For more on the foundations of the Cana Conference, see Jeffrey M. Burns, *Disturbing the Peace: A History of the Christian Family Movement, 1949–1974* (Notre Dame, IN: University of Notre Dame, 1999), 20–22, 35.
90. Burns, *American Catholics and the Family Crisis*, 255.
91. "Cana Conference for Engaged Couples Planned," *The Tablet* 38, no. 43 (December 21, 1946): 1. The Diocese of Brooklyn was the first diocese in the country to establish the Cana Conference as a Vatican-approved sodality. See "Rapid Growth of Cana Movement Noted," *The Tablet* 44, no. 49 (January 26, 1952): 1. See also "Cana Is . . ." *The Tablet* 45, no. 43 (December 13, 1952); 45, no. 44 (December 20, 1952): 11; and 45, no. 45 (December 27, 1952): 9.
92. "A Movement of and for Lay People," *Long Island Catholic* 1, no. 11 (July 12, 1962): 4.
93. "Cana Grows in Diocese: Plan New Conferences," *Long Island Catholic* 2, no. 40 (January 30, 1964): 1. See also "Active Role of the Layman," *Long Island Catholic* 1, no. 1 (May 3, 1962): 24–26; "18,000 Couples Attend Diocese Family Programs," *Long Island Catholic* 1, no. 9 (June 28, 1962): 4; "Diocese Cana Conferences to Mark 5th Anniversary," *Long Island Catholic* 1, no. 43 (February 21, 1963): 9.
94. "Cana: A Guide to the Future," *Long Island Catholic* 2, no. 20 (September 12, 1963): 8; "Cana Grows in Diocese," 1; "New Look for Cana Movement," *Long Island Catholic* 2, no. 41 (February 6, 1964): 7.
95. "Diocesan Cana Movement," *Long Island Catholic* 3, no. 40 (January 28, 1965): 1.

96. Antoinette Bosco, "Cana Program Labeled Essential," *Long Island Catholic* 3, no. 22 (September 24, 1964): 2; Burns, *American Catholics and the Family Crisis*, 260.
97. Antoinette Bosco, "Couple to Couple Approach to Marriage," *Long Island Catholic* 4, no. 52 (April 21, 1966): 4.
98. Nancy Dwyer, "Family Love Can Spark Revolution," *Long Island Catholic* 15, no. 45 (March 10, 1977): 1; "Nuptial Notebooks," *Time* 105, no. 14 (April 7, 1975): 68.
99. Leonard, *Richly Blessed*, 307–10.
100. In the early 1970s the Marriage Encounter movement in the United States split into two groups, the smaller National Marriage Encounter, and Gallagher's much larger Worldwide Marriage Encounter. For more see Burns, *Disturbing the Peace*, 208; "A Brief History of Worldwide Marriage Encounter," http://www.wwme.org/About-worldwide-marriage-encounter-mission-history.
101. Glenn Collins, "The Family; 1,700 Couples to Meet to Improve Marriages," *New York Times*, July 21, 1986, A14; Antoinette Bosco, "Marriage Encounter: Pros and Cons," *Long Island Catholic* 10, no. 40 (February 3, 1972): 1; Leonard, *Richly Blessed*, 309; "Marriage Encounter Convention," *Long Island Catholic* 17, no. 26 (October 26, 1978): 5; Ellen Mitchell, "Marriage Groups Encountering Criticism," *New York Times* (March 18, 1979): LI-1; *Blessed Sacrament Parish 25th Anniversary Journal*.
102. Antoinette Bosco, "LI Couples Say Yes to Marriage Encounter," *Long Island Catholic* 9, no. 52 (April 22, 1971): 18.
103. Liz O'Connor, "Marriage Encounter for Some Is a Whole Way of Life," *Long Island Catholic* 13, no. 26 (October 31, 1974): 10.
104. Bosco, "LI Couples Say Yes to Marriage Encounter," 18.
105. "CFM Aide Emphasizes Need for Concern for Family of Man," *Long Island Catholic* 8, no. 42 (February 12, 1970): 3. The same criticisms were made of the Cana Conference movement; see Burns, *American Catholics and the Family Crisis*, 321.
106. "Some Family Movement Reforms Urged," *Long Island Catholic* 8, no. 20 (September 11, 1969): 2.
107. "Family Movement on the March," *Long Island Catholic* 2, no. 22 (September 26, 1963): 2; "Area CFM to Discuss Politics and Race," *Long Island Catholic* 3, no. 17 (August 20, 1964): 2.
108. Msgr. Joseph Lawlor, interview by Sr. Joan de Lourdes Leonard, CSJ, December 11, 1981, transcript, p. 13, Box 226, Leonard Collection, ADRVC.
109. Thomas O'Gorman, "An Interview with Patty Crowley, Co-Founder of the CFM," *US Catholic Historian* 9, no. 4 (Fall 1990): 457–47; and see Johnson, "A Question of Authority," 220.
110. Antoinette Bosco, "Sing No Dirge for CFM, It's Still Alive on LI," *Long Island Catholic* 11, no. 15 (August 10, 1972): 1; Johnson, "A Question of Authority," 227.
111. Burns, *American Catholics and the Family Crisis*, 255.
112. "Couples Resent Being Forced to Attend Pre Cana," *Long Island Catholic* 11, no. 21 (September 21, 1972): 9.
113. Carol Speranza, "Priests, Young People Ruffle Pre Cana," *Long Island Catholic* 11, no. 21 (September 21, 1972): 9.
114. "CFM Aide Emphasizes Need for Concern for Family of Man," 3; Leslie Woodcock Tentler, *Catholics and Contraception: An American History* (Ithaca, NY: Cornell University Press, 2004), see esp. 176, 193–94, 273–76; Burns, *Disturbing the Peace*, 174–88.
115. Bosco, "Marriage Encounter: Pros and Cons," 1.
116. O'Connor, "Marriage Encounter for Some Is a Whole Way of Life," 10.

117. "Marriage Encounter," letter, *Long Island Catholic* 20, no. 38 (January 21, 1982): 6.
118. Msgr. Lawrence Ballweg, interview by Sr. Joan de Lourdes Leonard, CSJ, n.d. (ca. August 1981), transcript, p. 3, Box 226, Leonard Collection, ADRVC.
119. Joseph Cardijn who developed the Jocist method that inspired CFM, for example, was influential in the writing of Pope John XXIII's encyclical *Mater et Magistra* (1961) and, after being named a cardinal by Pope Paul VI in 1965, participated in the writing of *Apostolicam Actuositatem* (1965), the Second Vatican Council's Decree on the Apostolate of the Laity. For more, see Zotti, *A Time of Awakening*, 227, 262, 264.
120. "The Year of the Laity," *Long Island Catholic* 6, nos. 35-36 (December 28, 1967-January 4, 1968): 13.
121. "Laity Coming of Age," editorial, *Long Island Catholic* 6, no. 46 (March 14, 1968): 10.
122. "LI Laity Learn to Join in Preparing Real Celebration," *Long Island Catholic* 8, no. 47 (March 19, 1970): 8.
123. Sessa interview.
124. "Bishops May Allow Select Laymen to Distribute Communion," *Long Island Catholic* 10, no. 1 (May 6, 1971): 1.
125. "Laity May Assist at Distribution of Communion," *Long Island Catholic* 11, no. 3 (May 18, 1972): 2.
126. "2 Lay Communion Ministers Installed," *Long Island Catholic* 11, no. 12 (July 20, 1972): 1; "Extraordinary Ministers of Holy Communion to Be Commissioned," *Long Island Catholic* 11, no. 31 (November 30, 1972): 1.
127. "Extraordinary Ministers of Communion Well Received," *Long Island Catholic* 11, no. 34 (December 21, 1972): 2.
128. Antoinette Bosco, "What's Really Happening to Women?," *Marriage* (March 1971): 60. Bosco's other articles on the theme include "Image of Happy Housewife a Fraud?" *Long Island Catholic* 2, no. 32 (December 5, 1963): 9; Bosco, "Housewives' Jobs—Help or Hindrance?" *Long Island Catholic* 8, no. 25 (October 16, 1969): 4; Bosco, "Catholic Women on LI No Longer Fit Into Mold," *Long Island Catholic* 9, no. 10 (July 9, 1970): 4; Bosco, "Women Learn to Go It Alone Spiritually in Post-Conciliar Era," *Long Island Catholic* 9, no. 11 (July 16, 1970): 4. For analysis and context see Mary J. Henold, *The Laywoman Project: Remaking Catholic Womanhood in the Vatican II Era* (Chapel Hill: University of North Carolina Press, 2020).
129. Fr. Patrick Shanahan, "Parish School Boards as Policy Advisors," *Long Island Catholic* 10, no. 27 (November 4, 1971): 10.
130. Fr. Patrick F. Shanahan, "A Look Ahead: Parish Board of Education," *Long Island Catholic* 4, no. 17 (August 19, 1965): 15. Holy Family Parish in Hicksville, Sacred Heart Parish in Cutchogue, and St. Aidan's in Williston Park all founded parish school boards between 1965 and 1967; "3 Parishes of Diocese Have Lay School Boards," *Long Island Catholic* 5, no. 51 (April 27, 1967): 13.
131. "School Boards Sought for LI Parishes," *Long Island Catholic* 6, no. 46 (March 14, 1968): 1.
132. Richard M. Guilderson Jr., "Plans Released for Parish Council, School Boards," *Long Island Catholic* 6, no. 52 (April 25, 1968): 1.
133. "Parish Councils: A Report on Principles, Purposes, Structures and Goals," National Council of Catholic Men, Washington, DC, 1968, p. 1, Box 149, Chancellor's Collection, Priests' Advisory Council Minutes, ADRVC.
134. *St. Pius X Parish Twentieth Anniversary Journal, 1955-1975*, Archives of St. Pius X Parish, Plainview, NY.

135. Antoinette Bosco, "East Islip Parish's First Steps on a Thousand Mile Journey," *Long Island Catholic* 6, no. 19 (September 7, 1967): 4.
136. Antoinette Bosco, "Review of Findings on Councils," *Long Island Catholic* 8, no. 33 (December 11, 1969): 1.
137. "Great Care Taken at St. Matthew's to Begin with a Firm Foundation," *Long Island Catholic* 8, no. 37 (January 8, 1970): 1.
138. Bosco, "The Challenges of Change in the Parish," 15.
139. Bosco, "Review of Findings on Councils," 1.
140. Leonard, *Richly Blessed*, 311; Richard H. Dement of NCCM, letter to Bishop Walter Kellenberg, August 3, 1971, Box 32, Folder 4: Rockville Centre, NY, 1967–1971, Collection 10: National Council of Catholic Men, ACUA.
141. See Bonner, "Who Will Guard the Guardians?," 233. That parishes did not name the racial or ethnic makeup of their councils as a point of concern reflects the fact that Long Island's parishes were overwhelmingly white and that ethnic differences had indeed diminished in suburbia.
142. "Parish Council in Centereach First Fully Elected in Diocese," *Long Island Catholic* 7, no. 2 (May 9, 1968): 1.
143. Antoinette Bosco, "Council in Massapequa Emphasizes Need to Share," *Long Island Catholic* 8, no. 30 (November 20, 1969): 3.
144. Margaret O'Gara, "Few Young People on Parish Councils," *Long Island Catholic* 7, no. 11 (July 11, 1968): 1; Bosco, "Review of Findings on Councils," 1; Antoinette Bosco, "Parish and Community Dual Focus at St. Anne's Fledgling Parish Council," *Long Island Catholic* 8, no. 27 (October 30, 1969): 1.
145. Antoinette Bosco, "A Parish People 'Turn To'," *Long Island Catholic* 9, no. 27 (November 5, 1970): 1; "Parish Councils," letters, *Long Island Catholic* 15, no. 32 (December 2, 1976): 6.
146. Bosco, "Parish and Community Dual Focus at St. Anne's," 1; "St. Bernard's Unites Via 2 Approaches," *Long Island Catholic* 8, nos. 35–36 (December 25, 1969–January 1, 1970): 1; "St. Andrew's Parish Council Local Interests," *Long Island Catholic* 8, no. 40 (January 29, 1970): 1; Bosco, "Council in Massapequa Emphasizes Need to Share," 3.
147. Bosco, "Council in Massapequa Emphasizes Need to Share," 3; Bosco, "Parish and Community Dual Focus at St. Anne's," 1; Bosco, "Review of Findings on Councils," 1; Antoinette Bosco, "St. Jude 'Making Progress' Despite 'Enormity of the Task,'" *Long Island Catholic* 8, no. 29 (November 13, 1969): 1; "St. Elizabeth Responses Sought," *Long Island Catholic* 8, no. 34 (December 18, 1969): 9; "Youngest Parish Council Head Attacks Apathy with Gusto," *Long Island Catholic* 11, no. 2 (May 11, 1972): 1; Dorothy Crowe, "Parish Council," *St. Pius Digest* 1, no. 1 (March 4, 1973): 4; Stan Plaski, "A Closed Society," *St. Pius Digest* 1, no. 7 (November 1973): 7, Archives of St. Pius X Parish, Plainview, NY.
148. Bosco, "Parish and Community Dual Focus at St. Anne's," 1.
149. Antoinette Bosco, "The Laity's Role After Vatican II: LI Appraisal," *Long Island Catholic* 9, no. 31 (December 3, 1970): 1.
150. Ballweg interview, 6, 8, 9.
151. Bosco, "Council in Massapequa Emphasizes Need to Share," 3.
152. "Laymen Decide at St. Thomas More," *Long Island Catholic* 8, no. 41 (February 5, 1970): 1.
153. In 1958 Gallup polling found that 74 percent of US Catholics attended Sunday Mass in a typical week. By 1969, that number had fallen to 63 percent, a decline twice that

of Protestants; "7% Drop in Church-Going Reported in Gallup Poll," *Long Island Catholic* 8, no. 37 (January 8, 1970): 2.
154. See "Catholic Action, Time to Awake," *The Tablet*, 37, no. 26 (August 25, 1945): 10; "Developing Lay Leaders," *Catholic News* 66, no. 5 (September 22, 1951): 12.
155. "Apathy Seen as Primary Lay Problem," *Long Island Catholic* 5, no. 39 (February 9, 1967): 1.
156. "Talk about Apathy Causing More Apathy—or So It Seems," 1.
157. "LIC Survey on Vatican II Changes," *Long Island Catholic* 9, no. 28 (November 12, 1970): 1. In 1976 *Time* explored apathy and polarization in the American Church and highlighted conditions in St. Ignatius Loyola Parish in Hicksville: "A Church Divided," and "A Parish that Copes and Hopes," *Time* 107, no. 22 (May 24, 1976): 48–50, 55–56, 59.
158. Leonard, *Richly Blessed*, 303. The number of constituent groups eventually rose to eleven and included Christian Family Movement, Diocesan Council of Catholic Nurses, Diocesan Union of Holy Names Societies, Intra-Church Relations Committee, Kappa Gamma Pi, Long Island Association of Laymen, Long Island Catholic Alumni Club, Christian Life Communities, Teams of Our Lady, Young Christian Workers, and Young Christian Students.
159. "LI Lay Federation Established," *Long Island Catholic* 7, no. 45 (March 6, 1969): 2.
160. Dr. Raymond Zambito of the Federation of Lay Organizations in the Diocese of Rockville Centre, letter to Joseph O'Connell of the National Council of Catholic Men, August 15, 1969, Collection 10—NCCM, Box 32, Folder 4: Rockville Centre NY 1967–1971, ACUA.
161. Leonard, *Richly Blessed*, 306; "Island Laymen Adopt Constitution," *Long Island Catholic* 6, no. 38 (January 18, 1968): 2.
162. Antoinette Bosco, "LI Association of Laymen Succumbs," *Long Island Catholic* 9, no. 7 (June 18, 1970): 1.
163. James Harper, interview by Sr. Joan de Lourdes Leonard, CSJ, February 5, 1989 (hereafter Harper interview), transcript, pp. 1, 2, 6–7, Box 226, Leonard Collection, ADRVC.
164. "Island Laymen Adopt Constitution," 2.
165. "LI Association of Laymen," letters, *Long Island Catholic* 6, no. 39 (January 25, 1968): 10.
166. Bosco, "LI Association of Laymen Succumbs," 1.
167. Harper interview, 1, 2, 6–7.
168. Mrs. Therese Siller, interview by Sr. Joan de Lourdes Leonard, CSJ, n.d. (hereafter Siller interview), transcript, pp. 2–3, Box 106, Leonard Collection, ADRVC.
169. Bosco, "LI Association of Laymen Succumbs," 1.
170. "Theologians, Sociologists Explain the Present Crisis," *Long Island Catholic* 8, no. 10 (July 3, 1969): 4.
171. Richard Mauter, "Catholic Group on LI Suggests Liberal, Conservative Dialogue," *Long Island Catholic* 7, no. 2 (May 9, 1968): 1; and see "Forum Set March 19 to Discuss Liberal Conservative Polarization," *Long Island Catholic* 7, no. 45 (March 6, 1969): 3.
172. Diller interview, p. 2.
173. Mauter, "Catholic Group on LI Suggests Liberal, Conservative Dialogue," 1; Siller interview, p. 5; Fr. Paul Driscoll, interview by Sr. Joan de Lourdes Leonard, CSJ, n.d. (hereafter Driscoll interview), transcript, p. 11, Box 226, Leonard Collection, ADRVC. See also "Ecumenism Within the Walls," editorial, *America* 118, no. 21 (May 25, 1968): 693.

174. Driscoll interview, 11; Siller interview, 8.
175. "Dialogue More than Mere Word," *Long Island Catholic* 8, no. 46 (March 12, 1970): 1; Driscoll interview, 15.
176. The New York State Legislature expanded the number of exceptions to the legal prohibition of abortion in 1965 and debated legalization in the late 1960s. In 1970 New York became one of the first two states in the nation to decriminalize abortion, prior to the US Supreme Court's 1973 *Roe v. Wade* decision. See "NY Abortion Protests Rise," *Long Island Catholic* 5, no. 36 (January 12, 1967): 1; Antoinette Bosco, "The Abortion Push in New York," *Long Island Catholic* 5, no. 35 (January 12, 1967): 13; "Opposition Growing to Abortion Bills," *Long Island Catholic* 5, no. 38 (January 26, 1967): 1; "Abortion Debate Moves to State Legislature," *Long Island Catholic* 5, no. 49 (April 4, 1968); "Abortion Bill," editorial, *Long Island Catholic* 8, no. 50 (April 16, 1970).
177. Siller interview, 4, 7. For more on the role of Long Island Catholic women in the development of the national pro-life movement, see Taranto, *Kitchen Table Politics*.
178. Driscoll interview, p. 15.
179. "Update on Parish Councils," *Long Island Catholic* 23, no. 26 (October 18, 1984): 1.
180. Carol Anne Szel, "Diocesan Commission on Parish Councils in Final Stages," *Long Island Catholic* 23, no. 44 (February 28, 1985): 3.
181. "Final Report of the Diocesan Commission on Parish Councils," Diocese of Rockville Centre, 1985, pp. 7, 8, 14, Box 365A, Chancellor's Collection, Subject Files, ADRVC. In June 1987, Bishop McGann promulgated new guidelines for the councils, changing their name to parish pastoral councils in an attempt to reorient them from a political to a ministerial model; see Leonard, *Richly Blessed*, 312–13.
182. "Priest No Longer Has Absolute Authority in Parish," *Long Island Catholic* 23, no. 37 (January 10, 1985): 5; Jim Castelli and Joseph Gremillion, ed., *The Emerging Parish: The Notre Dame Study of Catholic Life Since Vatican II* (San Francisco: Harper and Row, 1987): 3. See also *Parish Life in the United States: Final Report to the Bishops of the United States by the Parish Project* (Washington, DC: United States Catholic Conference, 1983), 34–35.
183. *Diocese of Rockville Centre Quinquennial Report, 1983–1987*, Box 278: IX (2), Leonard Collection, ADRVC.

CHAPTER FIVE

1. Fr. Andrew Connolly, interview by Edward Thompson, May 31, 2004 (hereafter Connolly interview), transcript, pp. 49, 50, 58, 69, 70–71, Box 1672, Oral History Project, ADRVC.
2. Connolly interview, 12, 48, 50; "Wyandanch: An Area Isolated by Neglect," *Long Island Catholic* 7, no. 10 (July 4, 1968): 1; "New Parish Projects in Wyandanch Promise Bright '72," *Long Island Catholic* 10, no. 36 (January 6, 1972): 2.
3. Edward Smits, *Nassau Suburbia USA*, rev. ed. (Garden City, NY: Doubleday, 1990), 162.
4. Sharp, *History of the Diocese of Brooklyn*, 78.
5. Smits, *Nassau: Suburbia, U.S.A.*, 163.
6. Salvatore J. LaGumina, *Long Island Italian Americans: History, Heritage, and Tradition* (Charleston, SC: The History Press, 2013), 13, 15, 27; LaGumina, "Immigrants and the Church in Suburbia: The Long Island Italian-American Experience," *Records of the American Catholic Historical Society of Philadelphia* 98, nos. 1/4 (March–December 1987): 5.

7. LaGumina, *Long Island Italian Americans*, 22, 40, 41, 50, 52; LaGumina, "Immigrants and the Church in Suburbia," 8, 12, 13.
8. R. Alba, *Italian Americans: Into the Twilight of Ethnicity* (Englewood Cliffs, NJ: Prentice-Hall, 1985), 88.
9. LaGumina, *Long Island Italian Americans*, 9, 76; LaGumina, "Immigrants and the Church in Suburbia," 5; Smits, *Nassau: Suburbia, U.S.A.*, 199.
10. Salvatore J. LaGumina, *From Steerage to Suburb: Long Island Italians* (New York: Center for Migration Studies, 1988), 212; Herbert Gans, "Preface," in James A. Crispino, *The Assimilation of Ethnic Groups: The Italian Case* (Staten Island, NY: Center for Migration Studies, 1980), v.
11. Alba, *Italian Americans*, 89.
12. Richard Polenberg, *One Nation Divisible: Class, Race, and Ethnicity in the United States Since 1938* (New York: Penguin, 1980), 146–47; Alba, *Italian Americans*, 89; and see Will Herberg, *Protestant, Catholic, Jew: An Essay in American Religious Sociology*, rev. ed. (Chicago: University of Chicago Press, 1983); Andrew M. Greeley, *Why Can't They Be Like Us? America's White Ethnic Groups* (New York: E. P. Dutton, 1971); Benjamin Ringer, *The Lakeville Studies*, vol. 2: *The Edge of Friendliness* (New York: Basic Books, 1967).
13. Alba, *Italian Americans*, 90–91, 92; Nicholas J. Russo, "Three Generations of Italians in New York City: Their Religious Acculturation," in *The Italian Experience in the United States*, ed. Silvio M. Tomasi and Madeline H. Engel (New York: Center for Migration Studies, 1977), 197; Joseph LoPreato, *Italian Americans* (New York: Random House, 1970), 87, 90.
14. Russo, "Three Generations of Italians in New York City," 198; LaGumina, *Long Island Italian Americans*, 79.
15. LaGumina, *From Steerage to Suburb*, 90.
16. Louis Gesualdi, "A Comparison of the Attitudes and Practices of the Irish American and Italian American Catholics," in *Models and Images of Catholicism in Italian Americans: Academy and Society*, ed. Joseph A. Varacalli et al. (Stony Brook, NY: Forum Italicum, 2004), 48; Alba, *Italian Americans*, 92; Russo, "Three Generations of Italians in New York City," 203, 205.
17. Alba, *Italian Americans*, 92; Stefano Luconi, *From Paesani to White Ethnics: The Italian Experience in Philadelphia* (Albany: SUNY Press, 2001), 1:31.
18. Russo, "Three Generations of Italians in New York City," 208.
19. LaGumina, *From Steerage to Suburb*, 205.
20. LaGumina, *From Steerage to Suburb*, 180, 212; Richard Renoff, "Church Dedications of Italian-American National Parishes: Changing Types of Patrons, 1896–1960," in *The Saints in the Lives of Italian-Americans: An Interdisciplinary Investigation*, ed. Joseph A. Varacalli et al. (Stony Brook, NY: Forum Italicum, 1999), 124; LoPreato, *Italian Americans*, 91.
21. LaGumina, *Long Island Italian Americans*, 49; LaGumina, "Immigrants and the Church in Suburbia," 13, 15; LaGumina, *From Steerage to Suburb*, 206.
22. Gesualdi, "A Comparison of the Attitudes and Practices of the Irish American and Italian American Catholics," 40, 47.
23. Greeley, *The Church and the Suburbs*, 56, 264.
24. See Herberg, *Protestant, Catholic, Jew*, 157–58; David R. Roediger, *Working Toward Whiteness: How America's Immigrants Became White: The Strange Journey from Ellis Island to the Suburbs* (New York: Basic Books, 2006), 232; Jacobson, *Whiteness of a Different Color*, 188.

25. Danielle Battisti, *Whom We Shall Welcome: Italian Americans and Immigration Reform, 1945–1965* (New York: Fordham University Press, 2019), 114.
26. Richard Rothstein, *The Color of Law: A Forgotten History of How Our Government Segregated America* (New York: Norton, 2017), 70; Rosalyn Baxandall and Elizabeth Ewen, *Picture Windows: How the Suburbs Happened* (New York, NY: Basic Books, 2000), 171–90; Wiese, *Places of Their Own*, 98–99.
27. Sarah J. Mahler, *American Dreaming: Immigrant Life on the Margins* (Princeton, NJ: Princeton University Press, 1995), 192, 195.
28. Wiese, *Places of Their Own*, 268; Mahler, *American Dreaming*, 190. Long Island remains one of the ten most racially segregated areas in the country. In the fall of 2019 *Newsday* published the results of a three-year investigation uncovering widespread evidence of racist real estate practices: Ann Choi, Keith Herbert, and Olivia Winslow, "Long Island Divided," *Newsday*, November 17, 2019, 1.
29. Osborne, *American Catholics and the Church of Tomorrow*, 159. See also "The Secular City," *Commonweal* 83, no. 6 (November 12, 1965): 181–90; and Daniel Callahan, *The Secular City Debate* (New York: Macmillan, 1966).
30. Dennis J. Geaney, "Social Action in America," *Commonweal* 66, no. 21 (August 23, 1957): 514.
31. "Wyandanch: An Area Isolated by Neglect," 1.
32. "Diocese Residents in Rights March" and "A Great Peaceful Moral Demonstration," *Long Island Catholic* 2, no. 16 (August 15, 1963): 1; "One Man in the Crowd," *Long Island Catholic* 2, no. 19 (September 5, 1963): 5.
33. "3,000 from Island Participate in March," *Long Island Catholic* 2, no. 19 (September 5, 1963): 5.
34. "LI Conference Gives Racial Justice Guide," *Long Island Catholic* 2, no. 26 (October 24, 1963): 1.
35. "Catholic Interracial Council Is Formed for Long Island," *Long Island Catholic* 1, no. 19 (September 6, 1962): 1.
36. "The Dignity of Man in Suburbia," *Long Island Catholic* 1, no. 19 (September 6, 1962): 13; "Interracial Housing Discussed," *Long Island Catholic* 1, no. 2 (May 10, 1962): 4.
37. "What Happens When Negroes Move In?" *Long Island Catholic* 4, no. 2 (May 6, 1965): 14; "Real Estate and Race," *Long Island Catholic* 1, no. 29 (November 15, 1962): 3.
38. "LI Conference Gives Racial Justice Guide," 1.
39. Antoinette Bosco, "Massapequa Draws the Line: Rule Out Coercion of Black Family," *Long Island Catholic* 9, no. 21 (September 24, 1970): 3; "Racist Vandalism," *Long Island Catholic* 9, no. 24 (October 15, 1970): 6. See also "LI Racism Deplored," *Long Island Catholic* 6, no. 31 (November 30, 1967), no. 10; "Massapequa Rejects Hate," *Long Island Catholic* 9, no. 20 (September 17, 1970): 8; "Burnt Values," *Long Island Catholic* 17, no. 40 (February 8, 1979): 6; "Diocesan Office Deplores Cross Burning," *Long Island Catholic* 18, no. 17 (August 23, 1979): 2.
40. "Real Estate and Race," 3; "Fair Housing Parley Set in Garden City," *Long Island Catholic* 3, no. 52 (April 22, 1965): 20.
41. "Parish Gives Notice to Real Estate Men," *Long Island Catholic* 7, no. 3 (May 16, 1968): 1.
42. Letter by Florence P. Dowling of Garden City, "St. Aidan's on Real Estate," *Long Island Catholic* 7, no. 4 (May 23, 1968): 10.
43. Msgr. Edmond Trench, interview by Fr. Donald Diederich, July 1, 2004, transcript, p. 18, Box 1603, Oral History Project, ADRVC.

44. Antoinette Bosco, "Example Thunders in Race Relations," *Long Island Catholic* 3, no. 8 (June 18, 1964): 8.
45. Antoinette Bosco, "Candles Become Floodlights in Western Suffolk," *Long Island Catholic* 5, no. 24 (October 6, 1966): 4.
46. "Junior Interracial Unit Planned in Diocesan Schools," *Long Island Catholic* 3, no. 20 (September 10, 1964): 2; "Students Respond to Challenge," *Long Island Catholic* 3, no. 30 (November 19, 1964): 17.
47. "Teachers in Diocese Study Negro Background," *Long Island Catholic* 7, no. 21 (September 19, 1968): 2.
48. "Special Series on Black History Starting Oct. 9," *Long Island Catholic* 8, no. 23 (October 2, 1969): 1.
49. Pat McFaul, "U.S. Black History Seen as 'Weapon' in War on Bias," *Long Island Catholic* 8, no. 52 (April 30, 1970): 1.
50. "TV's Special Series Helped," *Long Island Catholic* 9, no. 15 (August 13, 1970): 15.
51. Nancy Dwyer, "The Diocese and Race: Pointed Statements on the Local Church's Progress—or Lack of It," *Long Island Catholic* 8, no. 28 (November 6, 1969): 1.
52. "Teachers in Diocese Study Negro Background," 2.
53. Dwyer, "The Diocese and Race," 1.
54. "Get with It, Black Priest Tells L.I. Council," *Long Island Catholic* 9, no. 1 (May 7, 1970): 5.
55. "After 10 Years Interracial Council Still Trying," *Long Island Catholic* 11, no. 52 (May 3, 1973): 9.
56. Marie Basile, "Small Audience Is 'Evidence' of Racism Problem," *Long Island Catholic* 21, no. 2 (May 6, 1982): 1.
57. Letter from Jeanette Mebus of Commack, "'Strong Words and Little Action' on Race," *Long Island Catholic* 8, no. 30 (November 20, 1969): 10.
58. "Wyandanch: A L.I. Community in Crisis," *Long Island Catholic* 7, no. 9 (June 27, 1968): 1.
59. "Wyandanch: An Area Isolated by Neglect," 1.
60. Francis X. Clines, "Violence Strikes L.I. Village Again," *New York Times*, August 3, 1967, 18; Clines, "Wyandanch Negro Youth List Complaints in Move to End Strife," *New York Times*, August 5, 1967, 8.
61. Fr. John B. Sheerin, CSP, "The Problem Is Much Greater than Brooklyn," *Long Island Catholic* 5, no. 15 (August 4, 1966): 14; "Racial Disturbances Plague the Nation," *Long Island Catholic* 6, nos. 13–14 (July 27, 1967): 15. Conflict between Black and white students twice forced the temporary closure of Bellport High School in October 1969 and January 1970, for example, Agis Salpukas, "Racial Disorders Force Bellport High School to Close for Day," *New York Times*, January 17, 1970, 32.
62. "Wyandanch: A LI Community in Crisis," 1; "Wyandanch: An Area Isolated by Neglect," 1.
63. "Wyandanch: L.I.'s Example," *Long Island Catholic* 7, no. 10 (July 4, 1968): 10; "Wyandanch: Action, Not Words," *Long Island Catholic* 7, no. 12 (July 18, 1968): 1; "New Concept Brings Center to Wyandanch," *Long Island Catholic* 8, no. 39 (January 22, 1970): 15; "Religion Can Lead," editorial, *Long Island Catholic* 7, no. 12 (July 18, 1968): 10.
64. "Wyandanch Revisited: A Ray of Hope Among Blacks," *Long Island Catholic* 8, no. 39 (January 22, 1970): 1.
65. "Church in Wyandanch Taking Active Role in Aiding the People," *Long Island Catholic* 9, no. 44 (February 25, 1971): 2.

66. Antoinette Bosco, "Wyandanch Housing Controversy Has a Statewide Import," *Long Island Catholic* 11, no. 31 (November 30, 1972): 1.
67. "Wyandanch Housing Gets Support," *Long Island Catholic* 12, no. 9 (July 5, 1973): 4; "Bishop Issues Support of Wyandanch Housing," *Long Island Catholic* 12, no. 8 (June 28, 1973): 4.
68. "Build It Here," editorial, *Long Island Catholic* 12, no. 8 (June 28, 1973): 6.
69. "New Wyandanch Housing," editorial, *Long Island Catholic* 11, no. 31 (November 30, 1972): 6.
70. Nancy Dwyer, "Public Hearing to Decide Fate of Wyandanch Housing," *Long Island Catholic* 12, no. 11 (July 19, 1973): 1; Robert Quinn, "Wyandanch Citizens Speak Out on Housing Proposal," *Long Island Catholic* 12, no. 15 (August 16, 1973): 2; Nancy Dwyer, "Babylon Town Board Rejects Wyandanch Housing Proposal Giving 8 Reasons; Hopes Dashed but Backers Will Continue Efforts," *Long Island Catholic* 12, no. 16 (August 23, 1973): 1.
71. "The Problem Is Still There," editorial, *Long Island Catholic* 12, no. 16 (August 23, 1973): 6.
72. Mahler, *American Dreaming*, 189.
73. Basile, "Black Catholics and the Church on Long Island," *Long Island Catholic* 18, no. 37 (January 17, 1980): 1.
74. Mrs. Barbara Horsham-Brathwaite, interview by Sr. Joan de Lourdes Leonard, n.d., transcript, p. 15, Box 226, Sr. Joan de Lourdes Leonard Collection, ADRVC.
75. Horsham-Brathwaite interview, 16.
76. Basile, "Black Catholics and the Church on Long Island," 1.
77. Basile, "Black Catholics and the Church on Long Island," 1.
78. Maria Basile, "Blacks Offer Diversified Talents to Strengthen Church," *Long Island Catholic* 18, no. 38 (January 24, 1980): 4.
79. Maria Basile, "No One Knows What It Is to Be Black Unless It's the Color of Your Skin," *Long Island Catholic* 18, no. 39 (January 31, 1980): 4.
80. Liz O'Connor, "New Office for Ministry to Black Catholics," *Long Island Catholic* 20, no. 24 (October 8, 1981): 1.
81. Mahler, *American Dreaming*, 123, 192, 195.
82. Antoinette Bosco, "Long Islanders Say 'Bienvenido' to Cubans," *Long Island Catholic* 5, no. 32 (December 8, 1966): 4; "Over 5,000 Cubans Now Live in Nassau, Suffolk Counties; Transition Smooth," *Long Island Catholic* 9, no. 8 (June 25, 1970): 11.
83. "W. Suffolk Workers Get Warm Welcome," *Long Island Catholic* 8, no. 18 (August 28, 1969): 3; Antoinette Bosco, "Squalor of L.I. Migrants 'Unbelievable,' says Nursing Sister," *Long Island Catholic* 8, no. 52 (April 30, 1970): 4; Antoinette Bosco, "L.I. Migrants Find Some Wonderful Friends," *Long Island Catholic* 10, no. 16 (August 19, 1971): 3.
84. Antoinette Bosco, "A Chance to Belong—Quest of Latin Immigrants," *Long Island Catholic* 8, no. 23 (October 2, 1969): 1.
85. "First Cursillo for Long Island," *Long Island Catholic* 4, no. 30 (November 18, 1965): 18; Carol Speranza, "Cursillistas: Not to Be Ignored," *Long Island Catholic* 13, no. 15 (August 15, 1974): 5; Speranza, "Cursillo Movement Thriving in Diocese," *Long Island Catholic* 13, no. 41 (February 20, 1975): 2.
86. Antoinette Bosco, "New Parish in Brentwood Is a Thriving One-Year-Old," *Long Island Catholic* 5, no. 21 (September 22, 1966): 11; *St. Luke's Roman Catholic Church 50th Anniversary Journal, 1965–2015*, p. 11, Archives of St. Luke Parish, Brentwood, NY.

87. Antoinette Bosco, "New Brentwood Neighbors Learn Poco a Poco," *Long Island Catholic* 5, no. 41 (February 16, 1967): 4.
88. Antoinette Bosco, "Learning in Brentwood's Operation Northwest," *Long Island Catholic* 5, no. 15 (August 4, 1966): 11; Richard Mauter, "'Operation' Resumes in Brentwood: Drive Swells Program's Enrollment," *Long Island Catholic* 6, no. 9 (June 29, 1967): 2.
89. Antoinette Bosco, "Poor to Be Aided—Pronto," *Long Island Catholic* 7, no. 41 (February 6, 1969): 1.
90. Marie Basile, "PRONTO Offer Social, Spiritual Services," *Long Island Catholic* 21, no. 18 (August 26, 1982): 5; undated PRONTO brochure, Pronto Collection: Folder 1, Archives of the Sisters of Saint Joseph.
91. Sarah J. Mahler, "Suburban Transnational Migrants: Long Island's Salvadorans," in *Migration, Transnationalization, and Race in a Changing New York*, ed. Hector R. Cordero-Guzman, Robert C. Smith, and Ramon Grossfoguel (Philadelphia: Temple University Press, 2001), 109–30.
92. Mahler, "Suburban Transnational Migrants," 111; Liz O'Connor, "Refugees Come with Dreams to LI," *Long Island Catholic* 21, no. 27 (October 28, 1982): 1; Sr. Joan de Lourdes Leonard, CSJ, *Richly Blessed: The Diocese of Rockville Centre, 1957–1990* (Marceline, MO: Walsworth Publishing, 1991), 225.
93. Mahler, "Suburban Transnational Migrants," 112.
94. Leonard, *Richly Blessed*, 224–27; "The Spanish Speaking Are Most Diverse of Immigrants," *Long Island Catholic* 13, no. 11 (July 11, 1974): 5; Carol Speranza, "Spanish Speaking and Church: Still a Gap," *Long Island Catholic* 13, no. 10 (July 4, 1974): 1. In the summer of 1974 the *Long Island Catholic* published a six-week series of articles on Long Island's Spanish-speaking Catholics from which this section draws heavily.
95. "CARA Catholic Poll," Center for Applied Research in the Apostolate, Georgetown University, Washington, DC, 2010, cited at https://www.usccb.org/offices/public-affairs/laity-and-parishes (accessed September 16, 2023).
96. Speranza, "Spanish Speaking and Church," 1.
97. Carol Speranza, "Parish Unity, Spanish Programs: Dilemma," *Long Island Catholic* 13, no. 13 (July 25, 1974): 2.
98. Antoinette Bosco, "Optimism Brightens Life of Brentwood Family," *Long Island Catholic* 8, no. 11 (July 10, 1969): 1.
99. For more on the mixed parish, see Brett C. Hoover, *The Shared Parish: Latinos, Anglos, and the Future of U.S. Catholicism* (New York: New York University Press, 2014); Tricia Bruce, *Parish and Place: Making Room for Diversity in the American Catholic Church* (New York: Oxford University Press, 2017).
100. "Hold on to Special Customs," *Long Island Catholic* 13, no. 11 (July 11, 1974): 5.
101. Carol Speranza, "L.I. Spanish Catholics Seek Spiritual Care," *Long Island Catholic* 13, no. 11 (July 11, 1974): 5.
102. Speranza, "Spanish Speaking and Church," 1.
103. Speranza, "Parish Unity, Spanish Programs," 2.
104. Liz O'Connor, "Salvadoran Are Our Brothers and Sisters," *Long Island Catholic* 21, no. 50 (April 14, 1983): 1. The diocese even reported to the Vatican that an "Immigration Sunday" held on January 9, 1983, was "not at all successful, even as a form of community consciousness-raising"; *Diocese of Rockville Centre Quinquennial Report, 1978–1982*, XIV (9). See also Speranza, "Spanish Speaking and Church," 1.
105. Speranza, "Parish Unity, Spanish Programs," 2.

106. The diocese found that the largest Spanish-speaking communities were in Brentwood, Wyandanch, Freeport-Hempstead, Patchogue, Long Beach, Five Towns, Great Neck, Roslyn, Oyster Bay, and Glen Cove.
107. Speranza, "Spanish Speaking and Church," 1.
108. Sr. Eve Gillcrist, OP, "Hispanics Raise Prophetic Voices," *Long Island Catholic* 23, no. 48 (March 28, 1985): 1, 13. See also "The Spanish Speaking Are Most Diverse of Immigrants," 5; Carol Speranza, "Fear Loss of Spanish Catholics," *Long Island Catholic* 13, no. 14 (August 8, 1974): 4; Speranza, "Spanish Speaking and Church," 1; Carol Speranza, "Spanish Social Services Seeks Community Self-Help," *Long Island Catholic* 13, no. 12 (July 18, 1974): 2.
109. For more on the white ethnic revival, see Thomas J. Sugrue and John D. Skrentny, "The White Ethnic Strategy," in *Rightward Bound*, ed. Bruce J. Schulman and Julian E. Zelizer (Cambridge, MA: Harvard University Press, 2008), 171–92; Greeley, *Why Can't They Be Like Us?*; Nathan Glazer and Daniel Patrick Moynihan, *Beyond the Melting Pot: The Negroes, Puerto Ricans, Jews, Italians, and Irish of New York City* (Cambridge, MA: Harvard University Press, 1970); Jonathan Rieder, *Canarsie: The Jews and Italians of Brooklyn Against Liberalism* (Cambridge, MA: Harvard University Press, 1985); Joshua M. Zeitz, *White Ethnic New York: Jews, Catholics, and the Shaping of Postwar Politics* (Chapel Hill: University of North Carolina Press, 2007); "The Troubled White American: A Special Report on the White Majority," *Newsweek*, October 6, 1969, 29; Matthew Frye Jacobson, *Roots Too: White Ethnic Revival in Post–Civil Rights America* (Cambridge, MA: Harvard University Press, 2008).
110. Polenberg, *One Nation Divisible*, 244–45.
111. Luconi, *From Paesani to White Ethnics*, 8; See Gans, "Preface," v, ix.
112. Luconi, *From Paesani to White Ethnics*, 5–6; Polenberg, *One Nation Divisible*, 246.
113. Battisti, *Whom We Shall Welcome*, 239.
114. Luconi, *From Paesani to White Ethnics*, 9; see Michael Novak, *The Rise of the Unmeltable Ethnics* (New York: Macmillan, 1972), 32, 58, 139.
115. Looker, *A Nation of Neighborhoods*, 261–62.
116. Looker, *A Nation of Neighborhoods*, 266, citing Italian American activists quoted in Arthur Mann, *The One and the Many: Reflections on the American Identity* (Chicago: University of Chicago Press, 1979), 36.
117. Looker, *A Nation of Neighborhoods*, 262, 266–68: in particular, they referenced the Vatican Council's defense of the individual's "inherent right to culture," and cited Pope Paul VI's 1971 apostolic letter *A Call to Action*, which "lamented the 'new loneliness' of the contemporary metropolis."
118. Fr. Andrew M. Greeley, "Second-Rate Ethnics?" *Long Island Catholic* 13, no. 42 (February 27, 1975): 6. See also "Sociologist Fr. Greeley Suggests Ethnic Study of U.S. to Help Solve Race," *Long Island Catholic* 7, no. 9 (June 27, 1968): 19; Fr. Andrew M. Greeley, "Rediscovering Cultural Pluralism," *Long Island Catholic* 10, no. 23 (October 7, 1971): 6; Greeley, "Dismissing Ethnic Thing Evidence of Pride," *Long Island Catholic* 10, no. 49 (April 6, 1972): 6; Greeley, "Ethnic Diversity Is a Benefit," *Long Island Catholic* 13, no. 32 (December 12, 1974): 6.
119. "Oktoberfest," *Long Island Catholic* 22, no. 19 (September 1, 1983): 1.
120. "Bishop McGann to Visit St. Isidore's," *Long Island Catholic* 16, no. 15 (August 11, 1977): 5; "Bishop Seeks to Heal the Differences at St. Isidore's," *Long Island Catholic* 16, no. 18 (September 1, 1977): 2.
121. "Long Island's Polish Parishes to Celebrate Czestochowa Feast," *Long Island Catholic* 21, no. 17 (August 19, 1982): 1.

122. "Italian-Style Festa in Centereach," *Long Island Catholic* 9, no. 47 (March 18, 1971): 9.
123. "San Gennaro Feast Set," *Long Island Catholic* 12, no. 18 (September 6, 1973): 14.
124. Bill Schmitt, "San Gennaro Festival—Food, Faith, Fun," *Long Island Catholic* 14, no. 19 (September 11, 1975): 4.
125. Marie Basile, "Priests Seek Ways to Serve Italian Parishioners," *Long Island Catholic* 20, no. 44 (March 4, 1982): 1.

CHAPTER SIX

1. Butler, *Our Lady of Grace Parish*, 12.
2. William F. Whelan, "A Brief Look at the History and Development of the Our Lady of Grace Roman Catholic Church West Babylon, New York," n.d., 5-6, 19-20, Archives of Our Lady of Grace Parish, West Babylon, NY; and see Antoinette Bosco, "The Parish that Was Born Big," *Long Island Catholic* 6, no. 43 (February 22, 1968): 11.
3. Bosco, "The Parish that Was Born Big," 11.
4. Fr. John E. Leonard, "From the Pastor's Desk," *Our Parish* 2, no. 4 (September 1967): 1, Archives of Our Lady of Grace Parish.
5. Whelan, "A Brief Look," 22-23; Silvio Impagliazzo, interview with the author, July 21, 2017, Our Lady of Grace Parish, West Babylon, NY.
6. William Goddard, "When a School Becomes a CCD Center," *Long Island Catholic* 6, no. 43 (February 22, 1968): 1.
7. Butler, *Our Lady of Grace Parish*, 12-13.
8. Goddard, "When a School Becomes a CCD Center," 1. The other parishes were St. Elizabeth in South Huntington and Immaculate Conception in Westhampton Beach.
9. Timothy Kelly has similarly argued that because dioceses were unable to provide sufficient desks in Catholics schools to keep pace with the suburban baby boom, Catholic parents doubted the rationale behind parochial schools, sent their children to public schools, and thereby helped collapse the walls of ghetto Catholicism well before Vatican II; Timothy Kelly, *The Transformation of American Catholicism: The Pittsburgh Laity and the Second Vatican Council, 1950-1972* (Notre Dame, IN: University of Notre Dame Press, 2009).
10. Joseph J. Casino, "From Sanctuary to Involvement: A History of the Catholic Parish in the Northeast," in *American Catholic Parish: A History from 1850 to the Present*, ed. Jay P. Dolan (New York: Paulist Press, 1987), 3.
11. Andrew M. Greeley, *The Church and the Suburbs* (New York: Sheed and Ward, 1959), 66; Sr. Joan de Lourdes Leonard, CSJ, *Richly Blessed: The Diocese of Rockville Centre, 1957-1990* (Marceline, MO: Walsworth Publishing, 1991), 73. In 1884, at the Third Plenary Council of Baltimore, the US bishops stated their expectation that every parish would build a school. For more on the Third Plenary Council of Baltimore, see Philip Gleason, "Baltimore III and Education," *U.S. Catholic Historian* 4, no. 3 (1985): 273-313. For more on Hughes's significant contributions to the expansion of American Catholic education, see Joseph J. McCadden, "Bishop Hughes Versus the Public School Society of New York," *Catholic Historical Review* 50, no. 2 (July 1964): 188-207.
12. Greeley, *The Church and the Suburbs*, 64.
13. Fr. Daniel E. Fagan, "The Catholics and Their Schools," *St. Pius X Digest* 7, no. 7 (March 8, 1964): 1.
14. Maureen O'Neill, "300 Wait All Night to Fill Class of 100," *Newsday*, April 7, 1959, 4; See also Leonard, *Richly Blessed*, 75.

15. *St. Aidan's Church Dedication Journal, 1961,* 17–19, Box 616, Seminary Library Collection, ADRVC.
16. *St. Brigid Centennial Journal, 1856–1956,* 20–21, Assorted Parish Journals, ADRVC.
17. Msgr. Edgar McCarren, interview by Sr. Joan de Lourdes Leonard, CSJ, April 3, 1982 (hereafter McCarren interview), transcript, pp. 3–4, Box 226, Sr. Joan de Lourdes Leonard Collection, ADRVC.
18. Msgr. Lawrence Ballweg, interview by Sr. Joan de Lourdes Leonard, CSJ, n.d. (hereafter Ballweg interview), transcript, p. 5, Box 226, Sr. Joan de Lourdes Leonard Collection, ADRVC.
19. *St. Barnabas the Apostle Church Dedication, 1959,* Box 903: Parish Journals, Bishops Office Collection, ADRVC.
20. Building Commission of the Board of Consultors, minutes for July 16, 1954, Binder 5, Diocesan Buildings and Property Office Collection, ADB.
21. *St. Martha's Ten Year Journal, 1949–1959,* Box 163A: Parish Files, Chancellor's Collection, ADRVC; *St. Martha's 25th Anniversary Journal, 1949–1975,* 18–19, Box 618, Seminary Library Collection, ADRVC.
22. *Holy Family Parish 25th Anniversary Journal, 1951–1976,* Box 163B: Parish Files, Chancellor's Collection, ADRVC.
23. Leonard, *Richly Blessed,* 75; "Add 4 New Schools in New Diocese," *The Tablet* 50, no. 28 (August 24, 1957): 1. The four new parish schools were: St. Martha in Uniondale, Our Lady of Peace in Lynbrook, Blessed Sacrament in North Valley Stream, and St. Joseph in Hewlett.
24. Leonard, *Richly Blessed,* 86; "Schools Outlook: More Seats, More Students," *Long Island Catholic* 1, no. 15 (August 16, 1962): 1.
25. The Diocese of Brooklyn, *Diocese of Immigrants: The Brooklyn Catholic Experience, 1853–2003* (Strasbourg, France: Éditions du Signe, 2004), 127. The six high schools, three in Brooklyn and three in Queens were Nazareth in East Flatbush, Bishop Kearney in Bensonhurst, Bishop Ford in Park Slope, Christ the King in Middle Village, Bishop Reilly in Fresh Meadows, and Mater Christi in Astoria.
26. Msgr. Florence D. Cohalan, *A Popular History of the Archdiocese of New York* (Yonkers, NY: United States Catholic Historical Society, 1983), 302. Among these new high schools were several operated by the archdiocese itself, including Archbishop Stepinac in White Plains (1948), Maria Regina in Hartsdale (1957), Our Lady of Lourdes in Poughkeepsie (1958), Cardinal Spellman in the Bronx (1959), Monsignor Farrell in Staten Island (1961), John A. Coleman in Hurley (1966), and John F. Kennedy in Somers (1967).
27. Leonard, *Richly Blessed,* 85, 86–87.
28. Leonard, *Richly Blessed,* 86; "Drive to End High School Lag," *Long Island Catholic* 2, no. 18 (August 29, 1963): 3. See also "Catholic High Schools," campaign brochure, Box 496, Folder: HS Campaign, Subject Files, Chancellor's Collection, ADRVC.
29. Msgr. Henry Reel, interview by Edward McCormack, n.d. (hereafter Reel interview), transcript, p. 6, Box 106, Sr. Joan de Lourdes Leonard Collection, ADRVC.
30. Thomas E. O'Brien, "Rockville Centre's High School Campaign," *Catholic Market* 3, no. 2 (April 1964): 54.
31. *St. Paul Church Dedication Journal, 1968,* Box 158, Chancellor's Collection, ADRVC; *Our Lady of Victory Fiftieth Anniversary, 1921–1971,* Box 163B, Chancellor's Parish Files, ADRVC.
32. Leonard, *Richly Blessed,* 65, 89–90.
33. "New High Schools Begin Classes," *Long Island Catholic* 5, no. 19 (September 18, 1966): 1; and see "Urgent Need for Catholic High Schools," *LIC* 2, no. 24 (October 10,

1963): 3; "Construction Begins on First of Four New High Schools," *Long Island Catholic* 3, no. 3 (May 14, 1964): 1; "More than 3,000 at High School Dedication," *Long Island Catholic* 5, no. 24 (October 6, 1966): 1; "Catholic High School Commemorative Insert," *Long Island Catholic* 5, no. 27 (November 3, 1966): suppl.; "Clear Sailing Ahead for New Schools," *Long Island Catholic* 6, no. 6 (June 8, 1967): 14.
34. Leonard, *Richly Blessed*, 78.
35. Holy Trinity High School in Hicksville had thirteen Sisters of Mercy and eleven Dominican Sisters; Maria Regina in Uniondale had ten Dominican Sisters and eleven Immaculate Heart Sisters; Holy Family in South Huntington had twelve Sisters of St. Joseph and twelve Ursuline Sisters; and St. John the Baptist in West Islip had eight Dominican Sisters and thirteen Franciscan Sisters. *Official Catholic Directory 1967* (New York: P. J. Kenedy and Sons, Publishers, 1967), 738.
36. Margaret M. McGuinness, *Called to Serve: A History of Nuns in America* (New York: New York University Press, 2013), 160, citing Marjorie Noterman Beane, *From Framework to Freedom: A History of the Sister Formation Conference* (Lanham, MD: University Press of America, 1993), 46.
37. "Call for Better Sister Training Programs," *The Tablet* 52, no. 3 (February 28, 1959): 8; Harold A. Buetow, *Of Singular Benefit: The Story of Catholic Education in the United States* (New York: Macmillan, 1970), 251-53.
38. Leonard, *Richly Blessed*, 78; "Sister Formation: Complete Training Aim of New Program," *Long Island Catholic* 1, no. 1 (May 3, 1962): 17; "Added Training Goal of New Building," *Long Island Catholic* 1, no. 1 (May 3, 1962): 3A. For more on the Sister Formation Movement, see Carol K. Coburn, "Ahead of Its Time . . . or, Right on Time? The Role of the Sister Formation Conference for American Women Religious," *American Catholic Studies* 126, no. 3 (2015): 25-44; Mary L. Schneider, OSF, "American Sisters and the Roots of Change: The 1950s," *U.S. Catholic Historian* 7, no. 1 (1988): 55-72; Beane, *From Framework to Freedom*; Darra Mulderry, "Educating 'Sister Lucy': Experiential Sources of the Movement to Improve Catholic Sisters' Education, 1949-1964," *U.S. Catholic Historian* 33, no. 1 (2015): 55-79; Amy Koehlinger, *The New Nuns: Racial Justice and Religious Reform in the 1960s* (Cambridge, MA: Harvard University Press, 2007).
39. Leonard, *Richly Blessed*, 82; "Open Nuns' College in Amityville," *Long Island Catholic* 4, no. 25 (October 14, 1965): 1. Molloy College was founded in Rockville Centre to serve Catholic laywomen; "Molloy College Dynamic Addition to Education," *Long Island Catholic* 1, no. 1 (May 3, 1962): 15.
40. McGuinness, *Called to Serve*, 160, citing Beane, *From Framework to Freedom*, 46.
41. "Last Class of Sisters to Receive Degrees from Brentwood," *Long Island Catholic* 10, no. 15 (August 12, 1971): 5.
42. McCarren interview, p. 4.
43. Leonard, *Richly Blessed*, 75; and for more on the Our Lady of the Angels fire, see David Cowen and John Kuenster, *To Sleep with the Angels: The Story of a Fire* (Chicago: Ivan R. Dee Publisher, 1998).
44. Koehlinger, *The New Nuns*, 29.
45. Leonard, *Richly Blessed*, 83; Patricia Byrne, "In the Parish but Not of It: Sisters," in *Transforming Parish Ministry: The Changing Roles of Catholic Clergy, Laity, and Women Religious*, ed. Jay Dolan (New York: Crossroad, 1989), 135-37. In the first five years of the diocese two parochial schools had opened with entirely lay staffs until a religious order could be found to provide at least some sisters for the school.
46. Leonard, *Richly Blessed*, 78, 82.

47. Leonard, *Richly Blessed*, 89.
48. "Writer of Ryan Book Forward Explains Stand," *Long Island Catholic* 3, no. 1 (April 30, 1964): 3.
49. Mary Perkins Ryan, *Are Parochial Schools the Answer?* (New York: Holt, Rinehart and Winston, 1964), 157, 163. These arguments echoed those made against Catholic schools in the late nineteenth century by Orestes Brownson and others; see Jay P. Dolan, *The Immigrant Church: New York's Irish and German Catholics, 1815–1865* (Baltimore: Johns Hopkins University Press, 1975), 109.
50. Robert E. Doyle, "Self-Examination by Catholic Educators," *Long Island Catholic* 3, no. 26 (October 22, 1964): 9; Fr. Barry McGannon, SJ, ed., *Christian Wisdom and Christian Formation* (New York: Sheed and Ward, 1964).
51. Buetow, *Of Singular Benefit*, 177–78.
52. Bruce J. Dierenfield, *The Battle over School Prayer: How Engel v. Vitale Changed America* (Lawrence: University Press of Kansas, 2007), 57, 54, 61.
53. Leonard, *Richly Blessed*, 95.
54. Antoinette Bosco, "From This . . . Came This . . ." *Long Island Catholic* 3, no. 10 (July 2, 1964): 11.
55. *St. Anne Parish 100th Anniversary Journal, 1895–1995*, Archives of St. Anne Parish, Brentwood, NY.
56. *St. Ignatius Loyola 125th Anniversary Journal, 1872–1983*, p. 16, Box 903: Parish Journals, Bishops Office Collection, ADRVC.
57. Msgr. Joseph Lawlor, interview by Sr. Joan de Lourdes Leonard, CSJ, December 11, 1981, transcript, p. 5, Box 226, Sr. Joan de Lourdes Leonard Collection, ADRVC.
58. Msgr. Frederick Schaefer, interview by Sr. Joan de Lourdes Leonard, CSJ, June 14, 1982 (hereafter Schaefer interview), transcript, p. 2, Box 106, Leonard Collection, ADRVC; Leonard, *Richly Blessed*, 97–98.
59. Antoinette Bosco, "The Pieces Come Together . . . The Result, A Parish," *Long Island Catholic* 5, no. 37 (January 19, 1967): 11; "St. Luke's Church Dedication to Mark Parish Milestone," *Long Island Catholic* 7, no. 2 (May 9, 1968): 1.
60. Leonard DeFiore, *Story of the Storm: Catholic Elementary Schools from the 1960s to the Present* (Arlington, VA: National Catholic Educational Association, 2011), 18.
61. "CCD Center Where Parish Does Its Thing," *Long Island Catholic* 7, no. 42 (February 13, 1969): 3; and see Antoinette Bosco, "Westhampton Beach Merge of Abilities," *Long Island Catholic* 3, no. 14 (July 30, 1964): 11; "L.I. Parish Dream Centers on Community," *Long Island Catholic* 7, no. 42 (February 13, 1969): 3.
62. "Centereach Confirmation, Dedication Set," *Long Island Catholic* 10, no. 3 (May 20, 1971): 2; "OL of Assumption Parish Dedicates New Center Nov. 7," *Long Island Catholic* 10, no. 27 (November 4, 1971): 2; see also Leonard, *Richly Blessed*, 101–2.
63. "New Schools of Religion," *Catholic Property Administration* 27, no. 11 (November 1963): 24.
64. "St. Elizabeth's Voters Favor Construction of CCD Center," *Long Island Catholic* 6, no. 28 (November 9, 1967): 1. See also "Religious Education Center Opens," *Long Island Catholic* 8, no. 5 (May 29, 1969): 1; "So. Huntington Religious Education Center Sees Impressive Future Ahead," *Long Island Catholic* 8, no. 5 (May 29, 1969): 1.
65. "Catechetical Centers Viewed as Inevitable," *Long Island Catholic* 6, no. 43 (February 22, 1968): 1; and see "Notre Dame Educator Backs Religion Centers," *Long Island Catholic* 6, no. 27 (November 2, 1967): 20.
66. Goddard, "When a School Becomes a CCD Center," 1.
67. Butler, *Our Lady of Grace Parish*, 12.

68. Whelan, "A Brief Look," 24; Mrs. Irene Lynch, interview with the author, July 22, 2017, Our Lady of Grace Parish, West Babylon, NY.
69. Sister Dorothy Fowler, "An Open Letter to Members of Our Lady of Grace Parish," *Our Parish* (March 1971): 4, and G. Neil Pike, "Plus 2," *Our Parish* (March 1971): 6, Archives of Our Lady of Grace Parish, West Babylon, NY.
70. Fr. John E. Leonard, "From the Pastor's Desk," *Our Parish*, September 1968, 1, Archives of Our Lady of Grace Parish, West Babylon, NY.
71. For an examination of the decline in vocations to women's religious communities in the United States, see Patricia Wittberg, *The Rise and Fall of Catholic Religious Orders: A Social Movement Perspective* (Albany: State University of New York Press, 1994).
72. McGuinness, *Called to Serve*, 173–74, citing Marie Augusta Neal, SND de Namur, *Catholic Sisters in Transition from the 1960s to the 1980s* (Wilmington, DE: Michael Glazer, 1984), 21.
73. Erick Berrelleza, SJ, Mary L. Gautier, and Mark M. Gray, "Population Trends Among Religious Institutes of Women," *CARA Special Report* (Fall 2014): 1. See https://cara.georgetown.edu/special-reports/
74. Colleen McDannell, *The Spirit of Vatican II: A History of Catholic Reform in America* (New York: Basic Books, 2011), 67–71, 169–71, 183; McGreevy, *Parish Boundaries*, 167–71, 218–19, 236, 338; Koehlinger, *The New Nuns*, 40–42, 48, 60.
75. McGuinness, *Called to Serve*, 179.
76. Leonard, *Richly Blessed*, 280.
77. See Koehlinger, *The New Nuns*, 10–11, 40–41, 212–13.
78. "Involve Laity in Catholic Schools," *Long Island Catholic* 8, no. 34 (December 18, 1969): 16.
79. Byrne, "In the Parish but Not of It," 170.
80. Nancy Dwyer, "Nuns Leaving Merrick School, But 'With Reasons,'" *Long Island Catholic* 9, no. 33 (December 17, 1970): 14; "Parish History," Parish Family of Curé of Ars, https://cureofarschurch.org/about-us/history.
81. "Nuns Gone: Laity Staff Tries in St. James," *Long Island Catholic* 9, no. 40 (January 28, 1971): 1.
82. Fr. Andrew Connolly, interview by Edward Thompson, May 31, 2004, transcript, p. 44, Box 1672, Oral History Project, ADRVC.
83. Fr. Patrick Shanahan, interview by Sr. Joan de Lourdes Leonard, CSJ, January 22, 1982 (hereafter Shanahan interview), transcript, pp. 4–5, Box 106, Leonard Collection, ADRVC.
84. "Lay Teachers' Strike Avoided," *Long Island Catholic* 15, no. 27 (October 28, 1976): 16.
85. "Lay Teachers Strike at Four High Schools," *Long Island Catholic* 16, no. 20 (September 15, 1977): 1; "Diocese and Lay Teachers Hold Firm to Strike Positions," *Long Island Catholic* 16, no. 24 (October 13, 1977): 4.
86. "Two-Year Agreement End Strike at Diocesan High Schools," *Long Island Catholic* 16, no. 26 (October 27, 1977): 9.
87. Marie Basile, "Lay Teachers Strike Diocesan High Schools," *Long Island Catholic* 20, no. 20 (September 10, 1981): 1; Maria Basile, "Strike Settled, All but 4 Teachers Return to Work," *Long Island Catholic* 20, no. 28 (November 5, 1981): 16.
88. Maria Basile, "Elementary Teachers Reject Union," *Long Island Catholic* 20, no. 28 (November 5, 1981): 1.
89. Timothy Walch, *Parish School: American Catholic Parochial Education from Colonial Times to the Present* (Washington, DC: National Catholic Educational Association,

2003), 177; "Catholic Schools: A Fiscal Crisis," *Time* 93, no. 13 (March 28, 1969): 42–43. See also "Enrollment Declines in 432 Schools of Archdiocese of New York," *Catholic News* 82, no. 47 (November 23, 1967): 1.
90. Walch, *Parish School*, 177–78, 180; "Rising Expenses Declining Enrollments Forcing Schools to Close," *Long Island Catholic* 7, no. 7 (June 13, 1968): 20; "Schools Close Consolidate in 4 US Dioceses," *Long Island Catholic* 8, no. 1 (May 1, 1969): 20.
91. *Holy Name of Mary 70th Anniversary Journal, 1902–1972*, Box 903: Parish Journals, Bishops Office Collection, ADRVC.
92. Robert M. Collins, "The Economic Crisis of 1968 and the Waning of the 'American Century,'" *American Historical Review* 101, no. 2 (April 1996): 401–2, 407, 412; and see Stephen B. Reed, "One Hundred Years of Price Change: The Consumer Price Index and the American Inflation Experience," *Monthly Labor Review* 137, no. 4 (April 2014): 22–23.
93. "Catholic Schools: A Fiscal Crisis," 42–43; and see "Public Schools Endangered If Parochial Schools Close," *Long Island Catholic* 9, no. 46 (March 11, 1971): 1.
94. Walch, *Parish School*, 180.
95. "Catholic Schools: A Fiscal Crisis," 42–43; "400 Catholic Schools Closed During Year Magazine Reports," *Long Island Catholic* 9, no. 51 (April 15, 1971): 5; and see Walch, *Parish School*, 180; Buetow, *Of Singular Benefit*, 286–87.
96. Neil G. McCluskey, SJ, *Catholic Education Faces Its Future* (New York: Doubleday, 1969).
97. Sr. Mary Chaminade, OP, "Restructuring of Catholic Schools," *Long Island Catholic* 9, no. 6 (June 11, 1970): 5, reviewing Fr. C. Albert Koob and Russell Shaw, *S.O.S. for Catholic Schools: A Strategy for Future Service to Church and Nation* (New York: Holt, Rinehart and Winston, 1970); and see Walch, *Parish School*, 181.
98. *St. Anthony's Parish, 1977*, pp. 11, 20, Box 903: Parish Journals, Bishops Office Collection, ADRVC.
99. *St. Frances de Chantal 50th Anniversary, 1952–2002*, Box 6: Miscellaneous, Archives of St. Frances de Chantal Parish, Wantagh, NY.
100. Russell David, "School Board," *St. Pius X Digest* 1, no. 2 (April 1973): 4, and 1, no. 1 (March 1973): 3, Archives of St. Pius X Parish, Plainview, NY.
101. Kevin Donohue, "St. Pius X School Board," *St. Pius X Digest* 2, no. 3 (March 1974): 5, and Cary Farmer, "St. Pius X School Board," *St. Pius X Digest* 2, no. 1 (January 1974): 2, Archives of St. Pius X Parish, Plainview, NY.
102. Mrs. H. Hurst and A. Orafferty, "For Parents Only," *Our Parish* 1, no. 2 (April 1966): 4, in the Archives of Our Lady of Grace Parish, West Babylon, NY.
103. "The Released Time Program at the Center," collection of essays and quizzes on the Center for Religious Education (October 1970); Rev. Ronald A. Barry, "Our Lady of Grace Center for Religious Education Progress Report, 1969–1970," Our Lady of Grace Collection, Folder 1, Archives of the Sisters of St. Joseph of Brentwood, NY.
104. "What Happened to Catechism," *Long Island Catholic* 9, no. 4 (May 28, 1970).
105. Lorraine Smith, "Sound Off," *Our Parish* (July 1972): 6, Archives of Our Lady of Grace Parish, West Babylon, NY.
106. Sue McRedmond, "Catholic Children or Guinea Pigs?" *St. Pius X Digest* 1, no. 5 (September 2, 1973): 3.
107. Greeley is quoted in "Catholic Schools Can't Do It All," *Long Island Catholic* 5, no. 15 (August 4, 1966): 17.
108. "Involve Laity in Catholic Schools," 16. Andrew M. Greeley, William C. McCready, and Kathleen McCourt, *Catholic Schools in a Declining Church* (Kansas City: Sheed and Ward, 1976).

109. Andrew M. Greeley, "Lots of Cowards," *Long Island Catholic* 15, no. 3 (May 13, 1976): 6.
110. Mary Perkins Ryan, *We're All in This Together: Issues and Options in the Education of Catholics* (New York: Holt, Rinehart, and Winston, 1972), x–xi.
111. Interviews by Sr. Joan de Lourdes Leonard, CSJ, in the Leonard Collection, ADRVC: Fr. David Farley, n.d., transcript, p. 3, Box 106; Msgr. John Bennett, September 29, 1988 (hereafter Bennett interview), transcript, p. 4, Box 226; Msgr. George Graham, December 11, 1981, transcript, p. 50, Box 226; Dr. Hugh Carroll, n.d., transcript, Box 226; Bishop Emil Wcela, n.d., transcript, p. 118, Box 106. Shanahan interview, 8. See also Ballweg interview.
112. Walch, *Parish School*, 231 citing Andrew M. Greeley and Peter H. Rossi, *The Education of Catholic Americans* (Chicago: Aldine, 1966); see also Buetow, *Of Singular Benefit*, 297–300; and Andrew M. Greeley and William E. Brown, *Can Catholic Schools Survive?* (New York: Sheed and Ward, 1970).
113. Msgr. James F. Coffey, interview by Sr. Joan de Lourdes Leonard, CSJ, August 7, 1981, transcript, pp. 8–9, Box 226, Sr. Joan de Lourdes Leonard Collection, ADRVC.
114. Unpublished report on the minutes of Diocesan Consultors' meetings in which high schools were discussed, and Bishop John R. McGann, letter to Most Rev. Pio Laghi, Apostolic Delegate to the United States, January 19, 1984, Box 506B, Folder: HS Closures, Education Office Collection, ADRVC.
115. Reel interview, 6.
116. Leonard, *Richly Blessed*, 212. In 1987 St. Agnes High School was taken over by the Marianist community from Chaminade High School in Mineola and was renamed Bishop Kellenberg Memorial High School. See also Liz O'Connor, "Bishop Sets Up New Secondary Education and Vocation Plans," *Long Island Catholic* 22, no. 33 (December 8, 1983); Ridgely Ochs, "Two Catholic High Schools and Seminary Prep to Close," *Newsday*, December 5, 1983, 3.
117. Bishop John R. McGann, letter to People of the Diocese, December 5, 1983, Box 506B, Folder: HS Closures, Education Office Collection, ADRVC.
118. Fr. Patrick E. Shanahan, Superintendent of Schools, letter to Diocesan High School Teachers, November 24, 1971, Box 506B, Folder: HS Closures, Education Office Collection, ADRVC; and see Leonard, *Richly Blessed*, 210.
119. Unpublished Report of the Diocese of Rockville Centre Business Office, "Diocese of Rockville Centre—Diocesan High Schools Enrollment History," December 12, 1983, Box 963, Folder: HS Closures, Education Office Collection, ADRVC.
120. Unpublished report on the minutes of Diocesan Consultors' meetings in which high schools were discussed; McGann, letter to Pio Laghi; Leonard, *Richly Blessed*, 211.
121. Fr. Donald Desmond, principal of Maria Regina HS, letter to Dr. Hugh Carroll, Superintendent of Schools, January 17, 1984, Box 506B, Folder: HS Closures, Education Office Collection, ADRVC.
122. For discussion of how the perceptions of high school seminaries had changed, see "New Look at Prep Sem," *Long Island Catholic* 8, no. 22 (September 25, 1969): 13; Antoinette Bosco, "Vocations: A Concern for Everyone," *Long Island Catholic* 6, no. 4 (May 25, 1967): 4; "Why Prep Seminaries?" *Long Island Catholic* 2, no. 4 (May 23, 1963): 3; and Joseph M. White, *The Diocesan Seminary in the United States: A History from the 1780s to the Present* (Notre Dame, IN: University of Notre Dame Press, 1989), 425.
123. Bennett interview, p. 8; Msgr. John F. Bennett, memo to Bishop John R. McGann, December 9, 1983, Box 506C, Folder: HS Closures, Education Office Collection, ADRVC. See also Ridgely Ochs, "Plan to Close 3 Catholic Schools Sparks Angry

Dissent, Walkouts," *Newsday*, December 7, 1983, 3; Geraldine Baum, "Sadness at Maria Regina," *Newsday*, December 7, 1983, 3; Geraldine Baum, "Foes of School Closings Dig in Heels," *Newsday*, December 9, 1983, 3.

124. Michael Hanrahan, "Is Diocese Off the Mark?" editorial, *New York Daily News*, December 11, 1983.

125. Msgr. John F. Bennett, memo to Bishop John R. McGann, January 25, 1984, summarizing content of the January 13, 1984, Coalition for Catholic Education Rally, Box 506B, Folder: HS Closures, Education Office Collection, ADRVC.

126. Dick Ryan, "Parents Rally to Rap School Closings," *National Catholic Reporter*, January 27, 1984.

127. James Renton, "Parents and Students Rally to Defend Catholic Education," *Wanderer*, January 26, 1984, 1, 7.

128. John W. Geis of Valley Stream, "Letter to the Editor: A Change for the Better," *Newsday*, February 3, 1984; Fr. John T. Uris, "Catholic High School Situation," *Notre Dame News and Views* 14, no. 1 (February 1984): 1, Box 506B, Folder: HS Closures, Education Office Collection, ADRVC.

129. Robert Fresco, "High Schools Deal with Fewer Students," *Newsday*, December 27, 1983, 3; "Enrollment Drop Leads to 146 School Closings in N-S," *Long Island Business Newsweekly*, January 4–10, 1984.

130. Geraldine Baum, "Catholic School Loyalty Is Strong," *Newsday*, March 14, 1984, 3.

131. Fr. Francis Thomas Keenan, SM, Provincial of Society of Mary, letter to Bishop John R. McGann, January 11, 1984, Box 506B, Folder: HS Closures, Education Office Collection, ADRVC.

132. Desmond, letter to Carroll.

133. Msgr. Daniel S. Hamilton, memo to Fr. Charles W. Swiger, Director of the Office of Research and Planning, February 16, 1984, Box 506B, Folder: HS Closures, Education Office Collection, ADRVC.

134. Msgr. John F. Bennett, memo to Fr. Charles W. Swiger, February 13, 1984, Box 506B, Folder: HS Closures, Education Office Collection, ADRVC.

135. For more on parish closures, see John C. Seitz, *No Closure: Catholic Practice and Boston's Parish Shutdowns* (Cambridge, MA: Harvard University Press, 2011); Thomas Rzeznik, "The Church in the Changing City: Parochial Restructuring in the Archdiocese of Philadelphia in Historical Perspective," *U.S. Catholic Historian* 27, no. 4 (Fall 2009): 73–90.

136. Geraldine Baum, "Fight for Catholic Schools," *Newsday*, December 18, 1983, 1; and see Joe Calderone, "Bishop Firm on School Closings," *Newsday*, December 12, 1983, 3.

137. McGann, letter to Pio Laghi.

138. Renton, "Parents and Students Rally to Defend Catholic Education," 1, 7.

139. Ryan, "Parents Rally to Rap School Closings."

CHAPTER SEVEN

1. Dr. Hugh Carroll, interview by Sr. Joan de Lourdes Leonard, CSJ, n.d., transcript, p. 9, Box 226, Sr. Joan de Lourdes Leonard Collection (hereafter Leonard Collection), ADRVC.

2. Msgr. Charles Swiger, interview by Sr. Joan de Lourdes Leonard, CSJ, September 17, 1981, transcript, p. 16, Box 106, Leonard Collection, ADRVC; "LI School Tax Revolt," editorial, *The Tablet* 52, no. 14 (May 16, 1959): 15. For even broader attacks on federal and state taxes, see "Schools and Taxes," editorial, *Catholic News* 67, no. 42 (June 6, 1953): 12; "Rescue Taxpayers," editorial, *The Tablet* 50, no. 3 (March 2,

1957): 10; "Taxation a Menace to Families," editorial, *The Tablet* 52, no. 1 (February 14, 1959): 10.
3. Barbara Maertz, "Can We Afford Our Schools? No!!" *Our Parish* (November 1971): 17, Archives of Our Lady of Grace Parish, West Babylon, NY.
4. Matthew J. Streb and Brian Frederick, "The Myth of a Distinct Catholic Vote," in *Catholics and Politics: The Dynamic Tension Between Faith and Power*, ed. Kristen E. Heyer, Mark J. Rozell, and Michael A. Genovese (Washington, DC: Georgetown University Press, 2008), 93, 95.
5. Joshua M. Zeitz, *White Ethnic New York: Jews, Catholics, and the Shaping of Postwar Politics* (Chapel Hill: University of North Carolina Press, 2007), 2.
6. William B. Prendergast, *The Catholic Voter in American Politics: The Passing of the Democratic Monolith* (Washington, DC: Georgetown University Press, 1999), 117.
7. Bernie Bookbinder, *Long Island: People and Places, Past and Present* (New York: Harry N. Abrams, 1998), 210; Bernice Schultz Marshall, *Running Nassau County* (Hempstead, NY: Hempstead Sentinel, 1944), In addition to the three towns of Hempstead, North Hempstead, and Oyster Bay, the county also comprises two cities, Glen Cove and Long Beach.
8. Bookbinder, *Long Island*, 201, 212; Rosalyn Baxandall and Elizabeth Ewen, *Picture Windows: How the Suburbs Happened* (New York, NY: Basic Books, 2000), 129.
9. Jon C. Teaford, *Post-Suburbia: Government and Politics in Edge Cities* (Baltimore: Johns Hopkins University Press, 1997), 29.
10. James C. Shelland, "The County Executive: A Case Study of the Office in Nassau County" (PhD diss., New School for Social Research, 1975), 101; Taranto, *Kitchen Table Politics*, 52; Richard Polenberg, *One Nation Divisible: Class, Race, and Ethnicity in the United States Since 1938* (New York: Penguin, 1980), 138–39.
11. Shelland, "The County Executive," 100, 103; Taranto, *Kitchen Table Politics*, 52; Polenberg, *One Nation Divisible*, 138–39; Lillian Dudkiewicz-Clayman, "Life of the Party: Unions and the Making of the Moderate Republican Party in Nassau County, New York" (PhD diss., Rutgers University, 2019), 90; Mollie Keller, "Levittown and the Transformation of the Metropolis" (PhD diss., Univ. of Michigan, 1990), 197–202, 225; Baxandall and Ewen, *Picture Windows*, 129.
12. Bookbinder, *Long Island*, 236–37.
13. Taranto, *Kitchen Table Politics*, 52, 53.
14. Bookbinder, *Long Island*, 236–38; Alfonse D'Amato, *Power, Pasta and Politics: The World According to Senator Al D'Amato* (New York: Easton Press, 1995), 55; Dudkiewicz-Clayman, 15, 18. See also Herbert David Rosenbaum, "The Political Consequences of Suburban Growth: A Case Study of Nassau County, New York" (PhD diss., Columbia University, 1967); Keller, "Levittown and the Transformation of the Metropolis"; Marjorie Freeman Harrison, "Machine Politics Suburban Style: J. Russel Sprague and the Nassau County (N.Y.) Republican Party at Midcentury" (PhD diss., Columbia University, 2005).
15. Taranto, *Kitchen Table Politics*, 53.
16. Bookbinder, *Long Island*, 237; Dudkiewicz-Clayman, 144–45.
17. Dudkiewicz-Clayman, 16, 148.
18. Dudkiewicz-Clayman, 16, 183, 196; Taranto, *Kitchen Table Politics*, 53.
19. Kevin M. Schultz, *Tri-Faith America: How Catholics and Jews Held Postwar America to its Protestant Promise* (New York: Oxford University Press, 2011), 119.
20. Bruce J. Dierenfield, *The Battle over School Prayer: How Engel v. Vitale Changed America* (Lawrence: University Press of Kansas, 2007), 72–73. Dierenfield does not define

affiliation or provide source information for these statistics. For more on the relationship between suburban Protestants, Catholics, and Jews and more details on the fight over religion in public schools, see chapters 4 and 6 of Schultz, *Tri-Faith America*.

21. Dierenfield, *The Battle over School Prayer*, 81; Baxandall and Ewen, *Picture Windows*, 155; Polenberg, *One Nation Divisible*, 144.
22. William R. Donaldson, "Long Island Extravaganza in School Expenditures," *The Tablet* 50, no. 27 (August 17, 1957): 15, and 50, no. 28 (August 24, 1957): 15.
23. Holman Harvey, "Do School Children Need Costly Palaces," *The Tablet* 50, no. 38 (November 2, 1957): 12. And see responses: "Do Students Have Costly Palaces," *The Tablet* 50, no. 44 (December 14, 1957): 24; "Costly Palaces?" letters, *The Tablet* 50, no. 45 (December 21, 1957): 6.
24. "Reprimand for School Palaces," editorial, *The Tablet* 51, no. 37 (October 25, 1958): 10.
25. Dierenfield, *The Battle over School Prayer*, 74. The Herricks Union Free School District covered Herricks, Garden City Park, Manhasset Hills, Searingtown, North Hills, Williston Park, and Albertson,
26. "How to Save $930,000," editorial, *The Tablet* 51, no. 42 (November 29, 1958): 11.
27. Schultz, *Tri-Faith America*, 118, 119.
28. Dierenfield, *The Battle over School Prayer*, 77.
29. "Decalogue, Anti-Religion," editorial, *The Tablet* 51, no. 4 (March 8, 1958): 11.
30. "Urges Decalogue Display in Schools," letter, *The Tablet* 50, no. 52 (February 8, 1958): 6; Dierenfield, *The Battle over School Prayer*, 78. See also "Support for Commandments in Classrooms," *The Tablet* 51, no. 3 (March 1, 1958): 1; "Decalogue, Anti-Religion," 11. For the role that calls for "local control" in suburban school districts played in conservative politics, see Campbell F. Scribner, *The Fight for Local Control: Schools, Suburbs, and American Democracy* (Ithaca, NY: Cornell University Press, 2016).
31. "Well-Organized Anti-Christmas Drive Reported," *The Tablet* 51, no. 40 (November 15, 1958): 1; see also "Christmas in Public Schools," editorial, *The Tablet* 51, no. 44 (December 13, 1958): 14.
32. Dierenfield, *The Battle over School Prayer*, 79.
33. Kathleen Holscher, "'A Decision that Spits in the Face of Our History': Catholics and the Midcentury Fight Over Public Prayer and Bible Reading," *Catholic Historical Review* 102, no. 2 (Spring 2016): 340–68. For more on the Knights of Columbus and the Pledge of Allegiance, see Anthony Hatcher, "Adding God: Religious and Secular Press Framing in Response to the Insertion of 'Under God' in the Pledge of Allegiance," *Journal of Media and Religion* 7, no. 3 (2008): 170–89.
34. Butler, *God in Gotham*, 225.
35. Dierenfield, *The Battle over School Prayer*, 67; "New York Regents Suggest Prayer as Class Start," *Catholic News* 66, no. 16 (December 8, 1951): 1. The prayer read: "Almighty God we acknowledge our dependence on Thee and we beg Thy blessings upon us, our parents, our teachers, and our country"; Don Zirkel, "No Proof Found That Many Are Against Prayer," *The Tablet* 52, no. 3 (February 28, 1959): 1.
36. Dierenfield, *The Battle over School Prayer*, 68, 71, 81; "Liberals Favor Censorship But Only of Prayer," *The Tablet* 51, no. 51 (January 31, 1959): 1. Parents in Plainedge petitioned that their schools use the Regents Prayer in the fall of 1959 after it had been ruled constitutional by the lower courts, but the school board voted four to three to wait until the US Supreme Court had heard the appeals; "School Prayer in Plainedge," *The Tablet* 52, no. 37 (October 24, 1959): 10.

37. Dierenfield, *The Battle over School Prayer*, 80, 81, 106. The board received 2,361 letters in favor of using the Regents Prayer. Of the 4,009 signatories endorsing the prayer, over 80 percent came from the heavily Catholic neighborhoods of New Hyde Park and Williston Park, and just 1 percent came from heavily Jewish Roslyn Heights. Most of the eighteen civic, fraternal, business, and religious organizations that supported the prayer were from Williston Park.
38. Dierenfield, *The Battle over School Prayer*, 83.
39. Dierenfield, *The Battle over School Prayer*, 93–95, 103; "Liberals Favor Censorship but Only of Prayer," 1; Zirkel, "No Proof Found That Many Are Against Prayer," 1.
40. "High Court Sees Regents Prayer Constitutional," *The Tablet* 52, no. 28 (August 29, 1959): 1; "Recitation of Public School Prayer Upheld," *The Tablet* 53, no. 37 (October 22, 1960): 1.
41. Dierenfield, *The Battle over School Prayer*, 122, 128–29; "Regents' Prayer Decision," *The Tablet* 55, no. 10 (April 28, 1962): 8; "NY Regents Prayer Held Unconstitutional," *Long Island Catholic* 1, no. 9 (June 28, 1962): 1; "The Court Decision Effects Are Widespread," *Long Island Catholic* 1, no. 9 (June 28, 1962): 1. Chandler had helped win both the *Everson v. Board of Education* (1947) and *Zorach v. Clauson* (1952) cases at the US Supreme Court.
42. "Black Monday Decisions," *America* 107, no. 14 (July 7, 1962), cited in Holscher, "A Decision that Spits in the Face of Our History," 344.
43. "In God We Trust?" editorial, *The Tablet* 55, no. 21 (June 30, 1962): 12. See also "Now Who's Hysterical?" editorial, *The Tablet* 55, no. 22 (July 7, 1962): 10; "High Court Ban on School Prayer Said to Strike at Heart of US," *Catholic News* 77, no. 26 (June 30, 1962): 1.
44. Schultz, *Tri-Faith America*, 136–37; "Bishop Kellenberg's Statement," *Long Island Catholic* 1, no. 9 (June 28, 1962): 1.
45. "Poll Shows Parents Favor School Prayer," *Long Island Catholic* 1, no. 16 (August 23, 1962): 6; "Narrowness of Regents Prayer Case Cited by NCWC," *Long Island Catholic* 1, no. 10 (July 5, 1962): 13.
46. "What Now? The School Prayer Decision," *Long Island Catholic* 1, no. 20 (September 13, 1962): 12.
47. "Secularists Attempt to Broaden Decision," *Long Island Catholic* 1, no. 10 (July 5, 1962): 1.
48. "In God We Trust?," 12.
49. Holscher, "A Decisions that Spits in the Face of Our History," 346.
50. Dierenfield, *The Battle over School Prayer*, 134, 141, 147, 149, 153, 156.
51. Timothy Verhoeven, "'I Am Not a Religious Crackpot': School Prayer, the Becker Amendment, and Grassroots Mobilization in 1960s America," *Journal of Social History* 55, no. 3 (2022): 773, 770; "What about the Becker Amendment?" editorial, *Christianity Today* 8, no. 19 (June 19, 1964): 20.
52. Verhoeven, "I Am Not a Religious Crackpot," 774–75, 779. For more on Schlafly and conservative women see Donald T. Critchlow, *Phyllis Schlafly and Grassroots Conservatism: A Woman's Crusade* (Princeton, NJ: Princeton University Press, 2008); Michelle Nickerson, *Mothers of Conservatism: Women and the Postwar Right* (Princeton, NJ: Princeton University Press, 2012).
53. Robert Wuthnow, *The Restructuring of American Religion* (Princeton, NJ: Princeton University Press, 1988).
54. Verhoeven, "I Am Not a Religious Crackpot," 782; Schultz, *Tri-Faith America*, 136–37; Dierenfield, *Battle over School Prayer*, 153; Holscher, "A Decision that Spits in the Face of Our History," 345–46.

55. Verhoeven, "I Am Not a Religious Crackpot," 783–84.
56. For more on the culture wars in general, see Daniel T. Rodgers, *Age of Fracture* (Cambridge, MA: Harvard University Press, 2011); Andrew Hartman, *A War for the Soul of America: A History of the Culture Wars* (Chicago: University of Chicago Press, 2015); James Davidson Hunter, *Culture Wars: The Struggle to Define America* (New York: Basic Books, 1991). For more on the place of educational debates in the culture wars, see Jonathan Zimmerman, *Whose America? Culture Wars in the Public Schools* (Cambridge, MA: Harvard University Press, 2002).
57. Henrik N. Dullea, *Charter Revision in the Empire State: The Politics of New York's 1967 Constitutional Convention* (Albany, NY: Rockefeller Institute Press, 1997), 219; John Cooney, *American Pope: The Life and Times of Francis Cardinal Spellman* (New York: Times Books, 1984), 310.
58. Sr. Joan de Lourdes Leonard, CSJ, *Richly Blessed: The Diocese of Rockville Centre, 1957–1990* (Marceline, MO: Walsworth Publishing, 1991), 90; Fr. Patrick E. Shanahan, Superintendent of Schools, letter to the Teachers of the Diocesan High Schools, November 24, 1971, Box 506B, File: High School Closures, Education Department Collection, ADRVC.
59. Holscher, "A Decisions that Spits in the Face of Our History," 354–55.
60. Neil G. McCluskey, SJ, made the case for Catholic schools in *Catholic Viewpoint on Education* (Garden City, NY: Doubleday, 1959). For a small sampling of the dozens of articles making this case in the Catholic press, from the 1940s through the 1970s, see "Catholic Schools Save Taxpayers $318,146,281," *The Tablet* 38, no. 28 (September 7, 1946): 2; "375,000,000 Saved Taxpayers Annually by Catholic Schools," *Catholic News* 62, no. 38 (May 15, 1948): 1; "Catholic Schools Save US Taxpayers $2.7 Billion a Year," *The Tablet* 54, no. 5 (March 11, 1961): 12; "Taxpayers Save Billions on US Catholic Schools," *Long Island Catholic* 1, no. 42 (February 14, 1963): 3. In Joanne Golding, SP, "State Aid to Nonpublic Schools: A Legal-Historical Overview," *Journal of Church and State* 19 (1977) see charts on pages 238–40 for the "Estimated Tax Savings for Public Schools by Virtue of Operation of Roman Catholic Parochial Schools" in each of the fifty states in school years 1969–70 and 1975–76.
61. Timothy Walch, *Parish School: American Catholic Parochial Education from Colonial Times to the Present* (Washington, DC: National Catholic Educational Association, 2003), 171.
62. Lynne Frederikke Zimmerman, "A Modern Religious Controversy: A Case Study of the Blaine Amendment at the 1967 New York State Constitutional Convention" (MA thesis, Columbia University, 1969), 1, 3; Harold A. Buetow, *Of Singular Benefit: The Story of Catholic Education in the United States* (New York: Macmillan, 1970), 157–58. For more on the nativist history of the Blaine Amendments, see Ray Allen Billington, *The Protestant Crusade, 1800–1860: A Study in the Origins of American Nativism* (New York: Macmillan, 1938); Philip Hamburger, *Separation of Church and State* (Cambridge, MA: Harvard University Press, 2004). For more on the history of New York's Blaine Amendment prior to 1968 see Harold A. Buetow, "Historical Perspectives of New York's 1967 Constitutional Convention and Article XI, Section 3 (The 'Blaine' or 'Know Nothing' Amendment)," *Catholic Educational Review* 65, no. 3 (March 1, 1967): 145–75; Charles E. Rice, "The New York State Constitution and Aid to Church-Related Schools," *Catholic Lawyer* 12 (Autumn 1966): 272–329. For a complete history of New York's 1967 State Constitutional Convention, see Dullea, *Charter Revision in the Empire State*.
63. Zimmerman, "A Modern Religious Controversy," 8.

64. "Supreme Court Gets Bus Issue," *The Tablet* 52, no. 9 (April 11, 1959): 8. In its 1947 *Everson v. Board of Education* decision the Supreme Court ruled 5–4 that a New Jersey law allowing public expense to pay for buses to parochial schools was constitutional; see Dierenfield, *The Battle over School Prayer*, 47.
65. "Passage of School Bus Bill Urged by Dem Leader in Albany," *Catholic News* 75, no. 9 (March 5, 1960): 13; "Sen. Speno Bill Would Modernize Pupil Transportation," *The Tablet* 51, no. 51 (January 31, 1959): 1.
66. "Speno Bus Bill Is Passed," *The Tablet* 53, no. 7 (March 26, 1960): 1; "5 Public School Leaders Favor Speno Bus Bill," *The Tablet* 53, no. 10 (April 16, 1960): 3; "Speno Bus Bill Is Approved," *The Tablet* 53, no. 13 (May 7, 1960): 1; "Governor Signs School Bus Bill for All Pupils," *Catholic News* 75, no. 18 (May 7, 1960): 1.
67. "Unbiased Book Aid Backed by CEF," *Catholic News* 80, no. 9 (March 4, 1965): 1; "Both Houses of NY State Pass Textbook Bill," *Catholic News* 81, no. 21 (May 26, 1966): 1; "Textbook Loans Win Approval with State Legislature," *Catholic News* 81, no. 27 (July 7, 1966): 1.
68. "Child Benefit Theory May Seal Fate of Blaine Amendment," *Catholic News* 82, no. 23 (June 8, 1967): 1. In 1982 Msgr. Edgar McCarren who had served as Rockville Centre's superintendent of schools from 1957 to 1965 evaluated that New York had "the best legislation in the country" for support of nonpublic schools; McCarren interview, 8.
69. Dullea, *Charter Revision in the Empire State*, 219.
70. Zimmerman, "A Modern Religious Controversy," 71.
71. Cooney, *American Pope*, 312; Andrew M. Greeley, "Twisting the Evidence," *Long Island Catholic* 17, no. 5 (June 1, 1978): 31.
72. Zimmerman, "A Modern Religious Controversy," 33, 78; Buetow, *Of Singular Benefit*, 334. For more on CEF, see Russell Shaw, "CEF: They'd Rather Fight," *The Sign* 45, no. 4 (November 1965): 13–16. The New York State Catholic Conference had encouraged the convening of a state constitutional convention as early as September 1965. Jack Balinsky provides a helpful summary of the committee's involvement in the 1967 convention in "A History of the New York State Catholic Conference, 1916–1968," https://jackbalinsky.org/uncover-the-history/a-history-of-the-new-york-state-catholic-conference-1916-1968.
73. Fr. Patrick Shanahan, interview by Sr. Joan de Lourdes Leonard, CSJ, January 22, 1982 (hereafter Shanahan interview), transcript, p. 16, Box 106, Leonard Collection, ADRVC; Zimmerman, "A Modern Religious Controversy," 30, 37. Shanahan noted that from Long Island, all but two of the delegates were Republicans and that Catholic education officials had worked with them on repeal.
74. Zimmerman, "A Modern Religious Controversy," 36. When the convention opened on April 4, 1967, Cardinal Spellman was present to give the invocation; Cooney, *American Pope*, 311.
75. Zimmerman, "A Modern Religious Controversy," 33, 78; Cooney, *American Pope*, 312.
76. Zimmerman, "A Modern Religious Controversy," 69; James F. Clarity, "Albany Delegates on the Value of the Constitutional Convention," *New York Times*, August 20, 1967, 76; Dullea, *Charter Revision in the Empire State*, 231.
77. For examples, see "Jewish Units Fight Blaine," *Long Island Catholic* 6, no. 7 (June 15, 1967): 1; "LI Minister for Blaine Repeal," *Long Island Catholic* 6, no. 7 (June 15, 1967): 1; "Protestant Weekly Seeks Blaine Repeal," *Long Island Catholic* 6, no. 15 (August 10, 1967): 1.

78. Richard L. Madden, "Foes of State Aid to Church Pupils Beaten in Albany," *New York Times*, August 16, 1967, 1; "Stage Set for Full Blaine Repeal," *Catholic News* 82, no. 32 (August 10, 1967): 1; "Delegates Vote 130–48 to Drop Blaine," *Catholic News* 82, no. 33 (August 17, 1967): 1;
79. Shanahan interview, 17.
80. Zimmerman, "A Modern Religious Controversy," 74; "G.O.P. to Urge a Separate Vote on School Aid at Charter Parley" *New York Times*, August 13, 1967, 55.
81. "Home Rule Powers Seen Abridged," *Long Island Catholic* 6, no. 20 (September 14, 1967): 14; and see "Debates Continue in Home Rule Dilemma," *Long Island Catholic* 6, no. 4 (May 25, 1967): 15.
82. Shanahan interview, 17; see also "Blaine's Fate Now Up to NY Voters," *Catholic News* 82, no. 34 (August 24, 1967): 1; "Con-Con Submits Single Package to the Electorate," *Long Island Catholic* 6, no. 22 (September 28, 1967): 23. The NYSCC had advised against a single ballot proposition for the referendum but when Travia was insistent Spellman refused to press what had become a partisan contention: Balinsky, "A History of the New York State Catholic Conference," 95; Dullea, *Charter Revision in the Empire State*, 323.
83. Zimmerman, "A Modern Religious Controversy," 14; Thomas P. Ronan, "2 Groups Support School-Aid Ban," *New York Times*, August 12, 1967, 23; Madden, "Foes of State Aid to Church Pupils Beaten in Albany," 1.
84. "Blaine Removal Would Curtail Rise in Non-Public School Costs," *Catholic News* 82, no. 25 (June 22, 1967): 1; Msgr. Edgar P. McCarren, "Central Problem of Catholic Education Today," *Catholic News* 82, no. 37 (September 14, 1967): 2. See also "Charter's Proposed Costs Deflated," *Long Island Catholic* 6, no. 24 (October 12, 1967): 14; "Forecast of New Charter's Costs Called Scare Tactics," *Catholic News* 82, no. 41 (September 21, 1967): 2; "Proposed Constitution Seen Helping Taxpayer's Pocketbooks," *Long Island Catholic* 6, no. 24 (October 12, 1967): 14.
85. Msgr. Edgar P. McCarren, "How Will Blaine Repeal Affect Public Schools," *Catholic News* 82, no. 38 (September 21, 1967): 2; McCarren, "Effect of Competition on the Public Schools," *Catholic News* 82, no. 39 (September 28, 1967): 2.
86. Msgr. Edgar P. McCarren, "Do Catholic Schools Really Promote Segregation," *Catholic News* 82, no. 40 (October 5, 1967): 2; and see "Parochial School Aid Linked to Integration," *Long Island Catholic* 6, no. 9 (June 29, 1967): 2. Suburban developments were more highly segregated but as the Diocese of Rockville Centre reported to the Vatican in 1982, "the population of the Catholic schools" on Long Island reflected "the same minority make-up as the general population" in the area; see *Diocese of Rockville Centre Quinquennial Report, 1978–1982*, X (5), Box 278: Diocesan Reports, Leonard Collection, ADRVC.
87. Msgr. Edgar P. McCarren, "Are Catholic Schools Really Divisive?," *Catholic News* 82, no. 41 (October 12, 1967): 2.
88. "Proposed Charter Will Aid Suburban Taxpayer," *Catholic News* 82, no. 44 (November 2, 1967): 1. During the summer of 1967 some 159 riots or uprisings had occurred among African Americans in cities across the nation, including most famously in Detroit (July 23–28) and Newark (July 12–17). See Malcolm McLaughlin, *The Long Hot Summer of 1967: Urban Rebellion in America* (New York: Palgrave Macmillan, 2014).
89. "LI Catholic Scores Another First," *Long Island Catholic* 6, no. 9 (June 29, 1967): 1.
90. "New Constitution," editorial, *Long Island Catholic* 6, no. 26 (October 26, 1967): 10. Still, the paper attempted to fairly outline the arguments in favor of and against the

new charter for readers to make an information decision: "Countdown on the State Constitution," *Long Island Catholic* 6, no. 26 (October 26, 1967): 14–15; "New Constitution . . . Pros and Cons," *Long Island Catholic* 6, no. 26 (November 2, 1967): 14–15.

91. Section III, *Catholic News* 82, no. 44 (November 2, 1967); "The Voters Decide," editorial, *Catholic News* 82, no. 44 (November 2, 1967): 8; and see "More Light, Less Heat, Less Scare," editorial, *Catholic News* 82, no. 43 (October 26, 1967): 1.
92. "Keep Church-State Separation," editorial, *New York Times*, August 14, 1967, 30. The Associated Press conducted a survey of the city's daily newspapers on October 19, 1967; Cooney, *American Pope*, 312.
93. See "Citizens for Educational Freedom" brochure and member registration form, n.d., Box 6 Miscellaneous, Archives of St. Frances de Chantal Parish, Wantagh, NY.
94. "Urge Intensified Blaine Repeal Fight as 15,000 Attend CEF Rally," *Catholic News* 83, no. 40 (October 5, 1967): 1; Balinsky, "A History of the New York State Catholic Conference, 1916–1968," 95; Cooney, *American Pope*, 317.
95. Cooney, *American Pope*, 311–13; Dullea, *Charter Revision in the Empire State*, 336.
96. Zimmerman, "A Modern Religious Controversy," 23; James F. Clarity, "Charter's Defeat Is Now Expected by Top Democrats," *New York Times*, November 4, 1967, 1.
97. "Critical Questions for the Church in NY State," editorial, *Long Island Catholic* 6, no. 29 (November 16, 1967): 10.
98. Msgr. Robert Emmet Fagan, interview by Sr. Joan de Lourdes Leonard, CSJ, September 4, 1981 (hereafter Fagan interview), transcript, pp. 19–20, Box 226, Leonard Collection, ADRVC; and see "Debates Planned on Aid to Non-Public Schools," *Long Island Catholic* 6, no. 3 (May 18, 1967): 3. In 1967 St. Aidan Parish in Williston Park ran adult education sessions on "Current Issues for the Layman." One six-week session addressed "Government in Private Education" and included a debate on the Blaine Amendment between Joe Fox of the Diocese of Rockville Centre's Education Department, and parishioner Tom Ford, a representative of the American Civil Liberties Union; "Adult Education Courses Emphasized by Parishes," *Long Island Catholic* 6, no. 22 (September 28, 1967): 39.
99. Shanahan interview, 17, 20.
100. Fagan interview, 19–20, 21.
101. "Charter Voted Down, Ban on Blaine Faces State Legislature," *Catholic News* 82, no. 45 (November 9, 1967): 1. For a complete vote tally by borough and county, see "Tally of Ballots on Statewide Issues and for New Jersey, Suburban, and Local Posts," *New York Times*, November 9, 1967, 30.
102. Sydney H. Schanberg, "Charter Vote 3-1," *New York Times*, November 8, 1967, 1.
103. Bernie Bookbinder, "Constitution Gets a 3-1 Drubbing," *New York Newsday*, November 8, 1967, 1.
104. Margo Dioguardi of Glen Cove, a mother of five Catholic school students, said that she opposed Blaine and hoped for its ultimate repeal but voted against the charter because she "resented being given the whole Constitution in a package deal"; "Repeal Blaine," letters, *Long Island Catholic* 6, no. 32 (December 7, 1967): 10.
105. Bookbinder, "Constitution Gets a 3-1 Drubbing," 1.
106. "Independent Voter Speaks," letters, *Long Island Catholic* 6, no. 33 (December 14, 1967): 10.
107. Fagan interview, 21.
108. "Critical Questions for the Church in NY State," 10.
109. Fr. John B. Sheerin, CSP, "Ecumenism Wounded in the Battle for NY," *Long Island Catholic* 6, no. 29 (November 16, 1967): 10; Richard Mauter, "Decision to Emphasize Blaine Opens Credibility Gap," *Long Island Catholic* 6, no. 29 (November 16, 1967): 1, 14.

110. "L.I. Laymen for Dialogue" and "Conservative Comments," letters, *Long Island Catholic* 6, no. 31 (November 30, 1967): 11.
111. In a letter to a constituent, State Senator Edward Speno stated: "I do not honestly feel that the proposed new Constitution was defeated only because of the Blaine Amendment but because of other controversial aspects"; State Senator Edward J. Speno, letter to Stanton Schneider of the State University of New York at Albany, April 2, 1970, Box 41, Folder 11: Education, Blaine Amendment, 1970–1971, Edward J. Speno Papers, Long Island Studies Institute Collections, Library Special Collections Department, Hofstra University, Long Island, NY.
112. "Self-Flagellation Necessary?" letters, *Long Island Catholic* 6, no. 32 (December 7, 1967): 10.
113. "Need for Education," letters, *Long Island Catholic* 6, no. 32 (December 7, 1967): 10. An October 19, 1967, article in the Diocese of Albany's newspaper celebrated the fact that the fundamentals of all ten of NYSCC's propositions regarding matters of health and welfare, education, citizen boards, housing and urban development, taxation, voluntarism, human rights, and collective bargaining had made their way into the draft constitution (Balinsky, "A History of the New York State Catholic Conference," 97).
114. Dullea, *Charter Revision in the Empire State*, 389. See also chapters 5 and 6 in Scribner, *The Fight for Local Control*.
115. Clarity, "Charter's Defeat Is Now Expected by Top Democrats," 1; Schanberg, "Charter Vote 3-1," 1 ; "Package Full of Defeat," editorial, *Catholic News* 82, no. 45 (November 9, 1967): 10 ; "Why the Resounding No?" *Long Island Catholic* 6, no. 29 (November 16, 1967): 14.
116. A week after the charter was voted down Spellman entered the Mayo Clinic and he died December 2, 1967. John Cooney states that with the defeat of the new charter "Spellman's power was broken" and "something seemed to have broken in the Cardinal." In reality, Spellman had not been in good health for some time (Cooney, *American Pope*, 325, 319).
117. Balinsky, "A History of the New York State Catholic Conference," 98.
118. Bookbinder, "Constitution Gets a 3-1 Drubbing," 1.
119. Greeley, "Twisting the Evidence," 31.
120. For more on taxpayer revolts see David T. Bieto, *Taxpayers in Revolt: Tax Resistance During the Great Depression* (Chapel Hill: University of North Carolina Press, 1989); David O. Sears and Jack Citrin, *The Tax Revolt: Something for Nothing in California* (Cambridge, MA: Harvard University Press, 1985); Isaac William Martin, *The Permanent Tax Revolt: How the Property Tax Transformed American Politics* (Palo Alto, CA: Stanford University Press, 2008).
121. Buetow, *Of Singular Benefit*, 283; Leonard Buder, "Education's Cost in Suburbs Stirs Growing Concern," *New York Times*, September 4, 1967, 1.
122. Agis Salpukas, "Nassau," *New York Times*, September 4, 1967, 22.
123. Buetow, *Of Singular Benefit*, 287–88; "Catholic Schools: A Fiscal Crisis," *Time*, March 28, 1969, 42–43.
124. George J. Marlin, *The American Catholic Voter: 200 Years of Political Impact* (South Bend, IN: St. Augustine's Press, 2004), 261, 276; Zeitz, *White Ethnic New York*, 140.
125. Shelland, "The County Executive," 109. In Nassau County in 1964 Republicans outnumbered Democrats 338,074 to 183,693.
126. Marlin, *The American Catholic Voter*, 267–68, 276.

127. Marlin, *The American Catholic Voter*, 278.
128. Zeitz, *White Ethnic New York*, 4, 3, 147, 155.
129. Prendergast, *The Catholic Voter in American Politics*, 155, 224; "Nation Must Aid Whites to Prevent Race Polarization, Catholic Leaders tell Nixon," *Long Island Catholic* 9, no. 17 (August 27, 1970): 3; Zeitz, *White Ethnic New York*, 143, 159.
130. Lillian S. Curley of Rockville Centre, "White Middle-Class a Whipping Boy," letter, *Long Island Catholic* 6, no. 52 (April 25, 1968): 10.
131. Mary White of Carle Place "The Abused Middle Class," letter, *Long Island Catholic* 8, no. 15 (August 7, 1969): 10.
132. "White Ethnic Groups Said to Be Forgotten," *Long Island Catholic* 9, no. 51 (April 15, 1971): 1.
133. David Paul Kuhn, *The Hardhat Riot: Nixon, New York City, and the Dawn of the White Working-Class Revolution* (New York: Oxford University Press, 2020), 250–51.
134. "The Catholic Vote: Big City Ethnics May Be Victory Key," *Long Island Catholic* 11, no. 10 (July 6, 1972): 1.
135. Laurence J. McAndrews, *What They Wished For: American Catholics and American Presidents, 1960–2004* (Athens: University of Georgia Press, 2013), 94, 120–21; Prendergast, *The Catholic Voter in American Politics*, 160.
136. Thomas J. Carty, "White House Outreach to Catholics," in Heyer, Rozell, and Genovese, *Catholics and Politics*, 183.
137. Prendergast, *The Catholic Voter in American Politics*, 156.
138. McAndrews, *What They Wished For*, 106.
139. Prendergast, *The Catholic Voter in American Politics*, 160.
140. McAndrews, *What They Wished For*, 123; Timothy Stanley, *The Crusader: The Life and Tumultuous Times of Pat Buchanan* (New York: St. Martin's Press, 2012), 67.
141. Prendergast, *The Catholic Voter in American Politics*, 160–61.
142. Campaign ad: "Nixon Reelection," *Long Island Catholic* 11, no. 26 (October 26, 1972): 14.
143. Polenberg, *One Nation Divisible*, 248–49; Marlin, *The American Catholic Voter*, 283; Carty, "White House Outreach to Catholics," 184.
144. Zeitz, *White Ethnic New York*, 194; and Marlin, *The American Catholic Voter*, 283.
145. Prendergast, *The Catholic Voter in American Politics*, 161; Marlin, *The American Catholic Voter*, 282; and Carty, "White House Outreach to Catholics," 183.
146. Annelise Orleck, *Rethinking American Women's Activism* (New York: Routledge, 2022), 57; Elaine Tyler May, *Homeward Bound: American Families in the Cold War* (New York: Basic Books, 2008).
147. For more on Schlafly, see Critchlow, *Phyllis Schlafly and Grassroots Conservatism*; Emily Suzanne Johnson, *This Is Our Message: Women's Leadership in the New Christian Right* (New York: Oxford University Press, 2019).
148. Andrew E. Busch, *Reagan's Victory: The Presidential Election of 1980 and the Rise of the Right* (Lawrence: University Press of Kansas, 2005), 81; Seth Dowland, *Family Values and the Rise of the Christian Right* (Philadelphia: University of Pennsylvania Press, 2015), 145; Orleck, *Rethinking American Women's Activism*, 199.
149. Taranto, *Kitchen Table Politics*, 51.
150. Taranto, *Kitchen Table Politics*, 52, 54.
151. Kenneth A. Briggs, "Carter and the Bishops," *New York Times*, September 3, 1976, A9; James M. Naughton, "Bishops 'Encouraged' by Ford on Abortion," *New York Times*, September 11, 1976, 1.

152. Carter campaign ad, *Long Island Catholic* 15, no. 26 (October 21, 1976): 14.
153. Andrew Greeley, "Catholics and Carter," *Long Island Catholic* 15, no. 18 (August 26, 1976): 6.
154. Campaign ad, "President Ford Sees the Family the Way Most Families Do," *Long Island Catholic* 15, no. 25 (October 14, 1976): 9.
155. "President Ford Sees the Family," 9; campaign ad: "To Get Aid for Parochial Schools, It Will Take a Few More People Like President Ford," *Long Island Catholic* 15, no. 26 (October 21, 1976): 10.
156. Marlin, *The American Catholic Voter*, 291–92.
157. Prendergast, *The Catholic Voter in American Politics*, 175.
158. Godfrey Hodgson, *The Gentleman from New York: Daniel Patrick Moynihan, a Biography* (Boston: Houghton Mifflin, 2000), 270.
159. Moynihan campaign ad, "Moynihan—U.S. Senator," *Long Island Catholic* 15, no. 20 (September 9, 1976): 8.
160. "Misleading," editorial; Arlene Doyle, "Mr. Moynihan's Record"; and Mrs. Patricia Corry, "The Moynihan Ad," *Long Island Catholic* 15, no. 23 (September 30, 1976): 6.
161. Hodgson, *The Gentleman from New York*, 270.
162. Buckley campaign ad, "Let's Look at the Record," *Long Island Catholic* 15, no. 27 (October 26, 1976): 5.
163. Hodgson, *The Gentleman from New York*, 272; Patrick Andelic, "Daniel Patrick Moynihan, the 1976 New York Senate Race, and the Struggle to Define American Liberalism," *Historical Journal* 57, no. 4 (December 2014): 1111–13.
164. Daniel Patrick Moynihan, "Government and the Ruin of Private Education," in *Counting Our Blessings* (Boston: Little, Brown, 1980).
165. Lawrence J. McAndrews, "Constricting Change: Jimmy Carter and Tuition Tax Credits," *Records of the American Catholic Historical Society of Philadelphia* 109, no. 3/4 (Fall-Winter 1998): 65–111.
166. Moynihan, "Government and the Ruin of Private Education," 236, 241; and see "Bullseye," editorial, *Long Island Catholic* 17, no. 51 (April 26, 1979): 6.
167. Kenneth L. Woodward, "Born Again! The Year of the Evangelical," *Newsweek*, October 25, 1976, 68. See Steven P. Miller, *The Age of Evangelicalism: America's Born-Again Years* (New York: Oxford University Press, 2014).
168. Most histories have understood abortion as the issue that galvanized evangelical political activism and the formation of the Religious Right. Randall Balmer and Anthea Butler have argued that racism was the crucial catalyst: Randall Balmer, *Bad Faith: Race and the Rise of the Religious Right* (Grand Rapids, MI: Eerdmans, 2021), 37, 45; Anthea Butler, *White Evangelical Racism: The Politics of Morality in America* (Chapel Hill: University of North Carolina Press, 2021), 58, 65–68.
169. May, *Homeward Bound*, xvii–xxvi; Dowland, *Family Values and the Rise of the Christian Right*, 119; Ziad W. Munson, *The Making of Pro-life Activists: How Social Movement Mobilization Works* (Chicago: University of Chicago Press, 2008), 85–86.
170. Dowland, *Family Values and the Rise of the Christian Right*, 111, 124.
171. Busch, *Reagan's Victory*, 81; Dowland, *Family Values and the Rise of the Christian Right*, 127.
172. Donald Granberg and James Burlison, "The Abortion Issue in the 1980 Elections," *Family Planning Perspectives* 15, no. 5 (1983): 232.
173. Tom Buckley, "After Javits the GOP Turns Right with D'Amato," *New York Times*, October 19, 1980, A41; Taranto, *Kitchen Table Politics*, 190.
174. Busch, *Reagan's Victory*, 106.
175. Taranto, *Kitchen Table Politics*, 190.

176. Frank Lynn, "Nassau Leads as Suburbs Gain Power in State," *New York Times*, December 21, 1980, A1. See also Lynn, "For Reagan and D'Amato, Island Is Likely Key to State," *New York Times*, November 2, 1980, LI1; Lynn, "New York GOP Sees Power Shift Within the Party," *New York Times*, November 6, 1980, A1.
177. Buckley, "After Javits the GOP Turns Right with D'Amato," A41.
178. Donald P. Baker, "Introducing the Distinguished Senator-Elect from New York," *Washington Post*, December 26, 1980, B1; Buckley, "After Javits the GOP Turns Right with D'Amato," A41.
179. D'Amato, *Power, Pasta and Politics*, 73.
180. Buckley, "After Javits the GOP Turns Right with D'Amato," A41.
181. D'Amato, *Power, Pasta and Politics*, 96, 99–100.
182. Taranto, *Kitchen Table Politics*, 210: "D'Amato took New York City (5,100 votes) and the upstate counties (2,000 votes) rather narrowly, but won a decisive victory on Long Island (63,000 votes, with 46,000 votes coming from his home county of Nassau)"; Buckley, "After Javits the GOP Turns Right with D'Amato," A41.
183. Ward Morehouse III, "D'Amato win in New York: No More 'Al Who?'" *Christian Science Monitor*, November 7, 1980, 5.
184. Busch, *Reagan's Victory*, 127; Marlin, *The American Catholic Voter*, 296.
185. Lynn, "For Reagan and D'Amato, Island Is Likely Key to State," LI1; Lynn, "New York GOP Sees Power Shift Within the Party," A1.
186. Taranto, *Kitchen Table Politics*, 213.
187. Prendergast, *The Catholic Voter in American Politics*, 178, 185.
188. Sara Diamond, *Not by Politics Alone: The Enduring Influence of the Christian Right* (New York: Guilford Press, 1998), 69.
189. Hodgson, *The Gentleman from New York*, 300–301, 326.
190. Carty, "White House Outreach to Catholics," 182, 186–87; Marlin, *The American Catholic Voter*, 299.
191. Lindsey Gruson, "Political Memo: D'Amato's Persistence Shows His Party's Shift," *New York Times*, March 1, 1992, 26.
192. "Election of 1980 Workshop Views a Range of Issues," *Long Island Catholic* 19, no. 22 (September 18, 1980): 1.
193. McAndrews, *What They Wished For*, 270.
194. Heyer, Rozell, and Genovese, *Catholics and Politics*, 6.
195. Streb and Frederick, "The Myth of a Distinct Catholic Vote," 93.
196. Heyer, Rozell, and Genovese, *Catholics and Politics*, 5; Prendergast, *The Catholic Voter in American Politics*, 27.
197. McAndrews, *What They Wished For*, 223, 270.

EPILOGUE

1. Andrew Greeley, "Mass Attendance Decline," *Long Island Catholic* 12, no. 29 [13, no. 28] (November 22, 1973): 2.
2. Carol Speranza, "LI Pastors Disagree with Survey on Mass Attendance," *Long Island Catholic* 12, no. 29 [13, no. 28] (November 22, 1973): 1–2.
3. Fr. John B. Sheerin, CSP, "The Drop in Sunday Mass Attendance," *Long Island Catholic* 12, no. 31 (December 6, 1973): 7.
4. Michael Hout and Andrew Greeley, "The Center Doesn't Hold: Church Attendance in the United States, 1940–1984," *American Sociological Review* 52, no. 3 (1987): 332, cited in Stephen Bullivant, *Mass Exodus: Catholic Disaffiliation in Britain and America Since Vatican II* (Oxford: Oxford University Press, 2019), 124.

5. Andrew Greeley, "It Looks Like a Catastrophe," *Long Island Catholic* 14, no. 24 (October 16, 1975): 6.
6. Andrew Greeley, "Church Attendance Down," *Long Island Catholic* 16, no. 38 (January 26, 1978): 6.
7. Center for Applied Research in the Apostolate, "Frequently Requested Church Statistics," CARA, 2023, https://cara.georgetown.edu/faqs.
8. Bullivant, *Mass Exodus*, 124 citing Rodney Stark and Charles Y. Glock, *American Piety: The Nature of Religious Commitment* (Berkeley: University of California Press, 1968), 195.
9. Andrew Greeley, "Return to the Churches," *Long Island Catholic* 17, no. 50 (April 19, 1979): 6.
10. Stephen Bullivant, *Nonverts: The Making of Ex-Christian America* (New York: Oxford University Press, 2022), 179, 187–88.
11. Bullivant, *Nonverts*, 187. For more on disaffiliation and the "nones," see Christian Smith and Patricia Snell, *Souls in Transition: The Religious and Spiritual Lives of Emerging Adults* (New York: Oxford University Press, 2009); Ryan Burge, *The Nones: Where They Came From, Who They Are, and Where They Are Going* (Minneapolis, MN: Fortress Press, 2021); Jim Davis, Michael Graham, and Ryan Burge, *The Great Dechurching: Who's Leaving, Why Are They Going, and What Will It Take to Bring Them Back?* (Grand Rapids, MI: Zondervan, 2023).
12. Bullivant, *Mass Exodus*, 195, citing Benedict XVI, "Responses of His Holiness Pope Benedict XVI to the Questions Posed by the Bishops" (2008).
13. Bullivant, *Mass Exodus*, 121, 208; Robert Wuthnow, *After the Baby Boomers: How Twenty- and Thirty-Somethings Are Shaping the Future of American Religion* (Princeton, NJ: Princeton University Press, 2007), 136–56.
14. Bullivant, *Mass Exodus*, 127, 70.
15. Fr. Patrick F. Shanahan, "The Church's Quest for Vocations to the Religious Life," *Long Island Catholic* 10, no. 49 (April 6, 1972): 10.
16. "Vocations Crisis," editorial, *Long Island Catholic* 11, no. 47 (March 29, 1973): 6.
17. "Catholic School Enrollment Shows Drastic Drop," *Long Island Catholic* 7, no. 44 (February 27, 1969): 20; "School Enrollment Down, Minority Numbers Increase," *Long Island Catholic* 23, no. 51 (April 18, 1985): 16.
18. Bullivant, *Mass Exodus*, 208–9; Christian Smith, Kyle Longest, Johnathan Hill, and Kari Christofferson, *Young Catholic America: Emerging Adults In, Out of, and Gone from the Church* (Oxford: Oxford University Press, 2014), 15.
19. Bullivant, *Nonverts*, 88.
20. Bullivant, *Mass Exodus*, 70; Robert D. Putnam and David E. Campbell, *American Grace: How Religion Divides and Unites Us* (New York: Simon and Schuster, 2010), 100–133; Michael Hout and Claude S. Fischer, "Explaining Why More Americans Have No Religious Preference: Political Backlash and Generational Succession, 1987–2012," *Sociological Science* 1 (2014): 423–37; David E. Campbell, Geoffrey C. Layman, and John C. Green, *Secular Surge: A New Fault Line in American Politics* (New York: Cambridge University Press, 2020).
21. Bullivant, *Nonverts*, 111.
22. Bullivant, *Mass Exodus*, 66, 70, 195; William J. Byron and Charles Zech, "Why They Left," *America* 206, no. 14 (April 2012): 17–23.
23. Bullivant, *Mass Exodus*, 195.
24. For early research on clergy sexual abuse see Jason Berry, *Lead Us Not into Temptation: Catholic Priests and the Sexual Abuse of Children* (New York: Doubleday, 1992); Richard

Sipe, *Sex, Priests, and Power: Anatomy of a Crisis* (New York: Brunner-Routledge, 1995); Philip Jenkins, *Priests and Pedophiles: Anatomy of a Contemporary Crisis* (Oxford: Oxford University Press, 1996). Scholarship from the post-Boston period of the abuse crisis includes Joseph P. Chinnici, *When Values Collide: The Catholic Church, Sexual Abuse, and the Challenges of Leadership* (New York: Orbis Books, 2010).

25. Mark M. Gray, "CARA Study Indicates Decline in Abuse Reports: Is The Worst Behind Us?," *America* 219, no. 6 (September 5, 2018): 1–4. And see John Jay College of Criminal Justice, *The Nature and Scope of Sexual Abuse of Minors by Catholic Priests and Deacons in the United States, 1950–2002* (Washington, DC: United States Conference of Catholic Bishops, 2004); John Jay College of Criminal Justice, *The Causes and Context of Sexual Abuse of Minors by Catholic Priests in the United States, 1950–2010* (Washington, DC: United States Conference of Catholic Bishops, 2011), 2.

26. Gray, "CARA Study Indicates Decline in Abuse Reports," 1–4.

27. Fr. Andrew P. Millar confessed to sodomizing a learning disabled fifteen-year-old boy in the bathroom of a beach pavilion at Tobey Beach on May 7, 2000, and was sentenced to a prison term of three years; "Retired L.I. Priest Is Charged with Sodomy Involving Teenager," *New York Times*, May 17, 2000, B-2; Rita Ciolli, "Group Wants Bishop Disciplined," *Newsday*, February 26, 2003, A-19.

28. Kevin J. Jones, "Reckoning with History, Long Island Diocese Names 101 Clergy Accused of Sex Abuse," *Catholic News Agency*, May 3, 2021, https://www.catholicnewsagency.com/news/247502/reckoning-with-history-long-island-diocese-names-101-clergy-accused-of-sex-abuse (accessed September 2, 2023).

29. Dietrich Knauth, "New York Diocese, Abuse Victims File Competing Bankruptcy Plans," *Reuters*, January 27, 2023, https://www.reuters.com/legal/litigation/rochester-diocese-receives-insurers-competing-201-mln-bankruptcy-plan-2023-09-01/ (accessed September 2, 2023); Dietrich Knauth, "US Judge Considers Ending Stalled New York Diocese Bankruptcy," *Reuters*, July 13, 2023, https://www.reuters.com/legal/litigation/us-judge-considers-ending-stalled-new-york-diocese-bankruptcy-2023-07-11/ (accessed September 2, 2023).

30. See Catherine R. Osborne et al., "Forum: Writing Catholic History after the Sexual Abuse Crisis," *American Catholic Studies* 127 (Summer 2016): 1–27; Peter Steinfels, "Vehemently Misleading," *Commonweal* 146, no. 2 (January 25, 2019): 13–26; Matthew J. Cressler et al., "Forum: Catholic Sex Abuse and the Study of Religion," *American Catholic Studies* 130, no. 2 (Summer 2019): 1–29; Brian Clites, "Breaking Our Silence: A Primer for Research on Clergy Sexual Abuse," *American Catholic Studies Newsletter* 47 (Fall 2020): 7–16.

31. Bullivant, *Mass Exodus*, 130.

INDEX

Page numbers in italics indicate figures or tables.

Abington v. Schempp (1963), 194, 196, 197
abortion, 99, 127–28, 185, 196, 204, 210–14, 216–17, 222, 272n176, 296n168
Abzug, Bella, 213
Ackers, Nita, 205
ACLU. *See* American Civil Liberties Union
activism. *See* charity/activism; politics
adult education, 109–13
advertisements, for homes, 44, *45*
affordable housing, 143–45, 149
African Americans: and Catholic education, 140–41, 145–46; suburban activism concerning, 137–44; as suburban Catholics, 131–32, 145–46; white flight as escape from, 30–31. *See also* race and ethnicity
agrarianism, 15–16, 26, *27*, 28–29, 34, 247n114
Alesandro, John, 89
Allen, James E., Jr., 191, 192
America (magazine), 13, 25, 28, 29, 60, 108, 127, 152, 194
American Civil Liberties Union (ACLU), 192, 195
American Federation of Labor (AFL), 24
American Jewish Congress, 192, 203
American Legion, 24, 25, 192
Antonucci, Dolores, 110
Archbishop Walsh Homes, Newark, NJ, 13–14
Archdiocese of Chicago, 116
Archdiocese of New York: building program in, 46; Diocese of Brooklyn's relationship with, 52–54, 56; education in, 196, 280n26; establishment of, 22–23; family apostolates in, 115; model home shows in, 43; size of, 23, 42, 53
Archdiocese of Philadelphia, 52
Archdiocese of San Antonio, 46, 52
archdioceses. *See* dioceses/archdioceses
assimilation, ethnic, 17, 21, 62, 134, 136, 151–52, 154
Assumption of the Blessed Virgin Mary Parish, Centereach, 123, 152–53
At Home Retreats, 87–88
Atlantic, The (magazine), 63
attendance. *See* church attendance

Babylon, NY, 144
Babylon Citizens for Home Rule, 144
Baldwin School District, 195
Ballweg, Lawrence, 76, 97, 125, 160
Balmer, Randall, 296n168
Bannon, Thomas, 72, 79
baptisms in Diocese of Rockville Centre, *231*
Baroni, Geno, 33, 152
Barrington, Leone, 95
Bauer, Burnie and Helene, 114
Becker, Frank, 195, 196
Bed-Stuy Youth in Action Home Study Project, 95
Behan, James J., 1
Bellarmine Discussion Group, 112
Belter, Leonard W., 203–4
Benack, Henry, 109

Bennett, John, 177, 181, 183
Berger, Peter, 114
Berkery, John, 262n5
Bermingham, Charles, 194
Bernardin, Joseph, 211, 218
Berner, Edna and Jack, *117*
Bible, 91, 96, 112, 174, 193, 194
Birch, Anne, 193
birth control. *See* contraception, debates over
Bishop Kellenberg Memorial High School, 281n39
bishops: and abortion, 211; authority of, 18, 218, 222; and education, 7, 157–58, 192–96; and funding for parish schools, 8, 10, 56, 188, 196–98; laity vs., 34, 157, 188, 203–4, 218; organization for, 111; political positions of, 24, 201–4, 218; and the postwar family, 24. *See also* priests
Black Catholic Lay Caucus, 146
Blaine, James G., and the Blaine Amendment, 197–206
Blessed Sacrament Parish, Valley Stream, 37, 79, 110, 118, 140
Bonner, Jeremy, 115
Bookbinder, Bernie, 205
Bosco, Antoinette, 64, 121–22
Boston Globe (newspaper), 222
Bovée, David, 16
Bradley, James F., 109
Brennan, John F., 192
Brennan, William C., 197
Brentwood College, 164
Brindel, Paul, "A Pox on Suburbia," 64
Brown, Lloyd, 70
Brydges, Earl W., 198–99
Buchanan, Pat, 208–9
Buckley, James, 213
Buckley, Jeremiah, 204
Buffalino, Lucille and Andrew, 120
Bullivant, Stephen, 220
Burke, Joseph, 43
Burns, Charles, 146
Burnt Hills School District, 197
Bush, George H. W., 214
bus transportation, government funding of, 195, 197
Butler, Anthea, 296n168
Butler, Jon, 236n11
Butler, William, 194

Byrne, John J., 70, 105
Byrne, Joseph, 158

Caffrey, Dorothy, 70
Caffrey, George, 70
Callan, Patrick, 91
Calvo, Gabriel, 116
Campion, Donald, 108, 152
Cana Conferences, 6, 114, 116, 118, 119. *See also* Pre-Cana Conferences
CARA. *See* Center for Applied Research in the Apostolate
Carbone, Michael, 194
Cardijn, Joseph, 267n83, 269n119
Carlino, Joseph F., 199
Carroll, Hugh, 172, 182, 187
Carter, Jimmy, 211–14, 216
catechetical centers, 8, 85, 155–57, 166–70, 174–77
Cathedral of St. Agnes, Rockville Centre, 37
Catholic Action, 21–22, 102
Catholic Building and Maintenance (journal), 46, 52
Catholic Charities, 93, 148; Office of Spanish Social Services, 147
Catholic Charities Review (magazine), 24
Catholic education, 7–8, 155–85; for adults, 109–13; African Americans and, 140–41, 145–46; CCD programs vs., 84, 158, 167, 169–70, 174–78; class sizes, 160, 164–65; costs and finances of, 7–8, 157, 162–63, 166, 170–74, 179–80, 187–88, 196–97, 205–6, 208–9; criticisms of, 164–66, 171, 181–84, *184*; decline of, 167–68, 172–74, 178–85, 205, 221; demand for, 157–60; and faith formation, 22, 84, 158, 166, 174–78; government aid for, 8, 188, 195, 197–206, 208–9, 212–13, 222; grade school students on Long Island, *232*; growth of, 3, 18, 160–63; in home settings, 82–86, *84*; Italian support of, 135; lay participation in, 107–11; numbers of students, *232*, *233*; parish schools and, 18, 19–20, 107, 108, 155–66, *161*, *168*, 170–74, 187, 196–206, 208–9, 212–13, 221–22; peak years of, 156–57; release time programs for, 158, 166–67, 195; school boards for, 122; secondary, 162, *163*, 178–85, *184*, 196–97, *233*; seminaries, 104; transformations in,

84–85; women's role in, 7, 245n105. *See also* catechetical centers; Confraternity of Christian Doctrine (CCD) programs; public education; teachers
Catholic Extension Society, 16
Catholic Hour, The (television program), 87
Catholic intellectuals: on Catholic subcultures, 32–33; commentary on suburbia by, 14, 34–35, 39; and urban life, 5; and white ethnic revival, 152
Catholic Interracial Council of Long Island, 94, 138–42
Catholic Interracial Council of New York, 30, 244n91
Catholicism: anti-Catholic sentiment, 17–18, 21, 158, 212, 213; criticisms of, 183; early American history of, 15; intergenerational transmission of, 19–20, 31, 62–63, 98–99 (*see also* faith formation); intrareligious socializing in, 134; in national and New York politics, 187–218; national identity of, 20; population and birthrate, 3–4, 15–17, 22, 23, 26, 28, 46, 149, 205; scandals in, 9, 183, 218, 222–23. *See also* bishops; Catholic education; conservative Catholicism; conversion; disaffiliation; fallen-away Catholics; grassroots Catholicism; laity; liberal Catholicism; nuns; priests; Second Vatican Council; suburban Catholicism; urban/immigrant Catholicism
Catholic Market (magazine), 52, 60
Catholic News, The (newspaper), 26, 201, 204
Catholic Relief Services, 54
Catholic War Veteran (newspaper), 25
Catholic War Veterans of America (CWV), 25, 43
Catholic Worker Movement, 16
Catholic Youth Organizations (CYO), 20
CCD. *See* Confraternity of Christian Doctrine
CEF. *See* Citizens for Educational Freedom
Center for Applied Research in the Apostolate (CARA), 105, 219, 222
Center for the Study of American Pluralism, 151
Center for Urban Ethnic Affairs, 151
Central Verein (organization), 16
Cervini, John, 96
CFM. *See* Christian Family Movement

Chamber of Commerce, 192
Chaminade High School, Mineola, 140, 146, 182
charity/activism: CFM and, 115, 119; homes as sites for, 92–95; NCWC and, 111; race as focus of, 137–44; shifting focus of, 92; women's political, 210–11, 214. *See also* politics
Chatham, Josiah G., 105
Chiara, Peter, 89
Christian Century (magazine), 195
Christian Coalition, 218
Christian Family Movement (CFM), 6, 90, 96, 114–19, 126, 147, 262n5
Christian Right, 214. *See also* Religious Right
Christopher, Joseph P., 53–54, 56
Christ the King Parish, Commack, 77, 79, 80, 83, 118, 167
church attendance, 17, 20–21, 99, 125, 219–20
Church of the Immaculate Conception, Long Island City, Queens, 25
Church Property Administration (journal), 52
church-state separation, 8, 188, 190–206
Cicognani, Amleto, 54
cities: rural living vs., 26–28; suburban living vs., 13–16, 30. *See also* urban/immigrant Catholicism
Citizens for Educational Freedom (CEF), 198, 201–4
civil rights movement, 32, 63, 132, 137–38
Clare Therese (nun), 158
Clark, Dennis, 30–31, 108, 138
Clark, Raymond, 159
clergy. *See* bishops; priests
Coalition for Catholic Education, 181, 184, 185
Coffey, James F., 178
Cohalan, Florence D., 53, 56
Cold War, 25, 31, 43, 189, 193, 210
Coles, Betty, 140, 141
Colgan, Thomas, 112
Collins, Robert M., 173
Colson, Charles, 208
Commentary (magazine), 208
Committee for Public Education and Religious Liberty (PEARL), 199, 204
Commonweal (magazine), 26, 60, 217
Commonwealth Housing Proposal, 144

Communism, 25, 43, 192–94, 206, 208, 210
community, sense of, 6, 33, 69, 75, 93, 95–98, 108–9
Concannon, Francis B., 138
Concerned Women for America, 211
Confession, 109
Confraternity of Christian Doctrine (CCD) programs: adult education component of, 111–13; criticisms of, 146, 176–77, 221; expansion of, 20, 107, 167–69; and faith formation, 157–58, 166, 174–78, 221; homes as sites for, 2, 83, 84, 91, 99, 108; lay teachers for, 2, 83, 101, 107–11; numbers of students, 233; religious education centers for, 85, 155–57, 166–70; traditional Catholic school education vs., 84, 158, 167, 169–70, 174–78; training of teachers for, 109–10
Congress of Industrial Organizations (CIO), 24
Conharty, Thomas I., 67
Connolly, Andrew, 131–32, 137, 142–44, 171
Connors, William J., 91
conservative Catholicism: liberal vs., 126–28, 181, 183–84, 188, 206–10, 217–18; Nixon and, 206–10; and the Republican Party, 208–18; rise of, 8, 188; and Second Vatican Council, 126; suburban, 188
Conservative Party (NY), 211, 215
constitutional convention (NY), 198–202
contraception, debates over, 8, 26, 99, 119–20, 212
conversion, 93, 232
Cooke, Terence, 209, 210
Cooney, John, 54, 123, 294n116
Cordes, Rose, 84
Corpus Christi Parish, Mineola, 139, 150, 160
Coston, Carol, 217
councils. *See* diocesan councils; parish councils
Cox, Harvey, *The Secular City*, 32
Croll, Edward T., 94
Crowley, Pat and Patty, 96, 114, 119
Cubans, 147
Cuddeback, Stephen A., 142
culture wars, 8, 10, 188, 196, 222
Cummings, Kathleen, 4–5

Cumminsky, Frank W., 125
Cuomo, Mario, 185
Curé of Ars Parish, Merrick, 127, 170–71, 210
Curé of Ars School, Merrick, 170–71
Curley, Lillian S., 207
Cursillo (retreat), 147
Cushing, Richard, 24, 29
CYO. *See* Catholic Youth Organizations

Daly, James J., 53–54, 56
D'Amato, Alfonse, 8, 215–17
Daugherty, Jeanne, 14
David, Russell, 174
Day, Dorothy, 16
DeLaura, Anthony, 136
Dember, Jean, 141
Dement, Richard H., 123
Democratic National Convention (Chicago, 1968), 90
Democratic Party: Catholic voters and, 209, 211–12, 215; liberalization of, 211, 215; in Nassau County, 189–90
Dennison, H. Lee, 190
DePasquale, Tess, 153
Depression, 23
Dermody, James J., 124
DeSiena, Phyllis, 153
Desmond, Donald, 113, 182
Diaz, Jose and Juanita, 149
Diocesan Catholic Charities, 94
diocesan councils, 6–7
Diocesan Liturgical Commission, 121
Diocesan Loan Funds, 20
Diocese of Brooklyn: and agrarianism, 28; Archdiocese of New York's relationship with, 52–53, 56; Diocese of Rockville Centre's relationship with, 56; division of, 37, 54, 56, 252n75; education in, 112, 159, 160, 162, 196, 280n25; establishment of, 22–23, 52; features of, 54; model home shows in, 43; parishes established/maintained in, 46, 70–72, 74, 76–77; priest assignments involving, 103–4; and race/ethnicity, 133; size of, 54, 59, 252n75
Diocese of Rochester (NY), 52
Diocese of Rockville Centre: baptisms in, 231; Board of Consultors, 180; community building in, 96–99; converts in, 232; Diocese of Brooklyn's relationship

with, 56; education in, 109–10, 112, 122, 159–74, *163*, 167, 177–83, 187, 197; establishment of, 4–5, 34, 37–39, 54, 56–61; family apostolates in, 115–17, 119; Kellenberg as bishop of, 54, 57–59; lay participation in, 86, 93, 121, 123, 126, 129; marriages in, *231*; as model suburban diocese, 4–5, 60–61; Office of Ministry for Black Catholics, 146; Office of the Spanish Apostolate, 147; parish councils in, 73; parishes established/maintained in, 1, 59–60, 71–72, 74, 77, 101, 135; population of, *229*; priest assignments and shortages in, 103–7; and race/ethnicity, 7, 132, 140–41, 147, 150–51; School Board, 192; Senate of Priests, 180; sexual abuse scandals involving, 222–23; size of, 59. *See also* suburban Catholicism

dioceses/archdioceses: competition/conflict between, 52–54, 56, 103–4, 251n63, 252n75; establishment of, 4, 15, 22–23, 52–60; finances of, 20; importance of, 4–5; metropolitan New York and surrounding region, *55*

disaffiliation, 8–9, 219–22. *See also* fallen-away Catholics

discussion groups, 91, 112–13

Dlag, Aloysius, 91

Dohen, Dorothy, 66

Dolan, Jay P., 3, 4, 92

Dominican Sisters, 147, 170–71, 173

Donaldson, William R., 191

Donovan, William, 97

Doughty, G. Wilbur, 189

Doyle, Edward, 191

Dri, Mrs. Frederick, 89

Driscoll, Paul C., 127–28, 210

Eagle Forum, 211

Early, Mr. and Mrs. Willy, 139

economic factors in growth of, 173

education. *See* Catholic education; Confraternity of Christian Doctrine (CCD) programs; public education

Eisenhower, Dwight D., 206

Ellis, Johnn Tracy, 32

El Salvador, 185

Engel, Steven, 194

Engel v. Vitale (1962), 194–97

Equal Rights Amendment (ERA), 196, 211, 214

ethnicity. *See* race and ethnicity

ethnic parishes, 7, 14, 17–20, 32–33, 68, 95, 99, 132–37. *See also* national parishes

evangelical Christianity, 10, 188, 210–11, 213–14, 216–18

Everson decision (1947), 195

faculty. *See* teachers

Fagan, Daniel E., 158

Fagan, Robert Emmet, 83, 105, 109, 202–3

faith formation: adult education and, 108, 126; educational experiences and, 22, 84, 157–58, 166, 174–78, 221; home as center of, 175–76; suburbanization's effect on, 61. *See also* Catholicism: intergenerational transmission of

Faivre, Mrs. Frank, 138

fallen-away Catholics, 93, 97–99, 194. *See also* disaffiliation

Falwell, Jerry, 214

family: Catholic church and the postwar, 24, 114–20; housing crisis and, 25–26, 29–30; as political issue, 188, 196, 210–14, 216; size of, 25, 29–30; suburban/rural vs. urban debate concerning, 26, 28–29, 35

family apostolates, 6, 102, 114–20

Family Life Bureau. *See under* National Catholic Welfare Conference

family liturgy, 85

feast days and festivals: ancestral traditions maintained during, 19; Italian sponsorship of, 135, 136, 153; suburban Catholicism and, 86; white ethnic revival and, 152–53

Feast of Saint Liberata, Patchogue, 136

Feast of San Gennaro, Island Park, 153

Feast of San Gennaro, Manhattan, 133

Feast of St. Rocco, Glen Cove, 133

Feast of the Assumption, Westbury, 133

Federal Communications Commission (FCC), 98

Federal Housing Administration (FHA), 39, 137

Federation of Lay Organizations of the Diocese of Rockville Centre, 126, 127

Ferraro, Geraldine, 185

FHA. *See* Federal Housing Administration

Fifth Avenue Drive-In, Brentwood, 67, 80–82, *81*
Figueroa, Carlos, 150
finances: dream homes as fundraising tool, 43; fundraising in suburban churches, 60, 73–76, *75*, 108; fundraising in urban churches, 19, 20, 60; national church support for, 20; parish, 60, 62, 73–76, 124. *See also* Catholic education: costs and finances of
Finegan, Scot, 194
First Communion, 90
Fisher, Theresa, 205
Fitzgerald, Maureen, 82
Flood, Frank, 124
Focus on the Family, 218
Ford, Gerald, 211–12
Four Hundred Years (television program), 141
Fowler, Dorothy, 176
Franks, Bettie, *184*
Fried, Philip, 193
Friedan, Betty, 63–64
Froehlich, John J., 71

Gallagher, Charles A., 117, 118
Gamm, Gerald, *Urban Exodus*, 9
Gangi, Salvatore, 191
Gannon, Robert I., 201
Gans, Herbert, 151
Garden Grove Community Church, California, 81
Gardiner, Althea, 138
Geaney, Dennis J., 60, 137
Geary, William R., 89, 118
GI Bill, 3, 28, 39, 137
Gilroy, Jane, 210
Glazer, Nathan, 152
Godfrey, William, 118
Goggin, Leo J., 123
Goldberger, Paul, 40
Goldwater, Barry, 206
Golphin, Vincent F. A., 146
Good Samaritan Hospital, West Islip, 143
Gorman, Daniel J., 182, 184
Gorman, John, 219
Gormide, Tomaz, 150
Grady, Frank A., 110
Graham, George, 177
Graham, Hugh H., 125
Graham, Robert A., 60–61

Grail Movement, 16
Grant, Ulysses S., 197
grassroots Catholicism: bishops vs., 34, 203–4; Second Vatican Council and, 120, 129; as source of political activism, 142; as source of religious reform, 11, 129. *See also* laity
Greeley, Andrew, 5, 30–31, 34, 61–65, 67, 92, 99, 106, 136, 152, 158, 171, 176–78, 204–5, 212, 219–20; *Catholic Schools in a Declining Church*, 177; *The Church and the Suburbs*, 9, 30, 61–64
Green, Thomas, 138
Griffin, James L., 147, 168
Guanill, Elizabeth, 148
Guerin, Matthew J., 115

Hamilton, Daniel S., 182–83
Hanrahan, Daniel U., 25–26
Hanrahan, Michael, 181
Hard Hat Riot (1970), 208
Harper, James, *117*, 118, 126–27
Harper, Madelaine, *117*, 118
Harrington, Donald S., 198–99
Harte, Mary, 193
Hartman, John, 79
Hartman, Thomas, 85
Harvey, Holman, 191
Hayden, Charles, 63
Hayes, Patrick Joseph, 57–58
Healey, Martin J., 112
Herberg, Will, 134, 238n34
Herricks Union Free School District, 191, 193–94
Hibernization, 135
Higgins, Ann, *175*
Higgins, Edward J., 25
Hill, Morton A., 28
Hispanic populations. *See* Latin Americans
Hoar, Edward P., 37
Hogan, Edward, 120
Holscher, Kathleen, 193
Holtzman, Elizabeth, 216
Holy Communion, 120–21
Holy Family Diocesan High School, 143
Holy Family High School, South Huntington, 163, 179–80, 184, 281n35
Holy Family Parish, Hicksville, 70, 78, 79, 80, 131, 160–62
Holy Hours of Adoration, 19

Holy Name of Jesus Parish, Woodbury, 77, 167
Holy Name of Mary Parish, Valley Stream, 37, 172
Holy Name Societies, 21, 86, 102, 107, 113–14
Holy Trinity Diocesan High School, Hicksville, 171
Holy Trinity High School, Hicksville, 152, 163, 179–80, 281n35
homemaker services, 93–94
homeownership, 14, 29–30, 40, 64
Home Owners Loan Corporation (HOLC), 23
homes: charity and activism originating from, 92–95; focus on worship in, 85–86; Masses held in, 80, 89–90; missions held in, 90–91; parish functions held in, 68, 82–91; religious education and prayer held in, 2, 82–91, 84, 108; retreats held in, 87–88
Home Visit Days, 94
home visits, 93
Homiletic and Pastoral Review (magazine), 105, 127
Horsham-Brathwaite, Barbara, 145
Horstmann, Dorothy, 87–88
House Visitation Program, 175
Housing Act (1949), 25
housing and race, 137–39, 143–44
housing crisis: affordable housing, 143–45, 149; Catholic responses to, 24–26; postwar, 23–24, 39
Housing Legislation Information Services (HLIS), 24
housing projects, 13–14
Howard, Theodore J., 80
Howes, Robert, 30
Hughes, John, 15, 17, 158
Hull, John B., 143
Humphrey, Hubert, 206
Hunter, Thomas, 126–27
Hurley, Neil, 30, 60
Hynes, Joseph J., 203

Ignatius of Loyola, Spiritual Exercises, 87
Imbiorski, Walter, 116
Immaculate Conception Parish, Westhampton Beach, 169
Immaculate Conception Seminary, Huntington, 251n63
Immaculate Heart of Mary Sisters of Scranton, 171
immigrants. *See* urban/immigrant Catholicism
Infant Jesus Parish, Port Jefferson, 101
intellectuals. *See* Catholic intellectuals
intermarriage, 134–35, 152
Interracial Council. *See* Catholic Interracial Council of Long Island; Catholic Interracial Council of New York
Interracial Review (magazine), 30
Intra-Church Relations Committee, 127, 210
Irish Catholics, 135–36
Italian Catholics, 19, 132–35, 153

Jackson, Curtis, 95
Jackson, Kenneth T., 9, 22, 80
Javitz, Jacob, 215–16
Jefferson, Thomas, 15
Jewish War Veterans, 25
Jews: and ethnicity in the suburbs, 134; and funding of public schools, 191; and government aid for religious schools, 195; and religion in public schools, 188, 190, 192–94, 198–99
Jocist Method, 115, 267n83
John Jay College of Criminal Justice, 222
Johnson, Lyndon, 33, 148, 173, 201, 206
Johnson, Philip, Crystal Cathedral, 81, 257n49
John XXIII (pope), 5, 32, 137; *Mater et Magistra*, 269n119
Joseph, Lazarus, 197
Judge, Thomas A., 148
juvenile delinquency, 20, 25–26, 192, 193, 196

Kane, Arthur J., 90, 169
Karvelis, William R., 90
Katz, Adelaide D., 64
Keenan, Francis Thomas, 182
Kelleher, Jean, *Halo for a Housewife*, 87
Kellenberg, Walter P., 37–38, 54, 56–61, 72–74, 77, 89, 91, 93, 98, 104, 111, 115, 121–23, 126, 131, 138, 141, 144, 147, 162, 165, 180–81, 195, 199, 201–3, 260n88
Kelley, Francis C., 16
Kelley, James Bernard, 29
Kelly, George A., 115, 199, 201, 202

Kelly, Timothy, 279n9
Kelly, William F., 28
Kenkel, Frederick P., 16
Kennedy, Joan and Jim, *117*
Kennedy, John F., 2–3, 32, 137, 194, 206, 208, 209
Kennedy, Robert F., 90, 202
Kenny, Patrick J., 72, 73, 78
Kerr, Jean, 254n97
Keyes, Joseph F., 80
Killilea, Marie, 254n97
King, Gerald, 191
King, Martin Luther, Jr., 90, 131, 207
Kirwin, Robert J., 125, 219
Knights of Columbus, 113, 193, 209, 217
Koehlinger, Amy, 245n105
Kohler, Edward M. *See* contraception, debates over, 118
Koob, C. Albert, 173
Krane, John, 150
Kruse, Kevin, 10

Ladies Home Journal (magazine), 63
LaFarge, John, 244n91
Laghi, Pio, 183
LaGumina, Salvatore, 208
LaHaye, Beverly, 211
laity: adult education for, 111–13; associations for, 18–19, 21 (*see also* parish societies/associations); bishops vs., 34, 157, 188, 203–4, 218; declining participation of, 125–26; discussion groups for, 91, 112–13; emerging significance of, 6–7, 11, 18–19, 21–22, 101–3, 105–6, 120–25, 129–30, 181; failure of hopes for prominent voice for, 103; family apostolates for, 114–20; Mass participation of, 88–89, 120–21; and parish councils, 122–25, 128–30; and politics, 126–28; priests' relationship with, 62, 101–3, 105–6, 118, 122–23, 125, 127, 130, 181–84, 203; retreats for, 87–88; Second Vatican Council's encouragement of leadership participation by, 101–2, 106, 120, 122–23, 125, 129–30, 181, 203, 210, 269n119; as teachers (CCD), 2, 83, 101, 107–11; as teachers (school), 156, 157, 165–66, 169–72, 179; in urban churches, 18–19. *See also* church attendance; grassroots Catholicism; homes
Langley, Harold F., 153

lapsed Catholics. *See* fallen-away Catholics
Latin Americans: immigration of, 132, 146–49; as suburban Catholics, 132, 147–51
Lauder, Robert E., 88
Lawlor, Joseph F., 110, 119, 167
lay associations. *See* parish societies/associations
leakage, 15
Lederhendeler, Eli, 30
Legions of Mary, 85, 86, 93, 98, 126
Lehman, Herbert, 167
Leonard, Joan de Lourdes, 155, *156*
Leonard, John, 109, 155–56, *156*, 169–70, 187
Levitt and Sons, 39–40
Levittown, NY, 29, 31, 39–40, 69
LIAL. *See* Long Island Association of Laymen
liberal Catholicism: conservative vs., 126–28, 181, 183–84, 188, 206–10, 217–18; criticisms of, 152, 176, 184–85; decline of, 8; and faith formation, 174, 176; and Second Vatican Council, 126; and urban Catholicism, 32–33
Liberal Party, 199, 216
liberation theology, 96, 152
Life Is Worth Living (television program), 87
Ligutti, Luigi, 26, 28–29
Lilly Foundation, 218
liturgical movement, 21–22. *See also* Masses; worship practices
Living Room Dialogues, 93
Loewe, Alfred, 193
Long Island. *See* suburban Catholicism; suburbs
Long Island Association of Laymen (LIAL), 126–27, 203
Long Island Catholic, The (newspaper), 2, 64, 77, 83, 87, 88, 92, 95, 97, 98, 101, 104, 106, 107, 111, 113, 114, 116, 117, 119–22, 126, 139–45, 150, 152–53, 162, 166, 182, 201, 203–4, 207, 209, 211–13, 221
Long Island Lighting Company, 141
Looker, Benjamin, 31
Looney, Francis J., 104
Lopez, Gail and Ralph, *184*
Lucas, Lawrence E., 141
Luna, Ann, 94

Maertz, Barbara, 187
Mansueto, Anthony, 123
March on Washington (1963), 138
Margiotta, Joseph, 190, 211, 215
Maria Regina High School, Uniondale, 163, 179–80, 182, 184, 281n35
Maria Regina Parish, Seaford, 77, 83, 105, 108, 109
Marriage (magazine), 122
marriage education and enrichment programs, 116–19, 134–35
Marriage Encounter movement, 6, 116–20, *117*, 145, 268n100
marriages in Diocese of Rockville Centre, *231*
Martin, Frank, 116
Marx, Walter John, 28
Masses: after Second Vatican Council, 88–89; attendance at, 17, 20–21, 99, 125, 219–20; homes as sites for, *80*, 89–90, 259n88; Italian-language, 136, 153; lay participation in, 88–89, 120–21; Spanish-language, 147, 149–50; transformations of, 120–21. *See also* church attendance; liturgical movement; worship practices
Matovina, Timothy, 4–5
Maurin, Peter, 16
McBrien, Richard, 217
McCarren, Edgar, 159–60, 164–65, 200, 204
McCarthy, Eugene J., 201
McCarthy, Joseph, 25
McCloskey, John, 17, 56
McCluskey, Neil G., 173
McCollum v. Board of Education (1948), 167, 195
McCormack, Ellen, 216
McCoy, Christine, 121
McEntegart, Bryan, 72–74, 78, 162
McEntegart, Joseph, 53, 54, 56
McGann, John, 99, 128, 172, 179–85, 263n7
McGannon, Barry, 166
McGean, James, 22
McGinley, Phyllis, 63–64, 254n97; *A Short Walk from the Station*, 63; *Sixpence in Her Shoe*, 64
McGovern, George, 209, 215
McGovern-Frazier Commission, 211
McGreevy, John, 14; *Parish Boundaries*, 9

McIntyre, James Francis, 58
McKeever, Paul, 56, 113, 140
McKenna, William J., 37–38
McLaughlin, Michael J., 139, 141
McQuade, Francis X., 107
McRedmon, Sue, 176
Meagle, Patricia, 109
Meany, George, 201
Meany, Mary, 164
Meese, Edwin, 218
melting pot. *See* assimilation, ethnic
Michael, Maureen, 147
Michel, Virgil, 21
Mignone, Ralph, 155
Mikulski, Barbara, 152
Milazzo, Caitlin, 237n28
Millar, Andrew L., 106, 222
Miraculous Medal novenas, 21
Molloy, Thomas E., 1, 46, 53–54, 70, 103, 162, 250n47
Molloy College, 112, 164, 281n39
Moral Majority, 214
Morewood Oaks Homes, East Northport, *45*
Morey, Roy, 208–9
Moses, Robert, 72
movie theaters, as site for worship, 1, 67, 80–81, 101, 221
Moynihan, Daniel Patrick, 152, 213, 217
Mundelein, George, 252n72
Murphy, Charles J., 90
Murphy, Gerald, 119
Murphy, James, 124
Murphy, William, 150
Murray, James G., 60
Murray, John E., 107

NAACP. *See* National Association for the Advancement of Colored People
Nassau Association for Public School Adult Education, 111
Nassau County, Long Island, parishes, 48–49
Nassau County Historical Museum, 141
Nassau County Human Rights Commission, 139
Nassau County politics, 189–90
Nassau Interfaith Committee for Interracial Visits, 94
National Association for the Advancement of Colored People (NAACP), 24, 138

National Catholic Education Association, 173, 209
National Catholic Reporter (newspaper), 185
National Catholic Rural Life Conference (NCRLC), 16, 26, 28–29, 85, 239n15; pamphlet, 27
National Catholic Welfare Conference (NCWC): Family Life Bureau, 85, 114–15; Social Action Department, 111
National Center for Urban Ethnic Affairs (NUE), 33
National Center of CCD, 169
National Conference of Catholic Bishops, 211
National Confraternity of Christian Doctrine, 93
National Council of Catholic Men, 87, 123, 171
National Council of Churches, 93
National Housing Conference, 24
National Marriage Encounter, 268n100
National Newspaper Association, 201
national parishes, 19–20, 28, 61, 133, 135–36, 149, 154. *See also* ethnic parishes
National Right to Life Committee, 214
NCRLC. *See* National Catholic Rural Life Conference
NCWC. *See* National Catholic Welfare Conference
Neighbor, Russell J., 169
Network (lobby), 217
New Deal, 8, 10, 23, 188, 206–7, 216
New Hyde Park School District, 192
New Republic, The (magazine), 189
New Right, 196, 217
Newsday (newspaper), 40, 57, 139
New York Board of Regents, 193
New York Catholic Benevolent Society, 21
New York Catholic Interracial Council. *See* Catholic Interracial Council of New York
New York City Planning Commission, 72
New York Civil Liberties Union, 194
New York Daily News (newspaper), 181
New Yorker, The (magazine), 63
New York Interstate Committee for Clergy and Laity, 184
New York Newsday (newspaper), 205
New York School of Theology for Laymen, 112
New York State Board of Education, 197

New York State Catholic Committee, 203
New York State Catholic Conference (NYSCC), 198–99, 204
New York State Council of Catholic School Superintendents, 205
New York State Court of Appeals, 52
New York State Supreme Court, 194, 197
New York Times, The (newspaper), 40, 64, 201, 202, 204–5, 208
Nickerson, Eugene H., 190
Nickerson, Michelle, 9
Nixon, Richard, 206, 208–10, 217
nones, 220, 222
Norwich-Green, East Norwich, 44
Notre Dame Study of Catholic Parish Life, 98, 129
Novak, Michael, 152; *The Rise of the Unmeltable Ethnics*, 33–34
novenas, 17, 20–21, 86, 135, 150
nuns: numbers of, 18, 170, 221; shortage of, 7, 83, 107, 109, 165, 169–70; as teachers, 2, 18, 163–65, 170–71, 179, 230; and urban/suburban ministries, 33, 148, 170, 217, 245n104, 245n105
Nyreen, Don, 115
NYSCC. *See* New York State Catholic Conference

O'Connor, John, 53, 185
O'Dea, Martin, 79
Office of Economic Opportunity, 33, 245n104
O'Grady, John, 24
O'Hara, Edwin V., 16
O'Malley, Walter, 54
Operation Northwest, 148
Operation Suburbia, 94–95
Oriano, Ernesto, 110
Orsi, Robert, 4–5
O'Toole, James, 235n10
Our Holy Redeemer School, Freeport, 73, 110, 158
Our Lady of Czestochowa, 153
Our Lady of Fatima Parish, Manorhaven, 91
Our Lady of Good Counsel, Inwood, 133
Our Lady of Grace Parish, West Babylon, 71–72, 75, 77, 78–79, 83, 85, 90, 106, 109, 110–11, 138, 153, 155–56, *156*, 169–70, 174–75, 187
Our Lady of Hope Parish, Middle Village, 78

Our Lady of Loretto Parish, Hempstead, 70, 73, 113, 147, 150
Our Lady of Lourdes Parish, Malverne, 140
Our Lady of Lourdes Parish, Massapequa, 78, 145
Our Lady of Mercy Parish, Hicksville, 70, 71, 83
Our Lady of Mount Carmel Parish, Patchogue, 134, 136
Our Lady of Ostrabrama Parish, Cutchogue, 153
Our Lady of Peace Parish, Lynnbrook, 37
Our Lady of Perpetual Help Parish, Lindenhurst, 155
Our Lady of Poland Church, Southampton, 153
Our Lady of Sorrows Parish, Corona, Queens, 96
Our Lady of the Angels School, Chicago, Illinois, 165
Our Lady of the Assumption Parish, Copiague, 133, 136
Our Lady of the Miraculous Medal Parish, Wyandanch, 1, 131–32, 137–38, 142–46, 155
Our Lady of the Snow, Blue Point, 90
Our Lady of the Snows Parish, Floral Park, 77
Our Lady of Victory Parish, Floral Park, 163
Our Lady Start of the Sea Parish, Staten Island, 43
Our Parish (magazine of Our Lady of Grace Parish), 90, 169, 174, 187

Pacelli, Eugenio, 252n72
Packwood, Bob, 213
Palko, Aloysius J., 83
parish associations. *See* parish societies/associations
parish councils, 6–7, 73, 75, 122–25, 128–30
parishes: changing attitudes toward, 95–98; establishment and growth of, 17–18, 20, 46, 47–51, 54, 59–60, 69–78; ethnic, 7, 14, 17–20, 32–33, 68, 95, 99, 132–37; finances of, 60, 62, 73–76, 124; homes used for activities of, 6, 11, 68, 79–80, *80*, 82–91; Masses and services offered by, 17, 19; national, 19–20, 28, 61, 133, 135–36, 149, 154; newspapers/magazines published by, 266n66; as sacred spaces, 68; schools run by, 18, 19–20, 107, 108, 155–66, *161*, *168*, 170–74, 187, 196–206, 208–9, 212–13, 221–22; suburban, 5–6, 60, 68–82, 95–99; temporary worship spaces for, 67, 78–82; urban, 17, 99, 134–37. *See also other terms beginning with* parish
parish missions, 90–91
parish plants, 1–2, 6, 20, 68, *71*, 82, 235n1
parish societies/associations: changing nature of, 102; decline of, 65, 113–14; in early suburban Catholicism, 107–8; participation in, as path to acceptance of children for parish schools, 107, 108; single-gender nature of, 102, 114; in urban churches, 19. *See also* family apostolates
parochial schools. *See* Catholic education; parishes: schools run by
pastors. *See* priests
Patterson, A. Holly, 37
Paul VI (pope), 269n119; *Humanae Vitae*, 8, 26, 113, 119
PEARL. *See* Committee for Public Education and Religious Liberty
Pelkowski, John and Helen, 71
Peyton, Patrick, 86
Pfeffer, Leo, 203
Piazza, Adeodato, 250n47
Picciano, Frank E., 192
Pius IX (pope), 52
Pius XI (pope), 21
Pius XII (pope), 54, 250n47, 252n72
Planned Parenthood Association of America, 29–30, 214
Pledge of Allegiance, 193
POAU. *See* Protestants and Other Americans United for the Separation of Church and State
Podhoretz, Norman, 208
Polish Catholics, 133, 136, 152–53
politics: of abortion, 127–28, 185, 196, 204, 210–14, 216–17, 222, 296n168; Catholic Action and, 21; Catholic realignment in Nixon era, 206–10; economic vs. racial factors in, 207; and education, 187–88, 190–206; family as issue in, 188, 196, 210–14, 216; the laity and, 126–28; local control as concern in, 203–4, 212; in Nassau County, 189–90; polarization in, 217–18; and the

politics (*cont.*)
  Reagan Revolution, 214–17; of religion in public schools, 190–96; Second Vatican Council and, 8; suburban Catholicism and, 8, 10, 187–218; taxes as issue in, 187–91, 204–8, 212–14; urban/immigrant Catholicism and, 19; white ethnic voters and, 190, 207–8, 210, 215–16. *See also* charity/activism; conservative Catholicism; liberal Catholicism; swing voters
Potterton, Daniel, 123
prayer: in home/neighborhood settings, 86–88; in public schools, 10, 191–96, 217, 221
Pre-Cana Conferences, 115–16, 119–20
President's Committee on Equal Opportunity in Housing, 139
Press Herald (Islip newspaper), 192
priests: assignment of, 103–4; brick-and-mortar, 18; changing expectations for, 105–7; criticisms of, 106, 107; demands on suburban, 62; foreign-born, 106–7; laity's relationship with, 62, 101–3, 105–6, 118, 122–23, 125, 127, 130, 181–84, 203; morale of, 106; number of, on Long Island, *230*; role of, 18; sexual abuse scandals involving, 9, 183, 218, 222–23; shortage of, 103–6; substandard/problematic, 103. *See also* bishops
Pronto, 148
proselytism, 93, 98
Protestantism: common conservative ground with, 196; evangelical, 10, 188, 210–11, 213–14, 216–18; interfaith dialogue with, 93, 193; and religion in public schools, 198–99; threat posed to Catholicism by, 15, 114, 193
Protestants and Other Americans United for the Separation of Church and State (POAU), 192, 195
public education: Catholic education outside of, 2, 20, 83, 91, 107, 109, 157, 166–70; Catholics' participation in politics of, 120; criticisms of, 158; declining enrollments in, 182; as option for Catholic parents, 7–8, 10, 18, 158, 173, 179, 187, 205–6, 279n9; politics and, 187–88, 190–206; programs on racial issues for, 141; release time programs in, 158, 166–67; religion's place in, 8, 10, 174, 188, 190–206, 217, 221; school boards for, 191–94; taxes supporting, 62, 187, 191, 197, 205–6. *See also* Catholic education
Puerto Ricans, 42, 147, 148, 149
Putnam, Robert, 96

Quealy, Peter, 37, 57, 252n72

race and ethnicity, 7; activism concerning, 137–44; backlash concerning, 10, 151–52, 188, 207; evangelical activism and, 296n168; flight to the suburbs, 30–31, 134, 137; and foreign-born priests, 107; housing and, 23, 137–39, 143–44; Marriage Encounter movement and, 118–19; politics and white ethnic voters, 190, 207–8, 210, 215–16; private and parochial schools and, 200; segregation based on, 7, 137–39; suburban churches and, 7, 94–95, 131–54, 270n141; transformations in ethnicity in the Catholic Church, 134–37, 149–54; urban/immigrant Catholicism and, 7, 9, 17–20, 32–33, 132, 134–37. *See also* African Americans; assimilation, ethnic; civil rights movement; Latin Americans; whiteness
Ramsey, Leroy L., 140
Reader's Digest (magazine), 191
Reagan, Ronald, 8, 185, 188, 211, 214–18
Reagan Revolution, 188, 214–18
Redemptorist priests, 91
redlining, 23
Re-Education for Mutual Acceptance in the Rockville Centre Diocese, 140
Reehill, Dan, 195
Reehill, Philip J., 101–2
Reel, Henry, 112, 162, 178–79
Reformed Church of America, 81
Regents Prayer, 193–95, 289n35
release time programs, 158, 166–67, 195
religious education centers. *See* catechetical centers
Religious Right, 196, 214, 218, 296n168
Reno, Muriel, 13
Republican Party: Catholic voters and, 208–18; evangelical Christians and, 213–14; in Nassau County, 189–90; in New York State, 210–11, 215, 217

Research Institute for Catholic Education, 200
restrictive covenants, 137
retreats, 87–88, 117, 147
Revitalization Corps, 94
Ribaudo, Charles A., 124
Richter, James, 89–90, 106
Right to Life Party (NY), 210, 215, 216
Rita Anne (nun), 171
Rivera, Lydia, 151
Rockefeller, Nelson, 197, 206, 210, 211, 215
Roethel, Barbara, 139
Roe v. Wade (1973), 196, 210
Roll, Bertin, 87
Roosevelt Raceway, Westbury, 86, 162
Rosary Crusade, St. Martha Parish, Uniondale, 87
rosary prayers, 86–87
Rosary Rally, Roosevelt Raceway, Westbury, 86
Rosary Societies, 102, 107, 108, 113–14
Roth, Lawrence, 194
Rowcroft, Kathryn, 140
Ryan, Gerald J., 116
Ryan, John A., 16
Ryan, John Barry, 237n28
Ryan, Mary Perkins, 85, 166, 177
Ryan, Peter, 91
Ryan, William, 121

Sacred Heart Parish, Cutchogue, 160
Sacred Heart Parish, Island Park, 83, 153
Saints Felicity and Perpetua Parish, Patchogue, 134
Salvadorans, 148–49, 150
Saturday Review (magazine), 63
Savastano, Anthony, 77–78
Schaefer, Frederick, 110, 111, 167
Schlafly, Phyllis, 196, 211, 214
Schlegel, Harry, 13
school boards, 122, 191–94
schools. *See* Catholic education; public education
Schryver, Mrs. Al, 64
Schuller, Robert, 81
Schuster, George N., 115
Schwebius, Louis J., 83
Second Vatican Council: and adult education, 109–13; anticipatory attitudes and practices to, 6, 11, 22, 32, 86, 102, 105–6, 111, 120, 130, 262n5, 279n9; *Apostolicam Actuositatem*, 269n119; Constitution on the Church in the Modern World, 143; discussion groups about, 113; and faith formation, 174, 176, 181; *Gaudium et Spes*, 32; interfaith dialogue encouraged by, 93, 193; lay leadership encouraged by, 101–2, 106, 120, 122–23, 125, 129–30, 181, 203, 210, 269n119; liberal Catholicism and, 33, 184; Masses after, 88–89; and politics, 8, 126; and public vs. private devotions, 86; and race, 137; theological changes of, 8; *Unitatis Redintegratio*, 93
secularism, 15, 32, 166, 192–93, 196
Seldin, Abe, 199
Sentner Daly, Joyce, "I Like Suburbia," 64
Serio, Joseph, 89
Sessa, Ann Matuza, 109
sexual abuse by clergy, 9, 183, 218, 222–23
Shanahan, Patrick, 122, 171, 177, 199, 202
Shapiro, Edward S., 247n114
Shaw, Russell, 173
Sheen, Fulton, 87, 201
Sheerin, John B., 219
Sheering, Bill, 158
Shelley, Thomas, 252n75
Shriver, Sargent, 209
Sign, The (magazine), 13, 28
Siller, Therese D., 127–28
Sillers, Marjorie, 64
Sister Formation programs, 164
sisters. *See* nuns
Sisters of Saint Dominic, 164
Sisters of Saint Joseph, 2, 148, 155, 164
slum clearance, 33
Smallwood, Mercedes, 146
Smart, Audrey L. J., 203
Smith, Al, 206
Smith, Art, 13
Smith, Dr. and Mrs. Joseph, 118, 120
Smith, Lorraine, 176
Smithhaven Mall, Long Island, 98
social unrest, 90
space: homes used for parish and worship activities, 68, 82–91; parishes as sacred, 68; of suburban Catholicism, 5–6, 67–68; temporary worship spaces, 78–82
Spalding, John Lancaster, 16
Spellman, Francis, 4, 37, 53–54, 56, 59, 104, 162, 194–95, 199, 201–4, 250n47, 294n116

Speno, Edward J., 197, 201
Sprague, J. Russell, 189
Ss. Cyril and Methodius Parish, Deer Park, 1–2, *3*, 97, 138, 167
St. Agnes Cathedral High School, Uniondale, 179, 285n116
St. Agnes High School, Rockville Centre, 146, 179
St. Agnes Parish, Rockville Centre, 57, *58*, 89, 115, 118
St. Aidan Parish, Williston Park, 110, 112, 139–40, 158–59, 193–94, 293n98
St. Albert the Great College, 164
St. Anne Parish, Brentwood, 67, 80–82, *81*, 89, 93, 113, 124, 147, 149–50
St. Anne Parish, Floral Park, 112
St. Anne Parish, Garden City, 160
St. Anne School, Brentwood, *165*, 167
St. Anthony High School, South Huntington, 179
St. Anthony of Padua, Rocky Point, 133
St. Anthony Parish, East Northport, 147
St. Anthony Parish, Oceanside, 173
St. Barnabas the Apostle Parish, Bellmore, 70, 160, 162
St. Bernard Parish, Levittown, 70, 79, 97, 106, 124, *175*
St. Bernard Parish, Mill Basin, Brooklyn, 72, 73, 78
St. Boniface Parish, Elmont, 113, 119
St. Brigid Parish, Westbury, 91, 133, 138, 151, 153, 159
St. Clare Parish, Queens, 72
St. Columba Parish, Marine Park, 74
St. Edward Parish, Syosset, 70
Steinfels, Margaret O'Brien, 217
St. Elizabeth Parish, South Huntington, 77, 83, *84*, 90
St. Frances de Chantal Parish, Wantagh, 70, *75*, 78, 113, 162, 174
St. Frances de Chantal School, Wantagh, *159*
St. Francis de Sales Parish, Patchogue, 134
St. Francis of Assisi Parish, Greenlawn, 80, 83, 95
St. Gerard Majella Parish, Terryville, *80*, 91, 101–2, 121
St. Gertrude Parish, Bayville, 125, 126
St. Hedwig Parish, Floral Park, Queens, 133
St. Hugh Parish, Huntington Station, 107
St. Hyacinth Parish, Glen Cove, 133, 153

St. Ignatius Loyola Parish, Hicksville, 69–71, 76, 90, 160, 167
St. Ignatius Retreat House, Manhasset, 91, 117
St. Isidore Parish, Riverhead, 152–53
St. James Parish, Seaford, *71*, 79
St. James Parish, Setauket, 80, 101
St. James Parish, Wantagh, 77
St. John of God, Central Islip, 148
St. John the Baptist High School, West Islip, 163, 179–80, 184, 281n35
St. Joseph Parish, Babylon, 155, 162
St. Joseph School, Kings Park, 171
St. Joseph the Worker Parish, East Patchogue, 119, 147
St. Jude Parish, Canarsie, Brooklyn, 74, 80
St. Jude Parish, Mastic Beach, 124
St. Ladislaus Parish, Hempstead, 70, 153
St. Laurence Parish, East New York, 74
St. Lawrence Parish, Sayville, 219
St. Luke Parish, Brentwood, 79, 113, 148, 167
St. Margaret Parish, Selden, 101
St. Martha Parish, Uniondale, 70, 73, 76, 87, 105, 160
St. Martin of Tours Parish, Amityville, 133
St. Mary Parish, East Islip, 89, 91, 122, 192
St. Matthew Parish, Dix Hills, 79–80, 113, 123, 131
St. Patrick Parish, Bay Shore, 148
St. Patrick Parish, Glen Cove, 112, 133, 147
St. Patrick Parish, Huntington, 113
St. Paul the Apostle Parish, Jericho, 70, 77, 79, 123, 163
St. Peter Claver Parish, Brooklyn, 95
St. Peter of Alcantara Parish, Port Washington, 92, 133
St. Peter Parish, Port Washington, 119
St. Peter the Apostle Parish, Islip Terrace, 91
St. Peter the Apostle Parish, North Great River, 77
St. Philip and St. James School, St. James, 171
St. Pius X Parish, Plainview, 70, 71, 79, 85, 87, 122, 124, 158, 174, 176
St. Pius X Parish, Rosedale, 72
St. Pius X Preparatory Seminary, Uniondale, 104, 140, 145, 178–81
St. Pius X Seminary, Uniondale, 158
St. Raphael Parish, East Meadow, 78, 121
St. Raymond Parish, East Rockaway, 37, 112

St. Richard Parish, Jackson, MS, 105
St. Rocco Parish, Glen Cove, 133, 153
St. Rose of Lima Parish, Massapequa Park, 79, 94, 121, 123, 124, 125, 139, 208
St. Thomas More Parish, Hauppauge, 87, 125, 219
St. Thomas the Apostle Parish, West Hempstead, 89
St. Vincent de Paul Society, 19, 143
St. Vincent Ferrer High School, New York City, 112
St. William the Abbot Parish, Seaford, 70, 77, 160, 162
suburban Catholicism, 1–5; agrarianism and, 15–16, 29, 247n114; anticipations by, of the Second Vatican Council, 6, 11, 22, 32, 86, 102, 105–6, 111, 120, 130; features and challenges of, 10, 38–39, 60–66, 220–21; fundraising in, 60, 73–76, *75*, 108; institutional expansion of, 44, 46–60; parishes for, 5–6, 60, 68–82, 95–99; pioneers of, 107–9; and politics, 8, 10, 187–218; population and birthrate, 23, 28–30, 38, 42, 59, 76–78, 103, 104, 124, *229*; postwar, 37–66; priestly authority in, 62, 102–3, 105, 123, 181–84; and race/ethnicity, 7, 94–95, 131–54, 270n141; scholarship and commentary on, 9–11, 32, 61–64, 95–98 (*see also* suburban Catholicism: urban vs.); and Second Vatican Council, 6, 11; spatial aspects of, 5–6, 67–68; urban vs., 11, 13–16, 30, 34, 63, 94–95. *See also* Catholic education; Diocese of Rockville Centre; parishes; suburbs
Suburban Fair Housing Conference, 139
suburbs: appeal of, 30–31; Catholicism's significance for, 10, 43–45; critiques and defenses of, 32, 62–64, 92, 96; economic factors in growth of, 31; growth of, 31, 39–42; prewar, 22–24; scholarship on, 9; urban living vs., 13–16, 30; white flight to, 30–31, 134, 137. *See also* suburban Catholicism
Suffolk County, Long Island, parishes, *50–51*
Suffolk County Development Corporation, 144
Suffolk County Health Department, 143
Suffolk Taxpayers Association, 191
Sugrue, Thomas, 4, 10

Sullivan, Charles L., 78
Sullivan, Joseph M., 204
Sullivan, Mary, 87–88
Supreme Court. *See* New York State Supreme Court; US Supreme Court
Swiger, Charles W., 182–83, 187
swing voters, 8, 188, 212, 217–18

Tablet, The (newspaper), 28, 34–35, 191, 192, 194, 195, 243n77
Taft-Ellender-Wagner Housing Act, 24, 25
Taranto, Stacey, 210
Task Force on Urban Problems, 218
taxes: deductions for nonpublic school tuition, 209, 212–14, 217; as political issue, 62, 187–91, 197, 200, 204–8, 212–14; public education supported by, 62, 187, 191, 197, 205–6, 214
teachers: in CCD programs, 2, 107–11; courses on racial issues for, 139, 140; laity as, 2, 101, 107–11, 156, 157, 165–66, 169–72, 179; nuns as, 2, 18, 163–65, 170–71, 179, *230*; for parish schools, 156; salaries of, 157, 166, 169, 171–72, 179; shortage of, 156, 157; training of, 164; unionization of, 171–72
Teams of Our Lady, 126
Tedesco, Louis, 121
Ten Commandments, 192
theaters. *See* movie theaters
Thomas, Sandra, 146
Time (magazine), 63, 173, 206
Tonelotto, Walter, 153
Town Crier (Islip newspaper), 192
Tracy, Mary, 184–85
Travia, Anthony, 198–99, 202–4
Trench, Edmond, 57, 74–75, 103, 140
Triumphant Hour, The (television program), 86
Truman, Harry S., 23, 24
Tschantz, Joseph J., 73–74
Tuition Tax Credit Act, 213

Unitarian Universalist Community Church, New York City, 199
United Federation of Teachers, 199
United Parents Association, 199
United States Conference of Catholic Bishops, 222
Urban Development Corporation (NY), 144

urban/immigrant Catholicism, 5; attendance of, 17, 20–21; emergence and growth of, 3, 14, 15–22; fundraising in, 19, 20, 60; housing projects and, 13; milieu of, 14, 16–22, 31; parishes for, 17, 99; and politics, 19; population and birthrate, 15–17, 26, 42; postwar, 31–34; prehistory of, 15; race/ethnicity and, 7, 9, 17–20, 32–33, 132; rural vs., 26–28; scholarship and commentary on, 9–10, 32–34, 65 (*see also* urban/immigrant Catholicism: suburban vs.); suburban vs., 11, 13–16, 30, 34, 63, 94–95; transformations of, 134–37. *See also* cities
urban renewal, 33
US Supreme Court, 8, 10, 167, 188, 194–95, 204, 209–10

Van Bourgondien family, 72
Vatican Apostolic Delegate to the United States, 183
Vatican II. *See* Second Vatican Council
Verbeeck, John, 72–73, 76, 105
Veterans of Foreign Wars (VFW), 25
Viccora, Mary Ann, 112
Vietnam War, 34, 113, 126, 141, 190, 198, 208
Vitale, William, Jr., 193

Wagner, Robert F., Jr., 25
Wallace, George, 206–7
Walsh, Edward, 181–82
Walsh, John, 141–42
Wanderer, The (newspaper), 182
War on Poverty, 33, 148
Watson, Joseph, 145
Watson, Nathaniel and Marie, 145
Wcela, Emil, 77, 83, 105, 108, 177
Wheatley Heights Civic Association, 144
White, Mary, 207–8
White, Theodore, 210
white flight, 30–31, 134, 137

whiteness: descendants of European immigrants and, 137; and escape to the suburbs, 30–31, 134, 137; ethnic revival of, 7, 33–34, 151–53, 207, 215; of Long Island suburbs, 137; and racial backlash, 10, 151–52, 188, 207; suburban Catholicism and, 132
Wilds, Betty, 143
Williams, Billie, 125
Wills, Andy, 138
Winter, Gibson, *The Suburban Captivity of the Church*, 32, 245n99
Wirthlin, Richard, 216
women: in Catholic education, 7, 245n105; as lay participants in Masses, 121–22; political activism of, 210–11, 214; and the politics of public education, 196; and urban ministries, 33, 245n104, 245n105; and worship in the home, 85. *See also* nuns
women religious. *See* nuns
Work, Martin H., 125
World War II, 136
Worldwide Marriage Encounter, 117, 268n100
worship practices: critiques of, 97; temporary spaces' effect on, 82. *See also* liturgical movement; Masses
Wuthnow, Robert, 196
Wyandanch, New York, 142–44
Wyandanch Community Development Corporation, 144
Wyatt, Wilson, 23

Young Christian Students, 262n5
Young Christian Worker Movement (Belgium), 21, 115, 262n5, 267n83

Zambito, Raymond F., 124–26
Zeitz, Joshua, 30–31, 207
zoning, 52, 144
Zorach v. Clauson (1952), 167, 195

www.ingramcontent.com/pod-product-compliance
Lightning Source LLC
Chambersburg PA
CBHW022032290426
44109CB00014B/837